Understanding Public Policy

Also by Paul Cairney

Scottish Politics: An Introduction (*with Neil McGarvey*)

Understanding Public Policy

Theories and Issues

Paul Cairney

First published 2012 by
PALGRAVE MACMILLAN

Palgrave Macmillan in the UK is an imprint of Macmillan Publishers Limited,
registered in England, company number 785998, of Houndmills, Basingstoke,
Hampshire RG21 6XS.

Palgrave Macmillan in the US is a division of St Martin's Press LLC,
175 Fifth Avenue, New York, NY 10010.

Palgrave Macmillan is the global academic imprint of the above companies
and has companies and representatives throughout the world.

Palgrave® and Macmillan® are registered trademarks in the United States,
the United Kingdom, Europe and other countries

ISBN 978-0-230-22970-9   hardback
ISBN 978-0-230-22971-6   paperback

This book is printed on paper suitable for recycling and made from fully
managed and sustained forest sources. Logging, pulping and manufacturing
processes are expected to conform to the environmental regulations of the
country of origin.

A catalogue record for this book is available from the British Library.

A catalog record for this book is available from the Library of Congress.

10   9   8   7   6   5   4   3   2   1
21   20   19   18   17   16   15   14   13   12

Printed in China

*For my lovely partner Linda, our beautiful children,
Evie, Alfie and Frankie, and our smelly but handsome dog
(who can be seen here –
http://smallvillagebigdog.wordpress.com/)*

Contents

List of Boxes, Figures and Tables

Boxes

Figures

Tables

List of Abbreviations

ACF	Advocacy coalition framework
AEC	Atomic Energy Commission (US)
AIDS	Acquired immune deficiency syndrome
BBC	British Broadcasting Corporation
BP	British Petroleum
BR	British Rail
BSE	Bovine spongiform encephalopathy (mad cow disease)
BT	British Telecommunications
CAP	Common agricultural policy (EU)
DSH	Dye–Sharkansky–Hofferbert (systems theorists)
EU	European Union
FCTC	Framework Convention on Tobacco Control
FDA	Food and Drug Administration (US)
FY	Financial year
GDP	Gross domestic product
HIV	Human immunodeficiency virus
HMO	Health Maintenance Organization (US)
IAD	Institutional analysis and development framework
IGR	Intergovernmental relations
IR	International relations
LA	Los Angeles
MLG	Multi-level governance
MNC	Multinational corporation
MSA	Multiple streams analysis
NEPA	National Environmental Protection Act (US)
NHS	National Health Service (UK)
NGO	Non-governmental organizations
NPM	New public management
OECD	Organisation for Economic Co-operation and Development
PE	Punctuated equilibrium (Theory)
PR	Proportional representation (electoral system)
Quango	Quasi-non-governmental organization
RCT	Rational choice theory
SARS	Severe acute respiratory syndrome
UK	United Kingdom
UN	United Nations
US(A)	United States (of America)
USDA	US Department of Agriculture
WM	Westminster model

Preface and Acknowledgements

I once met a fellow academic at a conference exploring ten years of devolution in the UK. Since the subject was fairly generic, the conference included people with a wide variety of backgrounds and so it is natural to meet people whose interests you do not share. However, I was still surprised to hear from a psephologist that he did not care about the study of public policy at all (despite the fact that several theories could be used to explain to him why he was no longer allowed to smoke his pipe indoors). It was something along the lines of: 'as soon as the election is over, I lose interest'. That would have been fine if left at that because he is a funny character who can get away with it. However, it then prompted our much more circumspect and thoughtful colleague to express very similar sentiments (something along the lines of: 'me too'). This confirmed in my mind the sad fact that not everybody shares my fascination with public policy. It then prompted me to ask the question: why? The first possible answer is that public policy is relatively unimportant when compared to other subjects such as elections. This does not ring true because the effects of public policy are everywhere. In fact, much of my undergraduate study led me to believe that, if anything, elections are relatively unimportant because the vast bulk of public policy is delivered routinely by organizations out of the eye line of elected officials. The second explanation is that public policy is just routine. Yet, while Richardson and Jordan's (1979) discussion of policy communities shows us how certain actors try to keep things *looking* routine and humdrum (to exercise power beyond the public eye), Baumgartner and Jones' *Policy Agendas Project* (http://www.policyagendas.org/) also shows us that such strategies are often spectacularly unsuccessful. The third explanation is that public policy is frustrating because it is difficult to study. It is complex, inherently messy and often unpredictable. This explanation *does* ring true and it prompts us to determine how to study it

There are a lot of excellent introductory public policy books which grapple with the need to mix the relatively inaccessible discussions of theory with what Birkland (2005: 3) calls the 'meat' of the book (i.e. the relatively 'concrete' discussion of the policy process and the actors and institutions involved). While in many cases the meat tends to win, my aim is to devote much more time to the theory (what would it be in this metaphor – the broccoli?) so that we can explore in more depth how these theories relate to each other. This approach leaves less (but still considerable) room for the type of extensive case study discussion found in other texts and thought to be essential to keep students interested in the theoretical material (Parsons' 1995 solution to this problem is to write a huge book). My aim is that, instead, this book can be used to encourage students to produce their own case study material. This is the approach that I have taken when teaching public policy at the University of Aberdeen. It allows students to make regular, original contributions to our seminar discussions and explore the extent to which the theories we discuss are useful to their studies. No-one complains too much. Some provide the occasional inquisitive look when I suggest that people can be lucky as well as powerful, but this is Brian Barry's and Keith Dowding's fault, not mine. Others groan when I point out how complex the policy process is and that there are no easy answers, but there comes a point at which you have to accept that statement. The same can be said for teaching civil servants. While theories could have the reputation of being too abstract to be of value to practitioners, my experience is that many civil servants welcome the chance to reflect on how their activities fit into a wider policy process. For example, how would they account for the fact that their political bosses generally pay no attention, but occasionally pay disproportionate attention, to their work? While it is tempting to just think that elected officials are feckless and opportunistic, punctuated equilibrium or multiple streams analysis provide a more convincing way to explain why policymaker attention often lurches from issue to issue without giving them the amount of attention required to solve problems in a meaningful way.

A bigger problem for me has been finding the time to complete the book in a world where the 'textbook' takes second place to original research (although this book, and related articles, shows that you can do both at the same time). I would like to thank the people who have helped me produce it. By far and away the most important contributor has been Allan McConnell because he not only read and commented on the whole book throughout the process (I have revised it considerably following his comments), but also did the same for the book I wrote with Neil McGarvey (*Scottish Politics,* 2008). At the risk of giving him a lot more work, I would recommend the substance and style of his comments to anyone. On the advice of Grant Jordan I have tried to get comments from the people associated with each theory. In some cases this was easy. For example, Frank Baumgartner is a regular visitor to Aberdeen and someone who has made some useful comments on more than one chapter. Hank Jenkins-Smith approved of the ACF chapter and suggested some further reading. In other cases it was moderately easy. For example, while multi-level governance is a vague term with a wide literature, Matthew Flinders is closely enough associated with it to make authoritative comments (which he did). With rational choice, it is relatively tricky because there are so many people to choose from. However, this chapter has been improved (and some glaring errors removed) following comments by some prominent contributors to the field – Andrew Hindmoor, Keith Dowding (who went well beyond the call of professional courtesy) and Iain McLean – as well as some very useful comments and book lending by colleagues in my department, Neil Mitchell and Patrick Bernhagen. Peter John gave some very useful comments on evolutionary theory. Martin Lodge and Oliver James gave some brief but useful comments on my ideas regarding policy transfer. Then there are people who went well beyond the call of duty to read multiple chapters just because I asked them to do so. Andrew Hindmoor provided some valuable input to the new institutionalism chapter. Darren Halpin commented (well!) on two chapters. Donley Studlar and Hadii Mamudu were very patient (I had to finish this book before co-authoring our book on Global Tobacco Policy) and Donley not only read and commented on chapters but also got his graduate students (including Stephanie Pratt) to follow suit. Mikine Yamazaki, my friend and colleague from Hokkaido University, gave me some good advice on the Japanese literature. Daniel Béland gave me advance copies of some chapters of Béland and Cox (2010). Last, but not least, thanks to Grant Jordan who has a reasonably balanced scorecard. On the one hand, his early 'retirement' led to me becoming head of department, slowing up the completion of the book. On the other, he has been a key driver for the development of my writing – reading and commenting on chapters, loaning me dozens of books and keeping me thinking about things when I thought I had cracked them enough to move on.

I would also like to thank people at Palgrave Macmillan. The first nod goes to Steven Kennedy for effectively turning my original proposal (a multiple lenses approach to tobacco policy) into two books – this one and (with Donley Studlar and Hadii Mamudu, 2012), *Global Tobacco Control: Power, Policy, Governance and Transfer* – and encouraging me to keep going. Although I managed to give this book the slip for a while, a serious chat at APSA 2009 was enough to refocus my mind. The second goes to Stephen Wenham who did a good job of prodding me (as did Helen Caunce) to make sure that things were progressing (and getting the first full draft reviewed). This is an important agenda-setting role when we have ten things that we could be writing or researching at any one time. The third goes to the anonymous reviewers, and particularly the final reviewer who read the whole book. This process never seems pleasant, but it seemed more constructive and positive than I expected. Final thanks to Andrew Seale, a conscientious 4th-year student at Aberdeen University, who agreed to sort out the bibliography (and then did so).

PAUL CAIRNEY

The author and publishers would like to thank the following for permission to use copyright material:

John Wiley & Sons for Figure 9.1 from Bryan D. Jones *et al.*, 'A General Empirical Law of Public Budgets: A Comparative Analysis', *American Journal of Political Science*, based on figure 2a, p. 861 (2001).

John Wiley & Sons for Figure 10.1 from Christopher M. Weible *et al.*, 'Themes and Variations: Taking Stock of the Advocacy Coalition Framework, *Policy Studies Journal*, pp. 121–40 (2009).

John Wiley & Sons for Figure 12.1 from David P. Dolowitz and David Marsh, 'Learning from Abroad: The Role of Policy Transfer in Contemporary Policy Making', *Governance*, p. 13 (2000).

Chapter 1

Introduction: Theories and Issues

The aim of this chapter is to identify the key themes that run throughout the public policy literature, and the book as a whole. We consider:

- *From the old to the new?* How contemporary theories draw on, or reject, the classic focus on policy cycles and 'bounded rationality'.
- *Power, agenda setting and public policy.* The role of policymakers and the actors that seek to influence how policy is made.
- *Governance and the power of the centre.* The extent to which power is concentrated within central government or dispersed to other types of governmental and non-governmental actors.
- *Individuals, institutions and environments.* The individuals that make decisions, the institutions in which they operate and the socio-economic pressures that they face.
- *Bureaucratic politics, policy networks and group–government relations.* The importance of 'sub-systems' or 'policy networks' in which relationships form between policymakers, civil servants and other policy participants such as interest groups.
- *The role of ideas.* The pursuit of policy goals may depend as much on the strength oif the argument, and the beliefs of the participants, as the strength of the participants.
- *Stability and instability; continuity and change.* Why policymaking involves stable relationships and policy continuity at one point, but instability and policy change at another.

Why do we study public policy?

We study public policy because we want to know why particular decisions are made. Why did so many governments decide to 'bail out' the banks, rather than let them fold, after the economic crisis in 2008? Why did many governments 'privatize' their industries and introduce private sector ideas to the public sector from the 1980s? Why did President Obama pursue healthcare reforms in the in 2009? Why have so many governments introduced major tobacco control policies while others, such as Germany, have opposed further controls? Why did the government introduce the 'poll tax' in 1989? Why did the Australian government reform gun laws in 1996 (McConnell, 2010: 149–53)? Why do countries go to war?

We study theories of public policy because we recognize that there are many different answers to these questions. These answers are based on different perspectives. We can focus on individual policymakers, examining how they analyse and understand policy problems. We can consider their beliefs and how receptive they are to particular ideas and approaches to the problem. We can focus on institutions and the rules that policymakers follow. We can identify the powerful groups that influence how policies are made. We can focus on the socio-economic context and consider the pressures that governments face when making policy. Or, we can focus on all five factors. Most contemporary accounts try to explain policy decisions by focusing on one factor or by combining an understanding of these factors into a single theory. However, there is no single unifying theory in public policy. Rather, we can take the insights from one and compare it with insights from others. The aim of this book is to outline major theories of public policy and explore how we can combine their insights when seeking to explain the policy process.

The use of multiple perspectives was pioneered by Allison (1969; 1971), whose aim was to explain why the US and Soviet Union made decisions that led to the Cuban missile crisis. Allison highlighted the limitations to 'realist' explanations based on treating a government as an individual with a single coherent understanding of its interests. He compared it with 'bureaucratic politics' accounts which focus on the pursuit of different interests in different parts of government, and 'game theory' accounts which focus on how each individual within the government behaves, to produce a more detailed understanding of the process (Box 1.1). Debates on the 'poll tax' in the UK perform a similar function. The decision to reform local taxation was a policy disaster and it contributed to the resignation of Margaret Thatcher as Prime Minister, prompting many to consider why the policy was adopted. For example, John's (1999) focus on the evolution and adoption of a powerful economic idea can be compared with McConnell's (2000) focus on the role of 'powerful socio-economic interests'. Cairney, Studlar and Mamudu (2012) explore major tobacco policy change. They ask why many developed countries had few policies on tobacco in 1950 but now have comprehensive tobacco controls which include high taxes and bans on smoking in public places. They discover a long-term process of reinforcement: the institution responsible for policy changed (the Department of Health has replaced the Treasury); there was a shift in the beliefs of policymakers and their understanding of the problem (it used to be treated as an economic good; now it is a health problem); the balance of power between tobacco companies and public health groups shifted; fewer people smoked, tobacco taxes fell and public opinion in favour of tobacco control rose; and, new medical knowledge and ideas on how to address the health risk became increasingly accepted within government.

Box 1.1 Essence of decision

Allison (1971) represents a pivotal attempt to compare multiple explanations for the same event. It combines discussion of three approaches to rationality: the 'neorealist' assumption of state rationality in which national governments are treated as 'centrally coordinated, purposive individuals'; the use of comprehensive and bounded rationality to examine the 'standard operating procedures' of the organizations that make up governments; and the use of game theory to discern an overall pattern of behaviour from the rational choices of key individuals (1971: 3–7; 257). Each approach provides different perspectives to explain the Cuban missile crisis. The value of multiple explanations is that they produce different (but comparable) answers to the same question and prompt us to seek evidence that we would not otherwise uncover (1971: 249). In Allison's case, we move from the type of explanation of state behaviour – in terms of the costs and benefits of action – that could be done by an 'armchair strategist' towards the pursuit of more detailed, relevant, evidence (1971: 251). Treating states as unified actors may produce parsimonious explanation, but only at the expense of more nuanced explanations based on organizational procedures, the decision-making environment and the need for all decision makers to bargain and accept compromise within government (1971: 253–4; see also Caldwell, 1977; Bendor and Hammond, 1992).

However, they also identify the idiosyncratic elements of policymaking: short term 'windows of opportunity' open (Chapter 11) and policy often only changes when a number of events happen at the same time (for other examples of multiple perspectives see Parker *et al.*, 2009; Greenaway *et al.*, 1992; Dunleavy, 1990; Gamble, 1990; Greener, 2002; Rosamond, 2000 and Mintrom and Vergari, 1996).

In each example, we find that a range of perspectives can be brought to bear on analysis. Our task is to explain policy decisions as fully as possible by drawing on that range. To that end, we first produce a series of questions to guide research. For example, consider what we would want to know about the decision of a government to 'bail out' its banks. How did policymakers analyse and understand the policy problem? How high was it on their agenda when compared to other issues? What arguments and economic ideas do they appear most receptive to? How were the issue and the decision processed within governing institutions? Which groups were consulted and listened to most? What socio-economic pressures did they face when making the decision? Second, we consider how these questions are synthesized by theories of public policy. For example, the advocacy coalition framework (Chapter 10) would identify the banking sector as part of a powerful coalition operating within a specialized part of the political system, maintaining close links to key policymakers and making sure that their economic ideas dominate policy debates even during periods of crisis. Further, by using the language of that theory we can compare the results of one study with a range of studies (on, for example, environmental or health policy) conducted using a similar research framework. Third, we compare the results with other theories that produce different, but often complementary, insights. Most of this book is devoted to often-abstract theories, but the ultimate aim is to help explain why decisions are made in the real world.

The general approach

Public policy is difficult to study but it is worth the effort. The policy process is complex, messy and often appears to be unpredictable. Further, the idea of a single process is a necessary but misleading simplification. When we scratch beneath the surface we find that there are multiple policy processes: the behaviour of policymakers, the problems they face, the actors they meet and the results of their decisions often vary remarkably. They often vary by region, political system, over time and from policy issue to issue. Indeed, we might start to wonder how we can make convincing generalizations about all public policy. That is why much of the literature employs the case study method just to make sense of very specific events.

However, there are well-established ways to make sense of the process as a whole. The first step is to define public policy, identify types of policy and then decide how to make the study of policymaking more manageable (Chapter 2). Traditionally, there have been two main ways to manage the study of policymaking. The first is to treat the policy process as a cycle and break it down into a series of stages such as agenda setting, formulation, legitimation, implementation and evaluation. The second is to consider a policymaking ideal – 'comprehensive rationality' – in which a policymaker has a perfect ability to produce, research and introduce her policy preferences. The modern history of the literature involves taking these approaches as the starting point, examining how useful they are as a way to organize policy studies, and considering how best to supplement or replace them with other theories. The main aim of this book is to identify those theories, explain how they work and assess their value. A further aim is to explore how their merits can be combined. For example, we can try to produce a single framework that combines the insights from more than one theory, or maintain the separation to encourage us to seek multiple perspectives. We might even compare the value of each theory as a way to choose one and reject another. If so, we might consider if we should choose the same theory each time, or if a particular theory is suited to particular types of case study.

The plan of each chapter is as follows. First, it sets out a key theory or concern of public policy. In some cases, such as punctuated equilibrium and the advocacy coalition framework, this is straightforward because the theory is linked to a small number of authors with a coherent research plan. In others, the chapter describes a rather disparate literature with many authors and approaches (institutionalism, rational choice, policy transfer, multi-level governance). Or, the chapter describes an important issue (defining policy, structural factors, bounded rationality, the role of ideas and power) and outlines key concepts or theories within that context. Second, it identifies the questions that each theory seeks to answer. Third, it considers the value of each theory in different circumstances. For example, we may explore its applicability to more than one political system. Many theories have developed from a study of the US political system characterized by a separation of powers; some thought is required when we try to apply their lessons in, for example, Westminster systems (see Chapter 4). Fourth, it explores how the key themes and issues raised by each theory relate to concerns raised in other chapters. We explore the language of policy studies and the extent to which theories address the same issues, and often come to similar conclusions, in different ways. Finally, Chapter 13 brings together this analysis and explores how best to combine the insights of public policy theories.

Theories of public policy: from the old to the new?

Public policy – the sum total of government action, from signals of intent to the final outcomes (but see Chapter 2).

Theory – a set of analytical principles designed to structure our observation and explanation of the world.

The way that we study **public policy** has changed significantly since the post-war period. A common narrative of policy analysis suggests that studies began, in the early 1950s, to focus on the 'policy sciences' and a belief that particular scientific methods should be applied to policy analysis (Lerner and Lasswell, 1951; Parsons, 1995: 16–28; Radin, 2000). In turn, policy analysis could be used by policymakers to better understand and make decisions. This led to a focus on two related forms of analysis: 'comprehensive rationality' and the policy cycle.

The idea of comprehensive rationality is that elected policymakers translate their values into policy in a straightforward manner. They have a clear, coherent and rank-ordered set of policy preferences which organizations carry out in a 'logical, reasoned and neutral way' (John, 1998: 33). There are clear-cut and ordered stages to the process (aims are indentified, the means to achieve those aims are produced and one is selected) and analysis of the policy-making context is comprehensive. This allows policymakers to maximize the benefits of policy to society in much the same way that an individual maximizes her own utility (as described by rational choice theory – Chapter 7).

Prescriptive or normative – relating to how things should be.

Descriptive – relating to how things are.

Ideal-type – an abstract idea used to highlight certain hypothetical features of an organisation or action.

While earlier accounts took this as an ideal to aspire to (when focusing on **prescriptive** or **normative** policy analysis), it is now more likely to be treated as an **ideal-type** or useful departure point when discussing how policymaking really works (when focusing on **descriptive** policy analysis). The phrase most used is 'bounded rationality' which Simon (1957) coined to describe a process in which people or organizations use decision-making short-cuts rather than comprehensive analysis, and seek satisfactory rather than 'optimal' solutions to policy problems.

Lindblom's (1959) theory of incrementalism emerged as both a descriptive and prescriptive alternative to comprehensive rationality. In a descriptive sense, incrementalism was a better fit with the evidence of the policy process. Decision makers did not look far and wide for policy solutions. Rather, their values limited their search and their decisions reflected decisions taken in the past. Indeed, policy analysis often involves merely solving the problems of past policies. Incrementalism also had a normative appeal for Lindblom (1959; 1979) who argued that more limited searches for policy solutions were efficient and less dispiriting. Further, existing policy represented a negotiated settlement between competing interests. Therefore, radical change would be inappropriate since it would require a government to ride roughshod over an existing policy consensus. As Chapter 5 suggests, the term 'bounded rationality' informs many contemporary theories and, while many follow Lindblom to identify incrementalism, others identify the potential for radical policy change.

The concept of policy cycles has a similar history. It was once employed prescriptively as a way to organize policymaking. The suggestion is that policymakers should divide the process into a series of stages to ensure policy success: identify policymaker aims, identify policies to achieve those aims, select a policy measure, ensure that the selection is legitimized by the population or its legislature, identify the necessary resources, implement and then evaluate the policy. The cycle is still employed in some policymaking circles (see Chapter 2). However, it is now generally used as an organizing framework for the study of policy. Few texts suggest that the policy process can be divided into stages unproblematically. Rather, the cycle metaphor suggests that the evaluation stage of policy 1 represents the first stage of policy 2, as lessons learned in the past form the basis for choices in the future. In other words, policymaking is a never-ending process rather than a single event. There are also distinct literatures dedicated to the study of agenda-setting, formulation and implementation stages.

Yet, fewer and fewer books begin with a discussion of comprehensive rationality and fewer authors structure their books around the cycles metaphor. Indeed, one of the most influential theories is built on a *rejection* of this approach (see Sabatier, 2007a: 7). Further, if you compare the contents pages of this book with those of Sabatier (2007a) and John (1998; 2012) you will see agreement on which theories and issues now deserve the most attention: new institutionalism, rational choice, multiple streams, punctuated equilibrium, advocacy coalitions, policy transfer, socio-economic factors, policy networks (and multi-level governance) and the role of power and ideas.

In this context, the aim of the book is to focus on theories of public policy at the expense of an approach which devotes a chapter to all or most stages of the policy cycle. Yet, I also demonstrate in Chapters 2 and 5 why a discussion of public policy is incomplete without comprehensive rationality and policy cycles. Most theories still draw on the concept of bounded rationality and most explore the consequences of cyclical decision making in which policy represents 'its own cause' (Wildavsky, 1980: 62; Hogwood and Gunn, 1984: 245). Studies of public policy are incomplete without this consideration of the context within which decisions are made, the limited resources that policymakers possess and their limited ability to change decisions made in the past.

Power, agenda setting and public policy

Power is a central concept in political science and the role of Chapter 3 is to set up the key issues. Its starting point is the 'community power' debate which explores different characterizations of power and the extent to which we can observe and measure it. At the heart of such discussions is the question of proof: how do we demonstrate that some are powerful and others are powerless? What is the evidence and where can we find it? For instance, power can be described in terms of reputations. It can relate to who we think or know is powerful. The most obvious illustration is elected policymakers who are, in principle, given the authority to govern by the electorate. Our aim in this context is to examine the extent to which that power is used in good faith. For example, we may examine the responsiveness of public policy to public opinion or the electoral and legal mechanisms used to keep policymakers in check. Yet, more attention is often given to the reputational power of *unelected* elites and organizations such as businesses and interest groups that represent business. We can see the importance of that focus if we return to the banking crisis example. Elected officials may make policy, and take heed of public opinion, but they are also acutely aware of the views and beliefs of the banking sector.

Discussions of power go well beyond Chapter 3. Most studies of public policy are based on an initial consideration of the concentration of power – is it concentrated in the hands of a few elites or dispersed more widely? In fact, it may be concentrated *and* dispersed. Public policy is broken down into a series of sectors and sub-sectors and most groups direct their attention to a small number of issues. Elites may dominate one sub-sector while other elites dominate others. The dominance of *particular* issues or aspects of policy is a key part of the study of public policy. Powerful groups often maintain their position by minimizing attention to certain issues. Policy change requires attention from policymakers and other interested participants but such attention is a rare commodity: a policymaker can only consider so many issues, a newspaper can contain only a handful of headlines and the public will only pay fleeting attention to politics. Power is exercised to make sure that important issues do not arrive at the top of the policy agenda.

This outcome may be achieved in several ways. First, issues are portrayed as not worthy of high-level or widespread attention. They can be portrayed as issues that were once important but have now been solved, with only the technical and unimportant issues of implementation to address. Or, they can be described as private issues that the government should not become involved in. Second, issues can be 'crowded out' of the policy agenda by other issues that command more attention. Third, the rules and procedures of government can be manipulated to make sure that proponents of certain issues find it difficult to command policymaker attention. We can find elements of all three in our banking example: the rules and regulations of banking are obscure and difficult for most of us to understand; banking rarely received critical attention when the economy was booming; issues such as banking bonuses have often been defended as a private matter (at least until governments bailed out certain banks); and, critics of the regulatory system have found it difficult (until recently) to be heard within government circles.

Governance and the power of the centre

Our discussions also relate to the concentration of power within government. Two related questions are explored throughout the book: is power concentrated at the centre of government; and, should power be concentrated at the centre of government? For example, the ideals of comprehensive rationality and policy cycles both suggest that power should be held centrally, perhaps because central policymakers are elected and implementers are not. In particular, a condition of 'perfect implementation' is that central policymakers have 'perfect control' and that the people who carry out their decisions display 'perfect obedience'

(Hogwood and Gunn, 1984: 198). Yet, this may be an inappropriate model because implementing officials may also be elected and have a legitimate and practical role in the making of policy. Or, in broader terms, a concentration of power in one place without checks and balances may be the best formula for its abuse.

The concentration of power is a key feature of discussions of federalism and multi-level governance (MLG) in Chapter 8. Both identify the absence of a single centre of government. Federalist studies identify a dispersal of power to multiple institutions and examine how they negotiate with each other (intergovernmental relations). MLG takes it one step further. It identifies a further dispersal of power to quasi and non-governmental actors and, in effect, blurry boundaries between formal and informal sources of authority. In some cases, such as the US and Switzerland, power is often devolved to a range of *elected* organizations. In others, power is often held by unelected quasi-non-governmental organizations (quangos), and policy is influenced heavily by non-governmental organizations. In our banking example, this might refer to the role of the central bank, which often operates independently of government, and financial regulators which are often quangos that work closely with the financial services industry.

Our main focus is on the difference that power diffusion makes to public policy processes and outcomes. MLG suggests that the process is messy: many actors may be involved at various levels of government and their relationships vary across time and policy issue. This makes policy outcomes difficult to predict because the formal responsibility for policy issues changes over time, different actors may become involved and there may be scope to influence and change policy at different stages of the process.

Individuals, institutions and environments

Policy conditions – refers to the nature or structure of the policy environment and hence the specific problems that policymakers face. Relevant contextual factors include a political system's size, demographic structure, economy and mass behaviour (Chapter 6).

Our understanding of power also informs our explanation of policy dynamics. When we seek to understand policy change, do we assign responsibility to the individuals that make policy decisions, the institutions in which they operate or the **policy conditions** and the socio-economic pressures that they face? Of course, the answer is: all three. In analytical terms, it is question of **structure** and **agency** (Chapter 6; Hay, 2002: 89). In practice, these processes are difficult to separate: policymakers act in accordance with institutional rules and their action depends partly on the nature of the

Structure – a set of parts put together in a particular way to form a whole. More importantly, the implications are: (a) that a structure is relatively fixed and difficult but not impossible to break down; and (b) it influences the decisions that actors make. Examples include economic structures and institutional rules.

Agency – refers to the ability of an actor to act to realize its goals. The implication is that this is intentional action based on an actor's thought process and ability to choose (rather than determined by the structure of the decision-making environment).

problem they face. Yet, these concepts still have an analytical value. They help us simplify and make sense of rather complex processes, and therefore help us draw generalizations and develop theories to explain other events and processes. Further, although we may agree that policy change results from a wide range of factors, theories often devote their attention to certain aspects: institutions (Chapter 4), the comprehensively rational policy-maker (Chapter 5), structural factors (Chapter 6) and the aggregate behaviour of individuals (Chapter 7).

In each case, if our focus throughout the book is on power, we must decide who or what can possess and exercise it. For example, we may attribute the exercise of power only to individuals because socio-economic and institutional structures do not act and therefore cannot exercise power. This appears to make things simpler, but it just raises another question: how else can we describe convincingly the importance of institutions and structures? Each chapter addresses these questions in different, but often complementary, ways. The rationality approach, explored in Chapters 5 and 7, focuses on the characteristics of actors such as policymakers. It identifies a series of assumptions about how individuals think and behave and identifies how much this explains, or explores what happens if these assumptions prove unrealistic (see Box 7.2 for a comparison of comprehensive rationality and rational choice theory). Rational choice theory employs 'methodological individualism' or a commitment to explain socio-political outcomes as the aggregation of the decisions of individuals. The basic aim is to establish how many, or what proportion of, political outcomes one can explain with reference to the choices of individuals under particular conditions.

These approaches compare with accounts that begin by considering the nature of the policymaking environment and how it impacts on the policy process. 'New institutionalism' (Chapter 4) treats institutions as sets of rules, norms, established practices and relationships that produce regular patterns of policymaking behaviour. Rules can be formal, such as the rules set out in the constitutions of political systems. Or, they can be informal, such as the common norms, understandings and expectations that people develop when they interact regularly with other people.

The basic premise of structural accounts (Chapter 6) is that powerful external forces determine, or at least influence, the way that individuals or governments make policy decisions. Or, policymakers are part of a large complex system that they have limited control over. There is a long list of examples and discussions to choose from. The socio-economic background of states may affect the size and scope of their welfare policies. There may be a strong imperative for governments to support the capitalist system and therefore the interests of the classes that benefit most from that system. We may identify the effects of 'globalization' – an imperative for governments to compete with each other to protect their economy and secure foreign direct investment, by reducing regulations, corporation taxes and public spending. We may explore the idea that policy represents 'its own cause': governments inherit massive policy commitments which constrain their ability to change policy beyond the margins; it is relatively difficult to introduce new policies and terminate others.

A combination of each approach suggests that we need to recognize the importance of structures and rules without saying that they determine behaviour. Contemporary theories of public policy address this issue by examining how policymakers and pressure participants adapt to their policy environment by, for example, using socio-economic shifts to set the agenda or 'learning' and adapting their beliefs to reflect those shifts (I use the term 'pressure participants' because not all participants are pressure or interest groups. They may also be businesses, organizations such as Universities, government agencies or different levels of government – see Jordan *et al.*, 2004). In our banking crisis example, we can identify the immense effect that the 'credit crunch' had on most governments. The issue rose to the top of their agenda and put incredible pressure on them to act. While most policymakers had, in theory, the ability to choose, they faced, in practice, a situation in which their choices were limited. In many cases, governments decided not only to bail out the banks but also to alter financial institutions, signalling their intent to change the rules in which the financial services industry operated and was regulated. Yet, few governments entertained a radical overhaul of the financial sector. Instead, they worked with, and amended, the system they inherited.

Bureaucratic politics, policy networks and group–government relations

A focus on big government and the inheritance of policy commitments suggests that many decisions are effectively outwith the control of individual policymakers. If they focus on one issue they have to ignore at least 99 others. As a result, most policies may change very little because they receive little attention. This theme can also be found in studies of 'subsystems' or 'policy networks'. Richardson and Jordan (1979) argue that policy change is generally incremental because most policy decisions are beyond the reach of policymakers. The sheer size of government, and the potential for 'overload', necessitates breaking policy down into more manageable units. Therefore, the policymaking world tends to be specialized, with the responsibilities of government divided into **sectors** and **sub-sectors**.

Sectors – broad policy areas, such as economic, foreign, agriculture, health and education.

Policymakers devolve the responsibility for policy management within these sub-sectors to civil servants who, in turn, rely on interest groups and other pressure participants for information and advice. These arrangements exist because there is a logic to devolving decisions and consulting with certain affected interests. Policymakers rely on their officials for information and advice. For specialist issues, officials rely on specialist organizations. Those organizations trade information (and other resources, such as the ability to implement government policy) for access to, and influence within, government. Consequently, much public policy is conducted primarily through policy networks which process 'technical' issues at a level of government not particularly visible to the public, often with minimal policymaker or senior civil service involvement. Participants tend to be specialists and we find in many fields that relationships develop between those who deliver policy and those who seek to influence it. Our aim is to establish how stable those relationships are and what effect they have on policy decisions.

Sub-sectors – specific policy issues or niches within sectors, such as (within agriculture) seed potato regulations or growth hormones in dairy production.

The policy networks literature suggests that most public policy is processed in relatively small policy networks that often operate out of the public spotlight. However, most approaches now try to capture a change in group–government relationships since the early post-war period. We have moved from a small, insulated 'clubby world' to a more competitive and complex political system, containing a much larger number of groups, experts and other policy participants, which makes it much more difficult for policy issues to be insulated from attention and for groups to restrict debate. This process is the focus for three chapters in this book, all of which seek to capture the changing group–government world in different contexts and with different concepts.

The multi-level governance literature (Chapter 8) links these changes to events and decisions made by governments in the past. For example, many governments reformed their public sectors from the late 1970s in the spirit of 'new public management', which describes (rather vaguely) the application of private sector business methods to the public sector. Many sold off previously nationalized industries and contracted the delivery of services to non-governmental organizations. The reforms have reduced the ability of central governments to deliver public services directly. They are now more likely to 'steer' rather than 'row', negotiating and making shared decisions with actors outwith the public sector. In countries such as the UK, the era of Europeanization, combined with the devolution of power to sub-national authorities, has further complicated the national government role. Decision-making responsibility is now shared across multiple levels of government, and with quangos and non-governmental actors. Consequently, the government is no longer able to centralize and insulate decision making. Rather, the policy process contains a much larger number of actors that central government must negotiate with to pursue its policy aims. Further, the group–government world has become much more complicated, with many groups lobbying and seeking to influence policy in multiple venues. The result is a rather messy policy process.

Punctuated equilibrium theory (Chapter 9) examines the changing group–government world to explain why political systems can be characterized as both stable *and* dynamic. Most policies stay the same for long periods while some change very quickly and dramatically. Punctuated equilibrium explains this dynamism with a combination of bounded rationality and agenda setting: since decision makers cannot consider all issues at all times, they ignore most and promote relatively few to the top of their agenda. This lack of attention to most issues helps explain why groups and officials can maintain closed policy communities and why most policies do not change. 'Policy monopolies' are created by 'framing' an issue in such a way as to limit the number of participants who can claim a legitimate role in the process. Groups argue that a policy problem has been solved, with only the technical and unimportant issues of implementation to address. If successful, the 'technical' description reduces public interest and the 'specialist' description excludes those groups considered to have no expertise.

Yet, in the smaller number of instances in which policymakers *do* focus on these issues, their levels of attention are disproportionate and their response is 'hypersensitive'. Change comes from a successful challenge to the way that an issue is framed, by finding other influential audiences with an interest in new ways of thinking. In many cases this shift can be explained by an increasingly crowded and multi-level policymaking process. When groups are excluded at one level, they 'venueshop', or seek influential audiences in other venues such as legislative committees, the courts or other levels of government. If they catch the attention of another venue, newly involved policymakers increase their demand for new information and new ways to think about and solve old policy problems. In a process of government characterized by interdependence between groups and government, and overlapping jurisdictional boundaries (in which many institutions can be influential in the same policy areas), these innovations can be infectious. The actions of one often catch the attention of others, producing a 'bandwagon effect' of attention and major policy change.

For the advocacy coalition framework (Chapter 10), the policy process is driven by actors attempting to translate their beliefs into public policy. Common beliefs bring people together within advocacy coalitions. In turn, different coalitions with different beliefs compete with each other within sub-systems. It identifies a complex and crowded political system and focuses on policy change over 'a decade or more' to reflect the importance of implementation. Widening the scope of study in this way means including multiple levels of government and a range of actors involved at various policy stages. The ACF partly represents an attempt to show how socio-economic factors are mediated by actors within policy networks. The idea is that within a policy sub-system these advocacy coalitions are not only jostling for position but also learning from past policy and revising their strategic positions based on new evidence and the need to react to external events. While many of these external factors – such as global recession, environmental crises and demographic changes – may be universally recognized as important, coalitions influence how policymakers understand, interpret and respond to them. They do so by adapting to events by drawing on their policy beliefs, and then promoting their understanding of the policy situation within the sub-system.

Overall, we have three major theories that draw on similar starting points – a focus on sub-systems and the relatively open nature of group–government relations – but take different positions on the factors that drive the policy process. The value for our focus on multiple perspectives is that each theory is applicable to more than one political system. While the ACF and punctuated equilibrium developed from studies of the US, they have been applied successfully to many other systems. While MLG developed from a study of the EU, it is applicable to other systems and has strong parallels to studies of federalism. It is therefore possible to consider the same case study from a variety of viewpoints, using each theory to draw our attention to different aspects of the same process.

In our banking example, MLG invites us to consider the deregulation of financial services and the development of policy networks of businesses and regulatory bodies outwith the public spotlight and often far removed from government attention. It may also highlight the need for governments to negotiate with (as well as, or rather than, merely compel) financial institutions to produce policy change. Punctuated equilibrium helps us track the effects of attention on policy. We can identify policy continuity when attention to finance was low, partly because long periods of growth helped groups present the policy problem as solved, with only experts interested in the technical details. Attention then rose dramatically following the credit crunch, prompting a huge number of groups to become involved in a range of policymaking venues.

Governments that had previously supported the market and deregulation suddenly came under pressure to guarantee deposits in, or buy shares in, banks to reinstate confidence and stop the major institutions from failing. The ACF helps us identify the role of beliefs and the way that they shape policy decisions. For example, we might identify two competing coalitions – an anti-regulation coalition that believes government intervention makes business less efficient, and a pro-regulation coalition that wants governments to curb the ability of businesses to take risks and regulate their behaviour to ensure particular ends (such as a cap on banker bonuses or more favourable rights for employees). We might expect that the anti-regulation coalition was relatively powerful until the economic crisis that undermined its belief system. A coalition unable to explain what went wrong may find itself out of favour with key government actors, prompting a shift in the balance of power within subsystems.

The role of ideas

As our focus on beliefs shows, policymaking is not just about people exercising power to pursue their interests. It is also about the role of ideas. A key concern of policy studies is to 'take ideas seriously' by recognizing the 'symbiotic relationship between power and ideas; to treat explanations for policy outcomes as more than the mere extension of power politics or the battle of ideas' (Kettell and Cairney, 2010: 302). This relationship can take many forms, reflecting the many ways in which we can define ideas. For example, ideas may be the shared beliefs that give people a common aim and a reason to believe that they have shared interests. They can represent the accumulation and establishment of knowledge within the political system, used to make policy decisions. Ideas may be paradigms, or the most established ways for people to understand their environment. Paradigmatic ideas are taken for granted and acted upon with little further thought. Ideas can be norms, or represent standards of behaviour that are considered to be normal and therefore acceptable. Ideas can be ideologies, or a more comprehensive set of political beliefs, used by individuals or groups as the basis for policy action. In each case, the exercise of power takes place in a context in which only certain beliefs or norms of behaviour may be considered acceptable. In this sense, ideas may represent a constraint on policy action. This understanding compares with the identification of ideas as more dynamic factors: 'viruses' that infect political systems; visions of political leaders used to 'carry' the electorate with them; or, policy proposals or new solutions that lead to policy change.

Combined, ideas represent both a constraint on, and a resource that can be used to encourage, policy change. It is this relationship between power and ideas, and conception of ideas as sources of stability and instability, which the literature tries to capture (Chapter 11). When we examine the role of ideas, we are looking for ways to identify: (a) the beliefs or thought processes of policymakers; (b) the factors that help maintain those beliefs; and, (c) the factors that might contribute to a change in beliefs, or how policymakers think and then act. When ideas are treated as 'viruses' we also consider the role of the 'host' and the ability of existing policymakers, with established beliefs, to resist 'infection'. Norms have a strong influence on behaviour but perhaps mostly when people exercise power to enforce them. Paradigms may represent the most established beliefs about what the nature of the policy problem is and how we should solve it, but crises also prompt policymakers to revisit, and often reject, those beliefs. In particular, Chapter 11 considers multiple streams analysis which suggests that, although the adoption of a policy solution may *seem* inevitable in retrospect, it requires the coming together of three factors at the same time: a problem is high on the agenda and 'framed' in a particular way, a solution already exists, and policymakers have the motive and opportunity to adopt that solution and translate it into policy. The relationship between power and ideas is also considered in other chapters: it is central to 'constructivist institutionalism' (Chapter 4); ideas are used to create a monopoly on the way that we understand policy issues (Chapter 9); and, beliefs are the 'glue' that bind coalition members in the advocacy coalition framework (Chapter 10).

Chapter 12 focuses on the transfer of ideas. The literature on policy transfer refers to the evidence for, and causes of, similarities in policy across political systems. This can relate to the transfer of ideologies and wholesale programmes, broad ideas, minor administrative changes and even negative lessons (when one country learns *not* to follow another country). Our discussion of ideas suggests that the scale and likelihood of transfer depends partly on the beliefs already held within the importing country. To take an extreme example, a capitalist and a socialist country may not find much to learn from each other about how to balance the public and private sectors or pursue economic growth. In less extreme examples, we may focus more on the rather technical reasons for the likelihood of transfer: if the borrowing country has an incentive to learn from another (for example, if they share a common problem and have a similar political system); if the policy is simple and easy to adopt; if the values of borrower and lender coincide; and, if their administrative arrangements are similar. Our discussion of power suggests that some countries may also become pressured to follow the lead of another. Chapter 12 explores the role of coercion, from the direct pressure of another country or supranational institution, to the feeling among an importing country that it should keep up with international trends. Overall, the study of transfer gives us the ability to explain not only why policy changes, but also the extent to which that change is common throughout the world.

In our banking example, we may identify in many countries some ideas that underpin policy, including 'economic growth is a key goal', to ideas that suggest the private sector is best placed to produce growth. Government adherence to such basic ideas can be used by economic groups to undermine policy solutions calling for a much greater involvement of the state (although most states actually regulate the economy rather extensively). Such attitudes will also influence the transfer of ideas and even the search for lessons elsewhere. For example, the UK and US rarely seek lessons on economic reform from China. Further, they might look to places such as Japan and Germany but find that their attitudes to business are different and that many lessons are not directly applicable. On the other hand, the economic example is further complicated by globalization and the interdependence between states. While governments may disagree about the solution to the financial crisis they are under some pressure to cooperate because their actions may have an effect on the actions of other governments.

Stability and instability; continuity and change

A central aim of most theories is to explain why policymaking involves stable relationships and policy continuity at one point, but instability and policy change at another. There is a discussion of policy continuity and change in every chapter. Policy cycle models identify decision points at which policy will change, but also that decisions made in the past constrain present options. Theories of power highlight the ways in which the powerful create or reinforce barriers within decision making, but also that these can be overcome. New institutionalism may focus on the constraints on policy change, often caused by events and decisions in the past, but also the extent to which rules and norms are challenged and reformed. Bounded rationality can produce both incremental and radical change. Structural factors are generally cited as sources of constraint, but developments such as demographic change can put immense pressure on policymakers to respond. Rational choice theory aims to identify points of equilibrium, in which there is no incentive for any individual to make a different choice, but much analysis seeks to explain the frequent absence of equilibrium and the potential for 'cycling'. MLG identifies new sources of 'veto points' within political systems, but also new sources of policy innovation and diffusion. Punctuated equilibrium uses theories of bounded rationality and agenda setting to explain long periods of stasis but bursts of innovation. The ACF identifies the core beliefs of advocacy coalitions, and the parameters of policy (such as fundamental social structures) as sources of continuity, but policy learning and external shocks to the sub-system as drivers for change. Ideas can represent paradigms that represent stability and continuity, but also new policy proposals that can be used to encourage change. We may also consider if decision makers seek lessons from elsewhere to pursue innovation or legitimize existing decisions.

In each case, the theories only tell us that policymaking *can* be stable or unstable; that policy *can* change or stay the same. We must also establish *what happens*, using theoretical constructs to guide empirical studies. In other words, it is up to us to identify what policy is and the extent to which it has changed. We use multiple perspectives to help us identify and then explain that change.

The structure of the book

The book is designed to introduce theories and concepts in a particular order. Chapters 2–4 introduce key concepts and background to the study of public policy:

- *Chapter 2*. We consider the meaning of public policy, describe the main ways to identify policy types and measure change, examine the role of models, theories and concepts and examine the classic starting point of policy analysis: the policy cycle.
- *Chapter 3*. We explore power as a key concept that underpins discussion in all subsequent chapters. We derive insights from the 'community power debate' to consider how to define power and consider the methods to identify power within policymaking systems.
- *Chapter 4*. We consider how to define institutions and identify the new study of institutionalism. We explore the role of institutions as the sets of laws and rules that govern the operation of policymaking systems.

Chapters 5–7 explore the role of structure and agency in policy studies:

- *Chapter 5*. We consider the second classic starting point for policy analysis: comprehensive rationality. We focus on policymakers at the heart of government and consider what conditions need to be met to ensure that they have the ability to research and articulate a series of consistent policy aims and then make sure that they are carried out. Our identification of 'bounded rationality' allows us to consider what happens when these conditions are not met.
- *Chapter 6*. We effectively start at the other end of the spectrum, identifying the role of factors that may be beyond the control of policymakers. Lowi's (1964) famous point is that too many people assume that policy analysis should begin with a discussion of 'rational' poli-

cymakers rather than the environment in which they operate. We explore the key 'structural' causes of policy outcomes (including the role of institutions), the extent to which policymakers are influenced by economics, the idea that policymakers inherit policy commitments and the idea that they form one part of a large complex policymaking system.

- *Chapter 7*. We consider the role of rational choice theory. While it appears to embody a primary focus on the role of individuals, it actually considers how they operate within structured environments. This can be demonstrated with 'game theory' which identifies the different ways that individuals act when faced with different incentives and constraints. Rational choice theory raises a series of important questions about the ability of individuals to 'free ride' (or enjoy the benefits of collective action without taking part) and how institutions can be structured to influence their behaviour.

Chapters 8–10 explore the relationships between policymakers and policy participants within policy networks or subsystems. Each chapter considers how to characterize the move from a small, insulated 'clubby world' to a more competitive and complex political system:

- *Chapter 8*. We identify multi-level governance, or the dispersal of power from national central government to other levels of government and non-governmental actors. We consider how do define governance and MLG, identify its origins in studies of the UK and EU, consider its applicability to other political systems and identify the links between MLG and other theories studying sub-systems.
- *Chapter 9*. We consider punctuated equilibrium theory, whose aim is to explain long periods of policy stability and continuity punctuated by short but intense periods of instability and change. Punctuated equilibrium theory is based on the study of bounded rationality, policy sub-systems and the literature on agenda setting. We explore the ability of interest groups to 'venue shop', or seek sympathetic audiences elsewhere, when they are dissatisfied with the way that policymakers understand and seek to solve policy problems.
- *Chapter 10*. We consider the advocacy coalition framework. It focuses on the role of coalitions driven by their common beliefs. Coalitions compete with each other, within sub-systems, to gain the favour of policymakers. Some coalitions can dominate the way that policy problems are understood and solved for long periods, but are also subject to challenge when external 'shocks' force them (and others) to reconsider the adequacy of their beliefs.

Chapters 11 and 12 consider the role and transfer of ideas:

- *Chapter 11*. Our basic premise is that policymaking is not just about power. Instead, we must identify how power and ideas combine to explain policy processes and outcomes. We consider how to define and identify ideas, explore the ways in which theories of public policy conceptualize the relationship between power and ideas, and outline the importance of 'multiple streams analysis' to capture both the explanatory power of ideas and ways in which ideas are promoted and accepted within government.
- *Chapter 12*. We consider the transfer of ideas from one policymaking system to another and consider the global spread of ideas. In some cases, transfer follows learning, when the knowledge of one system is used to inform policy in another. However, the transfer of ideas or policy programmes is also about power and the ability of some countries to oblige or encourage others to follow their lead. We consider what policy transfer is, who does it and why.

However, the chapters do not need to be read in strict chronological order. For example, Chapters 3 and 11 can be usefully combined to consider the role of power and ideas. Chapters 3 and 9 consider power and agenda setting. Chapters 4 and 6 have a common focus on structure and agency. Chapters 5 and 7 consider the role of rationality and agency in different but complementary ways. The role of Chapter 13 is to consider these multiple links in more detail and to consider how best to combine theories and concepts in public policy.

Conclusion

The most basic question we ask ourselves when studying public policy is: what do we want to know? The answer is that we want to know: what policy is; what policy measures exist; what measures have been taken; and how to best make sense of what has happened. In particular, we want to know what the most useful theories of public policy are, what each of them tells us, and what the cumulative effect of their knowledge is. We study theories of public policy because we want to ask why particular decisions are made, but recognize that there are many different answers to that question. The use of multiple theories allows us to examine the policy process, and build up a detailed narrative of events and decisions, using multiple perspectives. We focus on policymakers and seek to identify how they understand policy problems, how high the problem is on their agenda and which arguments and solutions they are most receptive to. We identify the political, social and economic pressures that they face when making decisions. We identify the main governing institutions and examine the rules they follow when they process issues. We identify policy networks and the relationships between interest groups and government. We also consider the extent to which policy is within the control of elected policymakers; how much is devolved to other actors such as civil servants and groups, other types of government and non-governmental organizations.

Each chapter sets out a key theory or concern of public policy, identifies its value and explores the questions that each theory seeks to answer. It then considers, where appropriate, how each theory or concept has been applied empirically and how much it tells us about different political systems, policy areas and time periods. The role of Chapter 13 is to consider how to best combine the insights of public policy theories. Theories can be synthesized to produce a single theory or kept separate to encourage multiple perspectives. Theories can also present contradictory analysis and empirical outcomes, suggesting the need to replace rather than accumulate our policy knowledge in some cases. In other words, we may identify common questions but different and perhaps contradictory ways to answer them. While we would like to combine the merits and insights of each theory, we must also consider whether this is a process of accumulating the knowledge gained from each theory or whether the results from one approach undermine those of another. Are these complementary or contradictory explanations?

Chapter 2

What is Public Policy? How Should We Study It?

The aim of this chapter is to:

- Consider definitions of public policy and policy analysis.
- Describe the main ways to measure policy change and identify policy types.
- Develop the idea of competing narratives to describe and explain the results of policy studies.
- Establish the role of theories and models of the policy process.
- Describe the 'stages' or 'policy cycles' approach to policy analysis.
- Explain why the policy cycles approach has been replaced by other theories.

'Public policy' is important because the scope of the state extends to almost all aspects of our lives. However, it is one of many terms in political science – like democracy, equality and power – that are well known but difficult to define. The problem of definition is more than semantic: it affects how we analyse and understand real policy issues. Different definitions, drawing on different aspects of the policy process, give us multiple perspectives. The first aim of this chapter is to explore such definitions. It does not construct a common definition from this discussion. Rather, it identifies key points that arise from the public policy literature: policy can refer to an aim, a decision or an outcome; it may refer to issues that policymakers do *not* to address; and, it is made and influenced by many actors who may or may not have formal authority. In other words, policymaking is a complex and far-reaching process that involves many individuals, groups and institutions. The second aim is to identify three complementary ways to simplify and make sense of its complexity: categorizing policy measures; producing narratives of policymaking; and, using analytical frameworks or theories to organize the study of, and explain, policymaking. These measures help us produce a checklist of methods to simplify and manage the study of complex policy processes.

A useful starting point is to draw on established ways to categorize policy measures, such as when Lowi (1964) famously compares regulation, distribution and redistribution. Such typologies show us that different kinds of policy have different characteristics and are associated with different styles of politics (John, 1998: 7–8). A key tenet of the public policy literature is that we need to identify and account for this variation. Policy outcomes and processes vary according to the political system and territory we study, the time period we choose and the policy area we focus on. Indeed, there may also be variation *within* policy areas when different issues display different characteristics.

This variation and complexity makes public policy difficult to measure or characterize. Although we can identify the types of policy instruments available to policymakers, the list of measures is long and it is difficult to know how significant each decision will be. Indeed, the more measures or decisions there are to choose from, the greater potential the researcher has to construct biased accounts of policymaking. There is always more than one way to interpret the significance and direction of policy from the evidence available. This point may prompt us to consider different accounts or 'narratives' of policymaking depending on which policy decisions we attach the most importance (Cairney, 2007a).

The problem of definition and measurement prompts us to consider how best to make sense of policymaking complexity. Models, frameworks and theories are there to help us analyse and explain complex policy processes. The model of the policy cycle is a good starting point for our analysis since many contemporary theories draw on the idea of a process that contains different stages. The model identifies a difference between a policymaker's intention and the policy outcome and has prompted a considerable literature devoted to the 'implementation gap'. A key way to understand this gap is to consider the stages through which a policy must pass before an authoritative decision is made and carried out: the agenda-setting stage is followed by policy formulation, the legitimation of policy, the assignment of the budget, the implementation of policy and policy evaluation. The cycle metaphor suggests that the evaluation stage of policy 1 represents the first stage of policy 2, as lessons learned in the past form the basis for choices in the future. In other words, policymaking is a never-ending process rather than a single event; different actors are influential at different stages and previous decisions often set the agenda for future decisions. Yet, it has also been subject to many criticisms and replaced by other theories. This chapter considers why it has fallen out of favour and how new theories build on (or reject) its insights.

What is public policy?

Hogwood and Gunn (1984: 13–19) identify different ways in which 'policy' can be understood: as a label for a field of activity (e.g. health policy); an expression of intent (e.g. 'we will improve healthcare'); specific proposals (e.g. a manifesto or white paper); decisions of government and the formal authorization of decisions (e.g. legislation); a programme, or package of legislation, staffing and funding; intermediate and ultimate outputs (e.g. more doctors, better medical care); outcomes, or what is actually achieved (better health); and a process, not an event, or a series of decisions, not a single decision. Box 2.1 provides further discussions of public policy and policy analysis, but the literature generally questions our ability to define policy (Smith and Larimer, 2009: 3–4; 25; 239; Colebatch, 1998: 72–3). The next best thing is to explore the issues that arise when we start with a simple definition. Defining public policy as the 'sum total of government action' raises four key questions.

First, does government action include what policymakers say they will do as well as what they actually do? Political parties produce manifestos and elected officials produce speeches setting out their policy plans, but should we wait until those plans are carried out until we call them public policy? This may seem appropriate because policymaking is 'often more symbolic than substantive' and statements are often made by policymakers to make it look like they are doing something when they are not (McGarvey and Cairney, 2008: 202; Althaus, Bridgman and Davis, 2007: 5; Dearlove in Colebatch, 1998: 9). Yet, it is difficult to know when to say that an aim has been pursued enough to constitute policy. Few would say that legislation is not policy until the budget is agreed to carry it out, but what about a consultation document officially setting out the government's plans (perhaps more common in parliamentary systems – Sabatier, 1998: 120)? This suggests that the identification of substantive policy measures is more of an art than a science.

Second, does it include the effects of a decision as well as the decision itself? We need to: (a) focus on policy outcomes as well as decisions; and, (b) recognize that those outcomes are influenced by factors outwith the control of policymakers. For example, they can ensure that money is put aside to pay for an *output* such as doctors or teachers. However, they can do less to ensure an *outcome*, such as an improvement on the health or education of the nation, because this also relies on the behaviour of the population (Colebatch, 1998: 114).

Third, what is 'the government' and does it include elected and unelected policymakers? It is worth considering how actors gain membership within the policy process (Colebatch, 1998: 16; Hale, 1988). They may have a recognized source of authority – such as presidents and elected members of the legislature. Or, they may have a recognized form of expertise that gives them policy influence, or be required to make sure that policy decisions are carried out – such as interest groups and civil servants (Colebatch, 1998: 18–22; 31–2). Policy is made by such 'policy collectivities' (1998: 23; Colebatch, 2006: 1). It is the 'joint product of their interaction' (Rose, 1987: 267–8).

Box 2.1   Discussions of public policy

The actions of government and the intentions that determine those actions.

(Cochran *et al.* in Birkland, 2005: 18)

Diverse activities by different bodies are drawn together into stable and predictable patterns of action which (as often as not) come to be labelled 'policy'.

(Colebatch, 1998: x)

'Policy' is a general term used to describe a formal decision or plan of action adopted by an actor ... to achieve a particular goal ... 'Public policy' is a more specific term applied to a formal decision or a plan of action that has been taken by, or has involved, a state organisation.

(Richards and Smith, 2002: 1)

Whatever governments choose to do or not to do.

(Dye in Birkland, 2005: 18)

Decisions by governments to retain the status quo are just as much policy as are decisions to alter it.

(Howlett and Ramesh, 2003: 5)

Attention should not focus exclusively on decisions which produce change, but must also be sensitive to those which resist change and are difficult to observe.

(Smith in Hill, 2009: 15)

Discussions of policy analysis

Public policy is hard to research as it is a composite of different processes that cross-cut most branches of government and involve many decision-makers.

(John, 1998: 9)

Given the staggering complexity of the policy process, the analyst must find some way of simplifying the situation in order to have any chance of understanding it.

(Sabatier, 2007a: 4)

Fourth, does public policy include what policymakers do *not* do (Box 2.1)? Policymakers may actively ignore an issue, or merely attempt to *look* like they are addressing it, because: it is low on their list of priorities; they do not have the means to solve the problem; and/ or, they know that they will face significant opposition if they try. Or, they may not pay attention to an issue because they do not consider it to be a policy problem. While some of these reasons may seem innocuous, they raise crucial issues of power and agenda setting discussed in Chapters 3 and 9. In many cases, issues are low on the agenda because actors exercise power to reinforce social attitudes, or manipulate decision-making proce-dures, to make sure they stay that way. In some cases, this absence of attention allows policy to be processed without a formal statement of intent by elected policymakers (Colebatch, 1998: 99), raising important questions about who is accountable for the outcomes.

If we combine the answers to these questions we find that our initial attempt to provide a simple definition of public policy is replaced by a lengthy discussion which highlights complexity. In this light, how do we make the task of policy analysis manageable?

Measuring public policy

The first solution is to identify different *types* of public policy and the wide range of policy instruments available to, and used by, policymakers (Cairney, Studlar and Mamudu, 2012; Birkland, 2005: 174–7; Howlett, Ramesh and Perl, 2009; Bardach, 2009; compare with Sabatier and Jenkins-Smith's 1993: 227 list of 'guidance instruments available to coalitions'):

1 Public expenditure. This includes deciding how to tax, how much money to raise, on which policy areas (crime, health, education) to spend and the balance between current (e.g. the wages of doctors) and capital (building a new hospital) spending.
2 Economic penalties, such as taxation on the sale of certain products, or charges to use services.
3 Economic incentives, such as subsidies to farmers or tax expendi-ture on certain spending (giving to charity, buying services such as health insurance).
4 Linking government-controlled benefits to behaviour (e.g. seeking work to qualify for unemployment benefits) or a means test.
5 The use of formal regulations or legislation to control behaviour.
6 Voluntary regulations, such as agreements between governments and other actors such as unions and business.
7 Linking the provision of public services to behaviour (e.g. restricting the ability of smokers to foster children).
8 Legal penalties, such as when the courts approve restrictions on, or economic sanctions against, organizations.
9 Public education and advertising to highlight the risks to certain behaviours.
10 Providing services and resources to help change behaviour.
11 Providing resources to tackle illegal behaviour.
12 Funding organizations to influence public, media and government attitudes.

13 Funding scientific research or advisory committee work.
14 Organizational change, such as the establishment of a new unit within a government department or a reform of local government structures.
15 Providing services directly or via non-governmental organizations.
16 Providing a single service or setting up quasi-markets.

There is also value in categorizing and identifying the nature of these instruments, if only to make the research process more manageable. The most famous attempt is by Lowi (1964; 1972; Smith, 2002) who distinguishes between regulatory, distributive, redistributive and constituent policies. It is built on the argument that 'policies determine politics': the nature of the policy measure, and the level of coercion required to implement it, determines how policy is made (Lowi, 1972: 299). For example, the politics of redistribution, in which one social group clearly benefits from public funding at the expense of another, may differ from distribution in which the trade-off is much less apparent (compare with Lipsky, 1980: 8–9). Or, distributive policy, providing a benefit to a social group, may differ from regulatory policies if the latter incur costs (to comply with regulations, or fines for non-compliance) on individuals and private companies (Lowi, 1964: 690–1). In each case, the likely effect of policy on individuals will influence their levels of opposition, the ways in which they mobilize to influence policy, and the amount of government coercion required to ensure success. In short, 'every category of policy has its own political dynamic' (Lowi, 1988: 726; McCool, 1995: 246–8).

The value of such typologies is *not* to show us that there are clear-cut distinctions in policy types. The boundaries between each type are blurry and many policy measures can include elements of each type (Steinberger, 1980; John, 1998: 7; Smith and Larimer 2009: 41). Policy measures also mean different things to different people, making it difficult for governments to predict and anticipate how individuals will mobilise in reaction to them (2009: 42). The idea that 'policies determine politics' should also be treated with caution; Lowi's point was that too many people assumed that policy analysis should begin with a discussion of policymakers rather than the environment in which they operate. Policymakers may act differently when they face different policy problems. Different policy areas often have different characteristics, present different problems to solve, have different participants, and are associated with different styles of policymaking. They also have different starting points based on the legacies of past decisions (John, 1998: 7–8; Smith and Larimer, 2009: 234; Hill, 2009: ch. 7).

While the nature of the policy environment does not *determine* how policymakers behave, they will take these things into account. For example, in healthcare the medical profession generally commands respect and the policy agenda is often driven by technological advance. In education, there is less of a role for technology and more scope for the public and policymakers to influence 'technical' aspects of policy such as the school curriculum. Environmental policy is heavily populated by environmental and business groups competing to influence regulatory policies, while the agenda is often characterized by lurches of attention associated with disasters (including the Exxon Valdiz oil spill in 1989 and the BP oil leak in the Gulf of Mexico in 2010). In agriculture, the issues generally receive less attention and are populated by fewer groups (John, 1998: 6). We may also see variations within policy areas. For example, the issues of healthcare, mental health and public health are populated by different actors who often compete for resources and attention to their policy aims. These types of variation are often unpredictable since they vary over time (e.g. the groups involved in, and the agendas of, mental health policy have changed radically in the post-war period) and according to political system (e.g. compare a tax-funded healthcare system in the UK with different health insurance-based systems in France and the US). Stable arrangements are also prone to challenge when issue-based worlds collide – such as when the spread of genetically modified crops gets environmentalists and the public more interested in agricultural policy.

Narratives of public policy

A focus on the range of policy instruments available to study suggests that we may come to different conclusions on the nature of policy when we examine different indicators (or interpret the same indicators differently). Our ability to analyse the policy environment will always be limited and we may have different ideas about which measures are the most important (see Lavis *et al.*, 2002, for a demonstration). For example, we may identify a high-profile policy measure that involves the use of legislation but does not have the money or resources behind it to ensure that the policy aim is fulfilled. Or, we may find more 'successful' examples of low-key, informal and unfunded agreements, between the government and other actors, to pursue a common aim. In practice, most areas will contain a complex mixture of such high and low profile, formal and informal, funded and unfunded, successful and unsuccessful decisions and the aim of the researcher is to identify the most important policies from a long list of potentially important actions.

The scope for different perspectives is demonstrated well by interview research. For example, I have interviewed interest groups, favouring tobacco control, who viewed UK legislation to ban tobacco advertising and smoking in public places as a *watershed* in public policy because previous regulatory measures were based on badly enforced voluntary agreements between the government and the tobacco and leisure industries. I have also interviewed government actors who argue that such legislation represents *incrementalism* because other policy instruments demonstrate a clear direction of travel towards tobacco control (Cairney, 2007a). Such competing accounts cannot be rejected simply because they are biased – *all* accounts are biased in the sense that they are based on a limited number of indicators, the decision to give some indicators more weight, and an interpretation of the motivation behind, or effect of, policy measures. The potential for bias comes from many sources, including:

- *The timeframe.* We may conclude that nothing much has changed in the short term but that a lot has changed in the long term, or vice versa. 'Vignette' studies focus in detail on one key event, while historical studies track policy change over decades.
- *The level or type of government we study.* Since policy can often be made by a wide range of organizations (executives, legislatures, courts, devolved authorities, agencies), and influenced by a range of non-governmental actors, the standard advice (which is easier said than done) is to focus on the policy rather than the jurisdiction. Yet, there is still an issue of focus. If we 'zoom in' we might miss the effect of the wider political system; if we 'zoom out' we might miss important details.
- *Our expectations.* When we identify policy change we link it, at least implicitly, to a yardstick based on how much we expect it to change (based on who is powerful) and how much we think policy should change under the circumstances (e.g. given the size of problem or the level of public attention). For example, Crenson's (1971) study seeks to explain why certain policymakers did not do enough to control pollution (Chapter 3).
- *Motivation.* For example, economic sanctions can be introduced to change behaviour or merely to raise money. Policymakers can introduce measures to satisfy a particular interest or constituency, ensure a boost to their popularity or fulfil a long-term commitment based on fundamental beliefs. The distinction is crucial if the political weight behind a measure determines its success.
- *Statistical comparisons.* We may describe spending on an issue as a proportion of GDP, a proportion of the government budget, a proportion of the policy area's budget, in terms of change from last year or over many years. In some cases the amount of money spent by government could be compared with that spent by industry (e.g. Cairney 2007a compares the health education budget with the amount that tobacco companies spent advertising their product). Or, the level of

fines or taxes could be compared to the incomes of individuals or organizations (e.g. imagine a $1m fine on BP or Microsoft).

*   *Contradictory and inconsistent policies*. Things become complicated when governments appear to pursue contradictory policies in one area, or policies in one field that have unintended consequences for another (such as when school expulsion policies affect youth crime).
*   *Excitement*! Richardson (1982a: 199) argues that most policy is processed in less visible and contentious arenas despite an under-standable tendency for case studies to focus on 'spectacular' policy activity.

Narrative – an account of a series of events; a non-fictional 'story'. An attempt to 'render various series of events into an intelligible whole' (Kay, 2006: 23).

One way to address this issue is to construct different **narratives** of policy development. It is possible to produce competing and equally plausible accounts of the type, speed and nature of change for the same policy issue or series of events. This recommendation is not particularly striking – indeed, this is effectively what happens when different theories are applied to the same case study. Yet, our choice of narrative has a crucial effect on the value of each theory. Put simply, theories of public policy that seek, primarily, to explain policy stability or continuity are reinforced by narratives highlighting incremental change but not by narratives highlighting radical policy change. An alternative way to make the same point is to say that the theories are only valuable if the evidence supports them – but the evidence is rarely incontrovertible; it is difficult to talk of *the* evidence with great certainty (Head, 2008).

Theories, models and heuristics

The final way to make sense of policy complexity is to apply models and theories. The initial aim of a model is to provide a simplified representation of a specific object or process. This need not be a completely accurate representation to have value. For example, think of a model car used to represent the real thing (McCool, 1995: x), or the iconic London Underground map (Parsons, 1995: 59–61). A model can be used as a guide to description; as a way to simplify and manage policy analysis by identifying the key features of a more complex entity. It serves as an **heuristic device** to help describe the real thing.

Heuristic device – a tool used to guide investigation; a learning technique based on direct investigation using models or ideal types.

A theory is a set of analytical principles or statements designed to structure our observation and explanation of the world. It sets out the object of study's essential features and the relationship between those features. In other words, theories tell us what to look for and then they help explain what we find. Our initial aim when we use theories is to identify policy decisions and their main causes. Our ultimate aim is to examine the extent to which we can identify the same causes in other situations and therefore generalize from specific to numerous instances. Their usefulness is based on the idea that, although the world is immensely complex, we can still identify a small number of factors that explain what happens within it (Sabatier, 2007a: 5; John, 1998: 8). We might also hope that the theory is parsimonious; it explains to us what is happening in an efficient and uncomplicated way.

The theory-building process can often be divided into two stages. First, we move from the detailed identification of key events and decisions in particular cases towards the identification of abstract ideas that apply across all cases. Second, we use those abstract ideas to inform our study of subsequent case studies and, in doing so, attempt to confirm or deny the value of the theory (a difficult task, to say the least – see Chalmers, 1999 on the philosophy of science before comparing Sabatier, 2007a: 5 with Della Porta and Keating, 2008a; 2008b on science and method). For example, Baumgartner and Jones' (1993) work on 'punctuated equilibrium' began as a means to explain why certain groups were able to exert power by monopolizing not only access to decision makers but also the way that people understood and addressed policy problems – producing case studies on tobacco, nuclear power, the environment and pesticides in the US. Then, Jones and Baumgartner (2005) developed the 'general punctuation hypothesis': a more abstract theory, based on the ability of policymakers to process information and pay attention to policy issues, with the potential to be applicable to all policy areas and beyond the US (Chapter 9).

However, no-one has managed to produce a theory applicable to public policy as a whole. Indeed, there is some debate in the field about whether or not we should try (Smith and Larimer, 2009: 15–17) because the world is too complex, and there are too many causes of outcomes (many of which seem exclusive to individual cases), to allow for parsimonious explanation. Or, parsimonious theories may be valuable but only explain part of the process (e.g. punctuated equilibrium primarily explains agenda setting, not implementation). Consequently, much of the public policy literature represents 'thick description' – a process of modelling or mapping out complex terrain (John, 1998: 8–9; Hill, 1997: 2). Overall, the choice may be between using models to *map* particular outcomes and theories to *explain* many outcomes, but the boundaries between the two are not always as clear as this suggests: both processes are based on the identification of the essential features of the world and how they relate to each other; and, the same model may be applicable to many cases, while some theories do not explain much beyond their initial case studies.

What is the policy cycle?

The policy cycle is the best known way to organize the study of policy-making (and the best way to introduce a discussion of policy theories). It is tempting to view the policy cycle as a theory because it is used to represent the policy process in multiple political systems. The same can be said for many of its stages – terms such as 'agenda setting' and 'implementation' are widely applicable. Yet, it is generally viewed as a simple model of complex processes because it does not explain directly what happens – for example, why issues arise on the policy agenda or why a particular decision is made (although these processes are explained by theories operating within the cycle model – Smith and Larimer, 2009: 34). It is a model in two related ways:

1 *Prescription* – a model for how policymakers *should* operate, to make sure that their decisions are made in a systematic way.
2 *Description* – a model to describe how they *do* operate, to simplify the study of how they make decisions (Hogwood and Gunn, 1984: 42–3).

It divides the policy process into a series of stages, from a notional starting point at which policymakers begin to think about a policy problem to a notional end point at which a policy has been implemented and policymakers think about how successful it has been before deciding what to do next. The image is of a continuous process rather than a single event. The evaluation stage of policy 1 represents the first stage of policy 2, as lessons learned in the past set the agenda for choices to be made in the future.

There is some variation in the literature regarding the number of stages in a policy cycle, but most describe the identification of policymaker aims, the formulation of policies to achieve those aims, the selection and legitimation of policy measures, implementation and evaluation. Lasswell (1956) is generally credited with setting the ball rolling with a short text highlighting: intelligence, recommendation, prescription, invocation, application, appraisal and termination. This was followed by Jones' (1970) book in which each stage commanded a chapter: from defining the problem, setting the government's agenda, formulating proposals, having a programme or coherent set of proposals legitimated by the legislature, assigning a budget, implementing and evaluating policy (see also Anderson, 1975; and Brewer and deLeon, 1983: 18–20; Smith and Larimer, 2009: 30; Parsons, 1995: 78–9).

Notably, most cycles texts were based on the US political system which enjoys a strong legislature and a budget process that must be agreed between the executive and legislative branches. This explains why the legitimation and budgeting stages receive more attention than they might in a study of centralized, parliamentary systems. However, in a more abstract sense, the model portrays how *any* government attempts to translate 'inputs' such as public demands into 'outputs' such as public policies (see Hill, 2009: 141–2 on Easton). Further, the idea that this is how the cycle *should* operate in a democratic system is widespread: the public will becomes known, elected policymakers then make and legitimize decisions at separate stages before civil servants and other bodies carry them out (Jann and Wegrich, 2007: 44). Attempts to provide a model for the UK or equally applicable to the US and UK (Hogwood and Peters, 1983: 8; Hogwood and Gunn, 1984: 7–11; Jenkins, 1978) and for Australia (Althaus *et al.*, 2007; Bridgman and Davis, 2003: 100; Howard, 2005: 10–11), produced a very similar list of stages (as set out in Figure 2.1 overleaf):

- *Agenda setting*. Identifying problems that require government attention, deciding which issues deserve the most attention and defining the nature of the problem.
- *Policy formulation*. Setting objectives, identifying the cost and estimating the effect of solutions, choosing from a list of solutions and selecting policy instruments.
- *Legitimation*. Ensuring that the chosen policy instruments have support. It can involve one or a combination of: legislative approval, executive approval, seeking consent through consultation with interest groups, and referenda.
- *Implementation*. Establishing or employing an organization to take responsibility for implementation, ensuring that the organization has the resources (such as staffing, money and legal authority) to do so, and making sure that policy decisions are carried out as planned.
- *Evaluation*. Assessing the extent to which the policy was successful or the policy decision was the correct one; if it was implemented correctly and, if so, had the desired effect.
- *Policy maintenance, succession or termination*. Considering if the policy should be continued, modified or discontinued.

While the use of the cycle as a framework for policy studies has diminished, many of the terms used to describe its stages are integral to the discipline – and this book – because they command their own literature. The study of policy formulation is a constant theme throughout the book and is discussed at length in Chapter 5. The study of agenda setting is really the study of power and, as such, is discussed in Chapters 3 and

9. The idea that governments consult primarily with interest groups, perhaps more than the public or legislatures, to legitimize their policies is discussed in Chapters 8–10. That leaves the less-discussed but just-as-important issues of implementation, evaluation and succession. A simple lesson from the cycles literature is that the study of public policy does not end when an issue has been raised and a decision has been made. Indeed, some of the literature describes this as just the *beginning of* the policy process.

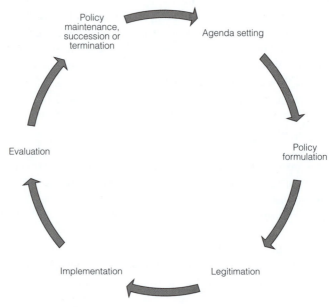

Figure 2.1   *The generic policy cycle*

Implementation

The study of implementation is based on the simple point that decisions made by policymakers may not be carried out successfully. Instead, we can identify an implementation 'gap' which represents the difference between the expectations of policymakers and the actual policy outcome (deLeon, 1999: 314–15; Hill and Hupe, 2009: 11). Hogwood and Gunn (1984: 197) attribute implementation failure to three main factors: *bad execution*, when it is not carried out as intended, *bad policy*, when it is carried out but fails to have the desired effect, and *bad luck*, when it is carried out and should work, but it is undermined by factors beyond the control of policymakers (Cairney, 2009a: 354, suggests that the gap is also wide because participants have unrealistic expectations). These explanations can be standardized in much the same way as the stages of a policy cycle. The common aim is to highlight the conditions that have to be met to ensure 'perfect' implementation success (Hood, 1976: 6; Hogwood and Gunn, 1984: 198; Sabatier, 1986: 23–4; Jordan and Richardson, 1987: 234–41; Birkland, 2005: 191; Cairney, 2009a: 357). The understanding is that, in fact, they explain why policies fail or achieve only partial success:

1 *The policy's objectives are clear, consistent and well communicated and understood.* A clear policy provides legal weight and acts as a 'standard of evaluation' (Sabatier, 1986: 23–4). A vague policy is subject to multiple interpretations and the potential for bad execution even by implementers with the best of intentions. For Hogwood and Gunn (1984: 204–6), perfect implementation requires that policy-makers: agree on a common understanding of objectives; fully specify those objectives in the correct sequence; and, coordinate the implementation process with no breakdown in communication.

2 *The policy will work as intended when implemented.* The policy must be a good solution to the problem, based on a 'valid theory of cause and effect' (if we do X, the result will be Y) (1984: 201).

3 *The required resources are committed to the programme.* Resources includes money, staffing and the 'real' resources necessary for success (such as the materials required for building programmes – 1984: 200). It also regards giving the task of implementation to an organization that 'would be supportive and give it a high priority', providing the right legal and economic sanctions and incentives to 'overcome resistance' (Sabatier, 1986: 23), and investing attention and political will to an issue over the longer term.

4 *Policy is implemented by skilful and compliant officials.* The term 'perfect obedience' (Hogwood and Gunn, 1984: 206) reminds us that we are discussing an ideal type; in fact, the discretion held by imple-menting officials with specialized jobs is 'unavoidable' (Sabatier, 1986: 23; Lipsky, 1980: 13–16; Hill and Hupe, 2009: 26).

5 *Dependency relationships are minimal.* There are few 'veto points' (Sabatier, 1986: 23) and the implementing agency does not rely on the cooperation of others (Hogwood and Gunn, 1984: 202).

6 *Support from influential groups is maintained.* The implementation process is long, and support from policymakers (and the interest groups that influence them) may be necessary to ensure that resources are maintained.

7 *Conditions beyond the control of policymakers do not significantly undermine the process.* Socio-economic conditions can often be unpre-dictable (such as oil crises and wars – Sabatier, 1986: 25) and affect the costs of, or support for, implementation (for example, consider the effects of an ageing population on pensions or personal care policies).

Pressman and Wildavsky (1973; 1979) draw on such factors to explain why the provision of US federal funds, for public works programmes to solve the problem of 'high unemployment and racial unrest', did not have the desired effect in Oakland, California. Many projects were not completed because: the building materials were not secured; there were too many 'decision points'; the implementing agencies relied on cooperation with many other authorities and private companies; the costs in some projects were higher than budgeted for; the legal framework was inadequate; there was disagreement about how spending money on training programmes would boost employment; the business loans programme contained incompatible aims; local groups opposed aspects such as low-cost public housing; and, the Economic Development Administration could not identify the influential groups from which it needed support (1979: 1; 35–6; 45; 51; 70–1; 87; 91–4; 98–100; 111).

We may suppose that some of these problems, such as interdependence, are specific to the US model of government in which power is shared by many organizations. However, examples from the 'majoritarian' UK demonstrate similar problems. Marsh and Rhodes (1992a) employ a similar framework to identify policy failures of the Thatcher government (1979–90): its privatization programme suffered because political objectives clashed with economic/ ideological objectives; monetarist economic policy suffered because the causal link between inflation and the money supply was suspect; the control of local authority budgets was undermined by local authorities; industrial relations policies lacked an adequate legislative framework; a policy to reduce social security spending was undermined by rising unemployment, and demographic effects (an ageing population) undermined the policy of healthcare financial stringency (although note that some of these policies, on privatization and industrial relations, are now considered by many to be successful).

In particular, they identify problems of interdependence exacerbated by the government's unwillingness to consult with interest groups before making decisions (1992a: 185). Those groups and agencies which were affected by policy, but not consulted, 'failed to co-operate, or comply, with the administration of policy' (1992a: 181). As Jordan and Richardson (1987: 242) show, there are four main advantages to consultation. First, it secures wider participation in the political system, and hence support for that system. Second, it creates a sense of involvement, and thus ensures greater commitment to the success of a policy. Third, it allows the government to benefit from the practical experience of those consulted. Finally, it allows some portion of responsibility for that success to be transferred to other participants. The argument that consultation allows a more informed government with fewer problems of agreement and compliance is almost universally applicable.

Top-down and bottom-up implementation

This approach is often labelled 'top down' because it is built on two related assumptions:

1 *Descriptive* – decisions are made at the 'top' (by central government or the legislature) and carried out at the 'bottom' (by implementing organizations).
2 *Prescriptive* – decisions should be made at the top and carried out at the bottom.

The 'bottom up' literature questions the assumption that central government is the main influence on policy outcomes. For example, Lipsky (1980) argues that policy is, to a large extent, made by the 'street-level bureaucrats' (including teachers, doctors, police officers, judges, and welfare officers) who deliver it. Bureaucrats are subject to an immense range of, often unclear, requirements laid down by regulations at the top, but are powerless to implement them all successfully (1980: 14). In other words, this is not necessarily an argument based on 'disobedience': committed workers do not have the resources to fulfil all of their job requirements (1980: xii). Instead, they use their discretion to establish routines to satisfy a proportion of central government objectives while preserving a sense of professional autonomy necessary to maintain morale. The irony is that the cumulative pressure associated with central government policy effectively provides implementers with a degree of freedom to manage their budgets and day-to-day activities. Therefore, policy change at the top will not necessarily translate to change at the bottom.

Hjern (1982: 213–16) argues that the assumption that policy is controlled by a single central actor with consistent aims exacerbates perceived and actual policy failure. Inattention to the complexity of implementation causes difficulties in the administration of policy, producing feelings of powerlessness when no one seems to be in charge. Instead, we should recognise *intra-departmental conflict,* when central government departments pursue programmes with competing aims, and *interdependence,* when policies are implemented by multiple organizations. Programmes are implemented through 'implementation structures' where 'parts of many public and private organizations cooperate in the implementation of a programme'. It is difficult to force decisions on actors within the structure who are employed by other organizations, so it is unrealistic to think that a sole central actor could secure its own aims and objectives irrespective of the actions of the others involved. Although national governments create the overall framework of regulations and resources, and there are 'administrative imperatives' behind the legislation authorizing a programme, the main shaping of policy takes place at local levels by implementation structures in which national considerations may play a small part (Hjern and Porter, 1981: 213).

The 'bottom up' alternative is summed up by Barrett and Fudge's (1981: 4) description of decisions made at the top as part of a bargaining process, with policy modified continuously as each actor involved in implementation, 'attempts to negotiate to maximize its own interests and priorities'. Central government may prove to be the most influential actor, but we should not assume so, particularly when it appears not to have a strong interest in the subject. Instead, we could shift our focus to the 'bottom' by identifying the implementing agencies involved and exploring how they operate (we should also not assume that implementers attach the same 'meaning' to policy measures as policymakers – Yanow, 1996; Schofield, 2004). Policy from the top may represent only one of many factors (including the lower level 'environment' in which local demands and needs arise) relevant to the deliberations and actions of those agencies (Barrett and Fudge, 1981: 25; Colebatch, 1998: 12; 28–9). Can we call the outcomes of practices so removed from the top 'government policy' (Colebatch, 1998: 30)?

These differences in approach led initially to the 'top-down versus bottom-up' debate. Their differences centred on *empirical issues* (e.g. the extent to which implementing actors can thwart the intentions of the centre), *research design* (should we focus on decisions made at the top or the implementation structure?) and *prescription* (who should make policy? How clear should the policy aim be? Who should implementers be accountable to?) (deLeon and deLeon, 2002: 474; Hudson, 1993: 392–5; Hupe and Hill, 2007; Hill and Hupe, 2009: 15–6). The debate was followed by 'third generation' studies that sought in vain to distil the vast range of variables, or causes of policy outcome variation, into a manageable and testable general theory (Goggin *et al.*, 1990; Smith and Larimer, 2009: 170–2; perhaps it was unsuccessful because implementation varies by policy type – Parsons, 1995: 480–1; Howlett and Ramesh, 2003: 90). There have also been attempts to combine the merits of top-down and bottom-up approaches (Hill and Hupe, 2009). The debate and search for synthesis reflect the biases inherent in each research design. A focus at the bottom highlights a multiplicity of influences and distance from central government, but does not tell us how many organizations meet targets set at the top; a focus at the top highlights the central control of a small number of issues, ignoring the bulk of government responsibilities which are delivered routinely and with minimal attention from elected policymakers (Cairney, 2009a: 360). Therefore, different approaches may be valuable in different circumstances (Matland, 1995: 165–7; Lundin, 2007; compare with Hill, 2009: 140).

Evaluation

Evaluation involves assessing the extent to which a policy was successful. A top-down approach might identify success if the implementation gap is small or if there is evidence of compliance (Matland, 1995: 154) and argue that policymakers at the top enjoy the most legitimacy when they are elected and accountable to the public (Linder and Peters, 2006: 31; Hill and Hupe, 2002: 71; Cairney, 2009a: 358–9). Indeed, in some cases, policy is implemented using top-down evaluation techniques: published targets provide an expectation of implementer behaviour (but often produce unintended consequences – Hood, 2007; Hoque *et al.*, 2004; Barrett, 2004) and dedicated units are created to monitor compliance (Lindquist, 2004).

Yet, things become more complicated when we identify incompatible or vague policy aims at the top that leave us searching for appropriate measures to judge success. There may also be competing forms of legitimacy, such as from local elected officials, that combine with the need to build some form of discretion into the policy design (to allow locally knowledgeable experts to adapt policies to particular circumstances), to produce an often unclear picture of the top–bottom relationship (see Matland, 1995: 154–5; Hogwood and Gunn, 1984: 207–8; 198; Colebatch, 1998: 68; deLeon, 1999: 320; deLeon and deLeon, 2002: 478). This normative dimension has been debated for some time in the US literature on intergovernmental relations, and now arises in studies of member state 'compliance' in the EU (Mastenbroek, 2005; Falkner *et al.*, 2004; Duina, 1997; Bache, 1999; Pülzl and Treib, 2007: 97–9). Devolved governments in the UK also point to the value of discretion and reject the direct link between success and adherence to top-down aims (Cairney, 2009a).

Evaluation is also complicated because success is difficult to measure. At the least, it involves the selection of a large mixture of measures that are hard to compare, or a small number of measures that are handpicked and represent no more than crude proxies for success (Cairney, 2009a: 369; Andrews and Martin, 2007). At the most, it involves a convoluted process that Marsh and McConnell (2010: 571; 580; see also Smith and Larimer, 2009: Chapter 6; Hogwood and Gunn, 1984: 224–40) heroically distil into seven factors. This includes consideration of the more practical issues, such as how long we should wait before evaluating a policy, how much information there is, how we can separate the effects of this policy from others and what the benchmark should be (e.g. the government's intentions, past outcomes, the success of other countries?). It also includes the more fundamental questions. For example, *whose* success are we measuring primarily – the government, its stakeholders or its target group (the 'social construction', of target groups is discussed in

Chapters 4 and 9)? Further, how should governments measure their own success? *Process* measures include a focus on a policy's legitimacy, *programmatic* refers to implementation success, while *political* refers to the effect of the policy on the government's credibility.

Such discussions demonstrate that evaluation measures are not 'objective' (Marsh and McConnell, 2010: 575) and that common evaluation terms such as 'effectiveness, efficiency and equity' give the misleading impression that they are technical (Box 7.3; Brewer and deLeon, 1983: ix). Any measure of success has to consider which measures we should select, who benefits the most from policy outcomes and what should be done following evaluation. Therefore, evaluation is 'an inherently political activity' (Taylor and Balloch, 2005: 1; Hogwood and Gunn, 1984: 221; Bovens, 'T Hart and Kuipers, 2006). It should not be considered as an afterthought in our policy analysis. Indeed, the likelihood of success may be the key reason that policymakers make particular decisions (see McConnell, 2010).

Policy maintenance, succession and termination

The notional final stage is when policymakers decide, on the basis of their evaluation, if the policy should be continued. The process reinforces the idea that 'policy determines politics' because new policies are often pursued largely to address the problems caused by the old (Wildavsky, 1980: 62). As Jones (1970: 135; 11) puts it, 'the end is the beginning', because government action results from the, 'continuing application and evaluation of ongoing policies' (perhaps with scope for larger departures during periods of crisis – I am writing this in the aftermath of the economic crisis which provided the 'window of opportunity' for decisions by many governments to reduce public spending dramatically; see Geva-May, 2004 on Kingdon). A decision made in the past also influences how the next decision will be made (Colebatch, 1998: 10–11). For example, it may be easier to amend a policy (and present it as new) than create an entirely new one. Hogwood and Peters (1983: 26–7) suggest that 'policy succession' is more likely than 'innovation' because most of the hard work has already been done: the issue is recognized as a legitimate problem for the government to solve; a service delivery organization exists; the policy has resources devoted to it; and, it has an established clientele. More significant innovations would require not only a process to establish these factors, but also the termination of another policy. Yet, termination has immediate financial costs, may produce the perception of policy failure, and may be opposed by interest groups, clients and the organizations that depend on the policy to survive (Hogwood and Peters, 1983: 16–17; 1982; Geva-May, 2004; Parsons,

1995: 574–5; deLeon, 1978; Hogwood, 1987). The policy cycle therefore tends to 'end' with the process of policy succession (Hogwood and Gunn, 1984: 61–84).

Beyond the policy cycle

The policy cycle has numerous good points. First, it is a simple model, understood by most students, suitable for systematic comparisons of policy processes (Howlett and Ramesh, 2003: 14). Second, the emphasis on recurring cycles captures the fluid nature of policymaking. Third, sometimes policymaking follows, chronologically, the sequence of stages (Anderson, 1975: 26–7; compare with Hill, 2009: 144). Fourth, it often represents a starting point for policymaking strategies. The idea that elected people make policy and unelected officials carry it out has normative weight (Colebatch, 1998: 77). In many policymaking circles it is still used to organize decisions or help civil servants to plan or describe their work (e.g. compare Bridgman and Davis, 2003, on Australia to Marchildon, 2001, on Canada, and the European Commission's (2011) description of the EU policy cycle). The fact that governments still attempt to separate stages such as policy formulation from implementation when delegating implementation to government agencies and the non-government sector makes it worthy of study (Chapter 8; Parsons, 1995: 458–9). In short, it represents the 'public face of public policies' (McConnell, 2010: 222).

However, the cycle model is not treated with the same respect that it used to enjoy. Sabatier (2007a: 7; see also Jann and Wegrich, 2007: 56; compare with Hogwood and Gunn, 1984: 6–11; Smith and Larimer, 2009: 235; Parsons, 1995: 80–1) argues that it has 'outlived its usefulness' for many reasons. First, it does not explain, or produce testable hypotheses on, how policy is made. Second, it is descriptively inaccurate because the stages often run in a different order and it is difficult to distinguish between them. Third, it has a top-down bias; it is largely designed to track how well choices made at the top are carried out at the bottom. Everett (2003: 65; see also Colebatch, 1998: 102) questions its value as a tool for policymakers, arguing that it is wrongly sold as the basis for a 'rigorous scientific method' which will produce good, equitable, policies. Instead, it is merely a framework that civil servants can use to 'smooth' policy once the difficult decisions have been made elsewhere (Everett, 2003: 66–8). Fourth, the top-down focus is misguided when policymakers administer 'placebo' policies, designed merely to look like they are being decisive, when they would rather delegate responsibility to other actors (Jordan and Richardson, 1987: 233) or policy is effectively made by administrators and legitimized by elected officials (John, 1998: 29). Fifth, it is simplistic as well as simple; a better theory would illuminate the interaction of 'multiple interacting cycles involving numerous policy proposals and statutes at multiple levels of government' (Sabatier, 2007: 7).

A final point is that the world in which the cycles model was introduced has changed profoundly – prompting the need for new theories to help us understand that new world. Radin (2000: 15; 34; see also Howard, 2005: 4) associates the policy cycle and comprehensive rationality models with the early post-war period of radical change. Policy scientists were able use those models because the overall direction of policy was driven by a small number of policymakers at the centre who relied on an elite group of policy analysts to produce 'objective' ways to gather facts, analyse and solve policy problems. This image contrasts with modern day policymaking characterized by four main factors. The first is a diminished sense of optimism regarding the government's ability to solve problems through objective scientific analysis; the status of policy analysis has diminished (John, 1998: 32–3) and policy scientists now have to compete with many other actors for policymaker attention.

The second is what Heclo (1978: 94) describes as an end to the 'clubby days of Washington politics' and Jordan (1981: 96-100) links, in other countries, to a shift from corporatism, in which group-government relations are centralized and exclusive, towards a more fragmented system with many more policy participants. The rise in government responsibilities not only mobilized more groups but also stretched the government's resources, producing its increased reliance on outside advice. This rise in activity from multiple sources, combined with the reduced exclusivity of policy analysis, often caused issues which were once 'quietly managed by a small group of insiders' to become 'controversial and politicized' (Heclo, 1978: 105). The third is a tendency for policy analysts and civil servants to spend long periods of time in the same department, becoming increasingly attached to policy programmes. This combines with a tendency of interest groups to focus their efforts on specific policy problems to produce a series of close relationships between policy specialists in and out of government. The fourth is the focus on not one but multiple centres of authority; the dispersal of power from a single central actor towards many organizations and sources of authority and influence.

Overall, we have a rather complex and shifting picture of the policy environment. On the one hand, it is a source of instability: populated by a fragmented government and many participants, potentially with different values, perceptions and preferences (Sabatier, 2007a: 3–4). On the other, groups often share close and stable relationships with government officials who operate out of the public spotlight. This is a picture that contemporary theories seek to capture and explain (see Chapters 8–10 in particular). Yet, we do not have to reject the stages approach to adopt these theories. Most cycles accounts recognize that the policy process is not simple (Jones, 1984: 214–7; Bridgman and Davis, 2003: 98; Hogwood and Gunn, 1984: 4–7; Brewer and deLeon, 1983: 23; compare with Howard 2005: 10; John, 1998: 23–7). Instead, its focus on legitimation and implementation stages merely helps us consider the policy process beyond the initial point of decision (Radin, 2000: 24; Jann and Wegrich, 2007: 44). This basic analytical distinction between formulation and implementation is crucial (Smith and Larimer, 2009: 36; Hill and Hupe, 2009: 4–6). Analytical distinctions are used in all public policy analysis – they tell us what is most relevant and worthy of our attention. The formulation/implementation distinction has value because it helps us reassess the usefulness of theories of public policy that mostly examine the former. A sole focus on policy formulation may exaggerate: the degree of power that certain political actors possess when making 'key decisions' (Chapter 3); the extent of policy transfer that takes place between political systems (Chapter 12); the effect of policy punctuations (Chapter 9); and the idea that major policy decisions are one-off events (produced, for example, during windows of opportunity) rather than as part of a wider process (Chapter 11).

While John's (1998: 30) ideal is for theories to consider the policy-making process 'in the round', there is a danger that this is not happening in a literature often dominated by agenda setting research (Schofield and Sausman, 2004: 235). Only the ACF considers a full policy cycle (although some accounts of policy networks identify changing patterns of group-government relations according to the cycle's stage – Richardson, Maloney and Rüdig, 1992; Judge, 1993: 131; Maloney and Richardson, 1995a; 1995b: Howlett and Ramesh, 2003: 232). Overall, it seems sensible to recognize the value of the idea of a cycle but to note the unrealistic simplicity of the model.

Conclusion

The study of public policy is challenging because the subject matter is so complex, with too many causes of variation in policy outcomes to make it as predictable as we would like. We can address this complexity by producing a checklist of methods to simplify and manage our efforts:

- *Observe, categorize and measure.* Seek ways to measure and describe the nature of public policy by considering basic distinctions (such as between aims, decisions and outcomes) and identifying policy instruments and types. We use these indicators to describe the nature of policy decisions and measure the extent to which policy has changed in each area. Although typologies are flawed, they help us move from an identification of complexity and variation towards stipulating what we expect to happen under particular circumstances.

- *Consider the factors that affect our narratives of policy development.* All narratives of public policy are 'biased' because they are based on our interpretations of a limited number of measures. We need to be self-aware when constructing narratives and be open to different accounts of empirical results. One way to encourage reflexivity is to produce more than one narrative and compare their outcomes – this should make one more sensitive to (rather than take for granted) some of the assumptions in one's favoured version of events. We may also find that particular narratives support particular theories of public policy (Cairney, 2007a).

- *Raise questions about power.* We can explore issues of power by establishing who has formal authority, identifying reputations, asking who makes and influences the most important decisions and considering why some key decisions seem *not* to be made (or why some problems and solutions receive attention, while others remain off the agenda). Of course, *measuring* power and linking it to policy outcomes is another matter – this is the focus of Chapter 3.

- *Map the policy environment.* We can appreciate the context within which decisions are made by considering the nature of the policy problem, the pressure that policymakers are under to address it, and the resources they can use to solve it. The idea that policy is influenced heavily by the nature of the problem is explored further in Chapter 6.

- *Consider the policy cycle.* The image of a cycle helps us consider the idea of 'policy as its own cause', the stages through which policies appear to go before an authoritative decision is made, and the difference between a policy decision and its implementation.

- *Use theories of public policy.* A general aim within science is to examine the proportion of outcomes that can be linked to the same causes. Our aim is apply this broad approach to public policy: to explain why certain policies exist, how they were made and what happens when they are made. To do so, we identify the most important factors in the policy process, such as: how and why choices were made; the role of institutions; the relationship between governments and interest groups; the socio-economic context; and the role of ideas. We then examine how they relate to each other by learning from the most established theories of public policy. Our aim is to examine how each theory of public policy gives us a better understanding of policy processes. To this end, most chapters (with the exception of 3 and 6, discussed above) outline a particular theory and describe what it tells us about the policy process; what factors we should identify and how they relate to each other. In most cases we consider the application of theories to a single policy process before considering how applicable they are in different countries (bearing in mind the likelihood of further variation by policy area and over time). Chapter 13 then considers what these theories tell us when considered together. It examines the extent to which we can combine their insights, the extent to which they are applicable in different countries and issues over time, and perhaps if different theories are most useful in different circumstances.

Chapter 3

Power and Public Policy

This chapter examines:

- How we define power.
- The community power debate.
- The three 'dimensions' of power.
- The right to exercise power and the issue of popular consent.
- The methods we use to identify power within political systems.

Although power may be the most important concept in political science, it is not the most clear. Its wide range of meanings and applications produces the need to be specific about its use in public policy analysis. It also highlights the importance of **methodology**, since a basic uncertainty about what power is may lead us to question how we gather knowledge of it. The aim of this chapter is to focus on power within the decision-making process. The question of power arises in its most basic form when we ask: who is in charge or who are the decision makers? Who is responsible for policy change? Who is *thought* to be in charge and who is *actually* in charge? We may also use discussions of power to explain why policies change or remain stable. For example, can power be exercised by policymakers to force (or resist) change in the face of opposition? Can power be used to 'set the agenda' and encourage policy change in some areas at the expense of others? Or, can more hidden forms of power such as the manipulation of knowledge and beliefs be used to restrict debate and minimize attention to the need for change? To answer these questions we often need to broaden our discussions from the exercise of power by individuals to the role of institutions, and from formal sources of authority to informal sources of influence.

Our starting point is the 'community power' debate. This underpins the modern study of **elitism** and **pluralism,** or the extent to which power is concentrated or diffuse within government and society. While Hunter (1953; 1980) and Mills (1956) identified the reputations of people

Methodology – the analysis of **methods** used to gather knowledge (based on epistemology, or a theory of what knowledge is and how it is created).

Elitism – power is concentrated in the hands of a small number of people or organizations that control policy processes.

Pluralism – power is diffuse; policy results from the interactions of (or competition between) many individuals and groups.

in powerful positions to theorize a ruling elite, Dahl (1958) questioned the importance of reputations as an indicator of power. Dahl suggests that power only has meaning when *exercised* and when we can identify the effects of one actor's power over another during key decisions. This approach suggests that the power of actors varies by policy issue. Each approach presents a different understanding of power and a different view on how to *observe* power. Therefore, the debate placed the issue of research **methods** to centre stage. It continued when Bachrach and Baratz (1962; 1963) questioned Dahl's focus on directly observ-

Behaviouralism has two broad claims: '(a) observable behaviour, whether it is at the level of the individual or the social aggregate, should be the focus of analytics: and (b) any explanation of that behaviour should be susceptible to empirical testing' (Sanders, 2010: 23).

able behaviour (Dahl's work is often linked to **behaviouralism**). Power is also exercised behind the scenes by 'setting the agenda' and limiting public debate. Or, people may feel powerless because they do not have the opportunity to contribute to key decisions – because they cannot find the arena to express their views or they feel unable to express them. The 'second face' of power describes a process of 'non-decision-making', or the less-visible actions taken to ensure that some individuals and groups do not engage.

The second face of power reinforces the importance of method because it is not easy to observe. Yet, these problems pale into insignificance when compared with the 'third dimensional' view. Lukes (1974; 2005) identifies a process in which some people benefit when others do not act according to their own 'real' interests. Their preferences are manipulated by other groups and institutions (such as governments) through the control of information and a process of socialization. Power in such instances may be furthered by a 'structure' or force, independent of the actions of individuals, such as a dominant ideology or set of rules within government that effectively blocks certain types of action. In broader terms, the exercise of power within institutions is rule bound and not reducible to the sum total of the actions of individuals. Thus, power can be observed, but it can also be theorized from a broader examination of social, economic and political relations (or the structured environment which affects how actors exercise power). This raises complex problems about the language used to describe the 'actions' of structures 'exercising' power and the methods we use to observe allegedly unobservable forms.

At the heart of such debates is the question of proof and measurement: how do we demonstrate that some are powerful and others are powerless? What is the evidence and where can we find it? The simplest

---

Box 3.1   Discussions of power

'Power' can refer to an incredibly wide range of concepts and arguments, including:

- The ability to get what you want despite the resistance of others
- The power to influence the choices of others
- The power to influence an actor's decision-making environment
- Power as a resource or capacity and the exercise of power
- Power based on popular support, used legitimately or illegitimately
- The power to change or obstruct
- Power as knowledge or embedded in language
- Reputational power
- The ability of a social class to realize its interests
- Decision or non-decision making
- The three 'dimensions' of power
- Sources of power – economic, military, governmental, cultural
- Power diffusion or centralization
- Who gets what, when, how?
- Power or systematic luck
- Inequalities of power related to gender, ethnicity, class, sexuality.

---

answer is that certain people benefit regularly from policy outcomes. However this can suggest at least three processes. First, they exercise power directly, to secure a policy outcome that benefits them at the expense of others. Second, they exercise power indirectly, to manipulate others into thinking that the outcome benefits both parties. Third, they benefit from an outcome without being responsible for it (Dowding, 1996, calls this 'luck').

While the community power debate represents an extensive discussion it is not exhaustive. In particular, this chapter considers the extent to which these discussions are based on a peculiarly Anglo-US focus on the extent to which power is measurable. In other fields our focus may shift to the extent to which the exercise of power is legitimate and how it lives up to an ideal of society unencumbered by inequalities of power.

Definitions of power

The concept of power encompasses a vast range of behaviours, including the ability to get what you want despite the resistance of others, the possession of authority based on consent and the inability to exercise autonomy when carrying out forms of class or 'structural' power. Power

Box 3.2 The language of power

Bachrach and Baratz (1970: 17–38) argue that if power is 'relational', then we need to know more about the motivations of A and B. They outline five main types (see also Arendt, 1986: 64–5):

Power – A achieves B's compliance using overt or tacit threats.

Influence – A achieves B's compliance without using overt or tacit threats.

Manipulation – A achieves B's compliance by restricting B's choices.

Force – A achieves her ends in the face of B's non-compliance by restricting B's choices.

Authority – B complies with A's request when she respects A's position and finds her commands reasonable.

may be: exercised visibly or hidden from view; used collectively or at the expense of others; concentrated or diffuse; and, used for legitimate or insidious purposes. It may be associated with visible reputations that affect clearly the actions of others, or more subtle inequalities with less obvious effects (Box 3.1; Lukes, 1986). In some discussions, power may encompass or be treated as synonymous with terms such as influence, authority and force; in others it may be differentiated from them (Box 3.2).

The key normative theme is that the use of power should not get in the way of democracy (for various meanings of democracy see McGarvey and Cairney, 2008: 220). While we accept that there are inequalities within politics and society, we hope that there are sufficient safeguards on governmental and non-governmental actors to limit their effects (Dahl, 1961). In this light, the study of power focuses on the extent to which inequalities in the possession of power translate into political outcomes. The key empirical themes are as follows. First, power can be understood as the capacity and potential to act; as a resource to be used. However, second, we may not know how much power an actor has until they exercise it and we analyse the outcomes. Third, it is relatively difficult to identify the exercise of power by actors who are not individuals. Therefore, can organizations, institutions and 'structures' act to exercise power? Finally, how do we study power? Should we use interviews to establish the reputations of elites or track the power of participants when key decisions are made? Should we deduce and theorize power relations from observed and unobserved behaviour? These questions are raised and answered within the 'community power' debate.

From community power to thought control: traditional approaches to power and politics

The community power debate

Many early studies of democracy sought to 'solve the problem' of elitism, based on the assumption that it is inevitable within society. While Schumpeter (1942) developed an economic theory of democracy to show that the electorate could still be involved by choosing between (and influencing the policies of) elites, this did not solve Lasswell's (1936) problem: a wider power structure less constrained by popular control. Power can be identified in a range of groups – the military, police, state bureaucracy, business and professions which control the communication of knowledge – and, if combined, could contribute to authoritarian rule (see Parsons, 1995: 248–50). The post-war period saw the publication of two books which came to represent the modern elitist position. Hunter's (1953) study of power in Atlanta, US, based on interviews asking respondents to list its most powerful people (who runs this community?), identified a small group of elites. Mills's (1956: 4) study, which was more theoretical than empirical, detected a US-wide male elite based on control of the 'big corporations', the 'machinery of the state' and the 'military establishment' (US President Eisenhower coined it the 'military–industrial complex'). This identification of a centralized order, contrasting with the formal US system of checks and balances, confirms Lasswell's greatest fears (Mills, 1956: 4–5). Elites at the 'top' have the means to control key events, while the fragmentation of 'mass-like society' at the 'bottom', combined with the ineffectiveness of 'middling units of power (such as political parties), undermines the potential for competition to influence policy outcomes (1956: 28–9; 361).

The key critique of this conception of power regards its method: how do we demonstrate its accuracy empirically? Dahl (1958; see also Polsby, 1960: 483; Kaufman and Jones, 1954: 207; Wolfinger, 1960) criticizes the 'ruling elite model' because it does not demonstrate the *exercise* of power. Rather, it posits an unobservable process of covert control which is 'virtually impossible to disprove' (Dahl, 1958: 463; 1961: 185; Polsby, 1960: 476). The statement '*A* has more power than *B*' has no meaning unless the groups have different preferences and the ruling minority's preferences are met at the expense of the other group (1958: 464). We must demonstrate that large and powerful organizations are controlled by elites and that inequalities in society translate into systematic advantages across the political system (1958: 465–6). Dahl's classic statement is that, '*A* has power over *B* to the extent that he can [or *does*] get *B* to do something that *B* would not otherwise do'. To demonstrate this power requires the identification of: A's power resources, A's means to exploit those resources, A's willingness to engage in political action, the amount of power exerted (or threatened) by A and the *scope* of that power – defined as effect of the action on B (Dahl, 1957: 202–3; 206; Polsby, 1960: 480). Overall, Dahl (1957: 214) points to the problems we face when we **operationalize** power.

Operationalize – to turn abstract concepts into observable and measurable quantities.

Dahl's main approach is to identify 'key political choices', involving a significant conflict of preferences and the outcomes of 'concrete decisions' (see also Polsby, 1960: 483–4). Using this test as part of a wider study of New Haven, US, Dahl (1961) identifies three main processes. First, there has been a shift since the eighteenth century 'from **oligarchy** to pluralism'. A ruling class based on the monopoly of elected positions by elites with high social status, education and wealth (the 'Notables') has given way to elections of the 'middle classes', 'ex-plebes' and formerly 'ethnic immigrant' populations whose status, wealth and education have also risen (1961: 11; 32; 44). Although there are still inequalities, they are 'dispersed' rather than 'cumulative': superior status and wealth no longer translates to a superior ability to control elected and unelected office (1961: 84). Although the power associated with money and status is significant, it now competes with the independent power of elected office and the vast range of political resources available to other actors – including time, esteem, support of the law and control of information.

Oligarchy the control of government by elites.

Second, there is an (albeit imperfect) democratic link between policy-makers and the electorate. Political participation – or entry into the 'political stratum' – is still highest among populations with the highest incomes, education and social and professional standing (Dahl, 1961: 282–3). The 'political stratum' is small and much more active and influential in politics than the 'apolitical strata'. Yet, it is not a closed group based on class interests; it is penetrable by anyone with the resources and motivation. Further, its members seek to build coalitions with the apolitical strata for straightforward practical reasons – as a means of re-election (1961: 91–2) or to avoid its wrath and *potential* to mobilize if provoked (1961: 310) – and for cultural reasons: 'democracy' is a powerful idea supported by the political stratum and the apolitical strata (1961: 316–7). The political stratum effectively acts *as if* the apolitical strata are involved by anticipating their reactions. Further, since the political stratum is now so heterogeneous, most groups in the apolitical strata can find a powerful advocate with a common interest (1961: 93).

Third, although there are significant inequalities in politics there is no overall control of the policy process. Although the Notables control policymaking positions in some sectors (or certain stages of the policy process) they do not control others. Public policy is specialized; the sheer size and fragmentation of political systems ensures that the reach of one actor does not extend across all areas: 'the individuals who spend time, energy and money in an attempt to influence policies in one issue-area are rather different to those who do so in another' (1961: 273–4; 126; 169; 180; see also Polsby, 1960; 482; Moran, 2005: 16). Therefore, the overall question to be asked is not: '"Who runs this community", but rather, "Does anyone at all run this community?"'(Polsby, 1960: 476).

The 'second face' of power

Subsequent debates were based as much on a critique of pluralist *methods* as the pluralist definition of power. Bachrach and Baratz argue (1962: 948; against Polsby, 1960: 477) that since there is no objective way for pluralists to identify key decisions we cannot demonstrate their representativeness. Therefore, the identification of pluralism in some case studies does not demonstrate pluralism overall (Crenson's 1971: 21 parallel argument is that the identification of an elected black woman does not demonstrate a lack of racism and sexism in electoral politics). Indeed, the modern study of agenda setting (Chapter 9) suggests that power is as much about the issues we do *not* identify or pay attention to. A powerful actor may successfully focus our attention on one issue at the expense of attention to others *without the need to engage* or discourage action in those other areas. Since policymaking attention is limited, the agenda-setting success of one group in one area may cause the failure of many groups in many others (Crenson, 1971: 25). Therefore, the pluralist focus on observable decision-making events does not take into account the second 'face' of power associated with the terms 'non-decision making', 'mobilization of bias' and 'un-politics'.

For Bachrach and Baratz (1970: 94), key decisions are not gauged by the size of the policy area or the degree of conflict, but by the extent to which a decision challenges the, 'authority of those who regularly enjoy a dominant position in the determination of policy outputs'. Power may be exercised to protect that dominant position; the strategy may be to restrict the attention of other actors to what the dominant consider to be 'safe' issues. Non-decision making suggests that power is exercised: 'when A devotes his energies to creating or reinforcing social and political values and institutional practices that limit the scope of the political process to public consideration of only those issues which are comparatively innocuous to A' (Bachrach and Baratz, 1962: 948). When A is successful, B is prevented from engaging in decisions which threaten A's preferences. It suggests that issues displaying differences between A and B are not necessarily important; B may 'win' decisions which are innocuous to A.

The less-powerful face two major barriers to engagement. First, they may be disadvantaged by the dominant view within society that favours some ideologies over others. For example, most may feel that an issue is not a legitimate problem for governments to solve (such as when issues of poverty were defined as a matter of individual responsibility) or that the solution proposed is not worth considering (such as a 'socialist' solution in a capitalist society). Power may be exercised to maintain this view of an issue in the knowledge that if an issue was more widely debated in more detail then more people would support intervention (Crenson, 1971: 180–1). Second, their grievances may be kept off the agenda by governing organizations and institutional procedures. For example, a government may fill unelected posts with people committed to the status quo or the most powerful may discourage the formal discussion of certain issues (Bachrach and Baratz, 1970: 54–9; 70; Hay, 2002: 175). *A* may contribute to a social or institutional climate in which there is a high chance of failure and/or a fear of sanctions for challenging the status quo, contributing to *B*'s inability or reluctance to engage (Hay, 2002: 175 draws parallels to speaking out against the 'local godfather'). Overall, Bachrach and Baratz (1970: 105–6) argue that the 'dominant group' manipulates the values of society and the procedures of government to ensure that the grievances of 'subordinate groups' are not aired. Political systems reinforce a 'set of values, beliefs, rituals and procedures' which cause an unequal distribution of 'benefits and privileges'. Such undemocratic rule by elites meets minimal opposition because those elites manipulate the decision-making process (Hindess, 1996: 5).

The main problem with the 'second face' of power (at least from the pluralist perspective) is that some aspects may be impossible to demonstrate empirically. Bachrach and Baratz's (1970) solution is to draw on Schattschneider's term 'mobilization of bias' to show that non-decision making can be observed. Schattschneider's (1960: 2–5) first point is that in any conflict the audience is more important than the original participants. Think of two fighters surrounded by a massive crowd – its composition, bias towards each fighter and willingness to engage are crucial. The outcome of conflict is determined by the extent to which the audience becomes involved. Since the audience is biased and only a small part will become engaged, the mobilization of one part changes the balance of power. This affects the strategies of participants: the 'loser' has the incentive to expand the scope of the conflict by encouraging a part of the audience to become involved; the 'winner' would prefer to isolate its opponent. Most political behaviour involves this competition to 'socialize' or 'privatize' conflict, often using widely held values such as 'equality' and 'social protection' versus 'individualism' and 'small government' (1960: 7–8). Or, the latter strategy may be summed up simply by the phrase 'this is a private matter'.

Schattschneider's second point is that the pressure group system is not pluralistic; a small proportion of the population – the well educated and upper class – is active and well represented by groups (1960: 34–5) The pressure system is largely the preserve of the business class seeking to minimize attention to 'private' disputes (1960: 30–7). Therefore, Schattschneider (1960: 12; 119) highlights the need for government to counteract imbalances based on economic power: 'Democratic government is the greatest single instrument for the socialization of conflict ... big business has to be matched by ... big democracy'. In this sense the government represents the audience to conflicts. However, there are more potential conflicts than any government or public can pay attention to. Therefore, most are ignored and the people are 'semi-sovereign' – only able to exercise their power in a few areas. Power is exercised to determine the issues most worthy of government attention; the structures of government, such as legislative procedures controlling debate, reinforce this process: 'All forms of political organization have a bias in favour of the exploitation of some kinds of conflict and the suppression of others because *organization is the mobilization of bias*. Some issues are organized into politics while others are organized out' (1960: 69). While Dahl (1961) treats the lack of political participation among the apolitical strata as a choice to be inactive and an issue of 'slack' (the *potential* to mobilize), Schattschneider (1960) argues that participants are *excluded* from participation. The ability of the business class to keep issues off the agenda means that we do not witness the systematic exercise of power by all participants in 'key decisions' (this process is not limited to business; see Box 3.3).

This argument is extended by Crenson's (1971) study of air pollution policy in US cities. His three basic points are that: (a) post-war levels of public attention to air pollution are low compared to the problem; (b) attention varies in different cities; and (c) while some cities have passed legislation to regulate air pollution during manufacturing, others have not. Crenson (1971: 5) seeks to establish if this inaction was 'random' or 'politically enforced'. For example, we could explain a shift from inaction to action in terms of the shifting politics in some cities. Government-driven attention may rise as **machine** politicians, used to dispensing patronage and favours 'in bits and pieces to individuals', are replaced by 'reform' politicians seeking to 'dispense favors' to the whole population (1971: 16). Since clean air can only be 'given' to the whole population, the issue may not arise until a population elects 'reform politi-

Machine politics – describes: (a) the tight control of a party or government by a few actors who (b) dispense favours or patronage to supporters as a means of reinforcing their power.

Box 3.3 Gender, power and public policy

Gender studies identify systemic exclusions of women and men within politics and society. For example, women may be excluded from formal positions of power and the production of knowledge and are less likely to possess economic, cultural and social resources. Power relationships may be reinforced in "'personal" relationships such as child-rearing, housework and marriage and in all kinds of sexual practices including rape, prostitution, pornography, sexual harassment and sexual intercourse' (Abbott, Wallace and Tyler, 2005: 35). These relationships are often exacerbated by other sources of inequalities – including class, ethnicity, sexuality and age – which reinforce social positions and undermine their ability to mobilize (indeed, some women may contribute to the subordination of others). Such issues produce an interesting counterfactual: how would the substance of policy change if more women were in positions of power? If we assume certain issues would be raised more often (such as the childcare for working families issue pursued by UK Prime Minister Gordon Brown) or different attitudes would be apparent (for example, a government less likely to engage in war) then we may reinforce gender stereotypes and contribute to inequalities of power. Further, if power relations are multi-faceted then gender may be replaced (by race, class, sexuality) as the main focus of inequality reinforced by others. The debate may also shift from the *power* to be equal to the *right* to be different without fear of the consequences (Bock and James, 1992). The key link to the community power debate regards the ability to 'socialize' or 'privatize' these 'personal' issues to place them on, or remove them from, the policy agenda. Indeed, the phrase 'this is a private matter' may have more weight in gender and family politics than in the increasingly politicized world of business.

cians'. Previously, 'machine' politicians may have ensured that their institutions were impenetrable to air pollution issues as a favour to local industries (1971: 19). Thus, in the case study of Gary (Indiana, US) we find evidence of non-decision making – when the Mayor delayed the study of air pollution, the study's authors (funded by manufacturing industries) underestimated the contribution of manufacturing to air pollution and anticipated the response of US Steel when recommending weak enforcement policies, and the City Council delayed its ruling on legislative proposals (1971: 64–5).

Overall, important issues are kept off the political agenda either by powerful interests who reinforce social attitudes and manipulate decision-making procedures, or (effectively) by the powerless who pay minimal attention to an issue or feel unable to engage. However, although Bachrach and Baratz (1970: 49–50) take the analysis beyond directly observable events, they share with pluralists a view on the limits to empirical analysis: one or more party has to recognize that a power struggle exists. If the researcher finds no grievance: 'the presumption must be that there is consensus on the prevailing allocation of values, in which case non-decision making is impossible'.

The third dimension of power

This statement represents the line between the second face and 'third dimension', which theorizes unequal power relationships despite the appearance of consensus (Lukes, 1974; 2005). The third dimension suggests that although all may seem to be in agreement, this is because B does not recognize her 'real' interests and that A benefits from the relationship at her expense. The **coun-**

Counterfactual – a statement used to explore what would happen if the opposite were true.

terfactual is that if given the chance (or made aware of a way to pursue her real interests) B would act differently.

The difference is highlighted to some extent by Crenson's argument that businesses in Gary did not have to engage in non-decision making. Rather, the population regulated itself and its government continued to promote weak regulations. These behaviours were based on their anticipation of an unfavourable reaction of business (Crenson, 1971: 67–70; 122–3). Gary was a town effectively built and kept alive by the company US Steel, which commands considerable loyalty. US Steel's strategy was to say very little in public to make sure that it did not contribute to the issue's salience (1971: 72). This, combined with the effect of US Steel's reputation on the population's behaviour, assured its dominance on the air pollution issue. US Steel's *inaction* was emulated by Gary (1971: 78). The issue was not raised even though unregulated air pollution represents a source of profit for the business and a source of severe ill-health for the population. By unwittingly accepting the pollution the population was not acting in its real interests (assuming pollution control would not cause unemployment – Lukes, 2005: 48). Further, made aware fully of the facts, the population would act differently to promote environmental regulations. Instead, its ability to articulate different preferences or support a new understanding of the situation (from economics to health) were undermined by an unfavourable 'political climate' (Crenson, 1971: 23). The population would not pay serious attention to the issue until given some sign that US Steel was supportive. When this support was not forthcoming, no action followed. Therefore, while this climate was effectively fostered by US Steel and Gary's political institutions, the different emphasis of the third face is that this process is not easily (if at all) observable. In this case, the 'possession of indirect influence permits industry to refrain from exercising its direct influence ... The mere reputation for power, unsupported by acts of power, can be sufficient to restrict the scope of local decision making' (1971: 125; 177). In this sense, Lukes (2005: 12) argues that it is a mistake to equate power with its exercise: 'Power is a capacity not the exercise of that capacity (it may never be, and never need to be, exercised)'.

The third dimension takes us full-circle to discussions of covert behaviour since 'power is at its most effective when least observable' (Lukes, 2005: 1). The behaviour of all concerned may suggest consensus rather than dominance, with no easy way to demonstrate one rather than the other. Indeed, it may be that B supports her own exploitation while A does not believe that she is acting against B's real interests (although the power of Lukes' argument refers more to the intended rather than unintended consequences of action). Yet, in some cases, the third dimension may still be visible if we can demonstrate that A manipulates B's beliefs. This is the power to:

> Prevent people, to whatever degree, from having grievances by shaping their perceptions, cognitions and preferences in such a way that they accept their role in the existing order of things ... Indeed, is it not the supreme exercise of power to get another or others to have the desires you want them to have – that is, to secure their compliance by controlling their thoughts and desires? (2005: 11–12; 27; 14)

The classic example of 'false consciousness' comes from Marxist descriptions of the exploitation of the working classes within a capitalist system: if only they knew the full facts, that capitalism worked against their real interests, they would rise up and overthrow it. In this scenario, they do not object because they are manipulated into thinking that capitalism is their best chance of increasing their standard of living. In effect, Lukes describes 'hegemony' in which the most powerful dominate not only state institutions but also the intellectual and moral world in which we decide which actions are most worthy of attention and which are right or wrong (Gramsci, 1971). In these terms, capitalist dominance is 'based on a combination of coercion and consent' (Hindess, 1996: 5). The 'most effective and insidious use of power' is to prevent conflict through the control of information and media, as well as a process of socialization (Lukes, 2005: 27).

Observing the unobservable

But how do we identify the third dimension if it is so difficult to observe? For example, does Lukes satisfy the pluralist focus on *demonstrable* power? From a pluralist standpoint, the answer is 'no'. Dahl (1958: 469) argues that if a 'consensus is perpetual and unbreakable ... there is no conceivable way of determining who is ruler and who is ruled'. Instead, concepts such as 'real interests' and 'false class consciousness' represent the imposition of a theorist's values on the research environment (Polsby, 1960: 479). Similarly, Polsby (1980: 97) argues that Crenson's argument regarding 'un-politics' is undermined by the potentially infinite number of non-issues, which requires a choice about which non-issues are the most important; it would be inappropriate for an outsider to call a particular issue important when the population doesn't.

Lukes (2005: 27) addresses the former problem by identifying third dimensional processes in Dahl's work – such as when the government shapes public preferences by restricting the flow of information or indoctrinates the population to ensure a widespread respect for the legitimacy of government and democracy. Crenson's (1971: 26–8) response to the latter is to compare levels of attention to the same problem by similar populations in different cities, asking why it is important in one but not the other. It predicts what a city's population would do by establishing the actions of an equivalent city's population in the absence of un-politics (1971: 33). This use of the comparative method is necessary to establish Dahl's focus on 'something that *B* would not otherwise do'. Crenson (1971: 80; 108; 182) also extends Dahl's argument that the political stratum acts in anticipation of the reactions of the apolitical stratum. If we accept that decision makers anticipate the reactions of the public to raise some issues, then we should accept that they anticipate the reactions of 'big business' to not raise others. This may not be observed in 'key decisions'. Indeed, the pluralist focus on air pollution policy in *other* cities would exaggerate non-business power because it would focus only on the examples in which the issue had become politicized (1971: 131). Therefore, the focus on observable decisions may be as misleading and biased as the decision to deduce power from less visible relationships.

Thus, non-pluralistic processes can be identified by extending pluralist methods – but has the burden of proof been met? In both cases, the answer from Polsby is 'no'. While Crenson's comparative method is commendable, Polsby (1980: 214–17) argues that no data provided by Crenson demonstrates that US Steel was powerfully inactive. Rather, given the importance of US Steel to Gary's economy, the population merely decided to trade-off clean air for employment. Lukes' (2005: 48) assumption that pollution control would not cause unemployment had no basis in fact (suggesting that it may not have been in their real interests to challenge the status quo), while Jones' (1975 in Polsby, 1980: 217) study of air pollution in Pittsburgh suggests that populations do not trade off their health for employment 'unwittingly'. Although Lukes (2005: 148) argues that Gary could act in its 'real interests' by pursuing US-wide regulations, this is based on the *assumption* that there would be no unintended consequences.

From empirical to normative: the right to exercise power

These debates introduce us to the fact that most empirical discussions of power are also normative. In the absence of 'all the facts', ideological norms fill the gaps – highlighting political practice within policy analysis. This argument is most clear in criticisms that the pluralist literature serves partly to legitimate the pluralist ideal by distracting us from the undemocratic role of elites (Hindess, 1996: 5; Hay, 2002: 175; but note that Dahl 1961: 3–5; **86**; 330–6 goes to great lengths to identify and measure inequalities, stating that: 'If the pluralist system was very far from being an oligarchy, it was also a long way from achieving the goal of political equality advocated by the philosophers of democracy'). However, we can make similar comments on bias within second face and third dimensional discussions. For example, Crenson (1971: 180) is really arguing that power gets in the way of democracy when elites do not compete over what *he thinks* are relatively important issues. Or, Marxists may bemoan the lack of working class awareness of their real interests because *they believe* that the capitalist system exploits them. They may be right or wrong but the 'facts' alone will not help us decide.

Although we may be able to witness manipulation or the shaping of preferences, we cannot decide with certainty if this is done to advance or thwart someone's 'real' interests. In this context, most attempts to separate completely the empirical and analytical from the normative seem doomed to failure (although see Hay, 2002: 187). For example, when Heyward (2007: 53) uses the example of a father denying his daughter education to illuminate the difference between dominance (power over someone which adversely affects her real interests) and potestas (power over someone with a benign effect) it becomes clear that we must first take a normative position (does this undermine her real interests because education should be available to all?) before deciding which form of power has been exercised. Indeed, such discussions of paternalism can be extended to the broader role of the state when constraining the freedoms of its citizens ostensibly for their own good. Similarly, while we may identify the government-driven socialization of its subjects in, for example, the promotion of 'citizenship', this may be more for legitimate reasons (to encourage participation in politics) than insidious (to foster passive consent) (Hindess, 1996: 72). Yet, this identification of a normative dimension is not necessarily a flaw of political science. Rather, wouldn't it be odd if academics became so divorced from the real or ethical world that they had no normative opinions?

The normative dimension suggests that power is about more than the *ability* to act. It is also about the *right* to act: how much power is exercised with the 'consent of those over whom it is exercised' (Hindess,

1996: 1; 11; see also Arendt, 1986: 62)? The identification of consent giving the capacity to exercise power over others may be most clear with democratically elected governments. In this sense, government action notionally combines the power of all who consent (1996: 15). As Hindess (1996: 13) suggests, at the heart of such relationships is the notion of a contract in which those vested with the right to exercise power are under certain obligations not to abuse that right, in part by upholding the values of those who consent. On the other hand, since one function of government is to regulate the attitudes and behaviour of its citizens for the collective good, it produces a circular effect: consent for government action is based on government-influenced attitudes (1996: 43). Governments may also weigh up the potential trade-offs between the welfare and liberty of their citizens. In this sense, government control and legitimacy may be assumed until citizens have the ability to give 'rational consent' (1996: 74; 118). Indeed, the criteria used to gauge an individual's or social group's ability to reason may also be determined by that government. Therefore, much political theory regards the appropriateness and effectiveness of such contracts and our ability to demonstrate that consent has been given in a meaningful way, usually via representative democracy, to an organization with a recognizable unity of purpose (and a clearly identifiable and accountable 'centre'). Similarly, discussions of democracy explore the extent to which other forms – such as participative, deliberative and pluralist democracy – provide more legitimacy and a clearer link between consent and the right to exercise power.

Anglophone versus continental European discussions of power?

This right to exercise power does not take centre stage in the community power debate. Indeed, Hay (2002: 170–1; 187–93; see also Hindess, 1996: 38) suggests that the debate represents a peculiar Anglo-US focus on the extent to which power is measurable. The main alternative extends beyond the third dimension to question whether power is so embedded in our language and practices that it is impossible to be liberated from it. Foucault (1977) presents two ways in which liberation may be impossible by drawing on the idea of society modelled on a prison. First, the power of the state to monitor and punish may reach the point in which its subjects assume that they are always visible. This 'perfection of power' – associated with the all-seeing 'Panopticon' – renders the exercise of power unnecessary (1977: 201; Hay, 2002: 191). Rather, individuals accept that discipline is a fact of life and anticipate the consequences of their actions (from colluding in crimes, cheating at school and slacking off at work, to forming political organizations that challenge the authority of the state) and regulate their own behaviour. Second, a broader form of control is so embedded in our psyches, knowledge and language, that it is 'normalized' and often rendered invisible. Consider, for example, mental health in which the 'knowledge' and identification of severe mental illness inevitably produces the perceived need for treatment. Or, we 'know' which forms of behaviour are deviant and therefore which should be regulated or punished (this is perhaps the most extreme form of socialization that we can imagine). Therefore, power is exercised not merely by the state, but also individuals who reproduce and reinforce this form of power by controlling their *own* behaviour as well as the behaviour of others. In other words, this is a ubiquitous form of social control in which the state is only one of many actors. Thus, any notions of collective or government power granted freely by the consent of individuals seems rather misplaced (Hindess, 1996: 145). Foucault's work contrasts with the idea that individuals are 'rational' or able to, for example, give consent based on their self interest and ability to reason (Chapter 7). Rather, agents may represent the ultimate hub of repressive power because individuals regulate their own behaviour rather than express their preferences (see Lukes, 2005: 91–3).

Such discussions may have been strangled at birth by the US pluralist focus on method because it is not clear how you could *recognize* this form of power far less theorize and measure it. However, they flourished within the 'critical' European literature which was less focused on power as a measurable and quantifiable entity (Hay, 2002). Instead, we see a focus on the ideal (or **ideal-type**) of the autonomous, rather than dominated), individual who, when compared with real life (which falls far short of the ideal), demonstrates that significant power is exercised through social forces that are relatively difficult to measure (Hindess, 1996: 95 uses Habermas' 'ideal speech situation' as a representative example). In other words, the common argument about this relatively hidden form of power may be: 'we know it is there even if we do not agree on how to identify it'.

Ideal-type – an analytical construct that serves as a comparator and point of departure for 'real world' descriptions of events and behaviour (compare with definition in Chapter 1).

Foucault's discussion may be problematic for some audiences because there is no real empirical focus and his theory once again gives the academic a unique position of enlightenment. However, at the very least it highlights the limits to our reliance on research methods focusing entirely on observable behaviour. The more individuals regulate themselves in the 'private' sphere, the less we can observe in public. Therefore, the sole focus on decision making *because it is observable* should remind us of the story of the drunk man searching for his keys under a lamppost – not because they are likely to be there, but because there is more light (Hogwood, 1992: 5). The most interesting forms of power may be the ones most difficult (or impossible) to research (Hay, 2002: 169)

Contemporary approaches to power and policymaking

How does the concept of power inform modern theories of public policy? Do new theories raise new issues or are their arguments based on the community power debate? The broad answer is that modern theories are influenced heavily by, and often seek to address, the arguments outlined above.

What is the power of ideas? Where does power stop and ideas begin?

Our discussion of power is really a discussion of power and **ideas**. Dahl's (1961: 310–17) 'democratic creed' refers to the beliefs held by the population on the importance of democracy as a guide to behaviour. Bachrach and Baratz's (1970: 54–9) first barrier to engagement is the dominant set of beliefs held within society. Luke's third dimension of power focuses on what people believe to be their real interests and the extent to which those perceptions can be manipulated. Foucault's social control is based on common knowledge of normality and deviant behaviour. So, there is often talk in political science conferences about 'bringing ideas back in' (a subject explored in Chapter 11), but our discussion of power shows that they never went out.

> **Ideas** – shared beliefs or ways of thinking (see Chapter 11 for a wider discussion).

The modern literature is largely devoted to conceptualizing this relationship between power and ideas (Kettell and Cairney, 2010; Béland, 2010). Discussions of agenda setting (drawing heavily on Schattschneider) focus on problem definition and the ability of groups to 'frame' issues to limit the number of participants in the policy process (Chapter 9). The advocacy coalition framework focuses on the shared beliefs of advocacy coalitions and charts their ability to establish a dominant way to interpret the policy evidence (Chapter 10). Hall (1993: 287) identifies policy paradigms, or ways of thinking about policy problems that are institutionalized or so ingrained in the psyche that they are often taken for granted (Chapters 4 and 11). The literature also explores what it would take to change those arrangements; how power could be exercised to challenge existing beliefs and change the way policymakers think and act. For example, the identification of extreme policy failures or external 'shocks' to the political system (such as a crisis or change in government) may prompt policymakers to engage in a fundamental rethink of their beliefs and seek out participants with new ideas. Or, the ideas and policies adopted by other governments may prompt policymakers to learn lessons and transfer policy (Chapter 12).

Ideas therefore perform two roles. First, they are used to limit policy change by excluding participants with challenging beliefs. Second, they are used by excluded groups to challenge barriers to policymaking engagement. Ideas can represent barriers to engagement but they can be overcome. As Bachrach and Baratz's (1970: 98) study of the politics of poverty in Baltimore suggests, these barriers *were* overcome over the longer term, as the previously excluded black population became increasingly powerful, buoyed by anti-poverty groups and more able, over time, to identify, become aware of and influence the 'arenas of conflict'. Similarly, the issue of air pollution now receives much more attention. Indeed, Crenson (1971: 69–71; 79) suggests that Gary shifted its policy first by learning lessons and transferring policy from Allegheny Pennsylvania, aided by federal government regulations which reduced the ability of large companies to play cities off against each other.

Structural and institutional power

The third dimension of power and, in particular, the example of the working classes unaware of their real interests, raises complex problems about the language used to describe how political structures influence behaviour. Poulantzas (1986: 146 and in Lukes, 2005: 54–6) defines power as 'the capacity of a class to realize specific objective interests'. In this context the state may be understood as an 'objective system of regular connections' to further the interests of a class and therefore represent a form of power which individuals merely 'bear' rather than exercise. In other words, this may be the ultimate expression of structural power if it is effectively exercised on behalf of classes by individuals with no autonomy (Miliband in Lukes, 2005: 56). However, such extreme conceptions have gained little support in political science.

For Dowding (1991: 9–10; 2003: 306) and Lukes (2005: 57) the term 'structural power' makes no conceptual sense because the 'exercise' of power requires the exerciser to have an ability to choose how they act – but structures cannot act. Only **actors** can act (and be held responsible for their actions). Dowding suggests that 'structural power' is used to explain outcomes in the interests of certain actors (such as capitalists) when those actors do not exercise power themselves. This point is central to Crenson's (1971: 125) argument that those with powerful reputations often enjoy favourable policy outcomes without exercising power. For

Actors – entities such as individuals, groups and governments with the means to consider information and make decisions.

Box 3.4   Power and luck

The term 'luck' conjures up an image of randomness and serendipity (Smith: 2009: 39; Lukes and Haglund, 2005: 49). 'Systematic luck' produces the suspicion that we are talking about someone who is randomly lucky a lot more than randomness suggests (i.e. non-random randomness!). Yet, in the way that Barry (1980a: 184) and Dowding (1996: 71; 2009) use the term there is no element of randomness. Rather, luck refers to someone who enjoys favourable political outcomes as the by-product of the behaviour of someone else. In turn, systematic luck occurs 'because of the way society is structured ... Actors denoted by their social location have powers based upon their social resources, and they also have luck based upon their social location' (1996: 71–2). Actors can be both lucky (by enjoying favourable outcomes caused by the actions of someone else) and powerful (exploiting one's position and resources to influence outcomes) but the analytical separation is important. For example, 'capitalists' benefit disproportionately from the decision by almost everyone, for their own reasons, to maintain capitalism (and support economic growth) rather than seek socialism. Socialist parties may know that the successful pursuit of socialism is impossible in the short term and will wreck their re-election chances, while the working classes may not want to endure decades of pain before securing long-term benefits (1996: 73). The resultant social structure proves far more beneficial to capitalists than other actors even though they did not determine the outcome. The crucial point to note is that the identification of 'luck' does not preclude the identification of power – capitalists are both powerful (when influencing the behaviour of governments and employees) and lucky unless they completely determine the actions of others. Similarly, other groups can be both powerless and unlucky. They may be powerless if they struggle to mobilize effectively and have no effective leadership or powerful sponsor (1996: 38–40); McLean, 1987: 66–7; compare with Lukes and Haglund, 2005: 50–2). Indeed, we should not assume that the pressure group world is pluralistic; mobilization on one side does not produce inevitable counter-mobilization from the other. They may be unlucky if they lose out when decisions are made. This may or may not relate to their inability to mobilize.

Dowding (1991; see also Barry, 1980a; 1980b; 2002) this may be better described as 'luck' (Box 3.4). People are 'lucky' when they benefit from policy outcomes (without exercising power) because their interests coincide with those of someone else exercising power. It may be used to explain why some groups appear to get more of what they want than their 'powers' would seem to suggest (Dowding, 2003: 316).

However, we still have two unresolved issues. The first is that we need to conceptualize the socio-economic pressures that policymakers face; the feeling that they often seem powerless or act in an environment that is often beyond their control (Chapter 6). In this context of structural power, Ward (1987: 602) highlights situations which appear to make 'certain acts unthinkable or physically impossible' or 'so costly that actors are structurally constrained from carrying them out'. This is not a million miles from Dowding's (1996: 44; contra. Hay, 2004a: 51) suggestion that 'we have no choice' really means that 'the best course of action seems obvious' (see also Hindess, 1988: 97; and Dowding 1991, 9: 'the power of individuals is in part determined (or rather structurally suggested) by their positions in the social structure'). There is widespread disagreement about how to theorize (and label) this relationship between structure and agency, but more agreement that individuals do not exercise power unconditionally and that some structures are more difficult to overcome than others.

The second is that we need to explain how institutions influence behaviour (Chapter 4). This process has two main aspects. First, the actions of individuals holding key posts may be said to be acting on behalf of organizations rather than themselves. Second, those individuals follow (and therefore reproduce) the customs and rules of that organization. Therefore, when we talk of institutions acting to exert power, we mean that it is difficult to reduce this process either to the rules governing institutions or the sum total of the actions of individuals. Rather, institutions are rule-bound entities which influence, but do not determine, the actions of the individuals. Or, using 'agency' terms, institutional action represents the sum total of the actions of individuals which follow and reproduce, or challenge and depart from, the rules governing institutions. For example, individuals may establish the constitution of an organization. In turn, that constitution may be followed long after the original participants have departed. In this sense, the rules of the organization survive and appear to take on a life of their own, highlighting two forms of power: the exercise of *direct* power to shape the conduct of others and *indirect* power to shape the future context in which others will operate (Hay, 2002: 186).

Is power centralized or diffuse? Should it be centralized?

The elitist position is that power is concentrated in the hands of a small number of actors, while pluralism suggests that no actors have overall control of the policy process because it is fragmented and specialized. These positions on the concentration of power are held, explicitly or implicitly, in all contemporary theories of public policy. They are perhaps most clear in discussions of incrementalism which often assumes a diffusion of power. Pluralism rests at the heart of Lindblom's (1959: 85) measure of 'good' policy which relates to the consensus reached by actors negotiating within the political system (Chapter 5). They also inform modern studies of policy networks and sub-systems (Chapters 8–10), although perhaps in a rather confusing way. On the one hand, the literature supports Dahl's argument that public policy is specialized; the sheer size and fragmentation of political systems ensures that the reach of one actor does not extend across all areas. On the other, it builds on Schattschneider's ideas about the exercise of power to limit debate within policy communities. Such discussions show that the dividing lines between elitism and pluralism are not clear. As Moran (2005: 16; see also Barry, 1980b: 350) suggests, pluralism may be elitism's 'close cousin'.

The debate on whether power is centralized or diffuse also has a normative dimension: *should* power be centralized? As Chapters 1 and 2 suggest, this is a perennial issue which began with the study of policy cycles and the 'comprehensively rational' policymaker and continues with discussions of multi-level governance (Chapter 8). The ideal of comprehensive rationality includes an assumption that power is held centrally by policymakers whose decisions are carried out by neutral bureaucrats or other organizations. While studies of implementation demonstrate that this assumption is unrealistic, many also suggest that complete top-down control would be inappropriate. This is particularly the case in federal systems with a separation of powers and formally recognized devolution of power to states, but also relevant to unitary states with elected local governments. The literature on multi-level governance (Chapter 8) further explores the distinction between power as *capacity* and the *exercise* of power. It suggests that while power may be concentrated formally, those decision-making 'centres' are surrounded by a myriad of actors exercising informal influence. It also takes the normative argument one step further, often suggesting that the dispersion of power to sub-state and non-state actors is more efficient and appropriate than centralization: 'Centralized authority – command and control – has few advocates ... the dispersion of governance across multiple jurisdictions is both more efficient than, and normatively superior to, central state monopoly' (Hooghe and Marks, 2003: 233). This position challenges the need for a clear and accountable 'centre' that seems necessary to make sense of the government's contract with those who consent to its power (see p. 59 above – 'the right to exercise power'). In the absence of such an arrangement, how do we hold policymakers to account?

Conclusion

Power has a wide variety of meanings, including the *capacity* for action: the ability to get what you want; the ability to affect the behaviour of others; and, the ability to alter the decision-making environment. In turn, this ability can be related to inequalities, or the relative powers of individuals, social groupings and institutions. Crucially, however, it also refers to the *exercise* of power. This distinction can be linked to the most important debates in the literature.

First, it underpins the community power debate. While the modern elitist position suggests that power can be inferred from reputations and the possession of powerful positions in government, business and society, the pluralist critique is that such power must be demonstrated and observed. This different approach to the use of research methods when studying power produced different conclusions: although power is dispersed unequally throughout society, this does not translate into overall control of the policy process. Rather, the control of elected and unelected office is diffuse and the sheer size and fragmentation of the state ensures that the reach of one powerful actor does not extend across all policy areas. This shift of attention from power-based reputations to policy outcomes in 'key decisions' raises empirical, methodological and normative questions that form the basis for the remainder of this book.

While many critics of the pluralist position accept the need to demonstrate the exercise of power, they argue that it ignores the role of *non-decision making*, in which the powerless are prevented from engaging in policymaking, and the *mobilization of bias*, in which some issues are 'organized out' of the policymaking process. Therefore, a focus on observable decision making in which one actor wins at the expense of another ignores the extent to which power is exercised, less visibly, to keep issues off the political agenda. This argument is extended in the 'third dimensional' account of power in which potential conflicts are minimized following the manipulation of people's beliefs. Although policy areas may *appear* to be consensual (suggesting that we can not observe winners and losers in 'key decisions'), this is because some actors do not recognize their 'real interests' and act accordingly.

Second, it informs debates on the role of structural power. Although there is a common recognition in the literature that the exercise of power is 'structured', there is less agreement on the extent to which structures possess power. Or, if structures do not have the ability to act, then it may make little sense to suggest that they *exercise* power. This goes to the heart of the way in which we theorize the power of institutions and the extent to which we can say that policymaking decisions are as a much a product of their environment as they are the actions of powerful individuals. It also relates directly to the issue of popular consent and the right to exercise power. For example, we may identify ideas which resemble structures – as dominant ideologies that restrict debate, forms of knowledge that undermine the rationality of individuals, and rules of government that limit popular participation in policymaking. We may also theorize that government power is only exercised legitimately on the basis of popular consent and that the presence of such structural constraints undermines the democratic link.

The difficulty raised by the latter approach is that the most important and interesting issues of power may also be the most difficult to research and demonstrate in a convincing way. Although we 'know' such power exists we do not agree on how to identify and theorize it. Therefore, what perhaps appears at first to be a rather dry and technical issue of methodology soon transforms into an issue that goes to the heart of the empirical and normative debate on who possesses, and who should possess, the means to exercise power. As the remaining chapters suggest, these issues of theory, method and evidence are addressed in a range of different ways by different models of public policy.

Chapter 4

Institutions and 'New Institutionalism'

The aim of this chapter is to examine:

- Institutions as the 'structures of government' that vary across policy-making systems.
- How we define institutions and institutionalism.
- Key variants of new institutionalism – historical, rational choice, normative, sociological, and constructivist.
- Is there more to unite than divide the new institutionalisms? For example, we consider the debate between 'empirical' and 'network' institutionalism and consider the argument that common policy styles can be found in most political systems despite their institutional differences.

The study of public policy would be incomplete without an understanding of policymaking institutions. The study of political science would also be incomplete without turning our understanding of terms such as 'institutions' upside down. The term may in the past have referred to the established organizations – such as legislatures, courts and executives – that we would intuitively associate with 'institution'. Indeed, in most cases we would have been able to *point* to an institution, or at least the building that symbolizes its existence (Judge, 2005: 2). Now, it refers to two related factors: regular patterns of behaviour and the rules, norms, practices and relationships that influence such behaviour. Institutions are not just the buildings or arenas within which people make policy – they are also the rules of behaviour that influence how they make policy.

These rules can be formal or informal. Formal rules of political systems include the US federal model and its constitution which sets out the rules governing the separation of powers between the executive, legislative and judicial branches and guarantees a degree of autonomy to its states. We may then compare these rules with those of other political systems, such as the 'Westminster model' which has an executive, within the legislature, that controls the autonomy of its territories. Or, a focus on particular rules may lead to comparisons of policymaking styles. For example, Lijphart (1999) differentiates between 'majoritarian' systems with first-past-the-post electoral rules and 'consensus' democracies which employ proportional representation. However, institutionalism can also refer to norms and non-statutory and informal rules. In this case, we focus on regular patterns of behaviour, the relationships that policy participants form and the common understandings that they develop about how to behave.

'New institutionalism' is the term used to describe this focus on rules rather than bricks-and-mortar institutions, and the concern with exploring norms and common understandings as well as statutory rules (although the differences between 'old' and 'new' are often overstated – see Peters (2005: 1–5); Thelen and Steinmo (1992: 3–5); March and Olsen (1984: 734–8) and compare with John (1998: 49); Adcock *et al.* (2006: 259–62); Rhodes (2006a: 95); Selznick (1996); Judge (2005: 5) and Peters (2005: 6–10)). This approach has boosted research into the institutions that we have always assumed to be central to political science explanation. However, it has also produced a significant problem: no-one is entirely sure what an institution is and what new institutionalism means.

The vagueness of institutionalism helps explain why there are so many variants. For example, Lowndes (2010: 65) lists a staggering nine approaches: normative, rational choice, historical, empirical, international, sociological, network, constructivist and feminist institutionalism. This suggests that the common term 'institutionalism' exaggerates the cohesiveness of the literature. It seems to represent an umbrella term or loose collection of approaches rather than a coherent theory (Hall and Taylor, 1996: 937; March and Olsen, 1984: 734). It may be held together by the belief that institutions are the 'central component of political life' and that 'they matter more than anything else that could be used to explain political decisions' (Peters, 2005: 164). However, we may have to work hard to make sure that we are talking about the same thing.

Identifying formal and informal institutions

Newton and van Deth (2010: 9) highlight the importance of institutions as 'structures of government'. Constitutions represent a 'set of fundamental laws that determines the central institutions and offices, and powers and duties of the state' (2010: 71). In this context, the list of constitutional rules and associated organizations is long, and the potential for different policy outcomes in different political systems appears to be considerable:

- *Confederal and federal.* Confederal arrangements can be found at the international level in which countries give some powers to supranational bodies to work in their common interests, but retain significant autonomy. Federal suggests a greater integration of territories, with common institutions more likely to have enforcement powers (Newton and van Deth, 2010: 107–9).

- *Federal and unitary.* In federal systems, there is a balance of power between the executive, legislature and judiciary and between central and territorial levels of government. The latter have powers and rights guaranteed to them in a written constitution. In unitary systems, the central government controls, and can reform or abolish, territorial government (2010: 109). These distinctions are blurred by a trend towards centralization in federal states and the 'quasi-federal' status of some unitary systems that guarantee some autonomy to regions (e.g. the UK and Spain) (2010: 114–15) .

- *Presidential, parliamentary and semi-presidential.* In presidential systems an elected president is head of government and state. Many systems are based on the US model in which the president heads the executive (where most policy is made) and can initiate but not control the progress of legislation. In parliamentary systems, the head of government is a prime minister or chancellor (the head of state is ceremonial). Many are based on the 'Westminster' model in which the executive forms part of, and is accountable to, the legislature. Most legislation is initiated and controlled by the governing party which tends to have a majority under a plurality voting system. In semi-presidential systems there is a fusion of executive and legislature, but the prime minister is chosen by an elected president. Presidential and semi-presidential systems are the most likely to distribute power and are often associated with inertia and 'deadlock', with parliamentary systems associated with strength or effectiveness (2010: 92–8; Weaver and Rockman, 1993: 2; compare with Chapter 5).

- *Unicameral and bicameral legislatures.* While many federal states (Australia, Belgium, Germany, Switzerland, US) have a 'strong' second chamber, most are 'weak' (they have limited powers to initiate and amend legislation or control financial matters) (2010: 79; compare with Galligan, 2006: 272–3).

- *The role of the judiciary.* Most states have a form of judicial review, but some also have constitutional courts (e.g. the EU, South Africa) and others have particularly active judiciaries (the US, Germany) (2010: 79–81).

- *Direct democracy.* This is important in countries such as the US and Switzerland with procedures for holding referendums prompted by popular local initiatives (Budge, 2006).

There are also a series of rules embedded within political systems, including:

- *Electoral systems*. In first-past-the-post systems, the candidate with the most votes (often a plurality rather than majority) in a constituency is elected. In proportional systems there is often more than one vote cast (or candidates are ranked in order of preference) to ensure a closer link between the share of votes and seats that political parties gain (Newton and van Deth, 2010: 248–9; Karp and Banducci, 2008).
- *Party systems*. The number of political parties is influenced by the number of 'cleavages' within society, such as between those representing labour or business, and ethnic and religious populations. Party systems are influenced heavily by electoral systems, particularly under plurality which exaggerates the results for the two largest parties at the expense of small parties (which are stronger and better represented under PR).
- *Rules of government formation and executive–legislative relations*. The need for minority or coalition government is more prevalent under multi-party PR systems (Newton and van Deth, 2010: 272–7). This combines with different rules in different countries regarding, for example, how long parties are given to negotiate government formation, how susceptible they are to motions of no confidence, and the extent to which parties can have policy influence in opposition (Strøm, 1990; Shugart, 2006).
- *Group–government relations*. 'Corporatism' refers to a close relationship between government and groups representing labour and business, in which 'umbrella' or 'peak' organizations are integrated within government policymaking structures. This is joint decision making, with the results often implemented by groups (e.g. by trade unions enforcing wage agreements on members). 'Tri-partism' is a similar but less formal arrangement. 'Pluralism' refers to a process in which groups compete with each other to influence government. In this case, informal 'rules of the game' are more important than formalized arrangements. Groups can also be 'para-governmental' when they receive money from governments to deliver public services (Newton and van Deth, 2010: 213–7; see also Martin and Swank, 2004; Martin and Thelen, 2007).
- *Structures of public bureaucracies*. Bureaucracies are subject to rules to ensure that they are powerful enough to be efficient but also accountable and not so powerful that they are autonomous. While such issues have inspired constant civil service reforms, so too has the wave of 'new public management' reforms based on the idea of applying private business methods to government (Kettl, 2006).

We may also identify a miscellany of rules which resemble policy decisions that have become 'institutionalized' in some way. *Economic institutions* refers to the system of state (country, not US state, level) rules governing the operation of economic organizations. For example, there may be a US (adversarial) or UK (self-regulation and oversight) model regarding the way government agencies regulate large corporations. There may also be Anglo-American, Rhineland and East Asian models of capitalism, each of which involve different relationships between the state and the market (Moran, 2006). *Regulatory state* refers to the collection of rules governing not only economic organizations but also interest groups, agencies and other organizations involved in the delivery of public services (Braithwaite, 2006) *Welfare states* represent a complex system of rules governing the provision of public and social services to the population.

In most cases, our analysis is complete only when we combine a study of formal institutions with informal rules, shared understandings and standard operating procedures. For example, the process of intergovernmental relations within federal and devolved systems involves not only written concordats and formal dispute resolution mechanisms (intergovernmental committees, the courts), but also informal contacts between political parties, civil servants and individuals (Horgan, 2004; Watts, 2007). In some systems, such as the UK, the norm is to avoid formal dispute resolution even if governments do not share a political party or know each other personally (Cairney, 2012; Chapter 8). While federal systems are 'cooperative' (in which the centre and states share power and must coordinate policy efforts) or 'dual' (in which powers are separated), in practice most are administratively and financially interdependent and tend to cooperate in similar ways (Newton and Van Deth, 2010: 114; Galligan, 2006: 274). The same can be said, to some extent, about central and local governments in unitary systems (John, 1998: 51–2).

But what exactly is an institution? What is institutionalism?

The *Oxford Handbook of Political Institutions* (Rhodes, Binder and Rockman, 2006) dedicates at least one chapter to the following institutions: the state, civil society, economic institutions, constitutions, federal and territorial institutions, executives, legislatures, courts, bicameral structures, public bureaucracies, the welfare state, regulations, local government, political parties, electoral systems, direct democracy, international and non-governmental institutions. If this is the list that most of us would produce (with the exception of one or two), then as institutionalists we have a common understanding of what to study when we analyse public policy. However, this may not be as promising as it looks, for two main reasons. First, we may only agree on what an institution is if we are taking the 'I know it when I see it' approach (and even then there are problems – see Thelen and Steinmo, 1992: 29, note 9; Peters, 2005: 74). Things will be different when we try to *define* an institution. Second, we may agree about what to study but not how to study it.

Rhodes *et al.* (2006: xiii) suggest that there is no 'singular definition of an institution on which students of politics can find wide agreement'. Dowding and King (1995: 10) warn against 'trivially true' definitions that make it difficult to find something that is not an institution. In other words, if 'institution' means everything then it means nothing (Rothstein in Lowndes, 2010: 72). Most importantly, we need to distinguish between an institution and an organization, which Simon (1976: xvii) defines as 'the complex pattern of communication and relationships in a group of human beings'. As Box 4.1 suggests, we can first understand an institution as an organization or arena within which decisions are made. Then, we can explore what it is about institutions that influence decision making. In most definitions the key focus is on regular patterns of behaviour and the rules and norms that influence that behaviour. If we adapt Simon's definition, our focus is on regular patterns of communication and action and the rules and norms underpinning human relationships.

Yet, this is still quite a vague endeavour, and we face more problems when we move from studying regular patterns of behaviour towards defining rules, identifying which rules are the most important, and assessing the extent to which rules are followed and *enforced*, or if most processes are characterized by shared understandings and agreements about how people should act. We need a language to describe institutions as influences on behaviour rather than forms of behaviour in their own right. One solution is to follow Hall's (1986; 1993) idea of 'standard operating procedures' which are recognized by participants and 'can be described and explained to the researcher' (Lowndes, 2010: 73; Ostrom, 2007: 23). Another is Ostrom's (2007: 23) attempt to distinguish between:

- *Rules* – 'shared prescriptions (must, must not, or may) that are mutually understood and predictably enforced in particular situations by agents responsible for monitoring conduct and for imposing sanctions';
- *Norms* – 'shared prescriptions that tend to be enforced by the participants themselves through internally and externally imposed costs and inducements'; and
- *Strategies* – 'the regularised plans that individuals make within the structure of incentives produced by rules, norms and expectations of the likely behaviour of others'.

Most discussions tread a fine line between saying that rules *influence* or *determine* the behaviour of individuals (Thelen and Steinmo, 1992: 3), but there is no common agreement on how to balance the two. For

Box 4.1 Discussions of institutions

These quotations give a flavour of the different meaning attached to 'institutions', from the identification of organizations and arenas, to the various rules and norms that may influence behaviour:

A major confusion exists between scholars who use the term to refer to an organizational entity such as the US Congress, a business firm, a political party, or a family, and scholars who use the term to refer to the rules, norms and strategies adopted by individuals operating within or across organizations. (Ostrom, 2007: 23)

Institutions are the arena within which policy-making takes place. They include the political organizations, laws and rules that are central to every political system and they constrain how decision-makers behave. (John, 1998: 38)

The formal rules, compliance procedures, and standard operating procedures that structure conflict. (Hall in Thelen and Steinmo, 1992: 2)

Institutions ...can be interpreted as reflecting habits and norms, more likely to be evolved than to be created. But institutions also may be seen as architecture and as rules that determine opportunities and incentives for behaviour. (Rhodes *et al.*, 2006: xiii)

Building blocks of social order ... organizing behaviour into predictable and reliable patterns. (Streek and Thelen, 2005: 9)

Humanly devised constraints that shape human interaction. (North in Sanders, 2006: 42).

example, March and Olsen (2006a: 3) suggest that an institution can be treated effectively as a structure because many rules often endure in the same basic form regardless of the individuals involved. Alternatively, Rhodes (2006a: 103) argues that 'Even when an institution maintains similar routines while personnel change, it does so mainly because the successive personnel pass on similar beliefs and preferences'. In this case, a rule becomes akin to a language: it only survives if there are enough individuals committed to its survival. Or, it is a 'tradition'; a 'set of understandings someone receives during socialization' (Rhodes, 2006a: 91).

This difference in language may seem trivial, but it highlights important debates which often divide the discipline (see also Box 4.2). For example, Bevir argued (in a seminar, 'Mark Bevir's "The Logic of the History of Ideas": Ten Years After' at the Political Science Association conference, Manchester, 2009) that the term 'institution' has a bewitching effect – it is misleading because it suggests a fixed entity or set of rules that we can all point to and understand in the same way; it is a meaningless and vacuous word devoid of content, which hides the real substantive differences in political practices ('Don't call practices institutions!'). It is not inevitable that institutions endure over time and we may question the extent to which institutions represent shared meanings and practices. Instead, they may be reproduced in different ways by individuals who understand those rules, and act, differently (Bevir, 2009). This makes the *identification* of institutions very tricky indeed. As Ostrom (2007: 23) argues, institutions 'exist in the minds of the participants and sometimes are shared as implicit knowledge rather than in an explicit and written form'. Further, the rules followed implicitly within organizations may even contradict the rules espoused explicitly in their written statements (2007: 23).

Therefore, while we can perhaps agree that institutions represent sets of rules and norms that guide behaviour, this may be where the agreement ends. As Rhodes *et al.* (2006: xiii) suggest, 'the range of theoretical approaches underlying the contemporary study of institutions is remarkably diverse, let alone the range of empirical and methodological orientations'.

Key variants: historical institutionalism

Historical institutionalism treats institutions as 'the formal rules, compliance procedures, and standard operating procedures' that 'structure conflict' (Hall in Thelen and Steinmo, 1992: 2) or 'structure and shape behaviour and outcomes' (Steinmo, 2008: 188). Its key terms are 'historical contingency', 'path dependence' (Thelen and Steinmo, 1992: 2) and 'critical juncture'. Historical contingency refers to the extent to which events and decisions made in the past contributed to the formation of institutions that influence current practices. Path dependence suggests that when a commitment to an institution has been established and resources devoted to it, over time it produces 'increasing returns' and it effectively becomes increasingly costly to choose a different path (Pierson, 2000a; Peters, 2005: 74; for a review of the path dependence literature see Greener, 2005; Kay, 2006). Therefore, institutions, and the practices they encourage, may remain stable for long periods of time.

A 'critical juncture' is the point at which certain events and decisions were made which led to the development of an institution. The timing of these decisions is crucial, because it may be the order of events that sets institutional development on a particular path (note the term 'sensitivity to initial conditions'). The analogy is a thought experiment with two

Box 4.2 Key questions for new institutionalism

Lowndes (2010: 65) and Schmidt (2006: 115) provide a list of new institutionalisms and explore the differences between them. However, there are no hard-and-fast distinctions between each version and it would be misleading to provide a table of definitions with strong dividing lines. There is too much disagreement on which texts fit into which camps (for example, see Peters, 2005: 108) and too much variation within those camps.

Instead, particular texts provide different answers to five key questions:

1 *What is an institution?* These are the rules, norms and 'standard operating procedures' that influence behaviour, but some accounts may identify formal rules or treat rules as fixed structures more than others.

2 *How does an institution influence individual behaviour?* Hall and Taylor (1996: 939–40) distinguish between the 'calculus' and the 'cultural approach'. 'Calculus' suggests that individuals make strategic decisions based on their preferences. Institutions affect behaviour by providing the payoffs or consequences of their actions (e.g. the 'penalties for defection'). 'Cultural' suggests that individuals follow 'established routines or familiar patterns of behaviour' based on their 'worldview' or 'interpretation of a situation'. Institutions affect behaviour by providing an important source of 'moral or cognitive templates' to inform that interpretation.

3 *How does an institution become established in the first place?* Different approaches may present different ideas regarding, 'intentional design, accident or evolution' (Goodin in Lowndes, 2010: 75–6).

4 *How does an institution change?* While most accounts suggest that institutions can be challenged or modified by agents, some treat institutions as structures that are relatively resistant to change, while others focus on the less-fixed rules agreed informally between participants or the institutionalisation of ideas.

5 *How does institutionalism inform comparative public policy?* While some 'empirical' accounts use institutions to explain country level differences, some 'network' accounts identify common institutional 'rules of the game'.

balls – one black and one red – in a container. What happens if, each time we take a ball from the container, we add another black or red ball to the container? If a black ball is chosen we add another black ball to the container and therefore increase the probability of a black ball being chosen next time (from 1 in 2 to 2 in 3). The more we choose, then the greater the cumulative effect of this first event. Choosing a black ball at this stage becomes self-reinforcing; it increases the chance of selecting a black ball next time. The immediate lessons from the experiment are: (a) that the initial event involved a degree of chance; and, (b) its cumulative effect was significant. Path dependence suggests both unpredictability and inertia, as relatively small events or actions can have large and enduring effects on institutions (Pierson, 2000a; Sanders, 2006: 39; Box

4.3). This may be a 'self-reinforcing process' or 'reproduction mechanism' as some decisions close off other options (Capoccia and Kelemen, 2007: 341; the usual example is the QWERTY keyboard – better systems now exist but the decision to adopt this keyboard in the past helps maintain its position now) and established organizations serve to uphold rules.

The wider lesson is that significant institutional differences are likely to develop in different countries. In each country, a different set of initial conditions produces a different set of actions and events which have a cumulative effect and set institutional development on a different path. Therefore, to give a full explanation for current institutional (and therefore policy) differences between countries we should look to the past to establish how and why they developed (Peters, 2005: 76). Historical institutionalism provides the 'theoretical leverage' to understand 'policy continuities over time within countries and policy variation across countries' (Thelen and Steinmo, 1992: 10).

A wide variety of publications – with different approaches (focusing on elite or social movement-driven institutions) and methods (single or comparative, small or large studies) – may qualify as historical institutionalist (see Sanders, 2006: 44; Schmidt, 2006: 104; Steinmo, 2008: 124; Peters, 2005: 75; Hall and Taylor, 1996: 938). Some studies seek to explain why institutions developed (Sanders, 2006: 51 identifies a focus on the role of labour/trade union movements in the formation of welfare states) or track the effect of existing institutions on things such as the success of interest group strategies or the translation of similar levels of public support for public services into different levels of taxation and sizes of welfare states (Steinmo, 2008: 124–5; see Rosamond, 2000: 116–17 on applications to the EU). Others explore the interaction between forces for change and relatively durable institutions, producing different levels and types of policy change in different countries.

For example, why do country-level differences in welfare state institutions endure in the face of strong socioeconomic pressures? Pierson's (2000b: 2–4; 2000c: 80–1) argument is that economic 'globalization' (see Chapter 6 for a full discussion and definition) may undermine the ability of countries to control their economic and monetary policies. Further, the rising costs of high unemployment, pensions and care for older people have put an immense strain on most countries' ability to maintain their welfare states. However, these pressures do not produce an inevitable 'race to the bottom', such as when countries radically reduce welfare provision and/or reduce corporation taxes and employment regulations to enable them to compete with other countries for foreign investment. Rather, different countries react differently according to: (a) the scope and popularity of existing welfare state institutions, and (b) political institutions which structure the interaction between political parties, interest groups and government.

Box 4.3   Path dependence and immigration

Bale (2008) combines a discussion of the common pressures on immigration policy in Europe with the identification of different policies which have endured for decades. Sources of common pressure include: the new freedom of movement of European Union nationals within the EU; the legacy of 'decolonialization' (many countries once colonized African and South American regions); a rise in asylum applications (particularly from people in Africa and the Middle East); attention to levels of unemployment and benefit-seeking in native and foreign born residents; rising 'Islamophobia' and new stereotypes of 'migrants and minorities as terrorists'; the rising popularity of radical right-wing parties seeking strong immigration controls; and, shifting ideas, from multiculturalism (the promotion of diverse cultures within states) to integration (the promotion of a common culture) (2008: 303–20). We can identify similar policies in many countries, such as the lack of attention to, or rejection of, the status of Roma travellers (2008: 331). However, we can also identify different policies based on their historical origins. For example, Germany's post-war policy of liberal immigration (initially to encourage Germans to return to Germany, followed by attempts to 'demonstrate its liberal credentials') but differential status (granting citizenship based on blood links, not birth or residence) has produced a population which includes 7 million 'foreigners'. While some policymakers have attempted to change policy on immigration and reform citizenship rules (i.e. to grant citizenship to many), this has proved difficult in a 'federal and consensual system that gives many "veto players" a say' (2008: 329). Bale (2008: 329) contrasts Germany with France, which has a history of granting citizenship more easily to 'illegal' immigrants (linked to issues such as decolonization in North Africa and previous fears about under-population). As a result, the new policy context is rather different and the agenda is more about being tough on illegal immigration and promoting national integration (in the context of a political system associated with a majoritarian rather than consensual style of policymaking) (see also Freeman, 2006).

Key variants: rational choice institutionalism

Rational choice theory is set out in detail in Chapter 7. It employs 'methodological individualism' or a commitment to explain socio-political outcomes as the aggregation of the decisions of individuals. Its aim is to establish what proportion of political outcomes one can explain with reference to the choices of individuals pursuing their preferences under particular conditions (the 'calculus' approach). This is where institutions come in. While preferences provide the 'motivation of individual action' we also need to know the 'context' within which they operate, to explain their choices (Dowding and King, 1995: 1). Individuals know that actions have different consequences in different contexts and this affects how they pursue their preferences. They act on the basis of what they expect to happen and institutions often provide that information. Individuals ask themselves, 'which action produces payoffs closest to my preferences?' and institutions affect behaviour by providing the payoffs or information regarding the consequences of their actions. For example, institutions may provide the 'enforcement mechanisms for agreements' and 'penalties for defection' (Hall and Taylor, 1996: 939–40). Overall, institutions represent sets of rules that influence choices, often producing regular patterns of behaviour. This regularity can be expressed in terms of equilibrium when we identify a stable point at which there is no incentive to divert from these patterns of behaviour.

Institutions may be treated as solutions to at least three public policy problems identified by rational choice. First, they may solve a collective action problem: the potential for choices made by individuals to have an adverse societal effect when there is an absence of trust, obligation or other incentives to cooperate with each other. The institution gives individuals that incentive if the rule dictates that they (and others) will be otherwise be punished (e.g. a rule dictating that individuals will be prosecuted if they flout the rules of the road), or if the rule acts as a positive inducement (e.g. individuals are rewarded financially if they recycle) (Peters, 2005: 49).

Second, institutions may reduce 'transactions costs'. In economics, institutions represent a set of (often formal and, if necessary, enforced) rules governing relationships between individuals or organizations. The aims are to maintain the trust required for them to reach agreements and reduce: the likelihood that agreements between actors are broken; uncertainty; and, the costs associated with wasted effort on joint tasks that are not fulfilled. In public policy, studies explore the relationship between legislative committees and government agencies, the rules of coalition government formation and the development of EU institutions governing the interactions between member states   (see Hall and Taylor, 1996: 943).

Third, institutions may address the problem of instability. As Chapter 7 suggests, there is no adequate rule to aggregate individual preferences into social preferences. Instead, there is always the potential for 'intransitive' electoral results or policy decisions for which there are 'majority-preferred alternatives' (Riker, 1982). If so, we might expect 'cycling' from one decision to another; as soon as one choice is made there is a more-preferred alternative ready to be selected as its replacement. In this case the role of an institution may be to 'channel preferences, slow the cycling process, and foster stability' (Dowding and King, 1995: 3). For example, a rule to ensure that elections take place once every four years reduces instability, while the formation of a governing majority with a relatively fixed policy programme may further limit the potential for alternative policy preferences to be considered.

The most prominent studies of institutional rational choice appear to treat rules effectively as structures that influence behaviour (Shepsle, 2006: 28; for examples, see Tsebelis, 2002; Dowding and King, 1995: 10; Ward, 2002: 86–7). Yet, rational choice institutionalism is much more than the study of formal design. We may also find informal rules and norms of behaviour that develop in a complex decision making environment. Shepsle (2006: 24–5) makes the distinction between the rules as 'exogenous constraints' (such as electoral systems which provide rules for when and how to vote) and the rules provided by the players themselves which may represent the 'equilibrium ways of doing things' (2006: 24–5). Rational choice accounts also suggest that institutions are subject to change by the individuals who follow and/or challenge existing rules (Hall and Taylor, 1996: 945).

Key variants: normative and sociological institutionalism

Peters (2005: 26) describes the work of March and Olsen as 'normative' because they identify the ability of 'norms and values within organizations' to influence behaviour. March and Olsen (1984: 739) reject the idea that we should explain political behaviour primarily in terms of choices based on the preferences of individuals. Instead, they refer to the role of political structures, defined as collections of 'institutions, rules of behavior, norms, roles, physical arrangements, buildings, and archives that are relatively invariant in the face of turnover of individuals and relatively resilient to the idiosyncratic preferences and expectations of individuals'. These structures act as a key reference point for political actors driven by duty: 'Members of an institution are expected to obey, and be the guardians of, its constitutive principles and standards' (March and Olsen, 2006a: 7). The 'rules of appropriateness' associated with each institution are 'transmitted through socialization' and 'followed because they are seen as natural, rightful, expected and legitimate' (March and Olsen, 1984: 739; 2006a: 7).

There are three main complications to such analysis. First, rules are often ambiguous and mean different things to different people. Second, different policy participants may be more or less willing or able to follow rules. Third, they may face a series of potentially contradictory rules associated with their role within one or more institutions. This leads March and Olsen (2006a: 9) to stress the role of an individual's identity and explore the link between forming a relatively strong attachment to one institution and adhering to its rules. This approach seems rather chicken-and-egg. Although institutions are structures that influence individual behaviour, 'individuals must pick and choose among influences and interpret the meaning of their institutional commitments' (Peters, 2005: 26). While the institution, as a structure, provides the 'rules of appropriateness', the individual appears to be in a position to judge which 'rules of appropriateness' are appropriate to follow. At the very least, to understand how people act within particular institutions we must identify both the rules and how they are understood by participants.

Peters (2005: 108) suggests that this focus on institutional norms and cultures originated in sociological institutionalism. Normative and sociological also share a rejection of 'functionalist' accounts of institutions. In sociology, functionalism suggests that 'societies have certain requisite functions that must be performed if they are to survive'; institutions represent the tools used by societies to produce the goods and services that they require (2005: 109). Similarly, in political science, institutions are 'functions of political life' (John, 1998: 39). Societies require that different institutions carry out different tasks to maintain an effective political system: 'legislatures make laws, executives take decisions, bureaucracies implement them and courts resolve disputes' (1998: 39; note John's reference to Easton and the policy cycle). In each case, institutions represent a neutral and efficient means for society to translate its values into political outputs.

Normative institutionalism rejects this idea that institutions have evolved to represent the most efficient way to solve the problems that societies face (March and Olsen, 1984; 1996; compare with historical – Hall and Taylor, 1996: 942). Institutional forms are not caused solely by the nature of their external surroundings and do not change inevitably to fit their new surroundings. Rather, institutions are to a large extent autonomous and, 'the paths they follow seem determined in part by internal dynamics only loosely connected to changes in their environment' (March and Olsen, 1996: 256). This reflects a wider literature in sociology and political science highlighting the ability of organizations to live on after their aims have been met or they no longer serve a useful purpose. Organizations may be able to maintain their standard operating procedures in the face of changing environments and the decisions of higher level policymakers (Peters, 2005: 110). Therefore, to understand how they operate we must study their 'culture' or the manner in which people within them understand their world (how it is and should be) (Hall and Taylor, 1996: 947; Peters, 2005: 111–15).

The most prominent description of this process refers to 'institutional isomorphism'. DiMaggio and Powell (1983, cited a staggering 12,000 times) revisit Weber's argument that competition among firms in a capitalist system, and between states, would cause bureaucracies to converge on the most efficient model. Hierarchical and unified bureaucracies, with strict rules to enforce formal roles, develop because they are 'technically' superior (Weber, 1978: 973). DiMaggio and Powell (1983: 147) argue that organizations become more alike without becoming efficient. For example, although government organizations initially form to address particular needs, based on the nature of the policy environment, they do not change efficiently as that environment changes (1983: 149). Rather, they become more alike to the other organizations that they compete with for resources, power and legitimacy within a common legal and political framework (e.g. they may emulate those organizations deemed to be successful). Or, they become increasingly driven by the rules and norms of public sector professions, developed through education and professional networks and encouraged by selective hiring practices (1983: 152). This is particularly the case when the aims of an organization are not clear and oversight is performed by people who are not particularly involved with, or aware of, the organization's activities. Although we might expect inefficient organizations to be 'weeded out' in a process of 'natural selection', economic efficiency is difficult to judge and organizations may be more likely to be judged on their political performance (1983: 157; compare with Hindmoor's 2006a: Chapter 6 discussion of rational choice and bureaucratic budgets). Or, they may be valued more for their symbolic or social value than their efficiency (Hall and Taylor, 1996: 949).

Key variants: constructivist (discursive) institutionalism

Constructivism is an approach to science that prompts us to consider the status of our knowledge: 'whether things are simply given and correctly perceived by our senses (empiricism) or whether the things we perceive are rather the product of our conceptualizations (constructivism)' (Kratochwil, 2008: 80). The latter suggests that the social world is artificial rather than real (2008: 86), but we should be clear about what this means. For example, Blyth (2002: vii–viii) relates it to the role of ideas as shared beliefs, arguing that if enough people believe a particular idea or argument then it becomes important as a means to explain behaviour regardless of its relation to the 'real' world. Indeed, shared beliefs may give people a common aim and a reason to believe that they have shared interests. In some cases, ideas or beliefs become institutionalized; they are taken for granted and rarely questioned, or at least accepted as the starting point when we consider policy problems. Constructivist accounts may identify path dependence, but relate this as much to ideas as governmental structures: 'it is not just institutions, but the very ideas on which they are predicated and which inform their design and development, that exert constraints on political autonomy' (Hay, 2006a: 65). As such, institutionalized ideas are not as stable as structures. Instead, they are 'constantly in flux, being reconsidered and redefined as actors communicate and debate with one another' (Béland and Cox, 2010: 4).

This argument suggests that institutions-as-ideas not only influence action but also 'exist' in terms of the way that actors understand them (see also Box 4.4). Hay (2006a: 65) notes that constructivists examine how actors 'interpret environmental signals'. Institutions represent 'established ideas' or 'paradigms' which act as 'cognitive filters' or the primary means through which people understand their environment. The agenda of constructivist institutionalism is to understand how such ideas are 'contested, challenged and replaced'. For Hay (2006a: 60) and Blyth (2002: 7; see also Streek and Thelen, 2005: 1–3) the aim is to explain often gradual institutional change from within institutions, rather than reverting to the notion of 'punctuated equilibrium' or radical change caused by an external shock. Institutional stability comes from the maintenance of dominant ideas, while change results from successful chal-

> **Discourse** – the verbal or written exchange or communication of ideas. In some cases, 'discourse' has a more ambitious meaning. For example, Foucault-inspired accounts link discourse to the power to decide which forms of knowledge are legitimate or acceptable.

lenges to those ideas. For Schmidt (2006: 113; 2010: 3; Schmidt and Radaelli, 2004: 193) this can involve 'coordinative' or 'communicative' **discourse**. 'Coordinative' refers to the role of individuals, groups or networks 'who generate the ideas that form the bases for collective action and identity' and compete with each other to have their ideas accepted. 'Communicative' refers to the use of those ideas in the wider public sphere – ranging from elites using policy platforms to persuade voters, to debate among social movements or local voters. In this sense, institutions represent the most

established ideas that are used to frame discussions and dominate debates, while coordinative and communicative processes suggest that these ideas can be challenged when they are debated.

The new institutionalisms: is there more to unite than divide them?

Ideas, inertia and change

The constructivist position is based on two related criticisms of the others. First, they are 'better at explaining continuity than change'. Historical, rational choice and sociological institutionalism treat institutions as constraints based on path dependence, structured incentives or a 'logic of appropriateness' bound to culture and norms (Schmidt, 2010: 2). They treat institutions as stable or relatively fixed, only to be changed radically before another stable institution is formed (Blyth, 2002: 7; Hay,

Box 4.4 Social construction theory

Social construction theory combines our focus on the institutionalisztion of ideas with discussions of power and agenda setting. Ingram, Schneider and deLeon (2007: 93) highlight two related factors: (1) the tendency of policy-makers to characterize populations to justify policy decisions (e.g. soldiers are heroes; big business is too powerful; the poor should make more effort to seek work; criminals are less worthy of policy attention); and (2) the power of groups to take advantage of, or compensate for, their positions in this definitional scheme. For example, the military is 'advantaged' because it is both powerful and given benefits by government, while big businesses are 'contenders' because they are often treated negatively but powerful enough to ensure 'hidden benefits and empty burdens'; the poor and homeless are too powerless to address their inadequate benefits, while criminals lack power and are burdened by government policy (2007: 102). In some cases, these characterizations become institutionalized as they are first incorporated into policy designs and then become 'hegemonic', 'natural' and 'seldom questioned'. In others, they are challenged successfully by, for example, interest groups representing themselves or social groups. The process is a 'continuing struggle to gain acceptance of particular constructions and their consequences' (2007: 95). This captures the argument that institutions-as-ideas influence behaviour but are also subject to challenge and reform.

2006a). The solution is to identify processes of instability or more regular institutional change by exploring the role of ideas. Second, they are 'overly structuralist' and do 'not grant purposeful actors a proper role' (Olsen, 2009: 3; Hindmoor, 2010). The solution is to explore not only how institutions influence agents, but also how actors challenge ideas and beliefs.

However, a key problem in assessing the role of ideas in other accounts is that ideas are difficult to define. Ideas range from mere policy proposals at one end of the scale to norms, paradigms and world views at the other. This suggests that they play a key part in normative and sociological institutionalism when norms influence behaviour. They are also present in many studies associated with historical institutionalism. For example, Peters (2005: 75) identifies medical knowledge and beliefs as the foundation of healthcare institutions in Immerguts' work, and the structure of belief systems as the explanation for stability and change in Hall's analysis (see Chapter 11). Indeed, Hall is cited by Hay (2006a: 66) as the main inspiration for constructivist institutionalism (see also Hall and Taylor, 1996: 942; Sanders, 2006: 42 and compare with Blyth, 1997: 229). In this light, Schmidt (2006: 113–14) suggests that constructivist may be viewed as a supplement to, rather than replacement of, other forms of institutionalism.

Formal and informal institutions

Streek and Thelen (2005: 10–11) focus on 'formalized rules that may be enforced by calling upon a third party'. In its absence, 'we are dealing *not* with an institution, but with a more or less voluntarily agreed social convention'. This differs from other accounts which include both formal rules as 'exogenous constraints' and the informal rules provided and enforced by the players themselves: 'simply the ways in which the players want to play' (Shepsle, 2006: 24–5). It is tempting to follow Schmidt (2006) and treat this as a representative divide between two types of institutionalism – historical and rational choice – but the lines between each type are too blurry, different authors take different approaches (Steinmo, 2008: 124) and there may be particular reasons for adopting certain definitions. For example, Streek and Thelen (2005: 11) use this approach to limit their coverage and solve a primarily practical problem: 'we exclude from our discussion empirical phenomena ... that would make our subject too broad to be meaningful'.

Preferences: exogenous/endogenous, fixed/unfixed

A common distinction between rational choice and normative is that the former explores how institutions affect the choices of individuals with fixed preferences, while the latter argues that institutions also influence their preferences. March and Olsen (1984: 739) make the strongest case that preferences change during the political process. They are 'moulded' by institutions as part of a 'combination of education, indoctrination and experience'. Thelen and Steinmo (1992: 8) make a similar distinction between historical and rational choice, arguing that the former explores not only the strategies of individuals but also how institutions affect their goals. Yet, the difference is qualified by Dowding and King (1995: 5): 'What rational choice may do is to assume that preferences are exogenous in one model and use another, complementary model to explain how the preferences were formed'. Again, this approach may be used primarily for practical reasons, to limit analysis to one particular aspect of behaviour. This suggests that the difference between the institutionalisms is often the *attention* they give to some approaches and explanations rather than their *contradictory* approaches.

Ontology

Constructivists suggest that the interests of actors are not as easy to establish as normative and historical accounts suggest: 'conduct is not a (direct) reflection of their material interests but, rather, a reflection of particular *perceptions* of their material interests' (Hay, 2006a: 68). In

Ontology – a theory of reality (is there a real world and how does it relate to the concepts we use to describe it?). Related terms are **epistemology** (a theory of knowledge and how we can gather it) and **methodology** (an analysis of methods used to gather knowledge – see p. 46).

this context, Schmidt (2008: 313) suggests that constructivism presents to 'older new institutionalisms' an **ontological** challenge: 'about what institutions are and how they are created, maintained, and changed'. Specifically, it makes the distinction between institutions that are real and represent structures that influence the interests of agents, and institutions as ideas that are created by agents and used to inform their perceptions of their interests. Hay and Wincott (1998: 952) make a similar point when urging historical institutionalists to reject the 'structuralism' of sociological and rational choice. Again, this is a question of structure and agency. The charge is that at least two variants do not identify a world in which the latter have a significant role; structures influence agents, but where is the discussion of agents reconstituting structures? The complication is that Hay and Wincott (1998: 952) only identify a 'tendency' within the literature to take this approach, rather than an inextricable link between institutionalism and structuralism. It may therefore be viewed as a *warning against* treating institutions as real, fixed structures. It suggests that there need not be a stark ontological division between each approach.

This somewhat artificial debate demonstrates a tendency within the literature to caricature each approach; in the absence of this process we can reach different conclusions. For example, Hall and Taylor (1996: 956) acknowledge that the 'calculus' and 'cultural' approaches are not necessarily polar opposites; proponents of each could acknowledge that 'a good deal of behaviour is goal-oriented or strategic but that the range of options canvassed by a strategic actor is likely to be circumscribed by a culturally-specific sense of appropriate action'.

Empirical and network institutionalism: do formal institutions determine policy styles?

The preceding sections highlight the danger that a focus on new institutionalism is the ultimate example of academic navel gazing; that we focus on increasingly esoteric language to describe a fairly straightforward subject. These discussions are interesting to some (including me), but do they also have a real world application? Can we take lessons from them and apply those lessons to policymaking case studies? This problem makes the debate on **policy styles** that bit more significant and interesting. Our overall question is: what are institutions and what difference do they make to policy outcomes? Our

Policy style – the way that governments make and implement policy.

specific question in this section is: what effect do they have on policy styles?

Policy style refers broadly to the way that governments make and implement policy, but it often refers specifically to the relationships that governments form with interest groups when making policy (Richardson, Gustaffson and Jordan, 1982: 2). A focus on styles allows us to compare the effects of formal and informal institutions on policymaking. For example, is policy made differently in political systems with rules that concentrate power at the centre? We have two main analytical choices: models which identify country-level *differences* in styles based on formal institutions within political systems, and models which highlight *similar* styles in different countries based on their adherence to common 'rules of the game'. The former is exemplified by Lijphart's (1999) *Patterns of Democracy* (one of the best known texts in political science, with over 3,000 citations). He sets up a simple distinction between 'majoritarian' and 'consensus' democracies according to their formal institutional make-up (Table 4.1).

Lijphart's (1999: 2) argument is that there are two basic models of political system design: those that concentrate power in the hands of the few (majoritarian) and those that 'share, disperse, and limit power' (consensus). In a majoritarian democracy the first-past-the-post voting system exaggerates governing majorities by (in most cases) granting a majority of seats in the legislature to a party which commands only a plurality of the vote. This result, combined with an imbalance of power towards the governing party's leadership, a weak second chamber and a unitary government, produces a concentration of power at the centre. Lijphart (1999: 2–3) associates majoritarian democracies with an 'exclusive, competitive and adversarial' mentality in which parties compete within parliament, interest groups are more likely to compete with each other than cooperate and governments are more likely to impose policy from the top down than seek consensus. In a consensus democracy, the proportional electoral system produces no overall majority and power is dispersed across parties, encouraging the formation of coalitions based on common aims. This spirit of 'inclusiveness, bargaining and compromise' extends to group-government relations, with groups more likely to cooperate with each other and governments more willing to form corporatist alliances.

An alternative approach to policy styles suggests that we cannot read-off behaviour simply from formal institutions. Richardson's (1982b) edited volume suggests that different political systems produce similar policy styles. Although the political structures and electoral systems of each country vary, they share a 'standard operating procedure' based on two factors: an incremental approach to policy (Chapter 5) and an attempt to reach consensus with interest groups, not impose decisions.

Table 4.1 *Lijphart's majoritarian–consensus dichotomy*

Institutional divisions	Majoritarian democracy	Consensus democracy
Executive power	Concentrated in single party majority cabinet	Shared in broad multiparty coalition
Executive-legislative relationship	Executive is dominant	Balance of power between executive and legislature
Party system	Two-party system	Multiparty system
Electoral system	Majoritarian and disproportional (based on a plurality of votes)	Proportional
Interest group system	Pluralist free-for-all competition among groups	Coordinated and corporatist, exhibiting compromise and concertation
Federal–unitary	Unitary and centralized	Federal and decentralized
Legislative power	Concentrated in unicameral legislature	Divided between two equally strong houses
Constitutions	Flexible constitutions that can be amended by simple majorities	Rigid constitutions that can be changed only by large majorities
Constitutionality of laws	Decided by legislatures	Subject to judicial review
Central banks	Dependent on the executive	Independent
Illustrative examples	New Zealand, United Kingdom	Switzerland, Belgium, the EU

Source: Lijphart (1999: 3–4).

The latter is based on two factors common to political systems. First, the size and scope of the state is so large that it is in danger of becoming unmanageable. Consequently, its component parts are broken down into policy sectors and sub-sectors, with power spread across government and shared with interest groups. Ministers and senior civil servants devolve the bulk of decision making to less senior officials who consult with groups and exchange access for resources such as expertise. Second, this exchange is based on the 'logic of consultation' with the most affected interests; it encourages group 'ownership' of policy and maximizes governmental knowledge of possible problems (Richardson and Jordan, 1979; Jordan and Maloney, 1997).

'Policy community' (Richardson and Jordan, 1979; Jordan, 1990a) describes this close relationship between civil servants and certain interest groups (but see Box 9.1 on different meanings of the term 'policy community'). Membership of that community is based in part on the willingness of its members to follow and enforce the 'rules of the game'. When civil servants and groups form relationships, they recognize the benefits – such as stability and policy continuity – of attempting to insulate their decisions from the wider political process. In some accounts, this stability hinges on socialization. Inclusion within the community depends on the gaining of personal trust; the learning process involves immersion within a 'common culture' in which there is strong agreement on the nature of, and solutions to, policy problems (Wilks and Wright, 1987: 302–3; McPherson and Raab, 1988: 55). In such cases we explain policy styles in terms of informal rules and norms of behaviour that transcend formal structures.

Evidence based on this research agenda suggests that countries often do not live up to their reputations. For example, Kriesi, Adam and Jochum's (2006: 345) study of seven Western European countries suggests that the British policy style is relatively consensual despite its majoritarian political system. In contrast, 'the Italian style of policy-making appears to be more unilateral' despite the fact that it, 'has institutions which are rather of the more consensus-democratic type', while the European Union is 'less co-operative than it appears at first sight' (Cairney, 2008 and Larsen, Taylor-Gooby and Kananen, 2006 present similar findings; see also Atkinson and Coleman, 1989; Bovens *et al.*, 2001; John, 1998: 42–4; Freeman, 1985). A similar approach is taken by Barzelay and Gallego (2010: 298) to criticize historical institutionalist accounts which focus too much on national character traits (in this case in France, Spain and Italy) at the expense of knowledge of their sub-systems.

Cairney (2009b) presents similar findings in his case study of mental health policy in Scotland and the UK. Much was made in Scotland of the potential for devolution to change policymaking radically. The argument was that a, '"top-down" system, in which power is concentrated within government, is not appropriate for a Scottish system with a tradition of civic democracy and the diffusion of power' (McGarvey and Cairney, 2008: 12). A proportional electoral system with a strong likelihood of bargaining between parties would replace a plurality system that exaggerates majorities and produces one party dominance. A consensual style of politics in Scotland would replace the adversarial style in the UK. Mental health policy appeared to confirm their respective images based on their formal institutions. The process associated with the UK Mental Health Bill from the late 1990s confirms the caricature of the top-down UK government and contrasts markedly with a consensual style in Scotland. The UK Government presided over a ten-year stand-off with groups, followed by limited legislation (just enough to be compliant with the European Convention on Human Rights); the Scottish Government oversaw a two-year consultation process that produced consensus and extensive legislation. Yet, further investigation reveals that a series of factors effectively had to be in place to cause what is really a departure from the 'normal' British style (see also Box 6.3). In the absence of these factors, policymaking returned to the normal consensual style which was very similar to that found in Scotland.

In other words, the evidence is very mixed. Formal political institutions are not a good predictor of the way that governments make and implement policy. The debate raises the possibility that political systems with different formal institutions may exhibit similar behaviour based on informal rules and common practices. A formal rule which is enforced by a third party may or may not be more important than a self-policed informal understanding when we seek to understand policymaking behaviour. As a result, we need to gather more evidence on, rather than make assumptions about, a country's policy style.

Conclusion

We no longer consider institutions to be the bricks-and-mortar arenas within which decisions are made. In their place, we study the rules, norms and conventions that influence individual behaviour. While this research agenda has raised the status of institutional studies, it has also produced much soul searching about what an institution is and how we should study it. We may agree that institutions matter and that they evolve and change, but explaining how and why is another matter. We can focus on the formal rules that are enforced, such as the written constitutions that set out a political system's separation of powers. Or, we can identify norms of behaviour and informal rules. We can regard institutions as sets of incentives used by individuals pursuing their preferences, or structures that influence those preferences. We can emphasize stability or change. Institutions can be relatively stable and durable structures that live longer than individuals, or unstable sets of ideas that are taken for granted on one day only to be challenged the next. We can treat them as structures that exist in the real world or as constructs that only exist in the minds of policy participants. We may identify historical differences to explain why public policy is different in different political systems or current practices which seem to be very similar.

These theoretical problems and debates have the potential to distract us from the value of institutional analysis. Alternatively, we can identify a basic common understanding (that institutions are important) and set of questions to guide public policy research (how are institutions formed by agents? Why, and under what circumstances, do agents accept or follow rules? What patterns of policymaking behaviour can we attribute to those rules?) (Peters, 2005: 156). The solution, then, for 'problem-oriented scholars' is not to ignore the debate; it is to get enough of a sense of perspective to allow us to continue to engage in theory-driven public policy research.

A key theme of this book regards the extent to which we can use the same theories to explain policy developments in countries with different institutions. For example, the policy process in a federal US may contrast with a devolved but unitary UK. While Germany has a federal structure, its size and relationship with the EU undermines direct comparisons with the US. Australia's system is federal but also parliamentary, not presidential. The checks and balances in the US system ensure a key policy role for the courts and a second legislative chamber; in the UK there have been few avenues for judicial policy influence (at least until EU legal procedures developed) and the second chamber is comparatively weak. The US' reliance on plurality voting (producing a two-party system) is shared by the UK (Westminster elections) and Canada but not Germany or Japan. Its 'weak' party structure, in which the main national parties do not control their state or local counterparts (Atkinson and Coleman, 1989), is shared by Canada but not Germany which has integrated parties and formal links to coordinate policy (Horgan, 2004).

Using these formal differences as a basis of comparison, we may produce questions relating to the application of theories of public policy to different countries. For example, are political systems with formal checks and balances the most conducive to pluralism (Chapter 3)? Are political systems with diffused powers and extensive 'veto points' less conducive to radical rather than incremental change (Chapter 5)? Is 'venue shopping' a feature of federal systems modelled on the US, but not unitary systems modelled on the UK (Chapter 9)? How does the study of rational choice vary among political systems with plurality (e.g. the median voter theorem) and PR (e.g. coalition and minority government theory) voting (Chapter 7)?

On the other hand, as the policy styles debate shows, countries with different institutions may produce similar 'standard operating procedures' when the behaviour of participants is driven by informal rules and norms. Further, much of the US literature combines a discussion of specific US institutions with *universal* themes. For example, Baumgartner and Jones' (1993) study is based largely on the bounded rationality of policymakers (Chapter 9). The advocacy coalition framework relates primarily to the belief systems that bind policy participants together (Chapter 10). Kingdon's (1995) multiple streams analysis explores policymaker receptivity to ideas (Chapter 11). The development of the EU has also increased the potential to bridge the gap between European and US models, with studies of EU multi-level governance and US federalism identifying similar processes and posing common questions (Chapter 8). The policy transfer literature combines a discussion of the widespread adoption of similar policy ideas with the institutional differences that ensure that they are formulated and implemented in different ways (Chapter 12). In other words, the remaining chapters recognize the difference that institutions make, but also highlight policy processes that transcend formal institutional boundaries.

Chapter 5

Rationality and Incrementalism

This chapter examines:

- How we define comprehensive and bounded rationality.
- The literature which uses comprehensive rationality as a point of departure.
- The argument that incrementalism is both a realistic description of how policy is made and how it should be made.
- How the study of incrementalism informs the big questions of political science, such as: how should we make policy? Should power be concentrated in the 'centre' or spread throughout political systems?
- The applicability of bounded rationality and incrementalist studies to multiple political systems.
- How the effects of bounded rationality are conceptualized by modern theories.

The classic method to study public policy is to select an ideal model and compare it to the 'real world'. The most established approach begins with the assumption of 'rationality'. Many models assume that rational actors 'maximize their utility' by weighing up the costs and benefits of their actions according to their preferences. The models contain a series of assumptions – preferences are fixed and able to be 'ranked' in order of importance; actors have perfect information and a perfect ability to make choices according to their preferences – which simplify rather complex decision-making processes. These assumptions are central to the empirical process in some discussions. For example, rational choice theory (Chapter 7) builds models and 'tests' their predictions against real world situations, assessing the extent to which the models correctly predict political outcomes.

Comprehensive rationality – an ideal type of decision making in which policymakers translate their values and aims into policy following a comprehensive study of all choices and their effects.

The study of **comprehensive rationality** takes a different path. It begins in a similar way by identifying a series of assumptions – about the preferences of policymakers and their ability to make and implement decisions – but they are treated as unrealistic from the beginning. It represents an ideal-type in two main ways. First, it is an unrealistic simplification of reality used to explore what really happens when policymakers make decisions.

94

Numerous models develop more 'realistic' accounts using comprehensive rationality as a point of comparison. Policymakers are subject to varying forms of **bounded rationality** in which their preferences are more difficult to pin down and their ability to make and implement policy decisions is more problematic. Second, it may be treated as an ideal to *aspire to*. A process in which elected policymakers identify problems, clarify their aims and carefully weigh up solutions before making a choice (based on perfect information and no resistance from unelected implementing officials) may resemble a common sense view of how democracies should operate. This double-ideal is what makes 'incrementalism' so interesting: it argues that comprehensive rationality is descriptively inaccurate and *prescriptively inadequate*; policymakers cannot reach this ideal and they should not try.

> **Bounded rationality –** a more realistic model which identifies the factors – such as uncertain aims and limited information – that undermine comprehensive rationality.

These issues are often simplified by focusing on (and exaggerating) the differences between the two most prominent scholars of comprehensive rationality in the twentieth century. While Herbert Simon focuses on the need to 'satisfice', or combine rational processes with **rules of thumb** to reach an acceptable proximity to the comprehensive ideal, Charles Lindblom appears to promote the practical and normative value of departing from it. Incrementalism suggests that the most realistic strategy for boundedly rational policymakers with limited policymaking resources is to make a succession of incremental changes to public policy based on the lessons of past decisions.

> **Rule of thumb –** a procedural shortcut that is easily learned and applied rather than completely accurate or reliable.

This debate is 'classic' but it is no less important now than it was in the early post-war period. It raises the big questions of political science regarding how we should make policy and to what extent power should be concentrated in the centre or core executive. Further, the identification of bounded rationality and its consequences is a fundamental part of most contemporary theories of public policy. It allows us to identify key sources of policy continuity and change in those theories. On the one hand, incrementalism is one of many discussions to highlight the limits to radical policy change by comprehensively rational policymakers. It is joined by 'inheritance before choice' which links policy inertia to the cumulative effects of incremental decisions, and some implementation studies which suggest that 'street level bureaucrats' often resist top-down innovation. On the other, punctuated equilibrium theory discusses incrementalism punctuated by rapid and profound shifts of attention and policy, while policy diffusion highlights the scope for significant change when boundedly rational policymakers emulate the policies of other governments.

What is comprehensive rationality?

The discussion of comprehensive rationality prompts us to question our assumptions about the power of the 'centre' to cause policy change, either as a single-decision maker, a 'core-executive' or governing organization:

- Do individual actors at the 'top' have the ability to research and articulate a series of consistent policy aims and then make sure that they are carried out?
- Can an organization act in the same manner as a rational decision maker?

Comprehensive rationality suggests that elected policymakers seek to translate their values into policy, aided by organizations which operate in a 'logical, reasoned and neutral way' (John, 1998: 33). The model includes a series of assumptions:

1 Organizations can separate values (required by policymakers to identify their aims) from facts (required by organizations to assess the best way to achieve those aims) when researching policy.
2 Organizations and policymakers can produce consistent policy preferences, and rank them, to help maximize societal gain (in the same way that an individual ranks preferences to help 'maximize utility').
3 Policy is made in a linear fashion. First, policy aims are identified in terms of the values of the policymaker. Second, all means to achieve those aims are identified. Finally, the best means are selected. There are clear-cut stages to the process – such as between agenda-setting (identifying aims), formulation (identifying choices and making decisions) and implementation (carrying them out).
4 Analysis of the decision-making context is comprehensive – all relevant factors and possibilities have been explored, and all theories regarding how the policy process works have been considered (Simon, 1976; Lindblom, 1959; Jordan and Richardson, 1987: 9–10; John, 1998: 33; Hill, 2005: 146).

Of course, since this is an idealized version of the policy process, the assumptions are unrealistic. Most approaches begin their analysis by identifying the limitations to comprehensive rationality. First, it is impossible to separate facts from theories and values in such an artificial way (Simon, 1983: 8 argues that the best way to demonstrate this point is to read the 'facts' in Hitler's *Mein Kampf;* see also Brinkmann, 2008; Etzioni, 1967: 386). Policy problems are always subject to interpretation and debate, there is often no widespread agreement on the cause and solution of the problem, and our knowledge of a policy's likely impact informs our attitude to it. Therefore, a combination of facts and values determines whether or not a policymaker identifies a problem to be solved.

Second, policymakers have multiple, and often unclear, objectives which are difficult to rank in any meaningful way. Therefore, they tend to pursue a small number of those aims which command their attention at any one time. Policy aims can also be contradictory – choosing a policy to address aim A may mean undermining a policy to address aim B, producing clear winners and losers from the policy process. These problems are multiplied when extended to organizations. Governments contain a mass of organizations pursuing policy aims relatively independently of each other, with little regard to the idea of centralized and ranked preferences or the trade-offs in policy choices (or little 'joined-up government').

Third, the policy process is not necessarily linear and it is difficult to separate the policy cycle into discrete stages. For example, implementing organizations have the discretion to make decisions which affect the nature of policy; change may depend as much on the values of implementing officials as policymakers. Or, the decisions made by policymakers at the top may merely legitimize practices at the 'bottom' (Chapter 2). The 'garbage can' model (Box 11.4) presents the most significant departure from an assumption of linearity, suggesting that the three processes – problem definition, solution, choice – appear to act almost independently, with the potential for a completely different order. It begins with solutions that already exist and then 'chase problems'. Then, policymakers select a solution that already exists to a problem defined for them.

Finally, policymakers are faced not only with incomplete knowledge of the policy environment and the likely consequences of their solutions, but also cognitive and time constraints which limit their ability to consider and understand every possible solution. Organizations do not have the capacity to consider every fact and solution; the cost of research forces them to set priorities. The search for theories to explain policy problems are limited by the values and emotions of policymakers (which predispose them to consider only some solutions) and organizational rules of thumb based on past experiences.

Bounded rationality

A more realistic view of the policy process is based on 'bounded' rationality:

1   Individuals and organizations cannot 'maximize' their utility; instead, they 'satisfice', or seek 'a course of action that is satisfactory or "good enough"'.
2   They have neither the ability nor the inclination to consider all facts; instead they use simple rules of thumb to focus on the factors considered to be most relevant and important (Simon, 1976: xxviii).

Simon's aim is, *as far as possible*, to use 'administrative science' to solve the problem of bounded rationality within organizations: by training officials in policy analysis to open their mind to new possibilities; fostering the development of specialization and expertise in information processing; teaching officials the most appropriate rules of thumb to make an organization more effective; and supporting the long-term goals of an organization by providing the right incentives (1976: 242–3; 1960). In other words, we no longer assume that officials within organizations are neutral. Rather, we seek to influence their behaviour to further policymaker aims. Simon's term 'satisfice' is appropriate, because this is not a straightforward process (Hill, 2005: 146–7; Parsons, 1995: 273–84). First, it requires an ability to identify the values of an organization and the policymaker it serves. Second, it assumes that a sole, central decision maker can control an incredibly complex policy process. When these conditions are not met, the recommendations act as a means to reduce the harm of (rather than solve) organizational complexity.

Incrementalism

Lindblom's model of incrementalism (Box 5.1) provides a similar critique of comprehensive rationality, stressing the limits to cognitive and problem solving abilities, the **opportunity cost** of comprehensive research, and an inability to separate facts from values. It also goes further by taking the role of politics more seriously and providing an alternative to the ideal of comprehensive rationality.

Opportunity cost – the value of option B which is forgone when we pursue option A. For example, the cost of a decision to study many policy options is the forgone chance to study fewer options in more depth.

When viewed through the lens of comprehensive rationality, the ability to identify problems, consider solutions and make choices seems unencumbered by politics. Yet, making choices is inherently political; it is about winners and losers. A policymaker has to consider not only her/his values but also, for example, the balance of power within the legislature and the reaction to policy changes by interest groups. Politics is often about making trade-offs between one's own aims and those favoured by other actors, or

Box 5.1   The meaning of incrementalism

The meaning of incrementalism is often clouded in three main ways. First, the meaning of 'incremental' is disputed. It is often equated with change through small steps. However, Lindblom (1979: 517) argues that increments can be large or small. The crucial distinction is between radical and non-radical change: does it follow logically from existing policy or mark a significant departure? This argument solves one problem but raises another: can we really separate radical and non-radical change in a straightforward way? Second, incrementalism can be a description of how policy is made or a discussion of the most useful strategies to pursue (or perhaps a confusing mix of both). Third, incrementalism can refer to analytical strategies, in which we decide how to (or study how organizations) overcome problems related to comprehensive rationality:

*   Simple incremental analysis – analysis limited to a small number of policy choices which diverge incrementally from the status quo; based on the argument that it is better to analyse a few issues comprehensively than seek comprehensive coverage of all issues.
*   Disjointed incrementalism – the simplifying strategies used by organizations (including simple incremental analysis, trial and error, parallel processing).
*   Strategic analysis – realistic policymaking strategies (including disjointed incrementalism and 'mixed scanning') used as an alternative to the 'futile attempt at superhuman comprehensiveness' (Lindblom, 1959: 88).

Or, it can relate to political strategies and how we produce policy agreement. For example, Lindblom (1959: 85) identifies 'mutual adjustment' – a process in which actors pursue their own interests and respond to the effects of other actors doing the same (by researching and anticipating their positions, using persuasion and seeking allies).

choosing policies that suit the aims of one actor over another. Policymaking is costly: it takes time and political will to persuade political parties, vested interests and the public that major policy change is appropriate (and to ensure that policy is implemented). It is also unpredictable: policymakers often react to events or solve problems caused by previous polices rather than devote the required time to major new policy initiatives. Consequently, boundedly rational policymakers are much more likely to introduce incremental policy changes – based on learning from past experience and addressing the unintended consequences of previous decisions – than introducing major new policy initiatives.

Lindblom suggests that policymakers do not begin by articulating their values, translating them into policy aims in rank order, and seeking the best means to achieve them. Rather, their willingness to trade off one aim for another only becomes clear when they make policy decisions. The analysis is not comprehensive, considering all of the empirical and theoretical implications. Rather, organizations analyse the effects of incremental change and ignore many important possible outcomes, alternative policies, theories and values. Consequently, we can no longer equate 'good' policy with its adherence to the values of policymakers. The test of 'good' policy shifts from its ability to satisfy wider policy objectives, to whether or not it commands agreement within the wider political system (Lindblom, 1959: 81). It suggests that an incremental strategy will generally be used as a rule of thumb: if a previous policy commanded widespread respect then policymakers will (and should) recognise the costs (analytical and political) of a significant departure from it.

Lindblom's prescription appears different from Simon's when he treats incrementalist strategies as reasonably efficient, sensible and democratic. First, it is efficient for government organizations to spend most of their time focusing on the effects of incremental departures from current policies; the more radical options are rarely given serious consideration by major political parties. Second, it is sensible for policy change to take place through a series of steps, to reduce the chance of making 'serious lasting mistakes'. The effects of non-incremental decisions are relatively unpredictable and more difficult to solve (1959: 86). Finally, to change policy radically may be considered undemocratic. Existing policy is based on, if not wide agreement, then at least a long-term process of negotiation, bargaining and adjustment. In a pluralistic system (Lindblom's analysis is based on the US political system), the values and policies pursued in one arena are counterbalanced by similar processes elsewhere. No single actor commands the policy process as a whole. Rather, multiple actors and agencies pursue their interests and command their own powerful 'watchdogs' to anticipate or redress 'damages done by other agencies' (1959: 85). This allows a process of 'partisan mutual adjustment' between a range of powerful interests (which accomplishes more than an all powerful central actor could – i.e. note Lindblom's comparison of the US to the Soviet Union). Overall, Lindblom (1965) recommends focusing intensely on a small number of policy options that depart incrementally from the status quo.

The normative debate: how should we make policy?

These issues prompted one of the most significant public policy debates in the post-war period. A common line held by Lindblom's critics is that incrementalism represents a more realistic model than comprehensive rationality, but has less to offer as a policymaking ideal.

Box 5.2 Periods of crisis: from the new deal to the credit crunch

As an example of crisis, Dror (1964: 154) highlights the US's New Deal period (the mid-1930s) in which a range of policies – to address unemployment, the welfare state, banking, industry and agriculture – were produced to deal with the Great Depression. The modern equivalent is the 'credit crunch', which describes the fallout from a period of international banking crisis, following the decision by many financial institutions to take excessive risks (particularly when supporting the 'sub-prime' lending market). The shock to political systems was so great that it undermined the ability of many to function (for example, Greece and Ireland were forced to accept large loans from the EU), and forced most governments to fundamentally reconsider their attitudes to the market, regulation and state intervention in a very limited time. Governments that had previously supported the market and deregulation suddenly came under pressure to guarantee deposits in or buy (often controlling) shares in banks to reinstate confidence and stop the major institutions from failing.

Dror (1964: 154) argues that Lindblom's normative thesis only holds if three conditions are met: existing policy is broadly satisfactory; the nature of the policy problem has not changed significantly; and there have been no significant advances in the means to solve problems. While these conditions hold during periods of social stability, they are not met: in newly developing states seeking to throw off the inheritance of an occupied past; during periods of crisis (Box 5.2); when attitudes change dramatically (such as when governments changed their approach to poverty or race); and when new technology requires change (otherwise, for example, a nation's armed forces will be 'excellently prepared for the last war' – Dror, 1964: 154). Our ability to learn from the past is diminished when the policy problem and its context is radically different. Overall, Lindblom's thesis legitimizes the bias towards inertia and conservatism in the US political system and discourages organizations from breaking their usual routine (Dror, 1964: 155). Given that governments already 'muddle through', Dror recommends a series of initiatives – such as brainstorming – to encourage them to plan their activities more efficiently, clarify their values, identify alternative policies and identify issues more worthy of comprehensive analysis (1964: 156).

Lindblom's (1964: 157) reply is that, while a 'disjointed incremental strategy' is not appropriate in *all* situations, *most* policy decisions (in liberal democracies and 'stable dictatorships' alike) meet Dror's criteria (see also Braybrooke and Lindblom, 1963). Further, it is only incrementalism that allows organizations to function effectively. Taking the comprehensive ideal seriously would 'paralyse' an organization by frustrating its staff and exhausting its resources before a decision is made (see also Etzioni, 1967: 386). In contrast, a regular routine affords it the chance to seek new directions without seeking the impossible (the analogy is the choice between pursuing unaided versus mechanical human flight). Lindblom's final defence is perhaps the most striking. Incrementalism should *not necessarily be equated with continuity and stability*: 'Logically speaking, one can make changes in the social structure as rapidly through a series of incremental steps as through drastic – hence less frequent – alterations' (1964: 157). If policymakers are inherently risk averse, they may be less likely to select radical policy choices but more likely to select options which may *appear* conservative but have a significant cumulative effect. Short-term continuity may mask long term change.

For Etzioni (1967: 387–8) this defence is limited for two related reasons. First, the idea of successive limited comparisons suggests that policymakers could take a circular path without more 'rational' direction. A move towards radical change through small steps assumes that policymakers refer to a long-term strategy when considering if the short term direction of policy is 'right' (Cairney, 2007a). Second, Lindblom treats the 'big' policy issues that do not conform to an incrementalist model as exceptional rather than worthy of the most study. Yet, incremental policy steps only make sense if we consider the fundamental decisions required beforehand. For example, the argument that defence spending is high and does not change much is incomplete without identifying the 'critical turning point' (such as a fundamental decision to go to war) which caused such high spending in the first place (Etzioni, 1967: 389). Organizations therefore need the ability to identify, and research comprehensively, the fundamental decisions which set the direction for incremental change. Etzioni's (1967: 389) solution is 'mixed scanning', which draws on the analogy of weather satellites to recommend a combination of broad scanning of the overall terrain and 'zeroing in' on particular areas worthy of more research.

In most cases this debate may be largely 'artificial' (Smith and May, 1993; see also Gregory, 1993). Lindblom's critics agree that incrementalism is a widespread phenomenon and that organizations do not change their behaviour beyond the margins, while Lindblom (1979: 518) argues that the dismissal of comprehensive rationality as an ideal does not mean a rejection of *better decision making*. Rather, the pursuit of a more realistic ideal would be more helpful. Lindblom's (1979) subsequent recommendation of 'strategic analysis', as a guide for decision makers, can include mixed scanning and Simon's discussion of 'administrative science'. The debate is also based on a rather unclear but crucial issue: the extent to which we can say that one change is radical while another represents stability and continuity. Since the nature of policy problems is open to interpretation and debate, there is no objective way to identify 'fundamental' policy issues or decisions (Smith and May, 1993: 203; indeed, many fundamental choices, such as decisions to go to war, appear to have been made incrementally – Hill, 2005: 151). The incremental/radical policy change distinction seems obvious, but where is the dividing line?

The normative debate: should power be concentrated in the 'centre'

Is the comprehensive ideal something to aspire to? So far we have discussed this question in a rather technical way, focusing on the limits to resources and cognitive abilities. In this section we explore its normative assumptions about power. The ideal of comprehensive rationality includes an assumption that power is held centrally by policymakers whose decisions are carried out by neutral bureaucrats or other organizations. In other words, a central decision maker *should* control the policy process. Or, the final word should rest with the chief executive of a particular organization. The ideal of comprehensive rationality has its critics because it suggests that power should reside in the hands of senior managers 'to the detriment of low ranking staff, clients and patients, whose perspectives are in practice neglected' (Smith and May 1993: 199). It takes us back to the concerns raised by top-down versus bottom-up forms of implementation: our need to balance the authority of the top with the local knowledge at the bottom; and, to dovetail the delegation of policymaking to people who know best how to do it with the maintenance of a meaningful degree of accountability for the outcomes (Chapter 2).

Lindblom's assumption of pluralism (1959: 85) has also been subject to considerable criticism. Incrementalism is tied closely to the suggestion that political consensus is the best measure of 'good' policy. What this may really mean is that 'good' policy will be decided by those most powerful if power is not as diffuse as Lindblom assumes. As Etzioni (1967: 387) argues, 'partisan mutual adjustment' does not guarantee equality, because 'partisans invariably differ in their respective power positions; demands of the underprivileged and politically unorganized would be underrepresented'. The more that resources within society are dispersed unequally, the less meaningful it becomes to talk of 'mutual' adjustment instead of coercion or dominance. Lindblom appears to accept these concerns in later work (1977; 1979), particularly noting the imbalance of power towards big business in a market system.

However, Lindblom argues that an unequal distribution of power in politics is not a good enough reason to reject 'partisan mutual adjustment'. A more centralized system may not redress this balance of power: 'strong central authority can be – and historically is, in case after case – an instrument for protecting historically inherited inequalities' (1979: 523). Indeed, the appearance of a comprehensively rational process may be used to minimize public, parliamentary and pressure group attention to inequalities. This allows us to revisit Dror's argument that incrementalism legitimizes the status quo: putting power in the hands of the few does not guarantee that it will be used wisely and in the spirit of benevolent neutrality that comprehensive rationality assumes.

Incrementalism: is it a universal phenomenon?

Incrementalism was based initially on a study of US politics, so how relevant is it to policymaking as a whole? The general themes are universal because they are based on a departure from comprehensive rationality. Further, as Lindblom (1979: 520) suggests, we should not confuse the advantages of incrementalism in politics (the management of policy by consensus and the minimization of unintended consequences) with inertia in politics (made more likely by the veto points in particular political systems combined with 'timidity' and 'ideological conservatism'). In other words, we need to separate the identification of inertia and veto, which may afflict some particular systems more than others, from the concept of incrementalism that may be applicable to all systems (compare with the discussion of policy styles in Chapter 4).

Commentators in the federal US, with a formal separation and devolution of powers, often refer to the UK's centralization of power as a source of much needed policy change (compare with Box 5.3). Hayes (2001: 2) outlines Burns' (1963) suggestion the US should be more like the UK, with: a two-party system and clear competition based on distinct manifestos, a winning party with a clear majority and therefore a legitimate mandate to introduce its policies, and a system which has more top-down levers and fewer checks and balances. In other words, the main hindrance to legitimate and swift policy change is the structure of government.

A similar rhetoric is found in 1990s discussions of Japan's political style – if Japan emulates the 'Westminster model' then it can address widespread inertia within the political system and re-establish faith in its politicians (Krauss and Pekkanen, 2004). In Italy and Germany there are fewer explicit references to Westminster, but similar criticisms of political systems which were once 'stable' but are now 'stagnating'. In Italy, 'institutionalists' pointed to the value of a consensual system of govern-

> ## Box 5.3   The shifting image of majoritarianism
>
> A significant irony, given the pro-Westminster rhetoric in the US and Japan, is that the opposite rhetoric was used in the 1990s to support political devolution in Scotland. A series of measures to link politics with the 'people' were devised, with the Scottish Parliament acting as a hub for new forms of engagement and a counterweight to strong central government; this new form of politics was designed to downgrade the role of political parties and reduce their ability to change policy radically in the absence of consensus. The Scottish experience was borne out of frustration with the Westminster model and the negative effect that top-down policy making had on public perceptions (McGarvey and Cairney, 2008; Jordan and Stevenson, 2000).

ment only when the country was deeply divided (in the aftermath of the Second World War and in the wake of the cold war). However, when policy conditions changed, the institutions of government did not, and a lack of party competition and choice (as a source of a mandate for significant policy change) contributed to the 'degeneration of Italian democracy' (Fabrini and Gilbert, 2000: 28). Similarly, Germany's stable political system was once considered to be an antidote to uncertain economic conditions in the rest of the world and conducive to the 'Golden Age' of post-war economic recovery. However, it now contributes to a, 'painfully slow, incremental process of political and economic change' which is ill equipped to deal with new political problems and unable to command the respect of its citizens (Kitschelt and Streeck, 2003: 2).

The common view seems to be that a majoritarian system puts power in the hands of the few and gives them more opportunity to pursue the comprehensive rationality ideal. However, an 'incrementalist view' suggests that the common theme in these countries is the attachment to unrealistic expectations about how quickly policy can change substantively within *any* political system. This leads to frustration at the lack of policy change and then disenchantment in politics and politicians. Hayes (2001: 3) draws on theories of incrementalism to suggest two constants in most mature political processes:

1   The necessity of bargaining and compromise between actors who have different information, different interests and conflicting views.
2   The need to build on past policies.

Incrementalist strategies may be used in most political systems for good reason: the identification of widespread bargaining and compromise is a sign of a mature and pluralistic process where the balance of power is not skewed towards some actors at the expense of others.

Radical change may be *worrying* since it suggests the ability of governments to ride roughshod over previous agreements. Therefore, instead of pursuing institutional reforms as a means to reinvigorate public confidence in politics, political elites should educate the public about the limits to (and problems with) radical change (Hayes, 2001: 3).

How do modern theories conceptualize bounded rationality? Is incrementalism inevitable?

The identification of bounded rationality is a fundamental part of most contemporary theories of public policy – but do they confirm Lindblom's argument that incrementalism is the main consequence? Incrementalism is certainly one of many discussions to highlight the limits to radical policy change by comprehensively rational policymakers.

The model of *policy communities* suggests that incrementalism transcends formal political structures. Regular changes of government do not necessarily cause wholesale shifts in policy, even in the 'majoritarian UK'. In part, this is because most policy decisions are effectively beyond the reach of ministers. The sheer size of government necessitates breaking policy down into more manageable issues involving a smaller number of interested and knowledgeable participants. Therefore, most public policy is conducted primarily through specialist policy communities which process 'technical' issues at a level of government not particularly visible to the public or Parliament, and with minimal ministerial involvement. These arrangements exist because there is a logic to devolving decisions and consulting with certain affected interests. Ministers rely on their officials for information and advice. For specialist issues, those officials rely on specialist organizations. Organizations trade information, advice and other resources (such as the ability to implement or 'deliver' a large group membership) for access to, and influence within, government. Further, the logic of this relationship holds regardless of the party of government. Therefore, we are unlikely to witness the types of radical policy shift often associated with a change of government (Richardson and Jordan, 1979; Jordan and Richardson, 1982; Jordan, 2005; Jordan and Maloney, 1997; Cairney, 2008).

Inheritance before choice in public policy extends the discussion of incrementalism to inertia (see Box 6.4 for a comparison of terms). The effect of decades of cumulative policies is that newly elected policymakers inherit a huge government with massive commitments. Most policy decisions are based on legislation which already exists and the bulk of public expenditure is spent on government activities (such as welfare benefits) that continue by routine (Rose, 1990; 1986; Rose and Davies, 1994). This theme of inertia is reinforced by *policy succession* and *path dependence*. The size and scope of the state is such that any 'new' policy is likely to be a revision of an old one following a degree of policy failure. New policies are often pursued merely to address the problems caused by the old. Policy succession is always more likely than innovation and termination. Indeed, incrementalism may be more about dealing with the legacies of past policies than departing incrementally from them. Even policy change in incremental steps does not guarantee that change is reversible, particularly when policy builds up its own clientele and interacts with existing policies (Hogwood and Peters, 1982; 1983; Geva-May, 2004). *Path dependence* (Chapter 4) suggests that when a commitment to a policy has been established and resources devoted to it, over time it becomes increasingly costly to choose a different path; the existing path demonstrates 'increasing returns'. Our focus of analysis is the 'critical juncture' which marked the beginning of a particular path and reduced the feasibility of alternative policy choices (Pierson, 2000a).

Multi-level governance expands the theme of power diffusion raised by US pluralism. Theories of governance (Chapter 8) extend it not only to the EU (which itself developed in a rather incremental way) but also more generally to large fragmented governments which lack a powerful centre (Kooiman, 1993: 4). This theme of power diffusion is extended by studies of *implementation*. Although legislation is made at the 'top', it is influenced heavily by the street level bureaucrats who deliver it (Chapter 2). Since they are subject to an immense range of (often unclear) requirements laid down by regulations at the top, they are powerless to implement them all successfully. Instead, they establish routines and use rules of thumb to satisfy a proportion of central government objectives while preserving a sense of professional autonomy necessary to maintain morale (Lipsky, 1980). Therefore, radical policy change at the top may translate into incremental change at the bottom.

On the other hand, many contemporary theories highlight the links between bounded rationality and non-incremental change. For example, *punctuated equilibrium theory* shows that political systems produce incremental and radical change. Boundedly rational policymakers have limited resources (including time, knowledge and attention) and cannot deal with all policy problems. So they ignore most and promote a few to the top of their agenda. This lack of attention to most issues helps explain why most policies do not change dramatically, while intense periods of attention to some issues may prompt new demands for change. The nature of policy problems is always subject to interpretation and debate because it is impossible to separate facts from values. Therefore, by 'reframing' issues, policy actors can draw the attention of policymakers to new ways of looking at (and solving) old problems. When successful, this produces a process of 'positive feedback', in which policymakers pay disproportionate attention to the issue, and a 'bandwagon effect', in which multiple actors in the policy process all pay attention to, and seek to influence, the same issue (Chapter 9; Jones, 1999, 2003; Baumgartner and Jones, 1993, 2009; Jones and Baumgartner, 2005).

Drawing on the 'garbage can' critique of comprehensive rationality (outlined above and in more detail in Box 11.4), *multiple streams analysis* suggests that radical policy change happens only when a 'window of opportunity' opens and three independent streams come together – problems, policies and politics. In most cases policy does not change radically because a policy problem does not receive enough attention, an adequate idea or solution is not available and/or policy-makers are not receptive to the idea. Yet, in many cases these streams *do* come together: a new or reframed problem gains attention, a solution gains currency within the policy community and policymakers have the motive and opportunity to translate the idea into policy. The model there-fore combines an overall assumption of policy continuity with a rather unpredictable process of change (Kingdon, 1984; Lieberman, 2002).

Theories of *policy diffusion* demonstrate that non-incremental change is consistent with the logic of incrementalism. Boundedly rational deci-sion makers develop rules of thumb to provide focus to their policy analysis and make the best use of their limited resources. One such rule of thumb is policy transfer, in which one region learns from the experi-ence of another. Diffusion studies suggest that some states merely emulate (rather than learn in detail from) others, on the assumption or brief impression that the innovating state was successful. Therefore, although bounded rationality may place limits on the ability of states to *innovate*, it may encourage most states to *emulate*. The wider *policy transfer* literature also suggests that some governments may be coerced into non-incremental policy change (Chapter 12; Berry and Berry, 2007; Dolowitz and Marsh, 2000).

Conclusion

Comprehensive rationality is used widely as an ideal type. The task is to identify its assumptions and consider the implications when these condi-tions are not met. Most build on the concept of bounded rationality which highlights: the inability of organizations to separate facts from values; unclear and conflicting political objectives; a non-linear deci-sion-making process; and, an incomplete search for knowledge com-bined with limited resources, time and cognitive abilities. From this model of constraint we then explore what happens (description, explana-tion) and what should happen (prescription, normative debates).

Generally, organizations 'satisfice', or seek solutions which are 'good enough', and use rules of thumb to make the decision-making process more manageable. While Simon uses this discussion to seek improvement to the decision-making process, Lindblom extends the analysis to a political context in which policymakers bargain with other actors. They use rules of thumb such as treating high levels of agreement in the political system as an indicator of good policy. Lindblom advocates this approach because it reduces the chances of governments making big mistakes that are relatively difficult to reverse, and ensures that they do not use their resources – *including political will* – unwisely.

The argument that incrementalism does and *should* happen produced by far the most debate in the literature. To some extent it began as a US-focused debate tied up in questions about pluralism and the sources of inertia in the US political system. Yet, this chapter demonstrates that the themes are universal. The use of incrementalist strategies to address the limits to comprehensive rationality is common to *all* political systems. All political systems face the need for bargaining and compromise and to build on past policies. The big questions of political science are universal: if comprehensive rationality cannot be achieved, what happens and what should happen? Should we spread analytical resources in an attempt to cover most areas or focus those resources on the issues most likely to receive policymaker attention? How do we identify the issues to pay most attention to and which issues can be ignored as a result? Should decision-making power be centralized to foster accountability or dispersed to make better informed local decisions? How do we balance both aims?

This is a 'classic' debate, but it is still relevant to contemporary theories of public policy. Most theories adopt an understanding of bounded rationality and seek to understand its consequences. Many theories reinforce the incrementalist argument by identifying the inability of the 'centre' to control the policy process and/or the inertia effects of big government which produce policy succession or inheritance before choice. Yet, most theories now explore the relationship between an overall picture of stability and significant episodes of rapid change. Bounded rationality may generally produce incremental change, but also far-less-frequent major change. It places great limits on governments but incrementalism is not an inevitable consequence.

As Jones and Baumgartner (2005: 119) suggest, incrementalism may *seem appropriate* to policy actors who want to be able to reverse mistakes more easily, establish 'stable expectations in a complex and uncertain environment', and address the spirit of compromise, particularly in political systems such as the US which have a formal separation of powers and 'overlapping, conflicting and interacting institutions'. Yet, as Hill (2005: 152) suggests, this does not mean that governments *will* act that way. Ideologically driven governments may still make radical policy choices even if their ability to produce a consistent and well-researched plan is out of reach (although whether or not these decisions are implemented is a different matter). Radical change may follow a window of opportunity, disproportionate attention to one issue at the expense of others, emulation or coercion – all of which suggest that bounded rationality should not necessarily be equated with stability, continuity or incremental change.

Chapter 6

Structural Explanations

This chapter examines:

- The main 'structural' sources of variation in the policy environment.
- The extent to which these factors 'determine politics' or represent the beginning of the 'funnel of causality'.
- The extent to which policymakers are constrained by their economic environment, drawing on discussions of Marxism, globalization and studies of public expenditure.
- The extent to which policymakers are constrained by the structures of government, drawing on idea of 'inheritance before choice in public policy' and that most policy change is 'policy succession'.
- Theories of complexity or complex systems.
- Our need to identify both the constraints of the policy environment and the ability of policymakers to influence, and make choices within, that environment.

When we seek to understand policy change, we attribute the exercise of power to the individuals that make policy decisions, but also recognize the institutions in which they operate and the pressures that they face. Chapter 6 examines the latter, focusing on the various ways in which we can describe the context of policymaking. In general terms we are interested in the policy 'conditions' or 'environment'. The policy environment may represent what policymakers take into account when identifying problems and deciding how to address them. They may be particularly aware of a political system's size, demographic structure, economy and mass behaviour. The policy environment may also represent a source of pressure or a direct influence on how policymakers operate. For example, an ageing population puts pressure on governments to address pensions policy and their provision of personal care, while an economic crisis almost inevitably rises to the top of a government's agenda (see Box 6.1 below).

The term 'structure' refers rather vaguely to a set of parts put together in a particular way to form a whole. In social science we tend to attribute two key properties to structures: they are relatively fixed and difficult but not impossible to break down; and, they influence the decisions that actors ('agents') make. Examples include the structure of the economy, the structure of rules within institutions, the structure of government (which includes its laws and the institutions which exist to implement them) and even the structured nature of some ideas (as introduced in Chapter 4 and revisited in Chapter 11). Our identification of 'structure' and 'agency' therefore raises a fundamental question: how much do policymakers shape, and how much of their behaviour is shaped by, their policy environment (Hay, 2002: 89)?

Policy studies may not always use the language of structure and agency directly, but they do supplement a focus on policymaker action by highlighting the policy context. We know that the decisions made by policymakers can have a profound effect on society, the economy and the structure of government. We also know that the choices they make are often based on policy problems that they have limited control over, such as: an increasingly global economy; demographic change; and, unpredictable events that propel issues to the top of their agenda (Chapter 9). There are limits on their ability to anticipate the effects of policy (Chapter 5) and the extent to which it is carried out successfully (Chapter 2). Policymakers operate within the context of institutions, or the rules, norms and cultures that influence their behaviour (Chapter 4). They also 'inherit' their government which represents the accumulation of all relevant policy decisions made in the past and carried out to this day (Rose, 1990). Indeed, such is the scope of the state that individual policymakers could not hope to have a full understanding of it, and their decisions while in office will likely represent a small part of overall government activity.

This context prompts us to consider a different perspective to 'comprehensively rational' decision making (Chapter 5) and the idea that the policy process begins with the decision by a policymaker to identify a problem to solve. Instead, we may envisage a world in which policies are already in place and the ability of policymakers to replace them are limited. This decision-making process takes place within the context of existing government policy and a huge infrastructure devoted to carrying it out. Further, the identification of problems often follows events that are out of the control of policymakers and appears to give them very little choice about how, if it is possible, to solve them. We can also link these perceived constraints to issues of power, because policymaking 'structures' may serve to protect the interests of certain groups or classes. Or policymakers may feel that their choices are limited because they will face powerful opposition if they attempt to reform well established structures or practices.

There are many ways to characterize this process, with different approaches striking a different balance between the role of structure and agency. While Chapters 5 and 7 begin by identifying the role of rational action, this chapter outlines accounts which focus on the *limits* to agency. It pays particular attention to the idea that policymakers represent one small part of a large complex system. Complexity theory suggests that we shift our analysis from individual parts of a political system to the system as a whole; as a network of elements that interact and combine to produce systemic behaviour that cannot be broken down into the actions of its constituent parts. This idea of a system captures the difficulty of policymaking and serves as a corrective to accounts that focus too much on the importance of individual policymakers and exaggerates their ability to single-handedly change policy. Instead, complex systems are 'non-linear'; they amplify the effects of some decisions but dampen the effects of others. Yet, we also consider if this theory comes at too much of a cost; if, like other structural accounts, it is too deterministic and does not recognize the importance of agency, or the ability of individuals to deliberate and make choices.

Do structural factors determine politics?

Box 6.1 outlines the main 'structural' sources of variation in political systems. These factors can be analysed in a variety of ways, with more or less stress on their ability to determine outcomes. For example, Hogwood (1992a: 191–208) simply compares demographic effects to the effect of changing parties in government and concludes that the former often had a larger effect on trends in public expenditure, employment and regulation than the latter. Lowi (1964) argues that 'policies determine politics' but, on further inspection, relies on the perceptions of policymakers and pressure participants to decide what the nature of those policies are likely to be (Chapter 2).

These accounts compare to stronger approaches, summed up by John (1998: 92):

> The simple idea is that the policy process, far from being a rational weighing up of alternatives, is driven by powerful socioeconomic forces that set the agenda, structure decision makers choices, constrain implementation and ensure that the interests of the most powerful (or of the system as a whole) determine the outputs and outcomes of the political system.

System – 'integrated group of interacting elements designed jointly to perform a given function' (such as a political system that functions to 'allocate values' – Dawson and Robinson, 1963: 267).

Many such accounts relate to **systems** theory, associated most notably with Easton (1953; 1965; see also Deutsch, 1970) and furthered by a series of empirical studies testing the statistical association between socio-economic variables and policy outputs ('Large-N comparative studies' – Blomquist, 2007: 261). Each study employs a simple model in which socio-economic factors produce demands that feed into the political system

---

Box 6.1   Structural factors

- Historic-geographic – factors such as the climate and stock of natural resources influenced how countries and regions developed; the population size of political systems may inform how institutions are set up; policies for dense, urban areas may not be popular in, or appropriate for, rural areas (Hofferbert, 1974: 228–9).
- Demographic – an ageing population puts pressure on the costs of social security and personal care; a 'baby boom' produces greater demand for schools.
- Economic – from the size of government tax income and cost of its policy programmes, to its ability to adjust interest rates and attract foreign investment.
- Social – social attitudes and behaviour influence the popularity and effect of policy measures; unhealthy behaviour in the population produces demand for healthcare services.
- Technological – the mass production of cars produced new demands on transport policy; medical advances produce demands for new medicines and equipment (Hogwood, 1992a: 191–208).
- Institutional – formal institutions set out the relationships between, for example, executives and legislatures, while informal institutions provide an understanding of norms and expected behaviour (Chapter 4).

(for visual representations see 2007: 266). Dawson and Robinson (1963: 269) question the argument that relatively competitive party systems in US states produce more 'liberal' social welfare policies. They argue that more variation is explained by the socio-economic composition of each state (income per capita, proportion of jobs not in agriculture, residence in urban areas). For example, the more urbanized populations demand more social welfare policies, while wealthier states are more able to afford them (1963: 285). These conditions also influence aspects of the political system, such as voter turnout and competition between parties. Dye (1966: 291) confirms that 'there are many significant linkages between economic development and policy outcomes', albeit with variations across policy areas. For example, wealthier US states spend more (overall, not as a proportion of wealth) on education, and attainment is most influenced by the level of education of their parents, but the levels of public hospital facilities vary less with income, while federal programmes often offset differences in welfare policy (1966: 288–9). Perhaps more importantly, Dye (1966: 293) makes a stronger case that political institutions may not necessarily exert an independent policy effect on outputs. Rather, those differences can be traced back to the socio-economic context.

A further case for the primacy of structural explanations comes from Hofferbert's (1974: 228–9) 'funnel of causality', based on the argument that 'history and geography are intricately woven into the actions of contemporary policymakers' (for an example, see Box 6.2). The funnel image gives the impression that at least four types of context feed into 'elite behavior', which represents the narrow exit hole out of which pours policy outputs. At the widest part of the funnel is the historic-geographic conditions that contribute to the socio-economic composition of a country or region For example, the climate and nature of local resources influence the population density, nature of employment and levels of prosperity of many regions (the explanation is clearest in oil, fish, agriculture and coal regions), while the concentration of particular social groups in particular areas may be traced back to historical events. In turn, the socio-economic composition of a region contributes to 'mass political behavior' such as voter turnout which influences the structure and fortunes of parties (1974: 230). All three factors combine with 'government institutions' to influence elite behaviour.

Yet, there is nothing particularly deterministic about these descriptions of the process. For example, Dye's (1966: 299–301) approach is very much like Lowi's: rejecting the idea that we explain outcomes solely by studying individual and group action, exploring how socio-economic factors might be studied and taken into account, then considering how the demands that arise from such factors are dealt with in the 'little black box labelled political system'. The latter is taken up more forcefully by Sharkansky (1972: 21) who explores how socio-economic signals are mediated by a system's legislature and executive administration. Hofferbert (1974: 231–3) argues that, while elites cannot ignore their policy environment, there is still scope for 'leadership' and 'vigorous action against strong historical and economic forces'. While structural factors may be important, their relevance to policymakers varies by policy area or type and over time, as issues rise and fall on the agenda (1974: 237–41). Further, systems theories portray the process as a cycle rather than a straight line: socio-economic variables influence outcomes, but the decisions made and the policy impact feed back to the policy environment.

Yet, the perception that systems theory downplayed the idea that 'politics matters' produced a strong academic reaction. Blomquist (2007: 270–1) links the reaction to a number of drawbacks to the 'Dye–Sharkansky–Hofferbert' (DSH) approach. For example, it effectively assumes a sole, central decision maker; it does not account for the multi-level and multi-organizational nature of political systems and the scope this affords for groups or policy entrepreneurs to venue shop, or for policy to vary markedly according to the decisions made at different times by different organizations. Further, it assumes that interests are relatively fixed; it does not account for the role of ideas and persuasion, or the ability for policymakers to make different decisions when problems are redefined and new interests are identified (2007: 276–8). In other words, he argues that it focuses too much on external factors at the expense of the policymaking process, which is often treated like a mysterious 'black box'. Consequently, later studies sought to 'bring politics back in' by comparing countries rather than states and finding a much clearer link between, for example, levels of social welfare spending and the role of political parties (John, 1998: 105–6; Blomquist, 2007: 264–5).

Overall, it is difficult to conclude that structural factors determine politics, for two main reasons. First, the structure and agency inspired policy literature generally presents a more dynamic process in which structures influence agents and agents often make or reconstitute the structural constraints within which they operate (Marsh and Smith, 2000: 5; Adler and Haas, 1992: 371; Jacobsen, 1995: 300) . While different texts describe this relationship differently (e.g. consider Hay's 2002: 118–21 discussion of Giddens), few present a completely structuralist account. Second, this is because it is difficult to present a convincing account of policymaking purely in terms of context and the constraints that policymakers face (Blomquist, 2007: 274–5). We must also explain how and why they acted; that they recognized or perceived certain constraints and felt that there was only one realistic choice. A key problem with the focus on structures and socio-economic forces is that we cannot define them objectively. Rather, they are subject to interpretation; different policymakers attach different meanings to what appear to the same socio-economic factors. They mediate the effects of external events by defining their importance and acting on them in a particular way. They are also subject to manipulation when pressure participants seek to convince policymakers that certain factors are causing a problem of crisis proportions (e.g. the 'demographic timebomb'). Consequently, policymakers may pay attention to some socio-economic factors and ignore others for long periods of time.

There are a few issues that, like a meteor about to fall on your head, simply can't be ignored. Yet, just as we can go too far in attributing outcomes to socio-economic pressure, so too can we go too far in highlighting the role of discretion and attention. Indeed, the fact that policymakers in most countries could choose to focus on any issue, but consistently focus on a small number of issues such as the economy, reinforces the importance of socio-economic factors.

A sensible way to address this problem *analytically* is to think in terms of the structure–agency mix, with some issues providing more or less constraint or role for choice than others. For example, the ageing population may give governments little choice but to plan for the consequences (although they can do so in a variety of ways), while technological-driven healthcare may perhaps be easier to resist, particularly if expenditure is limited and more cost-effective public health policies are available. Adapting to our physical environment also involves a complex

Box 6.2   Japan's nuclear policy

Japan's choice of nuclear power as a key source of electricity demonstrates the strong, but not determining, nature of the policy environment on decisions. In this case we are literally describing the policy environment because energy policy depends on two potentially competing factors. First, Japan has few indigenous sources of energy such as coal or gas, requiring it to import natural sources or rely on nuclear power. Second, it is vulnerable to natural disasters such as earthquakes that undermine reliance on nuclear power (even if considerable measures are taken to make them secure). The resultant policy, including nuclear as a key source, follows policymakers weighing up these sorts of constraints but without policy being determined by them. This case demonstrates how difficult it is to describe structural constraints. In the aftermath of the earthquakes in March 2011, one scientific commentator (on the rolling BBC news coverage) still maintained that Japanese governments effectively had to rely on nuclear power; that they had no choice. This type of example may be what Ward (1987: 602) has in mind when he describes situations which appear to make 'certain acts unthinkable or physically impossible' or 'so costly that actors are structurally constrained from carrying them out'. This constraint is far less apparent in most other countries, and the Japanese crisis has prompted many governments to reassess their energy portfolio (Pidd and Goldenberg, 2011).

mix of structure and perception. For example, coastal conditions may appear to force us to build protective barriers, but policymakers can also ignore the issue for some time (perhaps until the environmental conditions cause a human crisis).

However, there is no easy answer when it comes to the *method* we use to decide how impressive each constraint is. For example, we may explore methods that try to capture how policymakers perform a mediating role when they perceive and interpret their environment, make priorities when faced with a wide range of structural factors, and then act (as in Box 6.3). However, we also recognize that projects based on qualitative methods (such as elite interviews or participant observation) may be hard to secure and carry out (how much can we expect someone to rationalize accurately their reasons for acting?). Or, we can use quantitative methods that, while useful, may give a false sense of precision when it is often a rather blunt tool (Blomquist, 2007: 262; 268–70).

The economic context: Marxism and globalization

Marxism is perhaps the only term that can compete with behaviouralism or pluralism as the most criticized and misrepresented term in public

Box 6.3   Case study: mental health policy

The case study of mental health policy in the UK allows us to compare the role of institutions with the role of the policy environment. Cairney (2009b) compares the policy styles of the UK and Scottish governments, drawing on Lijphart's (1999) expectation that Scottish policymaking (in a PR system) would be more consensual when compared to the 'majoritarian' UK (see Chapter 4, 'Do formal institutions determine policy styles?', p. 87). Cairney suggests that this was only the case in one particular issue – regarding legislation to detain mentally ill patients against their will – when certain policy conditions were in place. In some cases the conditions are permanent: the smaller size and scope of the Scottish government allows it to coordinate policy across health and justice departments, and foster personal relationships between groups and government more easily. In other cases, they followed two events and decisions that occurred decades earlier. First, more psychiatric hospitals were closed in the UK from the 1960s, producing more agenda-setting cases of dangerously ill people 'roaming the streets' and a greater impetus for the UK to solve the problem. The experience reinforces the idea that policy represents 'its own cause'. Second, there has been no capacity to treat patients with 'personality disorder' in Scotland since the 1970s (when a patient killed three people when escaping from a secure hospital). As a result, the UK government would have found it much more difficult to introduce and implement the same policy in Scotland (2009b: 683–4). Therefore, two separate governments made different decisions partly because they faced different problems; they were operating in different policy environments. Of course, there are clear limits to such explanations because we also have to account for the role of agency and the ability of actors to make choices despite rules and restrictive policy conditions. In this case, nothing may have deterred a UK government driven strongly by ideology and its perception that an uncompromising policy position was popular.

policy. Many variants exist and Marx-inspired thought has gone so far beyond Marx that 'Marxist' is increasingly misleading. For our purposes, it is possible to construct a Marxist account of policymaking focusing on the role of elites. Our main aim may be to explain why the structure of government and public policy is so devoted to protecting the capitalist system of economic production and why business or economic interests tend to have a privileged position within the policy process. Further, our assumption may be that the capitalist system benefits one class of people (those who own or control capital) at the expense of another (the working classes). This can be done by identifying the role of elites in powerful positions in government and the relationships they share with business elites. For example, the ruling and capitalist classes share a common, privileged, background that predisposes them towards working with each other. Or, the world of business provides an incentive for policymakers to cooperate, either by presenting a key source of campaign funding or a source of employment in the future. In either case, the consequence is that government actors forge close networks with representatives of business, ensuring that while the latter do not rule directly, they dominate access to policymaking at the expense of other interests (John, 1998: 94). If we combine this argument with the recognition that it is in the interests of most governments or policymakers to ensure that the capitalist system runs smoothly, since this provides employment for its voters and government income through taxes, then we already have an attractive explanation for the position of business within the policy process (it doesn't even have to be Marxist – see Lindblom, 1977: chapter 13).

The problem perhaps comes when we consider this process of capitalist protection to be inevitable and almost immune from change; that agents merely function according to particular roles and have no real ability to make choices within this system (see Chapter 3 on structural power). This appears to be the case with 'structural' or 'functionalist' Marxist accounts that relate all significant policy developments to a functional imperative (although such accounts tend to be exaggerated – Hay, 2002: 116). For example, the new post-war economic imperative required that the healthcare system developed to maintain a functioning workforce, while education developed to socialize the workforce and give it the basic skills to operate as a relatively sophisticated working class. As John (1998: 96) argues, the basic problem with such arguments is that it is possible to interpret all policy developments in this way without much evidence and without demonstrating how the process works. Indeed, when we 'unpack' the process we find at least two problems. First, we have policies that appear to reflect the ideology of governments or the power or unions, such as the minimum wage or measures to protect union rights (we could say that they were provided to produce a more content workforce, but isn't this stretching the functional explanation too far?). Second, we can identify several types of capitalist class that may not share the same interests. For example, the issue of interest rates may divide the manufacturer and the banker.

The same can be said for 'globalization'; a rather vague and overused term that describes the international spread of processes which used to be confined to one or a small number of countries. It refers, most importantly, to economic integration in the form of global or deregulated financial markets, technology which allows greater interaction across the globe, and the role of 'global corporations' (Hill, 2005: 45; John, 1998: 103). It may also refer to the social and cultural integration which tends to follow greater interaction between countries and their populations (Parsons, 1995: 242–3). The identification of globalization may prompt us to examine what happens when nation states experience a diminished ability to control their own economic and monetary policies and to control the actions of large multinational corporations (MNCs). Governments appear to be forced to compete economically, react to widespread shifts and crises in international financial conditions (such as the 'credit crunch' – Box 5.2) and change to attract business from MNCs. As John (1998: 103; see also Quiggin, 2006: 536) highlights, the focus is on economics determining politics, with moves from the 1980s towards 'deregulation, privatization and cutting back welfare' representing a worldwide response to globalization (encapsulated by Friedman's (2000) term 'Golden Straightjacket').

As Hay (2002: 114) argues, such arguments are unconvincing unless they identify a clear causal process and some evidence. For example, we may identify an inevitable 'race to the bottom' as governments – acting on the belief that MNCs will not invest in countries with high taxes, a public sector-dominated economy, and restrictive labour and environ-mental regulations – reduce the size of the public sector and corporation taxes and deregulate to attract foreign direct investment. Yet, this race does not appear to have run, at least in the uniform way we might expect (for example, the overall size of the public sector has not diminished – Hay, 2006b: 591). Rather, different policymakers in different countries have reacted to their environment in different ways (Hoberg, 2001: 128–30; Hay, 2002: 253; Quiggin, 2006: 537). It suggests that 'structural forces' are important but they do not determine political behaviour; there is always some degree of choice. We may agree that one choice seems inevitable because it is much better than the rest. Or, the *appearance* of constraint and inevitability may be convenient for decision makers attempting to introduce unpopular policies or avoid responsibility for poor results (Hay, 2002: 259). However, there is choice nonetheless and 'the constraints of globalization are as much as anything else, what polit-ical actors make of them' (Hay, 2006b: 587). In this light, policy conver-gence focuses on the decisions of policymakers when they weigh up both external constraints to converge, and domestic pressures to diverge or stay different (a process explored further in Chapter 12). Indeed, a key reason for country-level policies to stay distinctive is that they are influ-enced by *other* structural factors, 'including distinctive national values, different political institutions, and the legacy of past policies' (Hoberg, 2001: 127; see also Sinclair, 2004).

The government context: inheritance before choice and policy succession

The 'legacy of past policies' is captured best by Rose (1990), who argues that the cumulative effect of decades of policies is that newly elected policymakers inherit a huge government with massive commitments. Since governments are more likely to introduce new than terminate old policies (Chapter 2), the cumulative effect is profound. Most policy decisions are based on legislation which already exists and the bulk of public expenditure is spent on government activities (such as welfare benefits) that continue by routine, carried out by public employees recruited in the past. This is not to say that policymakers have no choice or that their choices make no difference. Rather, current policymakers choose to 'uphold the laws of the land' before making new ones and the effect of their new policy choices is rather small in comparison to the sum of government activity (1990: 263). In other words, much government policy results from the choices made by former policymakers in the past (Rose and Davies, 1994: 229).

The logical implication of bounded rationality is that when policymakers pay attention to one issue they must ignore 99 others. When they invest a significant amount of effort and attention to policy change on one issue, they effectively accept that they cannot do the same for most other issues (Rose, 1986; compare with punctuated equilibrium in Chapter 9). Therefore, most of the day-to-day delivery of policy takes place without significant policymaker involvement. Most public sector organizations continue to implement policies that were legislated and budgeted for in the past (Rose, 1990: 264). This sometimes produces 'change without choice' when external effects, such as demographic changes prompting new demands for services, produce almost automatic changes in budgets (1990: 285). This argument supplements the suggestion, discussed in Chapter 2, that policy often represents its own cause. Policymakers often choose to address the 'consequences of inherited programmes that would not have been chosen by the current incumbents' (Rose, 1990: 264). It also reinforces Rose's (1984) suggestion that a new party in government may not make a major difference. In this case, parties not only inherit legislation but also a lot of draft legislation that tends to be passed regardless of the party in government (most legislation has cross-party support and is largely negotiated between civil servants and interest groups – Rose and Davies, 1994: 133).

Rose's argument comes with some very striking statistics when applied to the UK, such as: the Thatcher government of 1979 inherited 3,329 laws, of which 36 per cent were passed before 1900 and 56 per cent were passed before 1945 (1990: 266); 84 per cent of all government programmes in place in 1946 were still in place four decades later, accounting for 99 per cent of expenditure (1990: 273); and, the amount spent on new programmes by one four-year administration is approximately 2–4 per cent of total public expenditure (1990: 277). Rose and Davies (1994: 230–7) provide similar statistics on the US.

Box 6.4   Incrementalism and inertia

Incrementalism has much in common with a focus on inertia: the identification of limited cognitive and research capabilities within government; the rejection of the idea that rational decision makers consider all policy choices; the identification of marginal political changes; and, the idea that policies may cause as well as solve problems (Chapter 5; Rose and Davies, 1994: 31; Hogwood and Peters, 1983: 10–13). Lindblom (1979: 520) is careful to separate the advantages of incrementalist policymaking (the management of policy by consensus and the minimization of unintended consequences) with inertia in political systems (associated with veto points, 'timidity' and 'ideological conservatism'). However, Hogwood and Peters (1983: 12) question the ability of policymakers to minimize unintended consequences by rectifying mistakes. Rather, mistakes may only be identified after a series of incremental steps have been taken, while each step generates 'long-term commitments or entitlements which can be difficult to reverse or replace'. Rose and Davies (1994: 31) suggest that incrementalist analyses tend to be relatively short term; longer-term analyses show that marginal steps made in the past have produced 'massive commitments' such as the modern welfare state and tax systems. These policies are maintained and reproduced by government organizations that operate without requiring further authorization. If policymakers can only focus on a small number of issues, most mistakes will not even be considered far less rectified.

This theme of inertia is reinforced by the concept of 'policy succession', which is generally more likely than the combination of policy innovation and termination we might expect when new governments reject the old and bring in the new (Hogwood and Peters, 1983; compare inertia and incrementalism in Box 6.4). Policy succession is 'the replacement of an existing policy, program or organization by another' (1983: 1). While it may look new, and is different from mere 'policy maintenance', it is 'directed at the same programme and/or clientele' (1983: 18). Succession is increasingly likely for three main reasons. First, the size and scope of the state is so large that there are few issues in which it is not already involved in some way. Second, existing policy is often 'its own cause' (Wildavsky, 1980); the implementation of policy often throws up problems that command the time of policymakers. Third, the level of existing commitments are high and there is little scope to increase tax income (through growth or higher taxes) to fund new programmes (Hogwood and Peters, 1983: 2–5).

Succession is generally more likely than innovation because the conditions for the introduction of policy are already in place: the issue already has legitimacy because it has been addressed by government in the past; primary legislation may not be necessary; the resources for a service

---

Box 6.5 Case study: public expenditure

While we may not leave this discussion with the feeling that the actions of policymakers are determined by economic imperatives, we still recognize that most will perceive themselves to be in a rather constrained position. The economic issue is generally at the top of government agendas (not just when there are major crises, as in 2009), and it is no coincidence that treasury departments command a prominent role in most countries. At a very basic level, policymakers will be constrained by the need to maintain a reasonable balance between revenue and spending (the budget) and imports and exports (balance of payments) (Quiggin, 2006: 530–5). It is in the interest of many governments to support the economic system that favours capitalists. Governments also face an increasingly interconnected and competitive global economic system that produces new consequences for their behaviour. They inherit a huge budget that may be difficult to amend beyond the margins in any single year or term of office. The issue of public expenditure sums up the idea of inheritance because governments tend to make a 2–4 per cent difference to their overall spending patterns. However, it also demonstrates the degree of choice. For example, there are many ways to attempt to balance the budget, including running a deficit in one term of office, on the assumption that a future government will be obliged to produce a surplus (Quiggin, 2006: 540). The evidence also suggests that public expenditure as a percentage of GDP can vary quite markedly – for example from 54 per cent in 1982 to 36 per cent in 1999 in the UK (Hogwood, 1992: 43; Hindmoor, 2002: 208). More significantly, it fluctuates by policy area, as a combination of inertia and political choices produces minimal change in most areas but profound change in others (see Figure 9.1; John and Margetts, 2003: 421).

---

delivery institution have already been provided, and policy has an established clientele (particularly in areas such as social security). More significant innovations require not only a process to establish public and legislative legitimacy, but also policy termination to reduce costs before committing new resources (1983: 132–3; 225–6). Yet, complete termination is also rare because it has costs that many policymakers are reluctant to bear. As Chapter 2 suggests, termination has immediate financial costs, may produce the perception of policy failure, and may be opposed by interest groups, clients and the organizations that depend on the policy to survive (Hogwood and Peters, 1983: 16–17).

Again, these are not arguments about no choice or no effect (see also Box 6.5). For example, Rose (1990: 288; Rose and Davies, 1994: 5) argues that inherited commitments can be moulded to suit current problems, *some* programmes can be terminated or introduced, and the policy innovations made during the administration may have a long-term, cumulative effect. Further, many of the policy successions described by Hogwood and Peters (1983: 30), such as the introduction of the national health service in the UK, seem rather significant (in fact, they describe this as a hybrid of succession and innovation). Similarly, the significance of a decision to reform welfare policies by spending the same amount but changing the balance between recipients, may not be captured well by the term 'consolidation' (1983: 66). Rather, it shows us that any such reform may take a 'huge political effort' to produce 'marginal improvements' (1983: 129). It will not involve new money and will be carried out by the staff and organizations that the policymakers inherited (compare with Chapter 4 on institutions; Chapter 11 on first and second order change).

The policy process as a complex system

The image of a complex system captures well the idea that policymakers do not operate within a vacuum; they are one small part of a much larger process that they have limited control over. It is perhaps surprising, then, that portrayals of policy processes as systems fell into disuse, particularly since their proponents seemed to offer a general theory of political science (Dunsire, 1973: 123; 137–8). By the same token, it is not surprising that systems theory has enjoyed a recent renaissance. However, the size of this resurgence relates much more to its rise within the natural and physical sciences. Complexity theory offers a general theory of *all* science; it presents the idea that the same basic processes can be identified and explained in both the physical and social sciences.

Broadly speaking, the approach seeks to explain why complex or system-wide behaviour emerges from the interaction between 'large collections of simpler components' (Mitchell, 2009: x; Kernick, 2006; Blackman, 2001; Geyer and Rihani, 2010). Cairney (2010a: 3) identifies five common assumptions regarding how complex systems behave:

1   *The whole is greater than the sum of its parts.* A complex system cannot be explained merely by breaking it down into its component parts. Instead, we must shift our analysis to the system as a whole; as networks of elements that interact, share information, adapt and combine to produce systemic behaviour.
2   *The behaviour of complex systems is difficult to predict.* Complex systems exhibit 'non-linear dynamics' when they provide 'feedback' to particular actions; some forms of action are dampened (negative feedback) while others are amplified (positive feedback). As a result, small actions can have large effects and large actions can have small effects.
3   *Complex systems are particularly sensitive to initial conditions.* Initial events or decisions often produce a long-term momentum. The

'butterfly effect' captures this idea of seemingly insignificant factors producing consequences that have a profound cumulative impact.

4 *Complex systems exhibit 'emergence'.* Their behaviour often evolves from the interaction between elements at a local level rather than central direction. This may make the system difficult to control.

5 *Complex systems may contain 'strange attractors'.* Although complex systems are associated with unpredictable behaviour, they often display regularities of behaviour over extended periods (Bovaird, 2008: 320). 'Punctuated equilibrium' sums up this image of long periods of stability interrupted by short bursts of change.

In this light, a complex system is a large number of elements that interact with each other to produce system-wide behaviour. This process cannot be understood simply by breaking it down into its individual elements. For example, swarming behaviour in bees and coordinated behaviour in ants cannot be explained merely by the actions of individual insects. Rather, we must study their actions as a whole, the rules they follow, how those rules are communicated and the extent to which a small change in rules causes a large systemic change. The brain is also a complex system in which emergent processes, such as thoughts and feelings, are difficult to break down into the performance of individual neurons.

Unfortunately, the brain also makes it difficult to treat political or social systems in the same way. In other words, we should be cautious about the value of complexity theory to the social sciences because human behaviour, or 'the capacity to reflect and to make deliberative choices and decisions among alternative paths of action', makes the social world a different object of study than the natural or physical world (Mitleton-Kelly, 2003: 25–6). Its application to public policy is uncertain and often the term 'complexity' is used very loosely or denotes a metaphor or analogy (2003: 26; Kernick, 2006: 389; Bovaird, 2008: 321). So what happens when we try to use the term more directly, to identify a real, complex political system? Teisman and Klijn (2008: 288) highlight an initial difficulty: no-one is quite sure what a complex system is, beyond an intuitive reference to a collection of parts which may be analytically distinct but intertwined in practice and therefore difficult to separate when we observe their interaction. Jervis (1998: 5–6) suggests that 'We are dealing with a system when (a) a set of units or elements is interconnected so that changes in some elements or their relations produce changes in other parts of the system, and (b) the entire system exhibits properties and behaviours that are different from those of the parts'. He also recognizes the limits to such definitions and prefers to define by example (in accordance with the principle 'I know it when I see it'). This is not a problem in itself since most terms in the political science literature defy common definition, while many vague terms such as 'institutionalism' are used to represent a common focus. However, we still have to identify a common and distinctive scientific endeavour around the term 'complexity'.

For Teisman and Klijn (2008: 288) the endeavour in public policy is based on four broad insights. The first is that law-like behaviour is difficult to identify because the policy process is 'guided by a variety of forces', suggesting that X will only have an effect on Y under particular conditions that are difficult to specify. A policy that was successful in one context may not have the same effect in another. We need to know why it was successful in that instance, but the idea of complexity is that so many variables are relevant that it is difficult to account for them all. The second is that systems have 'self-organizing capacities', making them difficult to control; the effect of an external force may be large or small and this is impossible to predict from the external force alone. This lesson could be learned particularly by policymakers who otherwise would be surprised that their policy interventions did not have the desired effect. The third relates to the metaphor of the 'fitness landscape' or 'surroundings in which living beings exist and behave'. This landscape, which provides the context for the choices of agents, is unstable and often rapidly changing. Therefore, agents or organizations must adapt quickly and not rely on a single policy strategy (2008: 289; Mitleton-Kelly, 2003: 35–6). The fourth is that actors within complex systems are 'self-organizing, creating their own perception of what they want and how to behave in the landscape they are in' (Teisman and Klijn, 2008: 289).

Complexity is everywhere, but how can we study it?

The term 'complexity' sums up well the nature of modern policymaking. As Chapter 2 suggests, our aim is to conceptualize a rather complex and shifting picture of the policy environment which displays sources of stability and instability. The simple 'clubby days' of early post-war politics have been replaced by 'complex relationships' at multiple levels of government and among a huge, politically active population (Heclo, 1978: 94; 97; Baumgartner and Jones, 1993: 177–8; Jordan, 1981: 98). But can we identify the specific themes of complexity in more depth? There seem to be at least four key comparable discussions in the modern public policy literature (see also Klijn, 2008 on governance, multiple streams analysis and game theory).

First, punctuated equilibrium theory (Chapter 9) employs much of the language of complexity theory to explain shifts in group–government relationships. The 'general punctuation hypothesis' demonstrates, in a study of information processing, that policy processes exhibit non-linear dynamics and punctuated equilibria. Jones and Baumgartner (2005: 7) define information processing as the 'collecting, assembling, interpreting and prioritizing [of] signals from the environment'. Policymakers are effectively surrounded by an infinite number of 'signals', or information that could be relevant to their decisions (from, for example, interest groups, the media or public opinion). Since they are boundedly rational and do not have the ability to process all signals, they must simplify their decision-making environment by ignoring most (negative feedback) and promoting few to the top of their agenda (positive feedback). Negative feedback may produce long periods of equilibrium since existing policy relationships and responsibilities are more likely to remain stable and policy is less likely to change when the issue receives minimal attention from policymakers. Positive feedback may produce policy 'punctuations' because when policymakers pay a disproportionate amount of attention to an issue it is more likely that policy will change dramatically.

Second, the focus on sensitivity to initial conditions is a key tenet of historical institutionalism (Chapter 4). A 'critical juncture' is the point at which certain events and decisions were made which led to the development of an institution. The timing of these decisions is crucial, because it may be the order of events that sets institutional development on a particular path. Path dependence suggests that when a commitment to a policy has been established and resources devoted to it, over time it produces 'increasing returns' and it effectively becomes increasingly costly to choose a different path (Pierson, 2000a). The link between complexity theory and historical institutionalism is strong: both identify the same sense of inertia and unpredictability, as relatively small events or actions can have a huge and enduring effect on policy change that is very difficult to reverse (and both use the black-and-red-ball analogy outlined in Chapter 4) (Pierson, 2000a). Institutional explanations may also be relevant when our aim is to identify the rules governing systemic behaviour; complexity theory may add a new dimension when exploring the extent to which policy changes dramatically when those rules change (in much the same way that we explore a sudden shift of direction of a swarm of bees or an attitude shift in the brain).

Third, complexity theory's focus on 'emergent' behaviour in the absence of central control reinforces the implementation literature. Central governments face problems when they do not recognize the extent to which policy changes as it is implemented (Chapter 2). The level of interdependence between governments and implementing organizations has prompted the identification of 'self-organizing networks' (Rhodes, 1997: 50) and images of 'bottom-up' implementation through self-selecting clusters of organizations in which a variety of public and private organizations cooperate. While such arrangements have prompted governments to embrace new public management (the application of private business management methods to the public sector) and seek to impose order through hierarchy and targets, implementation structures may not be amenable to such direct control. The idea of a complex system reinforces the point that implementation problems cannot be related solely to the recalcitrance of service delivery organizations (see Teisman and Klijn, 2008: 294; Bovaird, 2008: 339). Constant reforms of service delivery functions may therefore be rather futile unless we recognize the non-linear and unpredictable nature of policymaking.

Fourth, the normative side of complexity theory may resonate with incrementalism. Sanderson (2009: 706) suggests that the implication of complexity is that we do not know exactly how any policy measure will make a difference. Therefore, policymakers should be careful when making interventions, making greater use of '"trial and error" policy making' and learning from pilot projects (2009: 707). It seems to represent a rejection of top-down control, giving implementing organizations the chance to learn from their experience and adapt to their environment (2009: 708; Haynes, 2008: 326; Bardach, 2006: 353). It also seems uncannily like the spirit of Lindblom (1959: 86):

> Making policy is at best a very rough process. Neither social scientists, nor politicians, nor public administrators yet know enough about the social world to avoid repeated error in predicting the consequences of policy moves. A wise policy-maker consequently expects that his policies will achieve only part of what he hopes and at the same time will produce unanticipated consequences he would have preferred to avoid. If he proceeds through a succession of incremental changes, he avoids serious lasting mistakes.

However, it is worth noting that our identification of complexity in the world does not necessarily mean that we should adopt the research agenda of complexity theory. Although anti-reductionism and whole-systems approaches sound very attractive, reductionist theories have a strong hold in political science. Indeed, our next approach – rational choice theory – may represent complexity theory's poplar opposite because it seeks parsimonious results based on a reduction of the social world into as few explanatory variables as possible. The old focus on systems was also remarkably simple, focusing on a small number of variables to explain a large degree of variation. This is as much a practical as a philosophical issue. While we may describe the world as a complex system, we may not have the ability to study it as one (Cairney, 2010b).

A return to structural determinism?

Unlike the old systems theory, complex systems theory does not appear to rely solely on producing quantitative tests on the relationships between socio-economic factors and policy outputs (Cairney, 2010a; 2010b). Yet, it still suffers from the same sense of determinism. This is a common complaint regarding most systems research, because it suggests that they have their own logics which 'operate in some sense independent of – and over the heads of – the actors themselves' (Hay, 2002: 102). The danger is that if the complex *system* is predominantly the causal factor then we lose sight of the role that policymakers play; there may be a tendency to treat the system as a rule-bound structure which leaves minimal room for the role of agency. What we need is an understanding of how agents perceive their decision-making environments; how they reproduce, accept or challenge the structural, institutional and wider systemic constraints that they appear to face when making decisions. This is the essence of the study of politics, explaining why different policymakers make different decisions under the same circumstances.

If we are being sympathetic to complexity theory we can treat its approach to structure and agency like Gidden's 'two sides of the same coin ... If we look at social practices in one way, we can see actors and actions; if we look at them another way we can see structures' (Craib, 1992: 3 on Giddens, 1984). On one side, we have 'self-organizing landscapes' (Teisman and Klijn, 2008: 289) or complex *systems* that adapt and change behaviour; behaviour is 'emergent' from the processes within systems and is not readily broken down to the agents within it. Further, much of the explanation for outcomes comes not from individuals but from the level of connectivity between them (Mitleton-Kelly, 2003: 28). On the other, we have the 'self-referential behaviour' of *agents*, reacting to 'external forces and changes' but also, 'creating their own perception of what they want and how to behave in the landscape they are in' (Teisman and Klijn, 2008: 289). However, each side appears to contradict the other: a focus on separable, independent actions by agents appears to contradict the idea that a complex system cannot be broken down into its component parts (Cairney, 2010a). Perhaps this is the true meaning of 'two sides of the same coin' – two arguments that represent each other's polar opposite. This problem is by no means unique to systems theory. Indeed, a common theme throughout the book is how to attribute explanatory power to entities that do not act but appear to influence heavily the actions of agents.

Conclusion

The term 'structural factors' is rather vague, can apply to a large number of developments, and is difficult to describe, so it is no surprise that a number of accounts vary markedly in their basic descriptions. The strongest structural accounts suggest that powerful external forces constrain the ability of individuals or governments to make decisions or that significant socio-economic change determines policy change. Yet, few contemporary theories take the latter approach. Rather, we can identify a range of approaches which try to strike the right balance between structure and agency. The DSH approach measures the association between socio-economic factors and policy outputs. Marxist accounts explore the strong imperative for governments to support the capitalist system and therefore the interests of the classes that benefit most from that system. Globalization suggests that governments may be forced to compete with each other to protect their economy and secure foreign direct investment. Inheritance before choice suggests that governments inherit massive policy commitments and tend to change policy only at the margins, while the pervasiveness of policy succession reflects the constraints on policy innovation and termination. Finally, complexity theory suggests that policymakers are part of a large complex system that seems to behave in ways that they cannot control.

The advantage of such approaches is that they highlight the context within which policy is made. We know that policymakers make choices, but recognize that policymaking does not begin with a blank slate or operate in a vacuum. Structural factors may influence what they pay attention to and how they act. There may be events and policy conditions outside of their control. There are limits on their ability to anticipate the effects of policy and the extent to which it is carried out successfully. They inherit a 'ship of state' that behaves more like a supertanker (which is notoriously difficult to turn round) than a rowboat. In short, this is a useful corrective to the idea, explored in Chapter 5, that politics begins when policymakers make choices.

The disadvantage is that such accounts often appear to favour structural explanations at the expense of a focus on agency. This is a particular feature of the Marxist accounts that highlight a degree of inevitability rather than choice, theories of globalization that do not explain how policymakers react to their decision-making environment, and theories which suggest that complex systems almost have a life of their own (or that politics takes place in a mysterious 'black box'). It is difficult to present a convincing account of policymaking purely in terms of context and the constraints that policymakers face. We must also explain how and why they acted. In some cases, policymakers have clear choices even when the decision-making context appears to provide only one realistic option. As the globalization debate shows, there is often a large gap between our assumptions on the inevitability of action and the actual evidence that such action has occurred. In other cases, we may feel that policymakers have no choice. However, this really means that 'the best course of action seems obvious' (Dowding 1996: 44). While it may seem like a fine distinction, it is one that separates the social from the relatively deterministic physical and natural sciences.

Most modern theories try to conceptualize this dynamic process in which structures influence agents and agents mediate or reconstitute the structural constraints within which they operate. They identify not only how socio-economic factors constrain behaviour, but also how policy-makers mediate these factors by interpreting or weighting their significance in different ways. The advocacy coalition framework is particularly notable because it seeks to incorporate the DSH approach into a wider analysis. Its flow diagram (see Figure 10.1) includes a discussion of 'relatively stable parameters', such as the 'basic distribution of natural resources', and 'external events' such as 'changes in socio-economic conditions', but it also seeks to explain the 'black box' by identifying the ability of advocacy coalitions to interpret external effects and compete to define the policy problem within sub-systems.

Chapter 7

Rational Choice Theory

This chapter examines:

- What rational means, what rational choice entails and what rational choice theory is.
- The role of game theory – what real world policy issues does it raise?
- The collective action problem in public policy and how we deal with it.
- The main debates between rational choice advocates and critics. RCT is controversial, and the debates go to the heart of how we understand science.

A key method to study public policy is to produce models and compare them to the real world (for discussions of the realness of the world, see Chalmers, 1999). The models, as descriptions of the real world's essential features, provide a means to deduce how people might behave within them and what the consequences of that action might be. Rational choice theory (RCT) adopts this approach by applying theoretical tools advanced in economics (also note the term 'public choice' – McLean, 1987: 1). Its key features are an adherence to **methodological individualism** and the **assumption** of rationality in individuals. The aim is to establish how many, or what proportion of, political outcomes one can explain with reference to the choices of individuals under particular conditions. However, beyond this description, a common understanding is elusive (Box 7.1).

> **Methodological individualism** – a commitment to explain socio-political outcomes as the aggregation of the decisions of individuals (or at least a belief that they *can be* reduced to the micro level).

> **Assumption** – an axiom or statement used (in RCT) to build a mathematical model.

While 'rational' refers to the ability to reason or apply logic, it is tempting to think that 'rational choice' refers to the pursuit of self interest. It may be better understood as a means to an end: rational actors seek to fulfil their preferences. Many RCT models also suggest that rational actors 'maximize their utility'. RCT models often contain a series of assumptions – e.g. preferences can be ranked in order of importance; actors have full information – which simplify rather complex decision-making processes. The ability to reason is not lost, since actors must be able to recognize the constraints of the environment within which they operate and make

Box 7.1   The key tenets of rational choice theory

There are few clear definitions that go beyond 'the application of the methods of economics to the study of politics' (Hindmoor, 2006a: 1; see also Eriksson, 2012; Parsons, 2005: 62 and Becker, 1976: 3). Most accounts focus on three methodological principles:

- The use of models and deductive reasoning. Deduction is often described as a departure from induction (an attempt to derive theories from observations of the world – Hindmoor, 2006a: 2). It creates models of the world based on a small number of propositions and a logical examination of their connections.
- Methodological individualism. Political outcomes are the product of an aggregate of the actions of, and interactions between, individuals. To act rationally requires the possession of preferences and beliefs.
- Instrumental rationality. Individuals fulfil their preferences according to their beliefs regarding the most appropriate means to achieve them. This is an 'intentional' explanation of behaviour based on the goals of individuals (Elster, 1985: 8) rather than motivation by 'habit, tradition, or social appropriateness' (MacDonald, 2003: 552).

Most also identify two variants (Dowding and King, 1995: 1). The first is an abstract exercise that gives individuals the ability to act optimally and predicts their likely behaviour and the resultant outcomes within a range of environments that provide different incentives to act. The aim is often to produce 'paradoxical results' (1995: 2) worthy of further study. The second involves more detailed assumptions regarding the preferences of individuals and how they relate to specific institutional settings. The aim is to explain outcomes. Many other variations can be identified, and some make more heroic claims about its scope and value than others. Rational choice advocates can be positivists, instrumentalists, realists or interpretivists (Hindmoor, 2006a: 212; although see Hampsher-Monk and Hindmoor, 2010; Hay, 2004a: 50). Methodological individualism can be used to downplay or demonstrate the role of social structures. Many models focus on agents such as organizations rather than individual human beings. Assumptions about rationality can be thin or thick, weak or strong (see below). Preferences can be said to exist 'prior to the social and political world' (John, 1998: 118) or merely be assumed, as a means to simplify analysis and delimit the scope of rational choice models (Parsons, 2005: 8–9). Agents can be calculating self-interested utility maximizers or just actors whose preference-seeking behaviour evolves from playing multiple games (Dowding, 2010; Ross, 2005; 'evolutionary game theory' often explores the actions of boundedly rational players who employ trial-and-error (Ward, 2002: 72–3). This degree of variation presents a problem for critics who are too quick to dismiss it based on a caricature (e.g. Stoker and Marsh, 2002: 6). On the other hand, the more that rational choice models are held to share only a slight family resemblance to each other, then the less claim there can be to 'universalism' rather than ad hoc explanations of different circumstances (Green and Shapiro, 1994: 29; see also Hay, 2004a: 54; but note that Laver, 1997: 8, is not too worried by this conclusion).

choices according to their preferences and their beliefs regarding the best way to satisfy them. In many cases these assumptions are central to the empirical process: simple models are constructed, the logical implications of their assumptions are deduced and their *predictions* may be tested in real world situations. This use of simplifying assumptions differs from our discussion of 'comprehensive rationality' in which we automatically treat them as unrealistic and examine the consequences

This departure from the comprehensive rationality approach raises an obvious question: why spend time constructing a model that appears so divorced from reality? The key answer is that the model is parsimonious rather than unrealistic; it extracts the *essence* of individual behaviour to produce a model of aggregate behaviour. Further, the best way to examine the value of its assumptions is to test their logical implications, by constructing models of political processes based on the behaviour of actors (as often explored through *game theory*) and examining the extent to which the predictions are analytically useful and/or confirmed by evidence from the real world.

Free ride – to enjoy the benefits of a collective resource without paying for them; to benefit from collective behaviour without engaging in that behaviour.

Our second question may be: what value does rational choice theory add to the study of public policy? The most relevant aspect is the 'collective action problem', or the potential for choices made by individuals to have an adverse societal effect when there is an absence of trust, obligation or other incentives to cooperate. While the action of one individual makes little difference, the sum total of individual actions may be catastrophic. In economics this may refer to 'market failure' when there is scope to **free ride** and therefore no incentive to purchase or contribute to **public goods** (such as national defences or clean air). This introduces us to a broader problem: although people may have common aims or interests, it does not ensure that they act collectively to achieve them. Rather, it may be rational to enjoy the benefits of a good or action without making a contribution.

Public goods – collective resources which are non-excludable (no-one can be excluded from enjoying their benefits) and non-rival (their use by one person does not diminish their value to another).

Principal–agent problem – a principal contracts an agent to act on its behalf, but the agent possesses more information on its activities and may not act in the principal's interests unless induced to do so (an action hampered by the principal's relative lack of information).

Collective action problems are often used to justify government intervention: if the effect of non-cooperation is that everyone is worse off, let's make people cooperate. Yet, institutional solutions are also beset by problems: civil servants may act in their own interests rather than according to the stated aims of government (producing a **principal–agent** problem); governments may encourage interest groups to devote resources to seek privi-

Box 7.2   What is the point of simplified assumptions?

There are at least four ways to use simplified assumptions when we study rationality:

1   The neorealist assumption of state rationality in which states are treated as 'centrally coordinated, purposive individuals' and we treat decisions 'as the more or less purposive acts of unified national governments' (Box 1.1; Allison, 1971).
2   The use of deliberately unrealistic assumptions to produce ideal types of policy processes. The aim is to state what conditions would have to be met to ensure a particular outcome and then explore the consequences of these conditions not being met (Chapter 5 on comprehensive and bounded rationality).
3   Microeconomics uses assumptions about individuals or firms to generate models of supply and demand and explore how markets work. On the demand side we may assume that individuals have perfect information, the cognitive ability to consider the consequences of all choices, and that their preferences are rank-ordered and transitive. They are able, as consumers, to fulfil their preferences within the confines of the market.
4   RCT applies this approach to the study of politics, often making similar assumptions about the rationality of individuals.

The key difference between (1) and (4) is the latter's adherence to methodological individualism (which challenges the notion of state rationality – see Allison, 1971). The difference between (2) and (4) is that the former rejects the assumptions while the latter uses them as the basis for further study. The main question is not 'how realistic do they seem?' but 'how do they aid deductive reasoning?' or 'how much do they explain'? In these terms, the use of more detailed and realistic assumptions to explain more of a particular event is not an inevitable consequence of finding out that a model's predictions are not completely accurate. RCT highlights the trade-offs between simplified models that produce generalizations about many instances, and detailed explanations that are difficult to apply elsewhere (Dowding and King, 1995: 16; Dowding, 1995a: 49; Dowding, 1995c: 82; Baumol, 1987: 155).

leged lobbying positions; and, perhaps most importantly, no government is able to make a decision that suits everyone based on an aggregate of the preferences of all individuals. Indeed, a large part of government activity involves coercing everyone (through taxes) to contribute to a policy that benefits only a small section of it, or regulating one group to benefit another (Wilson, 1980: 419–22). Such actions may be framed in terms of the 'national interest' but, if there is no such thing as a decision that suits everyone, such framing is merely an attempt to justify contentious policy decisions. Government solutions may also be expensive and produce unintended consequences, particularly when policymakers lack enough information to make good choices (Ostrom, 1990: 11). Therefore, RCT is not just used as a tool to justify government intervention. Indeed, it is often linked very closely to ideologies favouring market solutions and small government.

The applications of rational choice themes are extensive, often (but not always) because they are based on an intuitively appealing negative image of human beings that prompts inquiry into how to deal with them. It prompts the big questions in political science: how can we get people to cooperate for the common good (if it exists)? Should governments coerce people to pay for public goods? Do governments perform better than markets? Do we need big or small government? It leads to specific questions about institutions and how people operate within them: how do we deal with politicians who take money from businesses seeking preferential treatment? How can we hold people to account when they deliver public services? It also prompts policy-specific questions. The standard textbook question is 'how do we stop selfish people polluting the earth or over-exploiting natural resources?' but the reach of RCT is much further, including for example: what policies can deter terrorists (Sandler and Enders, 2004) and other criminals (Wright *et al.*, 2004)? We might also consider how the nature of the policy area affects the problem. For example, issues such as environmental policy may produce larger collective action problems when governments (and non-governmental actors) have a great need to cooperate to reach a unified policy but also a greater incentive to free ride on the efforts of others. In contrast, areas such as public health may display common problems that all must address (as well as strong professional networks that foster cooperation across jurisdictions), but global collective action may not be as important since policy need not be identical or made in the same way (think tobacco, alcohol or obesity policy rather than infectious disease control).

What does rational mean? What is rational choice? What is rational choice theory?

Instrumental – serving as a means to an end.

The most basic definition of rationality refers to the ability to apply logic and reason. There may also be some assumption about the *type* of reasoning; much of the history of Western philosophy regards what counts as valid and invalid reasoning (Oaksford and Chatter, 2007: 2). Rational choice theory has a rather neat solution to this problem – it assumes that actors have the ability to apply reason **instrumentally**. Rationality refers to how choices are made to serve particular ends, based on an actor's desires or *preferences* and her beliefs regarding how best to fulfil them

Utility – the satisfaction gained from fulfilling one's preferences (e.g. consuming a good or service).

(note: the preferences themselves are no guide to rationality – rationality refers to the way in which the person seeks to realize them). This is when it becomes tempting to deduce that rationality refers to the pursuit of self-interest since the 'end' or outcomes may be the maximization of **utility**.

There are two key qualifications to this statement. First, self-interest is a slippery concept since people may, for example, protect their families or give to charity to satisfy their preferences. Self-interest may not mean 'selfish in the ordinary sense of that word' (Shepsle and Bonchek, 1997: 16). Rational actors may be *egotistical* (self-centred) rather than *egoistical* (selfish) in the sense that they view the world from their own perspective and form preferences based on their interpretation of it (Dowding and King, 1995: 13–14). The main point to hold onto is that people have an order of preferences and they act to fulfil them, whatever those preferences may be. Second, self-interest is not what rational choice refers to. Rather, it describes how choices are made. In the most abstract models this involves two elements which Hindmoor (2006a: 182; compare with Tsebelis, 1990: 18) describes as 'axiomatic' and 'optimizing'. The axiomatic approach assumes that choices are 'rank-ordered' and 'transitive' (Griggs, 2007: 174). Rank-ordered means that actors can compare all their preferences and establish a hierarchy from most to least important. Transitive means that preferences are consistent in the sense that if A is preferred to B and B to C then A is preferred to C (preferences must also be 'reflexive', meaning that if my preference is x then I must prefer x or be indifferent to x and x – see Dowding, 2010 for a better explanation). The optimizing approach assumes that individuals will display optimizing behaviour. For example, a textbook assumption in microeconomics is that individuals have perfect information and no limitations on their ability to process or understand it – allowing them to pursue their preferences in an optimal way (this is now a much less common assumption in political science). If we employ both of these elements we can say that rational actors will make the best possible choices on the basis of their preferences and beliefs (reference is often made to Davidson's (1980) triangle of belief, desire and action; if we know two of them we can predict the third (Dowding, 1991; Parsons, 2005: 9; compare with Hindess, 1988: 89)).

The role of game theory and its relevance to public policy

Game theory furthers 'first principles' RCT by identifying collective action problems and prompting us to examine how institutions and public policies are created to address them. It examines the choices that actors make when situated within a strategic decision-making environment and faced with a particular set of 'payoffs' and the need to anticipate the choices of other actors. In the simplest games the assumptions are that all 'players' are instrumentally rational, each player knows that the others are rational, everyone understands the rules of the game and the payoff from each choice, and that everyone would make the same choice in the same circumstances (Hindmoor, 2006a: 106–7). Other games may introduce greater levels of uncertainty or different assumptions about the motivations of actors (see Box 7.3 on nested games; Harsanyi, 1986: 90; Chwaszcza, 2008: 154). The aim is to identify points of equilibrium when actors make a choice and stick to it, such as the 'Nash equilibrium' when players have made their best choice and there is no incentive to change behaviour. Note that 'best choice' refers to the 'best counter-strategy to what one expects the other person(s)' choice will be' rather than a choice which necessarily produces the best overall outcome (Chwaszcza, 2008: 145; what if we cannot tell what is the best choice? See Elster, 1986: 17).

The most famous example is the 'prisoner's dilemma'. While there are various discussions of the exact circumstances (I draw on Laver, 1997: 45–6), the basic premise is that two people are caught red-handed and arrested for a minor crime, placed in separate rooms and invited to confess to a major crime (the assumption is that they both did it and the

Box 7.3   Nested games

Tsebelis (1990) posits that the behaviour of individuals often seems suboptimal in one game until we take into account their involvement in a series of other games; it may be optimal to act 'irrationally' in the short term to support a longer-term strategy. For example, we may vote for a competing candidate in one round to ensure that one's preferred candidate has a better chance of success in the next (1990: 2). A constituency selection committee may reject a candidate (and lose a representative in Parliament in the short term) to establish a reputation and ensure better candidates in the long term (1990: 154). A Member of Parliament in a consociational political system (one that guarantees the representation of certain groups, to manage social conflict) can appear to 'lose control' of the people she represents in the short term to improve her position in parliament in the long term (1990: 174). The wider theme is that these games are played out differently if they are connected to other games. One may act differently in one game if one knows that there are consequences in another. This point applies to our prisoner's dilemma – it may be optimal to cooperate (stay silent) unilaterally if it ensures subsequent entry into the mafia rather than death. This suggests that the payoffs in Table 7.1 may not be accurate (1990: 8), since defection (confession) may produce an ultimate payoff of –50, or however many years the prisoner would otherwise have lived.

Table 7.1   *The prisoner's dilemma*

		Jill	
		Stay silent	Confess
Jack	Stay silent	**−1**, −1	**−10**, 0
	Confess	**0**, −10	**−8**, −8

Notes: The shaded area represents the Nash equilibrium. Most of the numbers are minus because they represent a loss (a deduction from Jack or Jill's life as free people), but be careful – many RCT analyses suggest that the numbers are *ordinal*; they tell us the order of preference but not that one outcome is, say, eight times as good as another.

police know it but can't prove it). The payoffs, as set out in Table 7.1, are as follows: if Jack confesses and Jill doesn't, then Jack walks free and Jill receives a ten-year jail sentence (and vice versa); if both confess they receive a much higher sentence (eight years) than if neither confesses (one year). The point of the game is to demonstrate a collective action problem: although the best outcome for the group requires that neither confess (both would go to jail for one year), the actual outcome is that both confess (and spend eight years each in jail). This point represents the Nash equilibrium since neither would be better off by changing their strategy unilaterally (assuming that they derive no utility from the shorter sentence of the other person – i.e. it is a *non-cooperative* game). To demonstrate, consider the incentives for Jack to act in anticipation of Jill's action, regardless of whether or not they agree to cooperate with each other: if he expects Jill to stay silent then his best choice is to confess and walk free (rather than stay silent and receive one year in jail); if he expects Jill to confess, his best choice is to confess and receive eight years (rather than stay silent and receive ten years). The incentives for Jill are identical and so both are driven to confess. The effect of Jack and Jill both acting rationally as individuals is that they are worse off than if they had cooperated successfully. In broader game-theoretical terms, both 'defect' when they should 'cooperate'.

In other scenarios the structure and payoffs of the game affect the preferences, and therefore the decisions, of actors differently. For example, in the 'chicken game', in which we imagine two people driving towards each other, there are greater costs when both defect (both crash and die) and therefore more likelihood that at least one will cooperate (by getting out of the other's way); in many 'assurance games' there is a greater benefit to unilateral cooperation and/ or a greater expectation by each player that the other will also cooperate (see John, 1998: 120–1; Hindmoor, 2006a: 109–11; Dowding and King, 1995: 8; Chwaszcza, 2008: 154; McLean, 1987: 127; Parsons, 2005: 21). Yet, individuals are not driven *inevitably* to cooperate.

These games may seem too detached from reality since few of us are criminals or recreationally reckless drivers (although most of us have seen cop shows in which prisoners might, say, confess the first time but stay silent the next). Luckily, we also have the 'tragedy of the commons'. The scenario is that a group of farmers share a piece of land which can only support so many cattle before deteriorating and becoming useless to all. Although each farmer recognizes the collective benefit to an overall maximum number of cattle, each calculates that the marginal benefit she derives from one extra cow for herself exceeds the marginal cost of over-grazing to the group. The tragedy is that if all farmers act on the same calculation then the common resource will be destroyed (Hardin, 1968: 1244). This may be a particular problem when the collective group is so large that it is difficult to track individual behaviour and so the ability to free ride is significant.

This problem is relevant to a wide variety of instances in which resources are scarce because the world's population is rising, there is no likelihood of a scientific solution, and a collective response is necessary but unlikely to be achieved without a degree of 'mutual coercion, mutu-ally agreed upon' (Hardin, 1968: 1247; Ostrom, 1990: 3). For example, we may value clean air and unpolluted water but feel that our small con-tribution to pollution will make minimal difference – much like the child who pees in the swimming pool. We may value the idea of a national parks, bountiful crops and sustainable fishing stocks but feel that our exploitation of those resources will make little difference. However, as anyone who has inadvertently tasted swimming pool water will testify, the aggregate effect of that feeling and selfish action by everyone is that the resource is spoiled. The same can be said for impending environ-mental crises. As a group we may fear global warming. As individuals, we contribute to the problem by burning fuel to keep warm, feed our-selves and produce goods and services (Sandler, 1997; 2004).

Overall, there is nothing to suggest that instrumentally rational indi-viduals have an incentive to cooperate even if it is in their interests and they agree to do so. This is a point related by Olson (1971: 2) to groups: 'unless the number of individuals in a group is quite small, or unless there is coercion or some other special device to make individuals act in their common interest, *rational, self-interested individuals will not act to achieve their common or group interests*'. These are dynamite conclu-sions that at one time would have blown out of the water 'the liberal idea that cooperation naturally follows from mutual interests' (John, 1998: 122). In the past they would have satisfied a key aim of rational choice analysis: to produce counter-intuitive (but plausible) results that force us to challenge our deeply held assumptions. The fact that they no longer seem counter-intuitive is a testament to the influence of rational choice analysis in political science. In effect, we are now faced with an intuitively appealing collective action problem that has a direct bearing on our study of public policy.

The relevance of rational choice theory to public policy

We may describe the initial collective action problem as follows:

1 There are situations in which the behaviour of rational individuals produces sub-optimal outcomes; the aggregate level of utility for a group (and each individual within it) would be higher if all individuals cooperated.
2 This can occur even when individuals are acting 'optimally' (i.e. it may not be a problem based on a lack of information or cognitive ability).
3 The solution is to give individuals the incentive to act in the 'collective' (and, as a consequence, their own) interest.

Institutional rational choice is built on the basic premise that: (a) each decision-making situation provides particular incentives for individuals to act; and (b) institutions, as formal and informal rules, can be used to change those incentives. However, the decision to create institutions is not straightforward. It depends on the context, our ability to influence individuals, our views on the extent to which people should be forced to act in the collective interest (*if it can be identified*) and the costs and unintended consequences of any solution. For example, if it proves 'irrational' to vote, should we provide incentives or oblige people to vote? If the outcome of individual private choices is 'market failure', should there be a role for government (and what should its role be)? Should we force or encourage people to recycle, conserve fuel, look after their health and obey the law? If the outcome of states acting rationally is that problems such as global warming and environmental damage are not solved, what should be the role of international agreements, laws and organizations?

Clearly, this is as much a normative as an empirical question (see also Box 7.4 on p. 147). In turn, much depends on how we 'frame' the problem – for example, as the logical solution to the collective action problem or as a solution that is much worse than the problem. Consider the contrast between the innocuous picture painted by Hardin's (1968: 1247) phrase 'mutual coercion, mutually agreed upon' (see also

McLean's 1987: 29–30 discussion of political entrepreneurs) and the image of a **Leviathan** which, although charged with enforcing collective agreements, uses its power to exploit its subjects 'without mercy for personal profit' (Laver, 1997: 43). It is presumably on the basis of the latter image that many RCT proponents seek solutions in terms of individual incentives rather than state determined outcomes (Hindmoor, 2006a: 4). As Ostrom (1990: 12) discusses, it could involve solving common resource problems by 'privatizing' them and assigning property rights. For example, individuals could invest in fencing equipment and the commons could be subdivided to remove any incentive to overgraze. However, it could also involve individuals seeking agreements with each other that could be enforced by a private rather than state authority – the commons would remain common and farmers would observe each other's behaviour and report defections to the third party that everyone pays for and agrees to respect (1990: 17). For Ostrom (1990: 20–2), the theoretical aim is to identify the conditions that have to be met for some groups to organize themselves to solve a collective action problem without state coercion, while the empirical aim is to identify concrete examples of this process.

Institutions, markets or collective agreements: what are the issues?

In this context, the first point to consider is that when the assumptions of game theory are modified the nature of the problem changes. In particular, the prisoner's dilemma is initially treated as a one-off decision, but in repeated games the players may know that there are longer-term consequences to defection. For example, the knowledge that player 2 will pursue a **tit-for-tat strategy** could provide player 1 with the incentive to cooperate (Axelrod, 1984; 1986) (or, for example, an incentive for some countries to reduce trade barriers). In other cases, high levels of trust and 'social capital' within particular political cultures may be used to solve collective action problems, particularly when participants share an understanding of their common interests and the costs of monitoring compliance are low (Keohane and Ostrom, 1995: 6; Ostrom, 1990; John, 1998: 124; Hindmoor, 2006a: 120–1; see Putnam 2001 on social capital). Both open up the possibility of 'anarchichal' solutions that are 'not enforced by any outside *Leviathan*' (Laver, 1997: 44).

The second point is that it is not always appropriate to coerce individual behaviour. It does not follow from Olson's (1971: 2) statement that *'rational, self-interested individuals will not act to achieve their common or group interests'* that they should be obliged to do so. Olson's collective action problem is that as the membership of an interest group rises so too does (a) the belief among individuals that their contribution to the group would make little difference and (b) their ability to free ride. While I may applaud the actions of an interest group, I can enjoy the outcomes without leaving my sofa, paying them or worrying that they will fail without me (the same argument applies to unions or notional groups such as the working class). Further, in a large group there is little role for strategies such as 'tit-for-tat' because I am unlikely to interact with those I do not cooperate with (Chwaszcza, 2008: 156–7; compare with McLean, 1987: 177–9). Thus, unless being an active member is beneficial ('process utility' could relate to the pleasing adrenaline of a protest, a feeling of moral superiority over less active citizens or the benefits of coffee mornings), group leaders must come up with other ways to persuade people to join (note the exception of trade union 'closed shops' and that many groups survive with patronage and without members – Jordan and Maloney, 1996: 674). Such 'supply side' solutions include 'selective incentives', or the provision of a benefit that only members can enjoy (the usual examples are silly mugs or discounts for services, but it could also refer to the commitment of a union to protect individual members).

The third point is that collective action problems may present a convincing argument for the role of 'institutions' but that institutions can come in many forms and encourage many types of behaviour, from the mere enforcement of norms to the development of governing institutions with considerable powers to tax and spend on public services (Dowding and King, 1995: 10).

Social choice theory

The fourth point is that we should not assume that an institutional solution can produce an *optimal* social or collective outcome. There are *always* winners and losers when policymakers make choices. Some preferences will be satisfied, while others will not. Indeed, a key theme of this book is power and agenda setting; the power to draw attention to some problems at the expense of others to make sure that scarce policymaking resources are directed to particular issues. Governments don't solve everyone's problems; they solve some, ignore some, and make others worse off. The best way to understand the wider analytical point is to begin with the idea that no voting system can aggregate individual preferences to satisfy the collective will unproblematically (McLean,

Intransitive – when preferences are not consistent. If A is preferred to B and B to C, A is not necessarily preferred to C.

1987: 10, 26). Instead, there is considerable potential for instability related to **intransitive** electoral results and policy decisions, or 'the selection of candidates or policies to which there are majority-preferred alternatives' (Riker, 1982; Hindmoor, 2006a: 80–7; Ward, 2002: 66; see also Ward and Weale, 2010). For example, a majority vote results in outcome A, only for us to find that the majority would prefer option C. There is no such thing as a 'public will' or 'national interest' that we can determine by merely adding up the opinions or preferences of the population.

For our purposes, its most famous illustration is the 'Arrow problem' (or impossibility theorem) (Dewan *et al.*, 2009: xxi). The context is the aim of welfare economics to explore our ability to maximize social welfare based on the welfare of individuals: *can some policies make everyone better off?* Two concepts are particularly relevant. The first is Pareto efficiency or optimality, which describes a point at which no one can be made better off without someone being worse off. This concept signalled a departure in economics from the assumption that society was inevitably better if overall levels of utility were higher. Instead, a 'Pareto improvement' only occurs if the overall rise did not make someone worse off. The second, Kaldor–Hicks compensation criterion is based on the argument that a change can appear to be Pareto inefficient but still appealing if: (a) the winner gains more than the loser loses; and (b) can compensate the loser while still gaining overall. If the winner compensates the loser fully, then the overall outcome is Pareto efficient. This argument relies on our assumption that the utility gained by one individual can be compared meaningfully to the utility lost by another (by measuring each individual's 'willingness to pay' for each outcome – see Just *et al.*, 2004: 6-7; Arrow, 1963: 4).

This is the context for Arrow (1963), who seeks to establish if any rule to aggregate individual preferences into social preferences can satisfy minimal normative criteria that most of us would agree with. His discussion is based on certain assumptions – that individuals are free to rank preferences as they wish, preferences are transitive, individuals either prefer one option to another or are indifferent, and that individuals only consider relevant or feasible choices – and the normative criterion that social choice is determined according to the preferences of all individual preferences rather than dictatorship (in which the preference of one individual represents the social choice). Notably, Arrow's theorem is based on a rejection of the ability to produce the interpersonal comparisons of utility necessary for Kaldor–Hicks compensation (Arrow, 1963: 59). On this basis, Arrow's finding is that no decision rule can be produced to satisfy his normative criteria (see also Dewan *et al.*, 2009: xxi; Hindmoor, 2006a: 83–4). It therefore undermines 'the idea that democracy is the implementation of the popular will represented by a social preference ranking' (Ward, 2002: 66). Instead, it is about policymakers making choices they know will benefit some and disadvantage others.

Institutions and unintended outcomes: bureaucracies and rent seeking

The final point is that we should not even assume that an institutional solution will produce a *better* outcome. Institutional solutions are costly and, ironically, may produce collective action and/or principal–agent problems. The first example refers to the strategies of civil servants (see Horn, 1995 for an extension of the principal–agent discussion to other public bodies). Niskanen (1971; 1975, building on Downs, 1967) argues that the supply of public services is inefficient when bureaucrats seek to maximize their own utility (in this case inefficient means that more costly services will be provided than by an equivalent provider in a competitive private sector). Most determinants of utility (salary, prestige, power, ease of implementing policy) increase in proportion to a department's budget. Therefore, bureaucrats will push for incremental increases in their budgets and will often be successful (particularly when only they can provide the services). While the 'principal' contracts the service and seeks to oversee its delivery, only the 'agent' knows how much it costs (note the US-centric assumption of bureaucratic oversight here; in the UK, departments are overseen by a powerful Treasury – Dowding, 1995c: 62).

Niskanen's work is remembered primarily because it was adopted by 'new right' governments keen to import private business practices to the public sector (see Box 12.1 on the global spread of 'new public management') (Hindmoor, 2006a: 152–3; Hay, 2004a: 59; Self, 1993; more important empirical work has been advanced by others – Huber, 2000; Huber and Shipan, 2002; Epstein and O'Halloran, 1999). In turn, this influenced rational choice accounts of bureaucracies. For example, one aim of Dunleavy (1985; 1991) is to explain why US and (particularly) UK governments were able to reform the civil service so significantly when previous attempts were undermined by powerful bureaucrats. In the US this was associated with reducing or freezing civil service numbers, while the UK government also 'hived off' executive agencies as part of a bigger project to inject competition in the public service (by introducing quasi-markets in healthcare, privatizing industries and contracting out many local authority and healthcare services). The answer expounded by Dunleavy (1985: 324; James, 1995) is that civil service reforms were not as inconsistent with bureaucratic self-interest as Niskanen would assume. Rather, they also value nonpecuniary advantages such as the chance to 'bureau shape' and embrace more enjoyable policy work by shuffling off responsibility for boring management tasks associated with large departments. Or, different civil servants have different preferences based on their role within the organization and the differences in payoffs to them from the same outcome – for example, 'top' civil servants were content to support privatization if it advanced their interests at the expense of the 'rank and file' (Dunleavy, 1986; John, 1998: 131–5; Marsh *et al.*, 2000; Dowding, 1995c: 79–80).

The second example is 'rent seeking' which relates to an intuitively appealing (but not necessarily accurate) notion that politicians are corrupt and that big businesses seek to bribe them to gain from policy decisions. Rent seeking is the 'investment of resources by firms and pressure groups in the expectation of securing economic privileges' (Hindmoor, 2006b: 87). It produces inefficiencies in the public and private sectors when organizations are distracted from their core activities (such as wealth creation). The argument begins with a discussion of the private sector in which we identify two types of inefficiency associated with monopolies: the cost to the consumer when companies restrict production and keep prices high; and the costs incurred by companies seeking monopoly positions (or other organizations trying to challenge them). Tullock (1967: 226–8) suggests that there are two further costs when the government creates or supports that monopoly – those associated with production when more efficient companies are blocked from entering the market (by taxes or tariffs); and, those incurred by organizations who lobby government to maintain or remove monopoly positions. Tullock's provocative parallel is the wasted cost associated with crime: the resources invested by criminals to steal and the expense of security measures to stop them. The main empirical problem is that rent seeking is difficult to identify because many group–government relations have a positive effect (Tullock, 1967: 228; 232; Hindmoor, 2006a: 163–4). To identify negative effects one must: identify and link the inefficiencies of public policy to rent seeking; show that government actors are not only selling favourable public policies to organizations but also devoting resources to framing public policies in a better light (such as when subsidies to farmers are framed as the public interest) and getting away with it (otherwise voters will punish governments that dispense favours – Dewan *et al.*, 2009: xxxiv); and show that groups are engaged in rent-seeking activity rather than providing information to improve public policy.

Both examples could be used to reinforce 'new-right' policies in favour of smaller government (employing fewer civil servants and dispensing fewer favours). Overall, it is not difficult to see the link between RCT, political individualism and an assumption against government solutions. Yet, this is not an inevitable progression. RCT merely prompts us to note that collective action problems will not be solved *unproblem-*

Box 7.4   What makes rational choice a normative theory?

There are normative elements to each approach to rationality identified in Box 7.2. While the aim of realism may have been to introduce a 'dispassionate' account of international relations, there is emphasis (particularly in 'neorealistic' accounts) on the positive role that international institutions play in addressing the anarchic international environment (Hay, 2002: 21). There is a strong normative dimension to the 'ideal' of comprehensive rationality and 'perfect implementation' (Chapters 1 and 5). We may also infer a normative dimension from economic concepts such as 'perfect competition' (which describes the conditions required to minimize prices within the market) and 'efficiency' (which entails a preferred outcome and means to achieve that outcome) which are often masked by technical language (Dowding and King, 1995: 15). In RCT, normative can refer to many things: that individuals should act rationally because otherwise they would lose out (Tsebelis, 1990: 30); the most efficient (and therefore most preferable) means to satisfy preferences (Elster, 1986: 1; compare with Moser 1990: 3); a discussion of what we should do (such as create institutions) when faced with collective action problems; or a belief by some rational choice theorists in political individualism (that the satisfaction of individual preferences should be 'the criteria by which policies and institutions are judged' – Hindmoor, 2006a: 4). Most RCT advocates appear to have a pro-market bias and an aversion to government action. Yet, Ward (2002: 67) also notes that rational choice informs the work of Rawls and Marxist thought (such as Roemer, 1988).

atically by government intervention: 'both markets and politics fail' (Buchanan, 1988: 13; see also Buchanan, 2005: 9; Hindmoor, 2006a: 178; Hindmoor, 2006b: 86).

The main debates between rational choice advocates and critics

Rational choice provokes regular debates between supporters and critics. This is partly for mundane practical reasons: both misrepresent each other's positions and many expect too much from a simple model of behaviour seeking to explain a complex political world (RCT defences are also often stated too provocatively – I outline this argument in more detail on my blog http://paulcairney.blogspot.com/2011/02/rational-choice-full-section.html). It is also because it raises one very obvious question: since people do not have the ability to behave in the way that rational choice theory suggests, why spend so much time and effort constructing a model divorced from reality? A defence of rational choice theory may come in two forms.

The first goes to the heart of how we understand science. The most robust defences of rational choice theory contrast it with the 'inductive' or 'empirical approach' which seeks to generalize from observed patterns of behaviour but, 'in the last analysis more or less says that the world is as it is because that's how it is' (Laver, 1997: 4; 10). Such accounts may be too detailed to be generalizable or too vague to ascribe explanatory power to a small number of core causal processes. Instead, rational choice theory produces models, based on a set of propositions about the real world, which can be tested by examining the extent to which their predictions are confirmed or refuted by the evidence. This requires that simplifications are made to aid deductive reasoning. In fact, as Ward (2002: 69) argues, simplification may be the main virtue of rational choice theory because: (a) the need to formalize one's argument (i.e. produce a set of rules which are abstract, or not applicable only to particular instances) forces one to be clear about one's assumptions which 'are often left implicit in verbal arguments'; and, (b) it forces us to choose what we think is most relevant and worthy of study. Further, a combination of simplification and formal logic establishes a clear link between cause and effect that can be demonstrated mathematically and then, if appropriate, used as a basis for testing empirically. This process – of model building, hypothesizing and testing – is the scientific way to decide whether or not a theory's assumptions are useful.

The second is that rational choice theory does not exclude the possibility of modifying those assumptions (and RCT has moved markedly in that direction in recent decades). Rather, different types of rational choice theory have different aims. Dowding and King (1995: 1) distinguish between 'first principles rational choice' which 'uses simplified models often with no obvious practical application to real world situations' and 'institutional rational choice' which engages with 'substantive political and social problems'. The former may be used as a way to generate models that approximate essential features of the real world and explore, deductively, the consequences of rational behaviour. The latter may be used to explore empirically the effect that specific rules, laws and norms have on the preferences and actions of individuals. Relatedly, the literature includes studies with simple and complex assumptions. A small set of simple assumptions, such as that actors optimize and that preferences are rank ordered and transitive, is 'thin'. Thickness refers to the extent to which more detailed and often specific assumptions regarding preferences and beliefs are posited (Tsebelis' (1990: 30) 'weak' assumptions also refer to consistency of preferences, while 'strength' suggests that the pursuit of such preferences in the real world will lead to optimizing behaviour). The literature also includes studies that model the effect that uncertainty and imperfect information has on the ability of individuals to pursue their preferences (compare Shepsle and Bonchek's (1997: 17–18, 33–5) upbeat solution to modelling uncertainty with those drawing on Simon's (1976) 'bounded rationality' to highlight habitual and 'satisficing' rather than maximizing behaviour – Hindess 1988: 69, 80; Parsons, 2005: 16–17, 58–62; see also Elster's 1986: 26 rejection of Simon's approach). But the decision to modify assumptions comes at a price and demonstrates the same basic trade-off in the sciences: between explaining a lot with a little or explaining a little with a lot. There is room in the social sciences for attempts to generalize across many cases or attempts to explain one case in great detail.

The consequence is that the validity of criticisms of rational choice theory varies. In particular, the statement that a model's assumptions are unrealistic is less relevant to 'first principles' discussions when the aim is to specify the results of hypothetical situations when certain conditions are met (Chwaszcza, 2008: 139). This approach is also less susceptible to criticism that its predictions are not borne out by the evidence because models may be better assessed according to their ability to highlight important causal processes deductively – formulating abstract propositions, establishing a logical relationship between propositions and considering their implications (Laver, 1997: 4, 11). A simple example is the 'paradox of non-voting' which suggests that the costs of voting (time, expense, inconvenience) are likely to exceed the benefits when the likelihood of an individual tipping the balance is miniscule and they can free ride instead. According to Green and Shapiro (1994: 50) this damages rational choice theory because the prediction of the model – people will not vote – is refuted by the evidence. Yet, this seems unfair if the initial aim of the model – to identify paradoxical behaviour or consequences – has been met. As Dowding (1991: 21) puts it, a part of any model's usefulness 'may result from the discrepancies between it and the real-life situation'. Similarly, Ward (2002: 70) suggests that the identification of outcomes based on the actions of the 'instrumentally rational, self-interested self' can be used as a 'standard ... against which actual behaviour can be compared' (such as when outcomes are influenced by the alternative, 'socially oriented, norm-driven self'; see also Laver, 1997: 9, but compare with Hindess, 1988: 52, 98–9). RCT raises questions that would not otherwise have been asked (Dowding, in correspondence).

The extent to which models explain real-world behaviour is more relevant to *substantive* rational choice accounts. In this vein, the most prominent critics are Green and Shapiro (1994: 179; see also Parsons, 2005: 51–2, 125–31; Udehn, 1996), who argue that the 'empirical contributions of rational choice theory' are 'few' and 'far between'. Rational choice accounts do not demonstrate: why people vote (1994: 68); that people 'free ride' (1994: 74); that intransitive policy preferences produce instability in public policy (1994: 111); or, why candidates stake out non-centrist electoral positions (1994: 169; there is also little evidence

Box 7.5   Wider rational choice applications in political science

Hindmoor (2006a) outlines a wide range of examples, including:

1 *Political business cycles*. The intuitive claim is that the popularity of incumbent governments relies heavily on the state of the economy and that they will seek to manipulate the economic cycle to make sure that it is booming before an election. Schultz (1995: 79–80) argues that there is little evidence to confirm this claim, in part because these strategies have longer term costs – both to the economy and the government's reputation – that popular governments do not need to bear. Therefore, the more popular a government appears to be before an election, the less likely it is to attempt to manipulate the economy (1995: 81; Hindmoor, 2006a: 46–7). John (1998: 128) suggests that this refined model demonstrates the value of empirical rational choice – only by testing the original theory, rejecting it and then confirming a new theory empirically did our understanding of this process progress (for a wider discussion of RCT and economic policy see Mueller, 2003: chapter 19).

2 *Riker's minimal winning coalition*. Self-interested politicians in political parties, primarily driven to seek office (or the power, prestige and income it entails), will seek to maximize the number of cabinet posts they control by attempting to form a minimum winning coalition (defined as half of the majority of parliamentary seats plus one) with one or more other party. The fact that this accounts for only one-third of all relevant instances in Western Europe contributed to a shift in explanation from office-seeking to policy-seeking. Models exploring a policy-seeking incentive often suggest that centre parties are pivotal and extreme parties might be excluded from coalitions (other parties would rather form a surplus coalition with a party closest to their views than minimal winning with a party with significantly divergent views) (see Hindmoor, 2006a: 56–8). Strøm (1990: 56; 69; 73) extends the policy-seeking assumption to argue that minority governments are more likely to form when the power of parliaments is high and opposition parties can pursue policies in opposition while waiting for incumbent governments to lose popularity.

3 *Party competition*. Political parties will compete in the centre ground to maximize their chances of election when certain conditions are met – including that there are two parties, there is only one dimension to voting choice (picture a simple left/right wing continuum), parties can move to any point on the continuum and there is 'perfect information' (2006a: 27). When these conditions are not met, we can say that there is a *tendency* towards the middle ground that is interrupted by factors such as the complexity of voting choice and the lack of information on what represents the centre ground. While this intuitively appealing model is difficult to demonstrate empirically (McLean, 1987: 52–3), Hindmoor (2006a: 47) suggests that this model is useful normatively because it demonstrates an incentive for political parties to 'formulate policies in order to please the voters rather than to please themselves'.

supporting Niskanen's model – compare John, 1998: 135 and Parsons, 1995: 311 with Dowding, 1995c: 55–65). Green and Shapiro (2005: 54) argue that RCT tends to be 'method-driven', not 'problem-driven'. In other words, instead of seeking to explain why policy decisions were made and what the outcomes were, it starts with RCT and seeks to explore its value. It is increasingly mathematically and methodologically sophisticated but decreasingly relevant to real world policy problems.

A more sympathetic reading of rational choice suggests that the empirical confirmation of a model's predictions will always be problematic and that Green and Shapiro are holding rational choice theory up to a standard that no other theory lives up to (John, 1998: 141; Ward, 2002: 83; Laver, 1997: 14–15). Further, rational choice models are built on the *ceteris paribus* assumption; that X will occur if all other things remain equal (or can be held constant or to have no effect) (Hindmoor, 2006a: 205). Yet, the social world is incredibly complex and difficult to predict; many factors do not remain equal. As a result, rational choice can only demonstrate a *tendency* towards particular behaviour (or an increase in the probability of certain behaviour). When such behaviour is apparent, rational choice theory can provide a convincing explanation of why it occurs (2006a: 212). Or, models can offer 'conditional predictions' rather than 'prophesies' (Hay, 2004a: 57; Dowding, 2001: 92). This does not necessarily mean that rational choice explanations have 'failed' (Hindess, 1988: 3) empirically if we do not believe that their aim is to explain all policy outcomes.

Conclusion

There is no chapter in this book that assesses a theory in terms of its ability to explain all or even most political life. Rather, our aim is to assess their usefulness and ultimately, the extent to which their merits can somehow be combined. In this spirit, we see that rational choice theory has a lot to offer. Ward (2002: 65) describes it as 'an indispensable part of the toolkit of political scientists', but one which relies on other theories to answer questions that it does not address directly: 'why individuals have the interests they do, how they perceive those interests, and the distribution of rules, powers and social roles that determines the constraints on their actions'. This position is consistent with our multiple theories approach.

But what direct application does RCT have to the study of public policy and real world policy problems? John (1998: 117; see also Hay, 2004: 46–50) suggests that detailed, empirical rational choice applications to public policy are rare because it is difficult to apply parsimonious explanations based on a small number of actors to a field characterized by 'inherently messy circumstances'. Yet, the *issues raised* by RCT inform many empirical studies. Indeed, RCT informs most aspects of public policy: the responsiveness of parties to voter preferences, the rules of government formation (including the effect that parliament has on policy), the power of bureaucracies, the formation and behaviour of interest groups, the extent to which institutions should be used to solve collective action problems and the inability of governments to make optimal decisions on behalf of their populations. Much comes down to whether we seek a general or a specific description or explanation of events and the price we are willing to pay for theoretical parsimony and reductionism (compare Hindess, 1988: 115 with Laver, 1997: 11–12). Further, the fact that collective action problems are often solved, or people do not always act in a self-interested manner (or even succeed in fulfilling their preferences when they do so) does not negate the value of this analysis. Rather, 'what if?' questions and the identification of tendencies towards particular behaviours and outcomes are essential to wider explanations of complex events.

Rational choice theory has, perhaps more than most, the potential to perform a normative prompt in public policy, prompting questions such as: how can we get people to cooperate for the common good (if it exists)? Do we need big or small government? How can we hold people to account when they deliver public services? RCT can be used to explore the consequences of our realization that government solutions may be expensive, cannot be 'optimal' and can produce unintended consequences. Rational-choice-inspired solutions are largely associated with new-right ideology and either a complete suspicion of governmental solutions to collective action problems (associated with the 'rolling back of the state') or the introduction of new public management techniques based on the assumption that public sector workers are self-interested and therefore need to be given the right incentives to act (as symbolized by the use of targets). The pervasiveness of NPM is explored in Chapter 12. Yet, RCT should not be seen as an inevitable inspiration for new right thinking. For example, Brennan (1996: 258–9; see also Hindmoor, 2006b: 94) questions the need to assume that all public sector workers are purely self-interested 'knaves' (a subject explored by Le Grand (2003) drawing on the work of David Hume). Further, Ostrom's work (1990) demonstrates the potential for non-market solutions to collective action problems based on trust and less impositional means (than institutions) to minimize the costs of monitoring and enforcing collective agreements. This approach has proved increasingly influential, winning Ostrom the Nobel Prize for economics in 1999 and demonstrating the direct policy relevance of RCT into the bargain.

The issues raised by rational choice are also directly applicable to our comparison, raised in the introductory chapter, between discussions of comprehensive rationality as an ideal form of decision making and other accounts which begin at the other end of the spectrum, stressing the messy nature of real public policymaking and exploring the extent to which we can make sense of this muddle. With regards to the former, the most directly applicable lesson comes from social choice theory and the simple argument that, because there will always be winners and losers when policymakers make choices, it is unrealistic to seek a rational-synoptic or technical solution to conflicts of preferences within society. With regards to the latter, several chapters explore the consequences when policy problems go beyond the boundaries of political systems and become hostages to complex decision-making arrangements that may undermine central control and simple institutional responses. They require new ways to solve collective action problems. Chapters 11 and 12 explore the role of factors such as the enforcement of norms and coercive policy transfer, but rational choice suggests that collective action problems may be exacerbated as well as solved by such measures.

Chapter 8

Multi-Level Governance

This chapter examines:

- How we define governance.
- The 'governance problem' as an unintended consequence of policy-making.
- How we pin down the meaning of multi-level governance.
- The applicability of MLG to the UK, EU and other political systems;
- The links between MLG and studies of federalism.
- The links between MLG and other theories such as punctuated equilibrium.

Multi-level governance describes the dispersion of power from national central government to other levels of government (hence multi-level) and non-governmental actors (hence govern*ance* rather than govern*ment*). The hook is that we are witnessing a major transformation in our object and focus of study: from national governing institutions to supranational and sub-national governing institutions; and, from central government to the different levels of government and non-governmental organizations that interact with them. MLG identifies blurred boundaries between formal and informal sources of authority which make it difficult to identify clear-cut decisions or power relations. In the international arena, it suggests that it is difficult to identify sovereignty within national governments. Rather, they are tied increasingly to the policies agreed between states and implemented by international organizations. In the domestic arena, the interdependence between public and private actors (and levels of government which share responsibility) suggests that governments do not rely solely on formal decision-making powers. Instead, they may choose (or be forced) to 'steer' rather than 'row', negotiating the delivery of public services with a range of organizations, when in the past they delivered them directly.

To some extent, MLG applies to particular political systems. For example, it began as a way to describe and explain major developments in the European Union policy process. The role of the EU (or the importance of agreements made and institutions established by member states) has become increasingly important, producing the need for new ways to conceptualize the policy process. MLG provides a new perspective to view key changes such as qualified majority voting and structural policy reform. It also helps us capture the true nature of policymaking in unitary and centralized systems such as the UK and France. For example in the UK, we can contrast the 'Westminster model' image of a strong, centralized state which acts unilaterally with MLG's image of a segmented, disaggregated state which is forced to share power and negotiate with other political actors (Bache and Flinders, 2004a: 38). Combined, MLG may be most useful to chart the fate of once-centralized-unitary, but now Europeanized, devolved and 'quasi-federal' political systems.

Yet, the themes raised by MLG are more widely applicable. In particular, MLG helps us compare the policy process in the EU with federal systems which have long enjoyed a separation of powers between the executive, legislative and judicial branches, and devolved power to subnational governments and policy specific jurisdictions. Further, MLG's reliance on the policy networks literature to describe the blurry boundaries between formal power and informal influence ties it to key theories of policymaking, such as punctuated equilibrium and the advocacy coalition framework, that began in the US before being applied to systems such as the EU and UK. In other words, a focus on MLG allows us to compare not only different political systems but also different theories of policymaking within those systems. MLG also extends our focus on the shift from a unified authority, acting rationally at the centre of government, towards a diffusion of power and 'multiple centres'. The world of government is changing, and theories such as MLG attempt to capture that change.

One consequence of this wide applicability is that MLG often seems like a rather woolly concept (Box 8.1) or a term used to bring together a wide range of studies with different assumptions and objects of study. For example, 'type 1' refers to a relatively clear separation of powers by territory (local, regional, national, supranational) while 'type 2' refers to the more complex diffusion of power according to policy issue, involving a wide range of organizations across various levels of government and the public and private sectors (Hooghe and Marks, 2003). The variation makes our normative discussions of policymaking (should there be MLG?) rather complicated. We may welcome MLG in systems such as the US and Switzerland which contain a plethora of planned, elected bodies. However, we may be less certain about systems such as the UK (and, to some extent, the EU) in which power often seems to be shared with bodies with less accountability following the unintended consequences of decisions made in the past.

We focus initially on the UK for two main reasons. First, the concept of a governance problem developed in the UK to describe a wide range of (intended and unintended) changes to politics and policymaking. Second, multi-level governance is best described analytically in contrast to its polar opposite, the 'Westminster model', which describes and explains a concentration of power in central government. The more realistic description of

---

Box 8.1   Key descriptions of (multi-level) governance

These quotations give a flavour of the woolly or 'slippery' nature of governance and MLG. We know that MLG refers to multi-level policymaking. We know that there may be blurry boundaries between formal and informal action, or between those formally responsible for policy and those who influence it. However, we also know that different texts describe the process in rather different ways or express doubt about their ability to go beyond the identification of fluid and unpredictable policy relationships:

> A system of continuous negotiation among nested governments at several territorial tiers – supranational, national, regional and local. (Marks, 1993: 392)

> We no longer have a mono-centric or unitary government; there is not one but many centres linking many levels of government – local, regional, national and supranational. (Rhodes 1997: 1)

> Governing issues generally are not just public or private, they are frequently shared, and governing activity at all levels (from local to supra-national) is becoming diffused over various societal actors whose relationships with each other are constantly changing. (Kooiman, 2003: 3)

> A key tenet of multi-level governance is the dispersal of authority and decision-making to a wide range of bodies through a process of negotiation. The net effect is that policy-making has been transformed from being state-centred and state-driven activity to become a complex mix of hierarchies, networks and markets. (Richards and Smith, 2004)

> While there is a view that states are losing control in the context of governance, the alternative view focuses on new state strategies for coping with the challenge of governance. (Bache and Flinders, 2004a: 36).

---

the UK as a quasi-federal state which shares power with other bodies shows us that the formal institutional differences outlined in Chapter 4 are less and less applicable to modern policymaking. Instead, policy styles are often very similar and the same theories can be used to compare policy-making processes across a wide range of countries. The *term* 'multi-level governance' may not be used much outside the EU, but the *processes it describes* are common features of many political systems.

What is governance?

Governance has numerous meanings. In the public policy literature, the term has been used to describe a range of practices or conditions, including:

- *A reduction of the size of the state.*
- *Good governance.* In the corporate world this refers to full disclosure, integrity and accountability, linked to the clarity of roles for managers. In government, these aims are combined with a diffusion of power to the judiciary and external auditors, a free press and respect for human rights.
- *The use of new public management.* NPM is the application of private sector ideas to the public sector. It includes setting standards of performance and gauging success by results, accountability to the 'customer', contracting out services and introducing quasi-markets in the public sector.
- *The 'socio-cybernetic system'.* Central government is one part of a wider system of governance which includes local and health authorities, quasi-non-governmental organizations (quangos – see Macleavy and Gay, 2005), and the private and voluntary sectors.
- *Policy networks.* Policymakers in government come together with other public and private sector actors to negotiate and make shared decisions. These networks are described as 'self-organizing' to reflect the government's limited capacity to control them (Rhodes, 1997: 46–53; Rhodes, 2006b).
- *Global governance.* The rise in importance of international organizations and agreements to reflect globalization and the growing interdependence between states (Box 8.2) (Kjaer, 2004).

Two related characteristics are most relevant to our purposes. First, there is interdependence between public and private organizations. Power is shared between actors formally responsible for making decisions and those they consult and negotiate with. Governments form policy networks with a range of interest groups and implementing organizations willing to trade their expertise and support for influence in the decision-making process. As a result, public policy is the 'joint product of their interaction' (Rose, 1987: 267–8). Second, governments often have the authority but not the capacity to make and carry out their own policies. They can influence but not control the networks of organizations that implement policy.

The governance problem

Both characteristics combine to create a new governance 'problem' which relates to the diminished ability of central governments to control the direction of policy (compare with discussions of implementation in Chapter 2). To some extent this problem has been created (or exacerbated) by governments when shifting 'the balance between government

---

Box 8.2 Global governance

Many of the world's major problems, such as climate change, economic crises and pandemics are 'transnational' and require some degree of cooperation across governments (Weiss, 2009: 254). Global governance, 'refers to collective efforts to identify, understand, or address worldwide problems that go beyond the capacities of individual states to solve; it reflects the capacity of the international system ... to provide government-like services' (2009: 257; see also Finkelstein, 1995; Slaughter, 2004). The concept of global governance suggests that the study of MLG shares similar concerns with studies of international relations. In many cases the difference is only linguistic. For example, in this chapter we ask: what is the 'Westminster model' and how does MLG compare? The WM describes a concentration of power at the centre and a high degree of state autonomy, while MLG describes the diffusion of power, multiple 'centres' and a form of integration that undermines sovereignty and autonomy. It ties in neatly with key concerns of IR, including: are states sovereign or interdependent? Is power centralized within states or shared with other levels and types of government and international organizations? In IR we can substitute the WM with neorealism. Neorealism treats the internal workings of states as 'black boxes', subordinating the importance of domestic political processes. It assumes that states are rational actors which exercise power according to self-interest in an anarchical international environment.

Both realism and the WM are challenged by new patterns of global politics in which power is increasingly diffused to supranational organizations, there is more international cooperation and interdependence, there is a rise of non-governmental and 'civil society' involvement in international policy (on issues such as land mines, torture and human rights), there is a greater adherence to international norms, and policing efforts are increasingly transnational (Welch and Kennedy-Pipe, 2004; Hooghe and Marks, 2003: 234; although see Chapter 12 – a lot of this activity may be driven by a small number of governments such as the US). A related theme is complexity. MLG conjures up the image of messy politics in which many actors are involved at many levels and types of government. In the wider international sphere, 'international regime complexity' captures the idea that multiple agreements shared, and international organisations created, by states has led to a messy and confusing process of international cooperation (Alter and Meunier, 2009).

---

and society away from the public sector and more towards the private sector' (Kooiman, 1993: 1). The process is associated with 'new public management' reforms, or the transfer of private business principles to the public sector (Gray, 2000: 283–4), including:

- *Privatization.* The sale of public assets, break up of state monopolies, injection of competition, introduction of public–private partnerships for major capital projects and charging for government services (Rhodes, 1994: 139; Goldsmith and Page, 1997: 150).

- *The introduction of 'quasi-markets'.* In the absence of privatization, internal markets may be introduced in which one part of the public sector competes with another for the 'business' of commissioning agencies (Day and Klein, 2000; Cairney, 2002; Wistow, 1992; Greer, 2004).

- *The reform of the civil service.* It includes attempts to make civil servants more accountable by giving them more responsibility to manage their own budgets, and separating the policymaking and delivery functions in government departments by hiving off the latter and creating executive agencies (Greer, 1994: 6; O'Toole and Jordan, 1995: 3–5; Massey, 2001: 21; OPSR, 2002).

- *The increased use of quangos* – public bodies sponsored by government, but operating at 'arms length' from elected policymakers and administratively separate from government (Greenwood *et al*, 2001: 153–7; Stoker, 2004: 32).

Much of the governance literature uses these developments to explain shifting policymaking processes in the UK (Hogwood, 1997: 715; Marsh, 1991; O'Toole and Jordan, 1995: 9–10; Cairney, 2002; 2009a; Richards and Smith, 2004; Flinders, 2009; DBERR, 2008: ii, 13). Yet, most of these processes can be seen worldwide. The privatization of 8,500 state-owned enterprises took place in over 80 countries between 1980 and 1992 (including Communist, post-Communist and developing countries) and the broad principles of 'new public management' are just as widespread (Box 12.1). Hooghe and Marks (2004: 15) report that a survey of 75 developing countries suggests 63 have undergone a process of decentralization (compared to half of the EU countries since 1980).

Perhaps the more significant difference in the UK is that governance is often treated as a problem created by government. In part, this problem is more apparent because public sector reforms were more radical in the UK than in many European countries (Kjaer, 2004: 35). It also *seems* more like a problem in the UK because governance compares with the 'Westminster model' (highlighting concentrated power in the executive) and suggests that the **core executive** is 'hollowing out' (Box 8.3). Peters and Pierre (2004: 78; see also Kjaer, 2004: 35; Kooiman, 1993) suggest that commentators used to centralized authority may view these new developments with suspicion. In contrast, in most European countries shared decision making is more established and welcome (compare with Lijphart's distinction between majority/consensus democracies in Chapter 4).

Core executive – the 'centre' of government, including senior ministers and the administrative arrangements which support them.

Box 8.3   Is the British state hollowing out?

Rhodes (1994; 1997) argues that the overall effect of new public management reforms (now combined with a process of devolution and Europeanization) is a decline in the capacity of central government to control public policy. The rise of new ways to deliver policy – from a unified civil service and accountable local government to a 'patchwork quilt' of quangos and non-governmental organizations – has produced service fragmentation and barriers to effective communication. It has also diminished accountability to Parliament via ministers, with much responsibility devolved to agencies, quangos and the private sector or lost to European institutions (see also Hogwood, Judge and McVicar, 2001: 97; Bevir and Rhodes, 2003: 6). However, the extent of the lack of central government control is heavily debated in political science. Many have questioned the 'hollowing out' thesis by pointing to the growing range of powers that the core executive enjoys, and exploring the extent to which changes at the centre have reinforced its power (Hogwood, 1997; Holliday, 2000; Marinetto; 2003). The government was never effective at controlling peripheral functions of the state such as the nationalized industries. Governance changes, such as privatization and civil service reforms, mark a return to core competencies, with the centre making strategic decisions and creating accountability mechanisms to ensure that these are carried out by others. In other words, we may be witnessing the shift from 'interventionist state' to 'regulatory state' (Hood *et al.*, 1999; McGarvey and Cairney, 2008: 150; see Majone, 1994 for an extension of this argument across the EU and its member states). Marsh (2008: 255; see also Marsh, Richards and Smith, 2003: 308) argues that 'strong government, although increasingly challenged' is a more realistic description than the 'hollowed-out state'. Although there is competition for power between multiple organizations, some are more powerful than others. While the government is dependent on other organizations to deliver policy, and is one of many organizations involved, it is also the most powerful organization.

Multi-level governance and the Westminster model

MLG is best described in contrast to its polar opposite, the 'Westminster model', which describes a concentration of power in central government. The WM is effectively an ideal-type (or **strawman**), useful as an analytical device to show what MLG is and *is not* (compare with Table 4.1). The main characteristics of the WM include:

Strawman – refers to the exaggeration of the properties of a concept to the point where it has become a caricature with no supporters. This makes it easier to criticize and its comparator more attractive.

• The reliance on representative, not participatory, democracy.

- The first-past-the-post electoral system which exaggerates the majority of the governing party and allows it to control Parliament.
- The power of the prime minister to control cabinet and ministers.
- A politically neutral civil service which acts according to ministerial wishes (Richards and Smith 2002: 3–4; McGarvey and Cairney, 2008: 23; Marsh *et al.*, 2001; Bevir and Rhodes, 1999).

So, power is centralized and government is top-down or 'one way traffic from those governing (the Government) to those being governed (society)' (Richards and Smith, 2002: 3). Bache and Flinders (2004a: 38) contrast this model with MLG. While the WM suggests a centralized, unitary state in which there are clear lines of accountability and hierarchical control, MLG suggests a disaggregated, quasi-federal state in which control is replaced by influence within a political system with multiple lines of accountability and uncertainty about where the 'top' (or centre) is in different situations. This loss of control is extended to the international arena, with 'absolute sovereignty' for one's foreign affairs replaced by interdependence and negotiation with other countries and international organizations. MLG therefore provides us with a new set of dictums when exploring policymaking. The diffusion of power vertically (across multiple levels of government) and horizontally (to non-state actors) suggests: negotiation not compulsion; fragmentation not centralization; and multi-level but not hierarchical relationships (see Table 8.1).

This contrast perhaps shows that it is easier to say what MLG *is not* (Jessop, 2004: 61). When we try to describe what it *is* we find different images. On the one hand, MLG could refer to a modest departure from state-centred politics in which regional and supranational governments have more powers, but in a relatively ordered system in which each level's responsibilities are fairly clear (suggesting multi-level govern-

Table 8.1 *Westminster model versus multi-level governance: key comparisons*

Westminster model	Multi-level governance
Centralized state	Disaggregated and fragmented state
Hierarchy and control	Power diffusion and negotiation
Clear lines of accountability	Blurry lines of accountability
Absolute sovereignty	Interdependence, unclear sovereignty
Unitary state	Quasi-federal state
Strong core executive	Segmented executive
Direct government	Delegated governance, 'steering' not 'rowing'

Source: Adapted from Bache and Flinders (2004a: 38).

ment). For example, the UK's devolution of powers to Scotland was accompanied by an extensive list of its responsibilities and a set of concordats to ensure that the governments coordinated their activities (McGarvey and Cairney, 2008: 2; Bache and Flinders, 2004a: 40). On the other hand, Rhodes' (1997) argument, that central government order has been replaced by a 'patchwork quilt' of organizations delivering services, points to much greater uncertainty about who is in charge. The importance of formal governing institutions, and the extent to which they can coordinate policymaking, are certainly issues yet to be resolved within MLG (Bache and Flinders, 2004b: 7; Hooghe and Marks, 2003: 234; 2001; Marks and Hooghe, 2000; Jessop, 2004; Peters and Pierre, 2004).

Multi-level governance, policy networks and the European Union

To some extent the woolly nature of MLG reflects the initial object of its study: the rapidly changing EU. A relatively fluid EU policy process, with levels of power diffusion varying across time and policy issues, requires a flexible theoretical framework to accommodate empirical studies.

The early literature on EU integration can be described as a contrast between two grand theories of international relations (Jachtenfuchs, 2001: 246; although see Rosamond, 2000: 145). Neofunctionalism suggests a political project in which incremental change is preferred to a federal approach setting out a formal constitution and separation of EU powers (Rosamond, 2000: 51). This begins with greater economic integration as trade barriers are removed, cooperation increases and countries become economically interdependent. Economic interdependence produces political integration incrementally (beginning with 'low politics', or the least controversial policy areas), with the logic of further cooperation in some policy areas contributing to a snowball effect in others. As this integration increases, so too does the role for supranational institutions to further the EU project. As the EU grows in power, groups representing 'social interests' shift their activities from states to European institutions (2000: 52). Overall, the creation of a political community in Europe is not only inevitable, but also a social good, reducing political conflict and the prospect of war (Haas, 1958). In contrast, intergovernmentalism suggests that member states remain the most important actors, as 'gatekeepers' controlling EU development. This follows a 'two-level game' in which domestic preferences within member states are taken to the EU bargaining table (Moravscik, 1993; Rosamond, 2000: 136–8). Supranational institutions have little independent influence and are given their power by states (Pollack, 2001: 225).

Both approaches proved to be flawed. The fundamental flaw of neo-functionalism is that its predictions did not come true (although see Box 8.4 on p. 164). In the short term, member states (such as France under Charles de Gaulle) blocked the 'inevitable' process of political integration (Dinan, 2004; Rosamond, 2000: 75; Haas, 1975). In the longer term, while political integration has progressed significantly (including 'high politics' issues such as monetary union), it is not uniform. The process of integration is better captured by MLG's focus on the variable diffusion of power by policy issue over time. Or, we may argue that it is more important to explain what the EU is and does now, rather than what it may be moving towards (see Rosamond, 2000: 106–9).

Intergovernmentalism has also proved less useful over time, as integration has affected domestic preferences and 'locked-in' each member state which is now one of many organizations within a complex set of multi-level governance arrangements (Pollack, 2001: 226–7). The EU is now a multi-level, not two-level, game (Rosamond, 2000: 147, with reference to Putnam's theory). Further, the more that supra-national institutions – such as the European Parliament, the European Court of Justice, and the European Commission – demonstrate decision making which is not dominated by the more state-centred institutions – the Council of Ministers and the European Council – then the more we can view the EU as moving away from the intergovernmentalist ideal (Asare *et al.*, 2009). Overall, states are caught in a web of interdependence that allows supra-national organizations and organized interests (including sub-national authorities) to influence both policy and integration. Policy outcomes are uncertain and dependant on levels of Europeanization, the entrenchment of member state laws and strength of the policy agenda in each jurisdiction (Marks, 1993).

For Bache and Flinders (2004b: 1–2) MLG began as a way to address a false boundary between the study of domestic and international politics in the EU, which:

Neither resembles domestic politics nor international organizations, and therefore defies explanation from approaches applied either to politics within states or politics between states…multi-level governance has been seen to capture the shifting and uncertain patterns of governance within which the EU is just one actor upon a contested stage.

The study of MLG developed as the EU itself changed and key developments established the importance of new levels of government in their own right. For example, the Single European Act in 1987 extended the use of qualified majority voting (and therefore a reduction in the ability of member states to reject new policies unanimously). It, combined with the development of powerful EU administrative and legal institutions,

---

Box 8.4　Neofunctionalism and interest groups

While neofunctionalism presents an incomplete explanation for EU development, its emphasis on interest group reorientation has merit. The EU has become an important hub for group-government relations (Mazey and Richardson, 2006: 248). It may further diminish state sovereignty because national governments have 'ceded sovereignty over large areas of public policy-making to the EU level' and interest groups are shifting their resources away from national governments towards the EU (2006: 251). Groups are 'increasingly engaged independently at the supranational level and see that level as a venue where they can pursue their own goals' (2006: 252). While the EU is a relatively open process, the ability of groups to exploit this new opportunity varies markedly (2006: 252). The level of resources between groups is unequal, with some possessing more money, expertise, personnel and legitimacy (depending on how the issue is framed). Therefore, many groups still lobby via member states. Representatives of member states are both lobbied by groups and lobbyists for them (2006: 253). Sub-national groups may also engage through sub-national governments and (where appropriate) their sister or parent organizations in the national arena (Keating, Cairney and Hepburn, 2009).

---

further established the role of the EU as an actor as well as an arena for intergovernmental relations (Bache and Flinders, 2004b: 2). At the other end of the governing spectrum, the reform of EU structural (regional aid) policy in 1988 advanced the ability of sub-national authorities to maintain direct links with the EU (Commission) as well as their central governments (2004b: 3). These developments highlight the scope for supranational and regional influence which is no longer conditional on national governmental support.

MLG also incorporates insights from the literature on policy networks to highlight the interdependence between governmental and non-governmental actors. The policy networks literature has long identified shared decision making as a key tenet of public policy. Following Habermas, Jordan and Richardson (1982: 84) highlight a 'rationality deficit' within modern government:

> Authorities with little informational and planning capacity...are dependent on the flow of information from their clients...thus unable to preserve the distance from them necessary for independent decisions.

The policymaking world is specialized, with the responsibilities of government divided into sectors and subsectors. As the scope of government has expanded and its departments have become more specialized (coinciding with the increase of 'particularistic' groups), civil servants have taken on a, 'larger and larger part of the policy making load' (1982: 86). Policymakers devolve the responsibility for policy management to civil servants. Given civil servants' lack of political legitimacy, they are, 'ill placed to impose and conflict avoidance is likely to result'. Further, given civil servants' lack of specialized knowledge, they are often dependent upon groups for information and advice. The result is policy networks, or policymaking relationships between those in formal positions of responsibility and those who seek to influence them. The process of specialized accommodation leads to a form of 'clientelism', in which civil servants form a bond with, and promote the interests of, certain groups within government. A bargaining relationship develops between groups and civil servants at various levels of government, based on an exchange of information for influence. It suggests that policymaking is too complex to be readily reduced to individuals and it is difficult to attribute responsibility for the exercise of power to make policy to those individuals. As Rose (1987: 267–8) argues, their activities are not separate but interdependent, and public policy, 'is the joint product of their interaction'.

Networks analysis, combined with the identification of multi-level policymaking, highlights informal relationships and the blurring of boundaries between public/private action and levels of governmental sovereignty. Decision-making authority is dispersed and policy outcomes are determined by a complex series of negotiations between various levels of government and interest groups. Our focus shifts from formal powers and the capacity to make and enforce decisions, to the much more messy and complex systems in which the distinction between formal and informal sources of authority becomes less meaningful. With decision-making responsibility shared across multiple levels of government (and with non-governmental actors), formal responsibility may be less important than a willingness to engage in policymaking and negotiate with other jurisdictions. In effect, MLG continues and extends a policy networks focus on the move from government sovereignty to a loss of decision-making control and the need to negotiate and share decisions rather than impose them.

Multi-level governance, federalism and beyond

A benefit of the MLG framework is that it brings together the study of unitary, federal and quasi-federal systems (Chapter 4). For example, it may aid comparisons between the federal US and the quasi-federal EU. Studies of federalism are drawn extensively (but not exclusively) from US experiences and MLG from studies of the EU, but both identify the absence of a single centre of government. Rhodes (1997: 1), describing governance, suggests, 'there is not one but many centres linking many levels of government' while Elazar (1971: 6), describing federalism, identifies 'the diffusion of power among multiple centers which must cooperate in order to govern' (both terms are also hard to define – Stein and Turkewitsch, 2008: 5)

The latter concern has produced an extensive literature on intergovernmental relations. It explores the entanglement of policy issues when power is vested in more than one actor. As Keating (2005: 18) discusses, multi-level government issues are common to most states with the dual aim of devolving decisions but maintaining central/broad control when appropriate. Although many political systems outline in detail the policy domains of each level or type of government, the boundaries between policy areas become blurred in practice. IGR often explores these issues by highlighting country-level differences according to institutional structures and the recourse to authority and formal resolution. It asks questions such as: is it a unitary, union, federal or quasi-federal state? What is the strength of the 'centre' and what is the frequency of formal dispute resolution? What is the role of parties, executives and courts in IGR (Watts, 2007; Horgan, 2004; Hueglin and Fenna, 2006: 215)?

In this sense, studies of federalism and MLG may diverge because the latter focuses more on informal relationships and the blurry boundaries between actions taken by policymakers and influential groups. In short, it shifts our focus from institutions towards policy networks and the idea that most policymaking takes place in specialized sub-systems in which direct accountability for policy outcomes is more difficult to identify (Stein and Turkewitsch, 2008: 10). Indeed, MLG may have more in common with theories, such as punctuated equilibrium, that developed from case studies of US policymaking within sub-systems. We therefore need to be very clear on what we are comparing: normative evaluations of governing types; types of political systems (federal, quasi-federal); particular systems (US, EU); or theories relating to policymaking in different systems.

Normative evaluations of MLG and federalism

A key link between MLG and studies of federalism is a common focus on the *necessity* of multi-level government; MLG is both a good description of how policy is made and perhaps how it should be made. Government is divided into different types and levels of government because 'no single centre could possibly do everything itself' (Newton and Van Deth, 2010: 105). Hooghe and Marks (2003: 233) point to a widespread feeling in the literature that, 'Centralised authority – command and control – has few advocates ... the dispersion of governance across multiple jurisdictions is both more efficient than, and normatively superior to, central state monopoly'. The devolution of policy responsibility provides:

- A greater ability to address the 'heterogeneity of preferences of citizens'.
- Closeness between policymakers and the affected population which helps make policy based on local knowledge.
- The benefits of competition between authorities.
- The scope for policy innovation within a larger number of authorities. (Hooghe and Marks, 2004: 16)

Comparing federal and quasi-federal systems

However, this argument alone does not take us very far because there are many types of multi-level government. The EU is unusual because it represents a modern-day confederacy, or at least a quasi-federal system, in which EU institutions resemble the executive, judicial and legislative branches (the European Commission, Court of Justice and Parliament) but member states are unwilling to cede sovereignty on key issues of economic, social and foreign policy (Newton and Van Deth, 2010: 109; Burgess, 2006: 226; Hueglin and Fenna, 2006: 13–16). Yet, it does not depart from a *norm* of federalism. Instead, we have many different types of federalism.

Federalist states combine national government with a constitutional arrangement that guarantees a degree of sovereignty to sub-national governments. This sovereignty may be justified in two main ways: to allow local decision making to supplement 'a distant centre of government' in large federations such as the US; and/or, to address (often geographically specific) political divisions 'based on language, ethnicity, religion, culture or history' in systems such as Canada and Belgium (Newton and Van Deth, 2010: 111–13). Federations vary according to the number of sub-national governments, the balance of powers between national and sub-national governments, the extent to which their respective responsibilities are spelled out, and the role of legislatures. They also have a different balance between national and sub-national shares of tax receipts and public employees (2010: 110–11; note that *almost all* tax receipts come from member state and subnational authorities in the EU – McKay, 2000: 31).

There are three main consequences. First, the division between federal and other systems is often unclear. Many unitary states seem quasi-federal because they retain power at the centre but devolve significant policy responsibilities to certain populations (Newton and Van Deth, 2010: 114). Indeed, our rejection of the Westminster model, and the idea of one single type of federalism, suggests that political systems are more similar than they first appear. MLG relates as much to the unitary UK as it does, say, the federal US. Second, different federations may provide different analytical links to, and policy lessons for, the EU. For example, Scharpf (1988) explores the potential for the EU to share with Germany a rather convoluted system of checks and balances which may stifle policy innovation (compare with Kitschelt and Streeck, 2003 in Chapter 5). Holland *et al.* (1996) draw similar links between inertia, federalism and environmental policymaking in Australia, Canada and the US. Church and Dardanelli (2005: 181) draw lessons for the EU on the move from confederalism to federalism in Switzerland (the 'near perfect embodiment of the federal idea'). McKay (2000) draws lessons from Australia, Canada, Germany, the US and Switzerland to determine if the EU can operate successfully as a system with almost no responsibility for raising taxes. Scharpf (1997) examines the scope for EU economic integration to mirror the development of 'regulatory competition' in the US. Overall, the lessons from 'federalism' are there, but the sources are far and wide.

Third, MLG shares with federalism the more open question about how multi-level government *should* operate. Hooghe and Marks (2003: 236; see also Hueglin and Fenna, 2006: 316) 'detect two contrasting visions' based on the following questions (and see Table 8.2):

- Should jurisdictions be designed around *communities* or policy *problems*?
- Should jurisdictions *bundle* competencies or be functionally *specific*?
- Should jurisdictions be *limited* in number or *proliferate*?
- Should jurisdictions be designed to *last* or be *fluid*? (Hooghe and Marks, 2003: 236)

With type 1, the dispersion of formal authority is limited to a small number of jurisdictions, with each enjoying an associated executive, legislature and court system. Devolution tends to be furthered on a *territorial* basis with a small number of discrete units of government and no overlap of membership. Policies are 'bundled in a small number of packages' at each level and the relationships are durable (Hooghe and Marks, 2003: 237). With type 2 we have a 'complex, fluid patchwork of innumerable, overlapping jurisdictions' (Bache and Flinders, 2004a: 39). Devolution takes place on a *policy* basis, with much larger numbers of authorities, memberships that span complementary policy areas, and less stable relationships as the arrangements are changed in response to changing policy conditions (Hooghe and Marks, 2003: 237).

Of course, the clear separation of types 1 and 2 will be difficult to find in the real world, suggesting that they are better seen as ideal types. Further, both provide different policymaking advantages. While type 2 exhibits the most flexible and dynamic arrangements, type 1 minimizes

Table 8.2   *Types of multi-level governance*

Type 1	Type 2
General-purpose jurisdictions	Task-specific jurisdictions
Non-intersecting memberships	Intersecting memberships
Jurisdictions at a limited number of levels	No limit to the numbers of jurisdictional levels
System wide architecture	Flexible design

Source: Adapted from Hooghe and Marks (2003: 236).

the coordination problems associated with a proliferation of bodies (2003: 39; type 1 may involve an asymmetry of power during intergovernmental relations – see, for example, McGarvey and Cairney, 2008: 163–6; Wilson, 2003). But does the evidence suggest that one type produces better policymaking systems overall? The most positive analysis of type 2 MLG derives from countries, such as Switzerland and the US, in which functionally specific bodies are *elected locally* and accountable to the populations they serve. This is particularly important in the US where the powers of states are guarded and strong centralization is deemed inappropriate in such a large area. However, it is a far cry from the UK in which there is a new form of 'distributed public governance' (Bache and Flinders, 2004a: 45) in which unelected quangos operate with minimal public and ministerial scrutiny, while executive agencies find themselves 'sitting on top of complex public–private relationships they may only vaguely understand' (Kettl, 1993 in Rhodes, 1997: 54).

Therefore, our normative conclusions are influenced by our empirical findings. The key questions become: is MLG *chosen* or an *unintended consequence* of government reform? Does type 2 MLG signal the devolution of power to elected local bodies or the loss of central control and accountability?

Comparing the EU and US

The term 'multi-level governance' is used rarely in studies of the US, but there have been some attempts to use federalist theory to compare the US and EU. For example, Keleman (2004; extending Majone's 1993; 1994; 1996 argument that the EU is a 'regulatory state') makes two main points. First, the vertical relationship (or the 'politics of competence') is similar in federal systems: most policymaking takes place at the federal (or central) level, while the responsibility for most implementation rests with the states (or sub-central authorities). Second, the extent to which the centre allows sub-central authorities the freedom to implement federal policy (the 'politics of discretion') depends on the levels of horizontal fragmentation within the central government. A highly fragmented system 'encourages an adversarial, litigious approach to regulation' (Keleman, 2004: 2). The competition between institutions makes them more protective of their authority and more likely to write detailed laws for the provinces to follow (what Keleman calls 'regulatory federalism'). In contrast, a concentration of power at the centre encourages 'discretionary federalism' or a 'less judicialized' approach (2004: 2). Written laws are broad, allowing for more flexibility in application by lower-level jurisdictions.

Treating the EU as federal-like allows us predict its behaviour according to its respective levels of horizontal fragmentation. The fragmentation of power in the EU is high, not only because two legislative chambers – the Council of Ministers and the European Parliament – compete with the European Court of Justice and the European Commission (Schain and Menon, 2007), but also because the Commission has limited powers to monitor implementation. Therefore, Keleman (2004: 2) predicts a form of *regulatory* federalism in which 'inflexible rulemaking and litigious enforcement' characterizes EU-member state relations. Kelemen effectively sets a research agenda for the EU based on previous studies of federal systems such as the US. So far, the evidence from EU policymaking is mixed. While Kelemen confirms his hypothesis in a study of environmental policy, Asare *et al.* (2009) present challenging findings in tobacco policy.

Comparing MLG and other theories

While the federalism and IGR literatures do relate to policymaking, I argue that more relevant comparisons to the EU-derived MLG come from the US-derived theories of public policy that engage more directly with the literature on interest groups and sub-governmental processes. Take, for example, the strong links between MLG and punctuated equilibrium theory (Chapter 9) which share a focus on bounded rationality, policy networks, policy complexity and policymaking in multiple, shifting venues (the importance of intergovernmental relationships should be equally clear in Chapter 10). The basic tenet of governance studies is that:

> No single actor has all knowledge and information required to solve complex, dynamic and diversified problems, no actor has sufficient overview to make the application of needed instruments effective, no single actor has sufficient action potential to dominate unilaterally in a particular governing model. (Kooiman, 1993: 4)

Therefore, the 'governance problem' exists in all political systems which face bounded rather than comprehensive rationality. There is not one, sole decision maker at the heart of government. The dispersal of power also makes it difficult to track the effects of policy measures taken at one level of government when it travels through a series of other 'centres'. This description takes us back to Chapter 3, in which we identified the difference between power as *capacity* and the *exercise* of power. While the centre is still powerful, its reach is limited when compared to the size of the state. While the government has the potential to intervene in the policy issues it is most interested in, its action in one area precludes the same degree of action in 99 others.

It is possible to infer policy continuity *and* change from this process. A degree of continuity can be found in the study of policy communities. The lack of policymaker attention to most issues, combined with the tendency of governments to process policy in specialist policy sub-sectors containing civil servants and interest groups, suggests that we will not witness radical policy change in many instances (Richardson and Jordan, 1979). Further, when viewed from the top-down, the problem of governance is an inability of central government to carry out its own policies directly (Pierre and Stoker, 2000: 43). Rather, the proliferation of governance organizations may produce a 'coordination dilemma' (Hooghe and Marks, 2003: 239) and an increase in the number of 'veto players' may 'make significant policy changes difficult or impossible' (Tsebelis, 2002: 7). Yet, continuity is not inevitable; there are many sources of major policy change in the EU context. First, the EU may impose new policies on member states that they would otherwise not entertain. Second, the diffusion of power and responsibility may encourage policy innovation in one territory, followed by emulation in the others (Hooghe and Marks, 2003: 236). Third, the spread of MLG increases the potential for interest groups to pursue their policies at different levels or types of government. If a group is dissatisfied with policy inertia at one level, it may find more success in another.

These issues of governance are discussed in the US but with some differences in language. Punctuated equilibrium theory identifies a similar starting point in bounded rationality: since policymakers cannot consider all issues at all times, they ignore most and promote relatively few to the top of their agenda. This lack of attention to most issues helps explain why most policies do not change. Instead, powerful interest groups are able to operate in relative anonymity within specialist policy sub-sectors. Yet, when policymakers *do* focus on these issues, their levels of attention are disproportionate and their response is 'hypersensitive'. In many cases this shift can be explained by an increasingly crowded policymaking process and the types of multi-level governance now identified in the EU. When interest groups are faced with 'negative feedback' at one level, they 'venue-shop', or seek influential audiences in other arenas

---

Box 8.5 An example of multi-level governance: EU–UK–Scotland–local

The example of Scotland within the EU demonstrates the shifting sands of policy responsibility. In some areas the EU level is clearly the most important. The Common Agricultural Policy and the Common Fisheries Policy are both set in the EU. While CAP allows implementation discretion (and Scotland has taken a different approach to the UK), there is less room to manoeuvre with fishing quotas. The EU generally controls environmental policy. For example, local authorities are responsible for the disposal of waste (often using private contractors), but follow an EU agenda, with a UK role in monitoring the Scottish Government's monitoring of local government. There is a greater mix of responsibilities in other areas. In tobacco policy, the EU has issued directives on minimum levels of taxation, maximum levels of tar, product labelling and tobacco advertising, but UK policies on these issues go beyond the EU requirements and apply to Scotland. In turn, Scotland was the first territory in the UK to introduce legislation to ban smoking in public places. It also controls NHS treatments such as smoking-cessation clinics and nicotine replacement therapy (Asare *et al.*, 2009). Similarly, while the EU is responsible for trade and the effects of different tax rates on alcohol, the UK sets its own tax (and therefore price) levels, while the Scottish Government controls licensing law, health education and funds NHS treatment for alcohol abuse (while also putting pressure on supermarkets to maintain high prices). In some areas the EU has a small but significant role. Most issues of healthcare are devolved to Scotland, with UK influence generally limited to professional standards. However, the UK controls the rules on financing new hospitals and the pressure to keep up with waiting-time targets in England prompted the greater use of private sector hospitals in Scotland. The EU's Working Time Directive limits the amount of time that doctors can work and be 'on-call'. This informed the renegotiation of Scottish medical contracts (coordinated at the UK level), increased the need for hospitals to centralize their services and undermined clinical cover in rural areas (see McGarvey and Cairney, 2008: 2; 160–77).

---

such as legislative committees, the courts or other levels of government. If they catch the attention of another venue, this produces 'positive feedback' in which the newly involved policymakers increase their demand for new information and new ways to think about and solve old policy problems. In a process of government characterized by interdependence and overlapping jurisdictional boundaries (in which many institutions can be influential in the same policy areas), these innovations can be infectious. The actions of one often catch the attention of others, causing a 'bandwagon effect' of attention and major policy change.

Punctuated equilibrium theory describes a process in which interest groups compete to set the agenda within multiple decision-making venues. Power is exercised to frame policy problems to ensure that they are dealt with in a particular decision making venue (Baumgartner and Jones, 1993: 32). Since most policies can be influenced by more than one level of government, the relative involvement of each jurisdiction depends as much on how the policy issue is understood and portrayed as the powers and responsibilities of each jurisdiction. The analysis shifts our focus from formal institutions and intergovernmental procedures towards policy networks and the idea that most policymaking takes place in specialized sub-systems. The identification of visible power relations is qualified by less visible competition to define policy problems and perhaps remove them from formal intergovernmental agendas. Punctuated equilibrium theory is therefore, in many ways, a better source of theoretical comparison with MLG (we consider the links between PE, MLG and the advocacy coalition framework in Chapter 13).

Conclusion

The concept of multi-level governance resembles the game of *Othello* which takes 'A minute to learn ... a lifetime to master'. It is easy to grasp: governance refers to shared decision making and the blurred boundaries between formal and informal sources of authority, while multi-level suggest that these processes take place above and below the nation state. Combined, we are witnessing not only a shift of power (in once-centralized political systems) to different layers of government, but also decision making which involves both government and non-government actors. For govern*ance* to have meaning this non-governmental involvement must also be meaningful (otherwise, we are really talking about multi-level govern*ment*). Yet, beyond this basic understanding, MLG is difficult to pin down and apply systematically or meaningfully. Within the literature we find varying degrees of uncertainty according to:

1. The role and power of the central state – are we witnessing strong government responding to new challenges, or weakened government operating in a world it can no longer control?
2. Types of MLG – from a stable, structured set of policy relations devolved by territory, to a fluid, flexible and more numerous set of bodies set up according to the logic of policy.
3. The links between empirical and normative discussions. There is no agreement on how MLG *should* be organized and many differences in how governments *are* organized.

As a result we may ask what value MLG adds when we seek a common description of governmental activity. MLG may be yet another umbrella term that describes a wide range of studies without bringing it together to form a coherent theory or research agenda. Yet, our discussions of the UK, EU and beyond demonstrate the value of MLG at explaining key policymaking developments. The UK government effectively created a new problem of governance. By privatizing the public sector, reforming the civil service, introducing quasi-markets and relying more on quangos it exacerbated the problem of central control. By no longer delivering public services directly, it became forced to cooperate with the many organizations now charged with the delivery of public services. This, combined with the diffusion of power upwards to the EU and downwards to the devolved and regional assemblies, has created a new decision-making environment for the UK's core executive. Multi-level governance describes its new position as one of many (public and private) organizations seeking to determine the path of public policy. Its research agenda is also straightforward, including the key questions: what tools does the centre have to control other organizations and how much can it 'steer' public policy (see also Bell *et al.*, 2010, on 'persuasion')?

To a large extent we should not be too worried by the problems we face when we extend issues of MLG to wider arenas such as the EU. In part, the confusion stems from the object of study: a relatively complex EU process which is still developing and difficult to explain. In this sense, Hooghe and Marks' (2003) types 1 and 2 can be seen as different but complementary lenses through which to study the same political process. If the EU as a whole defies the applicability of one overarching theory, then we should not be too surprised that the level of variation by policy area, territory and time should defy easy classification. MLG also goes beyond the literature, too focused on the big questions of international relations and integration, to focus on the more mundane, day-to-day business of European public policy.

The MLG literature allows us to make meaningful comparisons between the new quasi-federal systems, such as the UK and EU, and more established federal systems such as the US, Australia, Canada, Switzerland and Germany (even though the latter is complicated by Germany's inclusion in the EU). New studies of the EU tie in with older studies of federalism that favour a degree of decentralized government (although there is less agreement on how it should be organized), while theories of policymaking based on federalist studies may be applied to the new EU context. Perhaps most importantly, MLG may be compared usefully to other theories that began life in the federal US, that share a common focus on bounded rationality, interest groups, sub-systems and policymaking in multiple venues. These theories are discussed further in Chapters 9 and 10, with detailed comparisons following in Chapter 13.

Chapter 9

Punctuated Equilibrium

This chapter examines:

- The meaning of punctuated equilibrium, policy community and monopoly.
- The literature on agenda setting.
- The use of venue shopping to explain issue expansion, shifts of attention and policy change.
- The applicability of punctuated equilibrium within US and other political systems.
- The value of this theory to the wider concerns of this book, such as: how do we identify power within a political system; and, why does policy change?

According to punctuated equilibrium theory, political systems can be characterized as both stable *and* dynamic. Most policies stay the same for long periods while some change very quickly and dramatically. Or, policy change in a particular area may be incremental for decades, only to be followed by profound change which sets an entirely new direction for policy in the future. The aim of punctuated equilibrium theory is to explain these long periods of policy stability punctuated by short but intense periods of change. As Chapter 5 suggests, we can begin to explain it with reference to the limits of comprehensive rationality: since decision makers cannot consider all issues at all times, they ignore most and promote relatively few to the top of their agenda. This lack of attention to most issues helps explain why most policies may not change, while intense periods of attention to some issues may prompt new ways to **frame** and solve old policy problems. Further explanation comes from the power of participants, either to minimize attention and maintain an established frame of reference, or to expand attention to new audiences in the hope of generating the type of conflict and debate necessary to effect major policy change (True, Jones and Baumgartner, 2007: 157).

Frame – to define a policy's image (how an issue is portrayed and categorized).

Punctuated equilibrium can be described very simply as the novel combination of two approaches to the study of public policy: **policy**

Policy communities –
close relationships
between interest
groups and public
officials, based on the
exchange of
information for
influence (but see Box
9.1 on the European/
US usage). The links
endure if participants
establish a **policy
monopoly**, or a
dominant image of the
policy problem.

Agenda setting – the
study of public, media
and government
attention to policy
issues.

communities and **agenda setting**. In the former, the main focus is identifying stable relationships between interest groups and public officials. These relationships endure because the participants share a broad agreement about the nature of a policy problem and few other actors are interested in the issue (Jordan and Maloney, 1997). In many instances, those most involved are able to protect a **policy monopoly** by framing the issue in a particular way. At first this may involve the argument that the policy problem has largely been solved, with only the implementation to be addressed. Then, the issue may be portrayed as dull, to minimize external interest, or as technical, requiring a certain level of expertise, to exclude other actors. Group–government relations take place beyond the public spotlight since the issues are presented as too dull, technical or routine to invite attention, while most political actors do not have the resources to engage in this type of policymaking. As a result, policymaking tends to be incremental and based on previous agreements between a small number of participants.

In contrast, the study of agenda setting and public attention rarely identifies incremental change (Baumgartner and Jones, 1993: 10). A key focus is issues which attract high levels of attention. This could refer to a rise in attention following a crisis or 'triggering event' (Dearing and Rogers, 1996: 37–9). Or, it can be caused by interest groups trying to draw attention to 'their' issues. In particular, Baumgartner and Jones (1993: 32–7) connect shifts of attention to **venue** shift, in which an issue can become the jurisdiction of more than one institution at the same time. Groups excluded from policy monopolies will try to shift the debate from within by, for example, appealing to public officials and questioning the existing approach. If unsuccessful, they have an incentive to **venue shop**, or seek influential audiences elsewhere. It may involve an appeal to a different level or type of governing institution (such as a legislative committee or court) capable of making decisions on the same policy issue. Or, groups may seek to expand the size of the interested audience by making direct appeals to the public. When an issue reaches the 'top' of this wider political agenda it becomes processed in a different way: more participants become involved and more ways to look at (and solve) the policy problem are considered.

Venues – institutions
such as government
departments,
congressional
committees and the
courts, where
'authoritative decisions
are made'.

Venue shopping – the
attempt to seek
favourable audiences
in other venues.

A combination of approaches explains both continuity and change. Policies stay the same within policy communities because there is minimal external interest or a limited ability of outsiders to engage. Policies change when there is sufficient external interest to cause the collapse of previously insulated communities. External attention rises and the issues are considered in a broader political environment where power is more evenly spread and new actors can set the agenda. In both cases the key focus is the competition to define a 'policy image', or the way in which a policy is understood and discussed (Baumgartner and Jones, 1993: 31). While the successful definition of policy as a technical or humdrum issue ensures that issues may be monopolized and considered quietly in one venue, the reframing of that issue as crucial to other institutions, or the big political issues of the day, ensures that it will be considered by many audiences and processed in more than one decision-making venue.

Why 'punctuated equilibrium'?

The term 'punctuated equilibrium' was inspired from its use in the natural sciences to describe dramatic shifts rather than incremental development in evolution (Baumgartner and Jones, 1993: 19). In public policy, equilibrium (balance, or stability) is the result of: (a) dominance within government based on a supporting policy image and the enforcement of the status quo; and (b) political forces cancelling each other out. Punctuation refers to a policy change associated with: (a) the use of a competing policy image to mobilize previously uninvolved actors; and (b) imbalances between competing political forces. In other words, the often-misleading appearance of equilibrium refers to two things: first, the *creation* of institutions (such as policy communities) to support a policy monopoly; and, second, the *defence* of that monopoly by mobilizing against challenges by excluded groups. Punctuated equilibrium occurs if this strategy is unsuccessful and the policy monopoly is destroyed. It follows the successful promotion of a new policy image. The new approach to defining and solving a policy problem legitimizes the involvement of previously excluded groups and encourages previously uninvolved actors (often in different venues) to become involved. The result is constant change (cloaked by an overall picture of stability) as policy monopolies are created while others are destroyed. Note, however, that the term is used widely in political science, and we should not confuse it with the (albeit related) discussions of institutionalism we encounter in Chapter 4 (Hay, 2002: 161). We should also not necessarily equate punctuations with single events. Rather, events can prompt a long term 'explosive process' and we may not return to 'equilibrium for a very long time' (Baumgartner and Jones, 2009: 280–1).

Policy communities and policy monopolies

Marsh and Rhodes (1992a) identify a continuum of group–government relationships based on factors such as the number of participants and frequency and nature of contact. As Table 9.1 suggests, the concept of policy community sits at one end of the continuum, while the issue network represents its polar opposite. The term 'policy community' suggests a close, stable and often consensual relationship between a small number of groups and government (but see Box 9.1 on the Europe/US usage). In contrast, 'issue network' (discussed below) suggests a wide variety of links between the government and many groups, in which there is less agreement and less stability.

Important note: Baumgartner and Jones (1993: 7) use **policy monopoly** twice, to refer to the institutional arrangements (**policy community**) *and* the policy image: 'Policy monopolies have two important characteristics. First, a definable institutional structure is responsible for policy making, and that structure limits its access to the policy process. Second, a powerful supporting idea is associated with the institution'.

This spectrum of group–government relations sums up the focus of punctuated equilibrium in a nutshell. Baumgartner and Jones (1993) seek to explain the success or failure of attempts by certain groups to establish a policy monopoly. Policy monopoly refers to the 'monopoly on political understandings', or the ability of certain groups to

Table 9.1 *Types of policy network*

	Policy community	Issue networks
Numbers of pressure participants	Small – many are excluded.	Large – the barriers to entry are low.
Nature of consultation	Frequent, high quality.	Variable frequency and quality.
Nature of interaction	Stable and close.	Less stable. Access fluctuates significantly.
Levels of consensus	Participants share the same basic understanding of the policy problem and how to solve it. Members accept and support the outcomes.	A measure of agreement may be reached but conflict and opposition is more likely.

Sources: Adapted from Marsh and Rhodes (1992b: 251); see also Jordan (1981: 98).

Box 9.1   The changing world of group–government relations

The study of group–government relations has produced numerous approaches and a proliferation of terms to describe the nature and frequency of contact. They include: competitive pluralism, state corporatism, sub-government, iron triangles, policy whirlpools, sub-systems, policy communities and issue networks (Jordan, 1981; Baumgartner and Jones, 1993: 7; Jordan and Schubert, 1992). While issue networks are loose relationships between public officials and many interest groups, policy communities or iron triangles are close relationships between certain interest groups and public officials (but note that, in the US, 'policy community' may be understood very differently – as something more like an open advocacy coalition in Chapter 10).

'Policy network' became the generic umbrella term for group–government relationships in the UK, EU, Australia and Canada, while 'sub-system' is used more in the US. In Europe, early studies were linked to a focus on the putative differences between pluralism (bargaining with government and competition between large numbers of participants) and corporatism (formal collaboration between the state and a very restricted number of large groups representing, for example, business and labour). In the US, early studies identified relatively insulated and uncompetitive group–government relationships within a political system assumed to be pluralistic (iron, or cozy, triangles are closed relationships between implementing agencies, legislators, and favoured interest groups). Now, there is a greater focus on the need to explain instability and policy change. In the US, it may be a response to the identification, since the 1970s, of a more complex political system – containing a much larger number of groups, experts and other policy participants – which makes it much more difficult for policy issues to be insulated from attention and for groups to restrict debate. In the UK, it may follow the experience of the Thatcher government and the imposition of policy change in the face of widespread opposition, rather than through negotiation and compromise within closed communities. In the EU, it may follow the identification of a policy process which is 'more fluid and unpredictable – and less controllable – than seems to be implied by enthusiasts of the network approach' (Richardson, 2000: 1008). In each case, the group–government world appears to be changing and our aim is to explain this change.

---

maintain a dominant image of the policy problem (Baumgartner and Jones, 1993: 6). The maintenance of this monopoly requires a common adherence to the same policy image and an ability to exclude groups who do not sign up to this agenda. For our purposes, **policy community** is the venue or 'institutional arrangement that reinforces that understanding' (1993: 6; Jordan, 2005: 320). When civil servants and certain interest groups form relationships, they recognise the benefits – such as policy stability – of attempting to insulate their decisions from the wider political process (Richardson and Jordan, 1979). In some accounts, this stability hinges on socialization. Inclusion within the policy community depends on the gaining of personal trust, through the awareness of, following, and reproduction of 'rules of the game'. The learning process involves immersion within a 'common culture' in which there exists a great deal of agreement on the nature and solutions to policy problems (Wilks and Wright, 1987: 302–3; McPherson and Raab, 1988: 55).

What explains the 'insulation' of these communities from the wider political process? First, policies are broken down to such a level that few actors are interested or have the time or resources to become involved (particularly when the policy problem appears to have been solved). Second, a 'rule of the game' is that participants resolve issues within the network, rather than seeking change elsewhere. Participants know that while they may not agree with all decisions taken, it is counterproductive to highlight these grievances in other arenas where more involvement may dilute their influence. Third, the lack of wider political interest is furthered by defining issues as humdrum or technical, limiting attention and the ability of other groups to participate. If *successful*, they maintain a policy community which is characterized by:

- *A limited group membership*, based on the use of a certain policy image to exclude most participants and reduce the visibility of decisions;
- *Good quality relations* between groups and government, based on shared values or a shared understanding of the policy problem;
- *Policy and policy community stability*, based on a lack of external attention and the fruitful exchange of resources between groups and public officials. (Jordan and Maloney, 1997)

If the attempt to maintain a policy monopoly is *unsuccessful*, it suggests that the participants can*not* insulate the decision-making process from a wider audience and there is effective competition to define the policy's image (effectively as a problem that has *not* been solved). More groups become involved, there is greater competition for access to government, and there is greater political instability caused by group conflict. In other words, the breakdown of a policy monopoly is linked strongly to a movement away from policy communities (or, in the US literature, iron, or cozy, triangles) towards issue networks.

'Issue networks and the executive establishment'

Hugh Heclo's (1978) study of the US executive challenges the 'received opinion' which explains most public policymaking with reference to iron triangles linking 'executive bureaus, congressional committees and interest groups with a stake in particular programs' and excluding other political actors: 'the iron triangle concept is not so much wrong as it is disastrously incomplete ... Looking for the closed triangles of control, we tend to miss the fairly open networks of people that increasingly impinge upon government' (1978: 88). Heclo argues that the huge post-war rise in federal responsibilities (and the federal budget) was not accompanied by a proportionate growth in the executive's administration. Therefore, the administration became increasingly stretched as more groups became mobilized (in response to the growth of government and the consequences of policy). The simple 'clubby days of Washington politics' were replaced by 'complex relationships' among a huge, politically active population (1978: 94; 97; Baumgartner and Jones, 1993: 177–8; see also Jordan, 1981: 98 for similar trends in the UK). It suggests that if we focus on a small number of powerful actors then we overlook, 'the many whose webs of influence provoke and guide the exercise of power' (Heclo, 1978: 102).

In contrast with iron triangles, issue networks comprise a wide range of participants with 'quite variable degrees of mutual commitment', and participants 'move in and out of the networks constantly' (1978: 102). The boundaries of each network are indistinct and fluid. The barriers to entry are low, and based more on the ability to contribute to a discussion of the issues than material power or a common adherence to a policy image. The network is relatively unstable and resolutions to policy debate are conducted 'rarely in any controlled, well-organized way' (1978: 104). Overall, there is less evidence to suggest that iron triangles maintain policy monopolies. Issues which were once 'quietly managed by a small group of insiders' have now become 'controversial and politicized' as the role of policy activists increase and previously insulated policy communities collide (1978: 105). Baumgartner and Jones (1993: 45) provide a range of examples demonstrating this process. Policy communities 'relating to tobacco, pesticides, air and water pollution, airlines, trucking, telecommunications, and nuclear power were all destroyed or radically altered'.

However, a problem may occur if we exaggerate Heclo's position, focus too much on issue networks and assume that group–government relations are pluralistic. This wider political process may mask 'the real locus of decision' (Richardson, Gustafsson and Jordan, 1982: 2) and it is possible for a policy community to exist *within* an issue network (Read, 1996). Thus, Heclo's (1978: 105; see also True *et al.*, 2007: 158) qualification is crucial: while issue networks 'complicate calculations' and 'decrease predictability', it would be 'foolish' to argue that they replace 'the more familiar politics of subgovernments'. The 'politics of subgovernments' is still compelling. The sheer size of government means that most policy decisions are effectively beyond the reach (or interest) of government ministers or presidents (Richardson and Jordan, 1979; Heclo, 1978: 88). When decision makers focus on one issue they have to ignore 99 others. The policy process is broken down into more manageable issues involving a smaller number of interested and knowledgeable participants. Baumgartner and Jones (1993, following Simon, 1976: 242–3) call this **parallel processing**. Most public policy is conducted primarily through small and specialist policy communities which process 'technical' issues at a level of government not particularly visible to the public, and with minimal involvement from senior decision makers. These

Parallel processing – When many issues are considered at one time by component parts of a larger organization.

arrangements exist because there is a logic to devolving decisions and consulting with certain groups (Jordan and Maloney, 1997). Senior decision makers rely on their officials for information and advice. For specialist issues, those officials rely on specialist organizations. Those organizations trade that information/advice (and other resources such as the ability to implement government policy) for influence within government. Further, the logic of this relationship holds regardless of the party of government. Therefore, overall, we are unlikely to witness the types of radical policy shift associated with a change of government or president or a shift of party control in Congress.

On the other hand, these relationships often break down and policies *do* change. In such cases, parallel processing at a low level of government is replaced by **serial processing** at the 'macropolitical' (highest, or most senior) level (True *et al.*, 2007: 158–9). Therefore, any characterization of group–government relationships is a 'snapshot of a dynamic process' in which stable

Serial processing – when issues are considered one (or a few) at a time.

relationships are created and then destroyed (Baumgartner and Jones, 1993: 6). But what *causes* the movement from enduring and stable communities to a more fluid and unpredictable issue network process? Punctuated equilibrium theory suggests that policy change follows a mutually reinforcing process of increased attention, venue shift and shifting policy images (True *et al.*, 2007: 160). This is a key concern of the literature on agenda setting.

Agenda setting

The agenda setting literature focuses on: (a) levels of public, media and government attention to particular issues; and (b) what causes attention to rise or fall. It relates to three main factors. First, the pre-existing prejudices of the audience: different audiences will be

Policy issue – a focus of discussion, debate or conflict in politics.

At the top of the policy agenda – treated as the most important (or most immediate) policy problem to be addressed.

receptive to different **policy issues**. Or, different issues may occupy the **top of the agenda** in different arenas. This effect is more marked if we divide the policy agenda into smaller parts and measure issue attention in local, regional, national and supranational governments, the legislature or the courts. Yet, in many cases a range of audiences may be receptive to similar issues simultaneously if convinced that they are important. The media represents the 'privileged means of communication' between multiple venues which are often 'tightly linked', with 'shifts in attention in one ... quickly followed by shifts in others' (Baumgartner and Jones, 1993: 107; Lynas, 2008).

Second, the significance and immediacy of issues: some **policy problems** are more important than others, while some require quick decisions. For example, economic issues (such as unemployment, interest rates or tax) always remain high on the political agenda, while natural and human disasters focus the attention and demand an immediate response. Yet, since the attention of audiences is limited, and the number of potential issues is almost infinite, the significance of each issue and event is subject to interpretation, debate and competition (see Monbiot, 2008 for an entertaining critique).

Policy problem – a policy issue to be *solved*.

These qualifications point to the third main factor: the ability of political actors to draw attention to one issue at the expense of another. For Dearing and Rogers (1996: 1) agenda setting describes, 'an ongoing competition among issue proponents to gain the attention of media professionals, the public, and policy elites'. Baumgartner and Jones (1993: 11–12) focus on the effect this attention has on public policy. It includes what Kingdon (1984: 3–4) calls the *governmental agenda* (the problems that decision makers 'are paying some serious attention at any given time') and the *decision agenda* (the problems 'that are up for an active decision'). In this context, agenda setting can be summed up with two key statements:

1 There is an almost unlimited amount of policy problems that *could* reach the top of the policy agenda. Yet, very few issues do, while most others do not.

2 There is an almost unlimited number of solutions to those policy problems. Yet, few policy solutions will be considered while most others will not (Box 9.2).

Box 9.2   Participation in American politics: the dynamics of agenda building

Cobb and Elder's (1972: 10; 24–5; 28) main thesis is that there are numerous biases within the political system that restrict attention to certain problems and limit the consideration of solutions. First, the distribution of influence within society is unequal and participation within interest groups is limited (Schattschneider, 1960). Second, dominant interests in the political system promote 'non-decision making' or the use of social values and institutions to restrict the scope of debate (Chapter 3; Bachrach and Baratz, 1962: 948; Crenson, 1971; Gamble, 2000: 295). Third, the only policies given serious consideration are those which differ incrementally from the status quo, while the reaction to the consequences of previous decisions dominates the political agenda (Chapter 5; Lindblom, 1968; Hogwood, 1987: 35). Fourth, the problem may not yet be a legitimate area of concern because the state has never been involved (Cobb and Elder, 1972: 86; 93; Baumgartner and Jones, 1993: 46). Finally, the problem may seem too expensive or impossible to solve (Box 9.3). In this light, their question is: how can this bias towards the status quo be overcome?

Cobb and Elder (1972: 105–10) argue that the best chance for an issue to reach the top of the agenda is to maximize the size of its audience. They present the image of four different audiences as circles within larger circles. The smallest circle is the 'identification group' which is already sympathetic to an issue proponent's aims. If an issue expands, it gains the attention of 'attentive groups' (who are interested and easily mobilized only on certain issues), the 'attentive public' (high income, high educated people with general political interests) and finally the 'general public' which is 'less active, less interested and less informed' and therefore only becomes aware of an issue if it has a striking symbolic value (1972: 107–8). This symbolism is often far removed from the original dispute because only very broad goals allow different publics to become involved, while any technical or specific discussions would dissuade general public involvement. In many cases, a rise in attention is linked to 'triggering devices' or 'unforeseen events' such as natural disasters, riots and protests, while novel issues or issues amenable to piggybacking onto existing debates are the most likely to attract wider attention (1972: 84; 112–18). General public attention almost guarantees that an issue will be prominent on the government agenda (1972: 157). Therefore, while the idea of a politically active and knowledgeable public may be a 'myth', the 'agenda building perspective serves to broaden the range of recognized influences on the public policy-making process' (1972: 2; 164). Baumgartner and Jones (1993: 36–7) argue that gaining public attention is one of two strategies open to issue proponents. The second is venue shopping, or seeking more sympathetic audiences in institutions such as congressional committees, state governments and the courts. Therefore, while 'issue expansion' (the engagement of a wider audience) requires the reframing of policy problems in terms likely to attract new attention, this need not be in the broadest, least technical terms required by the general public.

Problem definition

Problem definition is central to an understanding of agenda setting in both cases. It refers to 'what we choose to identify as public issues and how we think and talk about these concerns' (Rochefort and Cobb, 1994: vii). The key point is that problems do not necessarily receive the most attention because they are the most important or immediate. There are no objective indicators to determine which 'real world conditions' are the most deserving of our attention. Further, the ability of decision makers to receive and act on 'signals' or information about the severity of policy problems is imperfect (Jones and Baumgartner, 2005: 8). Attention is linked more strongly to the ability of issue proponents to convince enough people that 'their' issues are the most worthy of discussion (Dearing and Rodgers, 1996). This may not involve a battle over the *accuracy* of 'facts', but to direct attention to *other* facts which support a rival policy image (Baumgartner and Jones, 1993: 107–8; 113). Attention-grabbing strategies depend on the following factors:

• *Framing*. Framing involves the definition of a policy's image, or how issues are portrayed and categorized. Issues can be framed to make them appear 'technical' and relevant only to experts, or linked to wider social values to heighten participation (Rochefort and Cobb, 1994: 5). To attract attention in the US, one may wish to link ideas to widely accepted values: 'progress, participation, patriotism, independence from foreign domination, fairness, economic growth' (Baumgartner and Jones, 1993: 7). However, core values may vary from country to country and over time (for example, compare the post-war and present day attitudes of most countries to the welfare state). More generally, issue expansion requires the reframing of an issue from a focus on self interest to a problem which the general public (or powerful sections within it) can relate to (Hogwood, 1987: 30). Framing is 'a mixture of empirical information and emotive appeals' (True *et al.*, 2007: 161).

Most policy issues are multi-faceted and can therefore command a wide range of images. For example, smoking may be framed in terms of health, health and safety, health inequalities, nuisance, employment, the economy, customs and excise, the role of multi-national corporations, civil liberties and even human rights. Yet, while there are many ways to frame the same problem, there is limited time and energy to devote to issues. So, highly complex issues are simplified, with very few aspects focused on at any one time at the expense of all the rest. This has policy consequences. For example, a focus on smoking as a health issue prompts governments to restrict tobacco use, while an economic image prompts governments to support the industry (Cairney, Studlar and

Mamudu, 2012). Baumgartner and Jones (1993: 109) suggest that while certain groups may exploit these limitations to create and protect a policy monopoly (based on one image for long periods), the agenda-setting process is too dynamic to expect this to go on forever. In particular, the news agenda is based on attempts to seek new angles to maintain the interest of a public audience. This new focus is accompanied by new journalists with different views, providing audiences for people who were previously ignored and creating interest within venues which were previously uninvolved. Indeed, the basis for creating monopolies – limited time, attention, cognitive abilities – also produces radical shifts of attention to different policy images.

• *Causality, responsibility and the availability of a solution.* For Kingdon (1984: 115), policy issues only become problems when there is a solution and 'we come to believe that we should do something about them'. This belief may follow new theories on the determinants of problems, who is to blame and who is responsible for solving the problem. For example, poverty became a public policy issue in the 1960s not because of a worsening of 'real conditions', but because of a shift in the issue's image 'from that of a private misfortune to a public problem amenable to government solutions' (Baumgartner and Jones, 1993: 28; Rochefort and Cobb, 1994: 15). Stone (1989: 282–3; 2002: 191) suggests that assigning responsibility is a strategy of organizations seeking to prompt or justify policy intervention. They use 'causal stories' which highlight the cause of the problem and who is to blame. For example, several studies shifted long-held beliefs about blame in health and safety (from the worker to the employer), environmental damage (from natural phenomenon to human pollution), and road safety (from careless drivers to car manufacturers). In each case, this shift of attention prompted equivalent shifts in public policy (this should not be confused with the 'blame game' following disasters such as Hurricane Katrina – Boin *et al.*, 2010).

However, in most cases there are likely to be competing sources of blame. Rochefort and Cobb's (1994: 1–4) discussion of the LA riots in 1992 highlights multiple causes: a justified reaction to police racism; poor immigration controls; a breakdown in law and order; the failure of Lyndon Johnson's Great Society measures in inner-cities; the Republican neglect of race relations; and, a 'poverty of values'. The same can be said for **valence issues**. While most agree that child, drug and alcohol abuses are problems, there is much less agreement on assigning responsibility and producing solutions (Baumgartner and Jones, 1993: 150).

Valence issue – an issue in which there is only one legitimate position and public opinion is uniform.

• *Crisis and triggering events*. In many cases, crises such as environmental disasters act as a 'triggering event', focusing public, media and government attention to an issue previously lower down on the agenda (but see Box 9.3 on p. 188). Or, they act as 'dramatic symbols of problems that are already rising to national attention' (Baumgartner and Jones, 1993: 130). For example, Western attention to environmental policy peaked in 1989 following the Exxon tanker oil spill in Alaska (Dearing and Rogers, 1996: 37–9) and following the BP oil leak in the Gulf of Mexico in 2010. This propensity to give disproportionate *attention* to disasters (rather than more 'mundane' events which cause more deaths) also means that issue proponents can highlight the *potential* for dramatic crises, such as a nuclear power plant disaster (Baumgartner and Jones, 1993: 118–21) or an outbreak of SARS (severe acute respiratory syndrome) or 'mad cow disease'. In other cases, the appearance of crisis depends more on a common belief that something has gone wrong. For example, in 2008 the financial crisis associated with the 'credit crunch' and sub-prime mortgages topped the agenda of many countries (BBC News, 2008). Or, problems are *labelled* as a crisis 'to elevate a concern when facing an environment overloaded with competing claims' (Rochefort and Cobb, 1994: 21).

• *Measurement*. Although the measurement of a problem may seem like a straightforward and technical matter, it is subject to as much interpretation and debate as issue framing. In some cases, it follows the complexity or ambiguity of the policy problem. For example, the measurement of poverty can relate to: a household or individual; mean or median incomes; absolute or relative poverty; income; wealth; and, inequalities in public service access. It may also have a different meaning in domestic and international settings: while the UK government defines the 'poverty line' as 60 per cent of the overall national median income ($450 per week in 2007) for two people with no children, the World Bank uses the figure of $2 per person per day to define absolute poverty and $1 to define extreme absolute poverty (Seager, 2008; Maxwell, 1999; World Bank, 2008; Jones and Baumgartner, 2005: 31).

Measurement debates have policy consequences. For example, the treatment of civil rights issues in the US changed significantly when the measure of racism shifted, from the need to prove a person's intent to discriminate, to statistical evidence proving that an overall selection process could not have happened by chance (Stone, 1989: 291). Governments can also change the scope of their measurements (and therefore policy responses) over time. For example, in the UK, unemployment means the number of people out of work and claiming unemployment benefit. However, from the 1980s the government introduced various policies to restrict the number of people who qualified for this

Box 9.3 Up and down with ecology: the 'issue-attention cycle'

Do peaks in attention cause policy change? Downs' (1972) thesis is that public attention is fleeting, even when this involves 'a continuing problem of crucial importance to society'. A rise in interest does not mean a worsening of the problem, while falling interest does not suggest that the problem has been solved. This point is a key tenet of the literature: 'Virtually every study of agenda-setting has found … that issues emerge and recede from the public agenda without important changes in the nature of the issues themselves' (Baumgartner and Jones, 1993: 47). The issue attention cycle has five stages:

- Pre-problem – a problem alarms experts but doesn't yet capture public attention.
- Alarmed discovery and euphoric enthusiasm – concentrated public attention is accompanied by a widespread hope that the problem can be solved quickly.
- Realizing the cost of significant progress – when the public realizes that the solution involves major costs or a significant change in behaviour.
- Gradual decline of intense public interest – people feel discouraged at the prospect of change and shift their attention to the next issue at stage two.
- Post-problem– public attention is minimal or spasmodic and the problem has been replaced by another issue.

Downs posits a weak link between public attention and policy change, since the public is rarely engaged long enough to see matters through. However, in many cases there is a policy response which creates new institutions that operate long after public interest has waned (Downs, 1972). This point is made more strongly by Peters and Hogwood (1985: 251; see also Hogwood, 1992b) who find a positive relationship between public attention and government reorganizations. As Baumgartner and Jones (1993: 87) argue, peak periods of organization change 'generally coincided with Gallup Poll data showing public concern with the same problems'. Therefore, 'the public is seriously involved in the agenda-setting process, not an ignored bystander' (Jones and Baumgartner, 2005: 269).

The policy responses from public attention may have long-term effects. A realization of the costs of policy change may occur only after legislation has passed and policy is being implemented (Peters and Hogwood, 1985: 239). New government organizations are created but 'do not simply "fade away" like public interest or media attention' (Baumgartner and Jones, 1993: 84–7; 191). For example, the 'euphoric enthusiasm' for nuclear power as a policy solution from the 1940s-led decision makers to support the industry and defer to their expertise. Since it took 20 years to 'realize the cost' of nuclear progress, by the time public opinion shifted against nuclear power the policy was too far advanced to reverse easily. It also took 10 years for mobilizations based on a negative image of pesticides to break down the institutional arrangements set up following post-war enthusiasm (Baumgartner and Jones 1993: 88, 97, 101, 169; Baumgartner and Mahoney 2005 also discuss Medicare, Medicaid, the Environmental Protection Agency and civil rights policies).

benefit. It included: excluding students and government trainees, giving unemployment benefit only to those who had made significant National Insurance tax contributions; and, making individuals prove that they were actively seeking work. The UK also has, when compared to the rest of the EU, a relatively high number of economically inactive people who claim sickness rather than unemployment benefits (Webster, 2002; Machin, 2004).

Problem definition and venue shopping

Baumgartner and Jones' (1993) discussion of venue shopping is inspired by Schattschneider's (1960) suggestion (Chapter 3) that power involves the competition to 'socialize' or 'privatize' conflict. Baumgartner and Jones (1993) highlight the role of government as a source for the socialization and privatization of conflict. For example, if iron triangles or policy communities (the 'winners') organize issues out of politics by creating a policy monopoly, their opponents (the 'losers') 'will have the incentive to look for allies elsewhere' (1993: 35–7).

Policy monopolies and communities are common, but so too is the ability to challenge monopolies and make authoritative decisions in other venues. Monopolies are created when institutional arrangements reinforce the relationships between certain interest groups and public officials in a single venue. The creation of a policy monopoly limits policy debate and the scope for policy change. The main options for issue proponents are two-fold. First, they can challenge the dominance of a monopoly within this venue. The attitudes of decision makers are susceptible to change according to the political circumstances they operate within. As Jones (1994: 5) argues, 'decision-makers value or weight preferences differently depending on the context in which they are evoked'. Decision makers have many (often contradictory) objectives, most issues are multi-faceted and there are many ways to solve policy problems. Therefore, it may be possible to shift the opinions of decision makers by 'shifting the focus of their attention from one set of implications to another' (Baumgartner and Jones, 1993: 30).

Second, if unsuccessful, they can venue shop and seek more sympathetic audiences elsewhere (the process is often trial-and-error rather than 'rational' – Baumgartner and Jones, 2009: 276). The consequence of a multiplicity of venues (across government and at different stages of the policy process) is that an issue may be viewed or framed differently in different arenas at different times (since each venue may be more receptive to a different policy image). The ability to venue shop has increased since the post-war period. An increasingly complex political system – containing a much larger number of groups, experts and other policy participants – makes it much more difficult for policy issues to be insulated from the wider political process and for policy monopolies to restrict debate (Baumgartner and Jones, 1993: 43). In most cases there is no natural jurisdiction for policy problems and no 'iron clad logic' for an issue to be considered at, say, the national rather than local level. It is also common for the decision-making responsibility for policy problems to shift over time (1993: 32–3).

This premise allows us to explain why policy change follows a mutually reinforcing process of increased attention, venue shift and shifting policy images. The key strategy is to involve the previously uninvolved. If issues 'break out' of these policy communities and are considered in one or more alternative venues, then the scope for new ways to examine and solve policy problems increases. As people come to understand the nature of a policy problem in a different way (and this new understanding of the problem is more closely linked to their priorities), more people become interested and involved (1993: 8). The more 'outside' involvement there is, then the greater likelihood of a further shift of the policy image, as new ideas are discussed and new policy solutions are proposed by new participants.

Case studies of punctuated equilibrium: 'some issues catch fire'

Baumgartner and Jones (1993) compare a range of case studies over several decades to demonstrate the creation of, and challenge to, policy monopolies. Environmental policy demonstrates the use of venue shopping to change a policy's image, with the new involvement of one venue producing a snowball effect. Environmental groups, who were unhappy at losing out on regulatory decisions made by a branch of the federal government, appealed to previously uninvolved members of Congress. Congress became more sympathetic to a new image of environmental policy and passed legislation (the National Environmental Protection Act, NEPA, 1969) to regulate business, allow groups greater access to the courts, and pave the way for a federal response (the creation of the Environmental Protection Agency) more in line with the new policy image (1993: 38).

In nuclear power, Baumgartner and Jones (1993: 59–82), describe the effect of a 'Downsian mobilization', or a period of public enthusiasm which prompts governments to solve policy problems (and then leave the details to experts). The government-inspired enthusiasm for nuclear produced a positive policy image – stressing the peaceful use of nuclear materials, reduced bills, independence from imported oil, employment, reduced air pollution and the economic benefits of new technology –

which supported the formation of a post-war policy monopoly. As the process moved from policy making to implementation, public, media and government attention fell and the details of policy were left to the (mainly private sector) experts, federal agencies (e.g. Atomic Energy Commission, AEC) and certain congressional committees.

However, from the late 1960s, there was increased opposition from environmentalists, local activists and nuclear scientists expressing concerns about safety. It suggests a 'Schattschneider mobilization', or an expansion of the scope of conflict (by actors previously excluded from iron triangles) to challenge a monopoly and change the direction of policy. This is most effective when internal scientific divisions and negative media attention are already apparent. The safety agenda was pursued through public hearings on nuclear licensing and, by the 1970s, public and media attention rose to reflect these new concerns (with the number of negative articles beginning to outnumber the positive). A range of venues became involved in the issue. The focus of Congress (and an increasing number of committees) became increasingly negative and NEPA reinforced the need for more stringent nuclear regulation. It was followed by a series of key decisions in the courts, including the retrospective application of NEPA to previous AEC licensing decisions, and supplementary action by state and local governments (including the use of planning laws to delay the building of nuclear plants). The new policy image was cemented in the public's mind by the accident at the Three Mile Island nuclear plant. The private sector lost confidence in the industry and no nuclear plants have been commissioned since 1977. Overall, the combination of interest-group opposition and venue shopping shifted the policy image of nuclear power from highly positive to overwhelmingly negative. The policy monopoly was maintained for over 20 years then destroyed. A post-war policy of power plant expansion was replaced by increased regulation (but note that the new context of climate change may shift its image once more – Baumgartner and Jones, 2009: 260–4).

In the early twentieth century, a tobacco policy monopoly was based on a positive policy image (economic benefits) and deferral to the experts in agriculture (with congressional oversight largely restricted to this arena). Tobacco consumption was high and media coverage was very low and generally positive, particularly during the Second World War when smoking had a glamorous image. However, from the 1950s there was significant issue expansion, with anti-tobacco groups increasingly setting the media agenda with a negative policy image. Tobacco consumption fell dramatically from the 1950s and in 1964 the Surgeon General's report cemented a new image based on ill-health. Congressional attention followed in the mid-1970s, with health committee hearings outnumbering agriculture and a range of public health groups increasingly involved and able to reframe the debate in negative terms (Baumgartner and Jones, 1993: 114; 210). By the 1980s, this new image was pursued through a series of high-profile court cases and by innovative states such as New York and California providing best practice and the scope for policy diffusion (Studlar, 2002). By the 2000s, tobacco control became much more restrictive (Cairney *et al.*, 2012) and the old pro-tobacco sub-system was completely 'destroyed' (Baumgartner and Jones, 2009: 280).

Also in the early twentieth century, a pesticides policy monopoly was based on a positive policy image (eradicating harmful insects, boosting agricultural exports, ending world hunger by boosting food production), public and media 'enthusiasm for progress through chemistry' and deferral to the experts in agriculture and the chemical industry (who enjoyed a close relationship with the Department of Agriculture, USDA, and the congressional agriculture committee – Baumgartner and Jones, 1993: 95). Environmental concerns were marginalized, consumer interests were generally ignored and the Food and Drug Administration (within the USDA) had no jurisdiction over pesticide control. However, the 'golden age' of pesticides was punctured in 1957 following the devastating failure of two large insect eradication campaigns and in 1959 following the FDA's decision to ban the sale of a crop tainted with pesticide residue. It shifted media and Congressional attention from the economic benefits of pesticides to their ineffectiveness, adverse health effects, and environmental damage. By the late 1960s, environmental groups had found support within multiple venues (Congress, the courts, executive and state agencies) and the enforced regulation of pesticide use rocketed.

The generalizability of punctuated equilibrium: (1) from case studies to theory

Jones and Baumgartner (2005: 278) address the possibility that punctuated equilibrium is merely a feature of policy monopolies and the case studies that they selected (see also Baumgartner and Jones, 2002 and True *et al.*, 2007: 163 for a list of case studies by other authors). Their focus shifted to more general theories about agenda setting and policy change. For example, 'disproportionate information processing' suggests that most government responses are not in proportion with the 'signals' that they receive from the outside world. Instead, political systems produce **negative** and **positive feedback**. While the former acts as a counterbalance to political forces, the latter reinforces those forces to

Negative feedback – a mechanism to 'rein back' forces for change. One change is resisted and goes no further.

Positive feedback – a mechanism to amplify forces for change; e.g. one change causes a 'bandwagon effect'.

produce radical change (Baumgartner and Jones, 2002: 8–16). This relates directly to the case study results: when policy monopolies are maintained, decision makers appear unreceptive to new information but, in periods of punctuation, decision makers appear to become hyper-sensitive to new information (Jones and Baumgartner, 2005: 8; 18). It also contributes to a much wider 'General Punctuation Hypothesis' (or the identification of 'disruptive dynamics' – Baumgartner and Jones, 2009: 253): although governing institutions receive 'feedback' on their policies (for example, from interest groups, the media or public opinion), they do not respond proportionately. The 'selective attention' of decision makers or institutions explains why issues can be relatively high on certain agendas, but not acted upon; why these powerful signals are often ignored and policies remain stable for long periods. Policymakers are *unwilling* to focus on certain issues, either because ideology precludes action in some areas, there is an established view within government about how to address the issue, or because the process of acting 'rationally' (and making explicit trade-offs between a wide range of decisions) is often unpopular (note: ideology suggests that a change in party of government may produce policy change, but a key point from punctuated equilibrium theory is that party changes are not the only source of 'policy disruptions' – Baumgartner and Jones, 2009: 287). They are also *unable* to give issues significant attention, because the focus on one issue means ignoring 99 others. Change therefore requires a critical mass of attention to overcome the conservatism of decision makers and shift their attention from competing problems (Jones and Baumgartner, 2005: 19–20; 48–51). If the levels of external pressure reach this tipping point, they cause major and infrequent punctuations rather than smaller and more regular policy changes: the burst in attention and communication becomes self-reinforcing; new approaches are considered; different 'weights' are applied to the same categories of information; policy is driven ideologically by new actors; and/or the 'new' issue sparks off new conflicts between political actors (2005: 52; 69). Information processing is characterized by 'stasis interrupted by bursts of innovation' and policy responses are unpredictable and episodic rather than continuous (2005: 20).

To demonstrate the applicability of this theory to policy change, the Policy Agendas Project (http://www.policyagendas.org/) extends the analysis from particular case studies to the dynamics of government budgets, elections and policymaker attention. Most notably, it produces a comprehensive analysis of post-war US public expenditure in the postwar period (Jones and Baumgartner, 2005: 111; True *et al.*, 2007) and the longer term (Jones *et al.*, 2009). Public expenditure changes have gener-

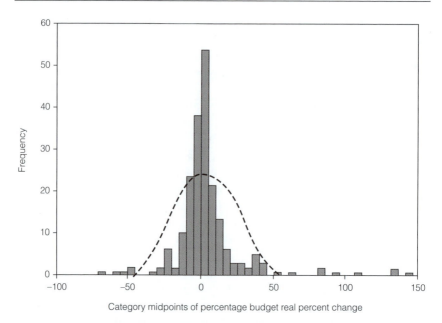

Figure 9.1   *A broad picture of the general punctuation hypothesis in action*

Source: adapted (normal curve added) from Jones *et al*. (2009: 861). It shows the percentage changes to US budgets from 1800–2000. See also the more detailed graphs in True *et al*. (2007: 170) and Jones and Baumgartner (2005: 111) which show an even higher central peak and longer tails when we analyse only the post-war budget changes (financial years 1947–93). Note that the latter figures track the amount dedicated (not the amount spent) and variation from the **mode** (a 4 per cent real annual rise is the most common) rather than the mean (Jones and Baumgartner, 2005: 110–11).

ally become key indicators in public policy because: (a) they allow us to measure policy changes in a systematic way; and (b) spending commitments are more concrete than more vague policy intentions (Chapter 2). The results are displayed in Figure 9.1 which highlights the annual percentage change of US budgets in each policy area (such as health, social security, and education). But what does the figure tell us and how should the results be interpreted? Jones and Baumgartner (2005) argue that if the overall nature of budgeting changes was incremental (and not punctuated), then the figure should display a **normal distribution**. This is a statistical term which usually refers to two things: (a) the **mean** figure; and (b) the **standard deviation** from the mean. A normal distribution suggests that most (68 per cent) of all the values are slightly different from the mean, while almost all (95 per cent) are no more than moderately different. In other words, while there will be a small handful of instances in which the values differ markedly from the mean, most values are bunched closely together, while some are further away from the mean, but not remarkably so (Box 9.4).

Box 9.4   Key terms for statistical analysis

Mean – the average, calculated by adding all values together and dividing by the number of values.

Mode – the average, calculated by identifying the most frequent value.

Standard deviation – a measure of statistical dispersion which generally denotes deviation from the mean (Figure 9.1 uses the mode). If all values are the same, then the SD is zero (e.g. the numbers 100, 100 and 100). The greater the dispersion (e.g. 0, 100, 200), then the greater the SD.

Normal distribution – denotes the level of SD from the mean. It suggests that 68 per cent of all values fall within a range of plus or minus one standard deviation from the mean, while 95 per cent fall within a range of plus or minus two standard deviations.

Leptokurtic – a distribution which is not normal because it has a higher central peak and more outliers. More than 68 per cent fall within ±1 standard deviation but less than 95 per cent fall within a range of ±2.

Outlier – a value which is further away from the mean than the normal distribution suggests.

Real increase – an increase in spending which takes inflation into account.

We may expect no more than a normal distribution because incrementalism suggests a common type of change in most policy areas: a small (or non-radical) change from previous years in most cases, combined with moderate change overall (2005: 120–3). Since there is some doubt about the size of an increment (Chapter 5), the normal curve accounts for a degree of variety of annual budget changes (up to ±80 per cent in the post-war period; up to approximately ±50 per cent in Figure 9.1). Yet, Figure 9.1 demonstrates that the distribution of values is **leptokurtic**. This has two main features. First, a higher central peak (note how much higher the bar reaches above the peak of the normal curve) and lower level of dispersion (note the space between the bars and the dotted line within the normal curve) than we would expect. In the vast majority of cases the **real increase** or decrease in annual spending is very low and the size of the increment is very small. Jones and Baumgartner (2005: 112) call this 'hyperincrementalism'. Second, there are many more **outliers** than we would expect under a normal distribution. For example, in their post-war data set with approximately 3,300 values we may expect approximately 15–20 outliers. Yet, there are many more. For example, the number of cases of annual change greater than +160 per cent is 75 (2005: 110). The analysis suggests that in a small but very important number of cases, 'programs received huge boosts, propelling them to double or triple their original sizes or more' (2005: 112). Overall, budget change is characterized by a *huge number of small changes* in each policy category, combined with a *small number of huge changes* (True *et al.*, 2007: 166).

This outcome results from 'disproportionate information processing'. Although there is no shortage of information, most issues are ignored or receive little attention, while some receive an intense level of attention which produces major policy consequences (2005: 112). The outcome also represents the most important confirmation of the general punctuation hypothesis, and '400,000 observations collected as part of the Policy Agendas Project' demonstrate that the hypothesis 'is a fundamental characteristic of the American political system (2005: 278). Indeed, the absence of a normal distribution is also a feature demonstrated by data on events such as US elections and congressional legislation and hearings (although the effect is most marked in budget data) (Baumgartner *et al.*, 2009: 611).

The generalizability of punctuated equilibrium: (2) other political systems

There is good reason to think that punctuated equilibrium theory applies mostly to the US. It was originally used to explain why the US political system 'conservatively designed to resist many efforts at change' also helped produce 'bursts of change' (True *et al.*, 2007: 157). Punctuated equilibrium suggests that the key features which explain stability – the separation of powers (executive, legislative and judicial), overlapping jurisdictions (between institutions or between federal, state and local government) and the pluralistic interaction between groups (in which the 'mobilization of one group will lead to the countermobilization of another' – Baumgartner and Jones, 1993: 4–5) – also help explain major punctuations. In most cases, these checks and balances combine with the ability of organized interests to 'counter-mobilize' to block radical policy change. However, in a small number of cases, mobilizations are accompanied by renewed interest among one or more venues. In such cases, 'the newcomers are proponents of changes ... and they often overwhelm the previously controlling powers' (True *et al.*, 2007: 157). Therefore, the diffusion of power across US government increases the scope for venue shift and helps groups form new alliances with decision makers capable of challenging monopolies.

Yet, the causal factors identified by punctuated equilibrium apply to a wide range of political systems. First, the separation of powers and/or existence of overlapping jurisdictions is not limited to the US. Indeed, the entanglement of policy issues (when decision-making power is vested in more than level of government) is common to devolved and federal systems (Keating 2005: 18; Cairney, 2006). Second, the multi-level governance literature demonstrates the increasing significance of multiple decision-making venues (and issue network rather than policy community relationships – Richardson, 2008: 25) in the EU and, more notably, countries such as the UK associated with a concentration of power via parliamentary government (Chapter 8). Third, the component parts of punctuated equilibrium – bounded rationality, information processing, complexity, agenda setting and group–government relations – are central to the policy literature as a whole. Processes such as 'disproportionate information processing' are universal; what we are really talking about is the effect of bounded rationality in complex policy-making environments.

Punctuated equilibrium has been applied extensively to policy change in Canada, the EU and many European countries (True *et al.*, 2007: 175; John, 2006; Baumgartner and Jones, 2009: 255; Baumgartner *et al.*, 2006) and continues to grow in importance as a truly comparative policy theory. For example, Jones *et al.* (2009: 855) identify the same basic distribution of budget changes in the US, UK, Canada, France, Germany, Belgium and Denmark: 'budgets are highly incremental, yet occasionally are punctuated by large changes'. Further, Baumgartner *et al.* (2009) show that variations in the data may relate as much to the stage of the policy cycle as the political system. Much depends on the levels of 'friction', or costs related to coordination, which are lower at the beginning of the policy cycle than the end. So, for example, it is easier for legislative committees to come together to focus on new issues than for large governments to shift their budgets to reflect new priorities. Consequently, the former will display lower levels of kurtosis (change is effectively more 'normal') than the latter (which displays relatively high levels of both minimal and dramatic changes) (2009: 609).

Conclusion

The aim of punctuated equilibrium is to explain long periods of policy stability punctuated by short but intense periods of change. A combination of bounded rationality and agenda setting explains how policy monopolies can be created and destroyed. While there is an infinite number of ways to understand policy problems, there is only so much time and energy to devote to issues. So, highly complex issues are simplified, with very few aspects considered at any one time at the expense of all the rest. Problem definition is crucial because the allocation of resources follows the image of the policy problem. Policy stability depends on the ability of policy communities to maintain a policy monopoly. The production of a policy monopoly follows the successful definition of a policy problem in a certain way, to limit the number of participants who can claim a legitimate role in the process. As the examples of pesticides and nuclear power suggest, this often follows a burst of wider public and governmental enthusiasm for policy change. Such 'Downsian mobilizations' produce a supportive policy image, based on the idea that economic progress and technological advance has solved the policy problem, allowing policy communities to operate for long periods with very little external attention. After the main policy decision is made, the details are left to policy experts and specialists in government. This allows the participants to frame the process as 'technical' to reduce public interest or 'specialist' to exclude those groups considered to have no expertise. The lack of attention or external involvement allows communities to build up a policy-delivering infrastructure that is difficult to dismantle, even during periods of negative attention.

Policy change is explained by a successful challenge to policy monopolies. Those excluded from monopolies have an interest in challenging or reshaping the dominant way of defining policy problems. This may come from within, by ensuring that new ideas or evidence force a shift in government attention to a new policy image. Or, if this new image is stifled, then groups attempt to expand the scope of conflict and promote it to a more sympathetic audience. 'Schattschneider mobilizations' can extend to other decision-making venues and/or to the wider public. In either case, the successful redefinition of a policy problem prompts an influx of new actors. As the examples of pesticides and nuclear power suggest, the new policy image based on safety concerns produced a snowball effect. It began with rising dissent among experts within a policy community, followed by increased media coverage critical of the *status quo*. Previously excluded interest groups exploited this shift of focus to attract the attention of decision makers in other venues. The adoption of the safety agenda in one venue had a knock-on effect, providing more legitimacy for the new image and creating an incentive for decision makers in other venues to become involved. The result was profound policy change following a burst of new regulations by Congress, the courts and multiple levels of government. Policy change therefore follows a mutually reinforcing process of increased attention, venue shift and shifting policy images. As people come to understand the nature of a policy problem in a different way, then more people become interested and involved. The more 'outside' involvement there is, then the greater likelihood of a further shift of the policy image, as new ideas are discussed and new policy solutions are proposed by new participants.

The 'general punctuation hypothesis' suggests that this effect is not limited to policy communities. Rather, the case studies highlight a wider process of 'disproportionate information processing'. Most government responses are not in proportion with the 'signals' that they receive from the outside world. They are either insensitive or hypersensitive to policy relevant information. As a result, most policies stay the same for long periods because decision makers are unwilling or unable to pay them sufficient attention. However, in a small number of cases, policy changes radically as decision makers respond to a critical mass of external attention. The burst of governmental attention is accompanied by a sense of policy malaise and a need to play 'catch up'. New ideas are considered, different 'weights' are applied to the same kinds of information, and the 'new' issue sparks off new conflicts between political actors. These bursts of attention produce short bursts of radical policy change. The best demonstration of this picture of stability and change can be found in budgeting. Budget change is characterized by a widespread 'hyperincrementalism' (or a huge number of small annual budget changes), combined with a small number of huge changes to annual budgets. Overall, the picture is more dynamic than incrementalism suggests, even if most policymaking appears to be incremental. Although most policy issues display stability and there are many policy communities, these are constantly being created and destroyed. Therefore, any snapshot of the political system will be misleading since it shows an overall picture of stability, but not the process of profound change over a longer period.

Chapter 10

The Advocacy Coalition Framework

This chapter examines:

- The key aspects of the ACF, including the role of beliefs, the composition of sub-systems and external sources of stability and change.
- The meaning of 'belief systems', the distinction between core, policy core and secondary beliefs and the role of policy-oriented learning.
- How the ACF has been revised over time.
- The applicability of the ACF to political systems outside of the US.
- The value of this analysis to the wider concerns of this book, including the study of group–government relations, policy cycles, socio-economic factors and the role of ideas.

A key aim of policy analysis is to understand and explain a complex world: the policy process contains multiple actors and levels of government; it displays a mixture of intensely politicized disputes coupled with technical and routine decision making, and; the full effects of major policy decisions may not be clear for at least a decade (Sabatier, 2007a: 3–4). According to the advocacy coalition framework (ACF) the best way to understand this world is to focus on a process driven by actors promoting their beliefs: 'policy participants hold strong beliefs and are motivated to transfer those beliefs into actual policy ... before their opponents can do the same' (Sabatier and Weible, 2007: 192; 196). Beliefs act as the glue which binds actors together within **advocacy coalitions**. In turn, different coalitions compete with each other to secure policy outcomes consistent with their beliefs. This competition takes place within specialised **policy sub-systems**. These processes often display long-term stability and policy continuity because the 'core' or 'policy core' beliefs of coalitions are unlikely to shift and one coalition may dominate the subsystem for long periods.

Advocacy coalitions – 'people from a variety of positions (elected and agency officials, interest group leaders, researchers) who share a particular belief system – i.e. a set of basic values, causal assumptions, and problem perceptions – and who show a non-trivial degree of coordinated activity over time' (Sabatier, 1988: 139).

Policy sub-system – a 'set of actors who are involved in dealing with a policy problem' (1988: 138; for more detail, see McCool, 1998: 558).

200

There are two main sources of change in this framework. First, coalitions adapt continuously to their policy environments and engage in policy learning to remain competitive. This process often produces minor change because policy learning takes place though the lens of deeply held policy beliefs. In other words, coalitions learn on their own terms – selecting the information they hold to be most relevant and acceding only to change which does not undermine the coalition's main source of cooperation. Second, external 'shocks' – such as the election of a new government with different ideas or the effect of socio-economic change – affect the positions of coalitions within sub-systems. Shocks may produce major change as coalitions are forced to question the fundamental nature of their beliefs in the light of new evidence and/or one coalition's source of dominance is undermined. For example, a competing coalition may adapt more readily to its new policy environment and gain the favour of the sub-system's **policy brokers** or **sovereign**. The ACF thus represents an attempt to show how external sources of change in the political system are mediated by the actors that represent a source of stability within sub-systems. While many of these external factors – such as global recession, environmental crises and demographic changes – may be universally recognized as important, coalitions influence how sovereigns understand, interpret and respond to them.

Policy brokers – actors within sub-systems that seek to minimize conflict and produce workable compromises between competing advocacy coalitions.

Sovereign – the governmental authority or ultimate decision maker within a sub-system.

The main value of the ACF is that it combines a novel discussion of at least four key processes and relationships within public policy. First, it recognises the importance of policy networks, but challenges the idea that policy is controlled by a small number of groups and government actors. Rather, it identifies a wider variety of players, including journalists, academics and actors across various levels of government. Second, it shares with the literature on policy cycles the view that policy change must be analysed over the longer term and not just at the point of decision. However, it is also driven by a critique of artificial distinctions between stages in the policy cycle (Chapter 2). Third, it highlights the importance of socio-economic factors, but attempts to go beyond the 'black box' approach (Chapter 6) to explain how those factors are addressed within the political system. Fourth, it adds to our understanding of the role of ideas by demonstrating how beliefs are promoted within government. The ACF encourages us to analyse public policies in the same way we consider beliefs; a policy choice is based not only on a belief about what the outcome should be, but also why we should desire that outcome and how it will achieve its aim (Sabatier, 1998: 99). While policy debates involve the exercise of power, they are also driven by debates on the best measures of, and how best to interpret, a policy problem (Sabatier, 1988: 158, drawing on Majone, 1980; compare with Radaelli's 1999: 664 discussion of policy narratives).

A picture of the advocacy coalition framework

As Figure 10.1 suggests, the main focus of the ACF is on a policy subsystem within a wider political system. It shares with the policy networks literature a focus on the types of group–government relationships that develop when the reach of government has extended to most aspects of society. Governments deal with the potential for 'overload' by breaking policy down into more manageable sectors and sub-sectors and devolving decision-making responsibility to less senior, but often more knowledgeable, officials. In turn, those officials gather policy knowledge in consultation with actors such as interest groups, who trade their expertise and advice for access to government and the chance to influence policy. The system effectively produces 'enormous pressures for specialization' and it is unusual for groups to have enough relevant knowledge to compete in more than one or two sectors (Sabatier, 1993:

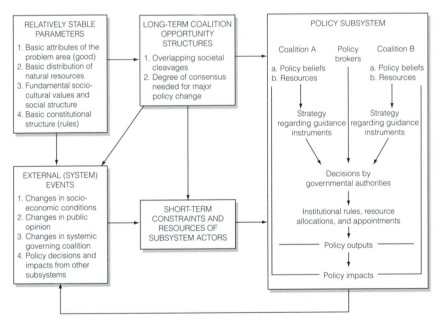

Figure 10.1   *The advocacy coalition framework flow diagram, 2007*

Source: Weible, Sabatier, and McQueen (2009: 123). Note that there may be more than two coalitions within a sub-system. The insulation of sub-systems from each other is also a simplification – see Sabatier and Weible (2007: 193; Weible *et al.*, 2009: 134) for a discussion of overlapping sub-systems.

23; Sabatier, 1988: 138; Sabatier and Weible, 2007: 192; compare with Dahl in Chapter 3). Much of the early post-war literature suggests that this pressure produced specialized and exclusive 'policy communities' or 'iron triangles' (Jordan, 1981; Richardson and Jordan, 1979; Weible and Sabatier, 2005) (see Box 9.1 on terminology). However, the ACF follows Heclo's (1978: 94–7) departure from a focus on the simple 'clubby days of Washington politics' towards 'complex relationships' among a huge, politically active population. Issues which were once 'quietly managed by a small group of insiders' have now become 'controversial and politicized' (1978: 105; compare with McCool, 1998: 554–5).

In the ACF, the politicization of issues is more common than in policy communities which promote shared norms and maintain a policy monopoly to exclude potential participants (Chapter 9). Indeed, advocacy coalitions often exhibit the opposite behaviour by identifying and 'activating latent constituencies' (Sabatier, 1993: 24). The ACF also highlights a systematic role for actors not usually considered to be part of insulated policy communities:

> Our conception of policy subsystems should be broadened from traditional notions of iron triangles limited to administrative agencies, legislative committees, and interest groups at a single level of government to include actors at various levels of government, as well as journalists, researchers and policy analysts who play important roles in the generation, dissemination, and evaluation of policy ideas. (Jenkins-Smith and Sabatier, 1993a: 179; see also Sabatier, 1993: 24–5; Sabatier and Weible, 2007: 192)

This set-up requires policy analysis over 'a decade or more' for two main reasons. First, it is necessary to capture the longer term 'enlightenment function' that actors contribute through policy research. The role of beliefs is central to the cohesiveness of advocacy coalitions, and policy researchers are a welcome source of ideas. Indeed, a key aim of the ACF is to 'integrate the role of such technical analysis into the overall process of policy change' (Jenkins-Smith and Sabatier, 1993b: 41). Second, it highlights the role of actors at all levels of government by analysing policy over a full 'cycle'. The ACF draws on the literature on policy cycles to reject the analysis of policy formulation without tracking its implementation, and to highlight the role that actors outwith the national level of government contribute to policy innovation. The inclusion of actors from multiple levels of government reflects the frequency of their interactions and strength of their relationships: US federal programmes are generally implemented by state or local governments; 'intergovernmental transfers constitute a significant percentage of most state and local government budgets'; state and local government representatives have a strong presence within the policy networks surrounding the legislature and executive agencies; and, interest groups tend to lobby 'a variety of agencies at different levels of government ... A coalition doing poorly in Washington is not helpless but instead can focus its efforts at subnational levels where it is more powerful' (Sabatier and Jenkins-Smith, 1993: 215–16; 230; Sabatier, 1993: 36; compare with 'venue shopping' in Chapter 9). However, the ACF rejects the artificial distinctions between stages of the policy process. Rather, the main focus of analysis remains the policy sub-system, with actors in national and subnational governmental arenas operating as part of a common advocacy coalition (Jenkins-Smith and Sabatier, 1993a: 5).

One consequence of this approach is that the boundaries between competing coalitions, policy brokers and governmental authorities (or 'sovereigns') are more fluid than Figure 10.1 suggests. Coalitions may 'seek to alter the behaviour of governmental institutions', but those institutions may already be predisposed to the coalition's 'policy cores' (Sabatier and Jenkins-Smith, 1993: 227). Governmental authorities may be formally responsible for policy decisions, but they may also be members of advocacy coalitions (compare with the blurred boundaries between formal authority and informal influence in MLG – Chapter 8). Indeed, different actors within the same authorities may be members of competing coalitions. Similarly, policy brokers may also have a 'policy bent', while some members of coalitions may be driven strongly by a desire for compromise and sub-system stability. The 'distinction between "advocate" and "broker" ... rests on a continuum' (Sabatier, 1993: 27). Effectively, the details become empirical matters to be investigated in case studies.

Belief systems and power

The ACF suggests that actors are motivated by their beliefs to form long-term coalitions, rather than simple 'short-term self-interest' which produces a tendency towards 'coalitions of convenience' (Sabatier, 1993: 27). The reason that members of advocacy coalitions stay together is that they have similar 'belief systems', which represent a complex mix of theories about how the world works, how it should work and what we should do to bring the former closer to the latter (compare this to discussions of world views, ideologies and policy proposals in Chapter 11). Beliefs also relate specifically to policy action, influencing which problems coalition members feel, 'should receive the highest priority, the causal factors that need to be examined most closely, and the governmental institutions most likely to be favourably disposed to the coalition's point of view' (Jenkins-Smith and Sabatier, 1993b: 41). The importance of a common belief system, or 'set of basic values, causal assumptions, and problem perceptions', is that it helps explain, in a parsimonious way, why a wide range of different actors exhibit 'coordinated activity over time' (Sabatier, 1993: 25). There are three main types of beliefs (although the boundaries between the first two are sometimes fluid):

- *Deep core beliefs.* These regard an actor's 'underlying personal philosophy' (Sabatier, 1993: 30). Examples include: beliefs on whether people are evil or socially redeemable; how we should rank values such as freedom and security; whose welfare should count the most; and, the basic left/right wing divide (Sabatier, 1998: 103).
- *Policy core beliefs.* These regard 'fundamental policy positions'. Examples include: the proper balance between government and market; the proper distribution of power across levels of government; what causes policy problems and whether or not society can, and should attempt to, solve them (Sabatier, 1993: 31; 1998: 110).
- *Secondary aspects.* These relate to the funding, delivery and implementation of policy goals and the information gathered to support the process (1993: 31).

There is a hierarchy of beliefs according to their scope, how strongly they are adhered to, how they influence learning and how susceptible they are to change in the light of new experiences and events. Core beliefs span most policy areas and are the least susceptible to change. Indeed, a shift in core beliefs within one policy cycle would be 'akin to a religious conversion' because they are 'largely normative issues inculturated in childhood and largely impervious to empirical evidence' (Sabatier, 1993: 31; 36). However, they tend to be too broad to guide policy-specific behaviour. Instead, policy core beliefs are employed within particular sub-systems. Although policy core beliefs are more susceptible to change, this may not happen within a cycle because: the 'enlightenment function' may take place over decades, many beliefs are 'primarily normative – and thus largely beyond direct empirical challenge'; and, 'powerful ego-defense, peer-group, and organizational forces create considerable resistance to change, even in the face of countervailing empirical evidence or internal inconsistencies' (Sabatier, 1993: 44; 33). In some cases, a coalition may revisit its view on the 'overall seriousness of the problem' when compared to other issues, or regarding the most appropriate role of government (Sabatier and Jenkins-Smith, 1993: 221). For example, environmental coalitions may shift their beliefs about the best way to achieve their policy goals, from a top-down command-and-control approach towards education and the provision of economic incentives. However, in most cases, change refers to 'secondary aspects'; policy learning usually takes place when beliefs on the routine delivery of specific policies are refined according to new information gathered during the policy cycle (Sabatier and Jenkins-Smith, 1993: 31; 221; compare with May's 1992 distinction between instrumental, social and political learning).

While the centrality of beliefs and policy learning gives prominence to the role of ideas, the ACF also incorporates a discussion of power. The ability of advocacy coalitions to push policy in their favoured direction is dependent on their resources, including 'money, expertise, number of supporters and legal authority' (Sabatier, 1993: 29; compare with Dahl's sources of power in Chapter 3). Coalition power depends on: their numbers and the status of members 'in positions of legal authority'; their ability to 'garner public support'; their grasp of 'information regarding the problem severity and causes and the costs and benefits of policy alternatives'; their ability to spin their arguments convincingly (without losing respect from policymakers); their 'mobilizable troops', or members willing to initiate public demonstrations and fundraisers; the money they have to fund research, 'bankroll sympathetic candidates' or otherwise gain policy access and disseminate their message; and the ability of their leadership to present an 'attractive vision for a coalition' and exploit the opportunities for policy change prompted by external shocks (Sabatier and Weible, 2007: 201–3).

Beliefs and resources reinforce each other. Members of an advocacy coalition seek as many allies as possible. Beliefs act as the glue to bind participants, while the coming together of a range of allies creates 'pressures for common positions, which tend to harden over time' (Sabatier, 1993: 26). Further, legal authority and institutional rules are resources that can be used to establish or reinforce the centrality of particular beliefs within sub-systems (although note the other strategies used by coalitions – Sabatier and Jenkins-Smith, 1993: 227). The establishment of authority and rules often produces stability and tends to reinforce the balance (or asymmetry) of power between coalitions that is mediated by policy brokers. In turn, stability often leads to policy continuity, since a battle of ideas is replaced by a focus on secondary aspects.

The dynamics of 'policy-oriented learning'

For Bennett and Howlett (1992: 275), the concept of policy learning supplements theories that explain policy change as the result of social pressures (Chapter 6) and the exercise of power (Chapter 3). The mediation of external pressures and the exercise of power are based partly on the knowledge held and used by participants. However, they argue that learning can refer to at least five related processes and authors: governments adapting to the success or failure of policy (Hall); governments reacting to their environment (Heclo); organizations developing better policymaking functions (Etheridge); governments drawing lessons from the experience of governments in other regions (Rose); and coalitions engaged in learning based on their existing beliefs (Sabatier) (Bennett and Howlett, 1992: 277; note the distinction, explored in Chapter 12, between learning and 'copying'). May (1992: 333) also discusses the 'trial-and-error' learning associated with incrementalism and implementation studies.

While these processes may be related, the models of learning are not interchangeable. They differ in their answers to three questions: 'who learns, what is learned, and what effects on resulting policies emerge as a result of learning?' (Bennett and Howlett, 1992: 278). For example: Heclo's model suggests that the main driver for change is societal pressure and that government and party officials act as 'policy middlemen'; Etheridge focuses on the role of state institutions, with learning driven by 'bureaucrats'; and, Sabatier 'attempts a marriage of interest-based and knowledge-based public policy theory' (1992: 279–80). The ACF suggests that coalition actors are much more than 'middlemen' between external forces and policy. It identifies different strengths of beliefs that affect the type of learning that takes place. Secondary aspects are modified easily in light of experience, while policy core beliefs may only change following external 'shocks'. In the absence of shocks, it is policy core beliefs ('selective perception and partisan analysis' – Sabatier, 1993: 34) that determine the focus of learning and the way that information is used.

Sabatier (1998: 104) defines policy-oriented learning as: 'relatively enduring alterations of thought or behavioral intentions which result from experience and/or new information and which are concerned with the attainment or revision of policy objectives'. Learning *within* coalitions is based on three key processes: (1) individuals within coalitions use new information to inform and adjust their beliefs; (2) coalitions experience a turnover of members; and, (3) members of coalitions interact and influence each other's views (Jenkins-Smith and Sabatier, 1993b: 41). A typical process of change, over several years, involves the dissemination of new ideas within coalitions by new members or existing members using new evidence. The diffusion of, or resistance to, new ideas depends on factors such as the 'rate of turnover, the compatibility of the information with existing beliefs, the persuasiveness of the evidence, and the political pressures for change'. In most cases, learning follows the routine monitoring of policy implementation, as members consider how policy contributes to positive or unintended outcomes and whether their beliefs regarding the best way to solve the policy problem are challenged or supported by the evidence.

Learning *across* coalitions resembles a form of adaptation by (the members of) coalition A to the beliefs of coalition B, particularly when

B's views become 'too important to ignore' (1993b: 43). Learning is a political process and 'not a disinterested search for "truth"' (1993b: 45; Sabatier, 1988: 151). First, learning is not straightforward because information on the success of policy is difficult to obtain and subject to framing by each coalition. In some cases, there are commonly accepted ways to measure policy performance. In others, it is a battle of ideas. Second, technical information is often used 'primarily in an "advocacy" fashion' when the exercise of power is not enough to secure a coalition's policy. For example, a manufacturer accused of excessive pollution may 'challenge the validity of the data concerning the seriousness of the problem', or produce data on the costs of regulation, rather than merely lobby to minimize regulation (1993b: 45; Sabatier, 1988: 152). Third, competing coalitions may refuse to engage on each other's terms, particularly when the 'level of conflict' is high and each coalition's claims threaten the core beliefs of the other. Data may be used as 'ammunition' rather than something to exchange and learn from (unless the debate can be restricted to professional scientific arenas – 1993b: 49; 54). Fourth, dominant coalitions are unlikely to simply accept the arguments of other coalitions and adopt their preferred policies. Rather, they seek to incorporate those points in a way that acknowledges the flaws of their own approach but maintains, as far as possible, the link between their core beliefs and policy measures. For example, a coalition may favour amending a piece of legislation instead of replacing it. Therefore, non-incremental change may require an external shock that undermines the position of that coalition within the subsystem (1993b: 43–4). Otherwise, a coalition can successfully challenge the data and the technical basis for policy change and delay the process of policy innovation for years (Sabatier, 1998: 104).

Stability and instability, continuity and change

These dynamics explain periods of policy stability and continuity: established sub-systems contain the same small number of coalitions (Sabatier, 1993: 26 suggests there will generally be two to four) exhibiting relatively fixed beliefs and fundamental policy positions (at least over the period of one policy cycle of a 'decade or so' – Sabatier and Weible, 2007: 193). Although coalitions will engage in policy learning according to their evaluations of policy impacts, this tends to affect the secondary aspects of policy rather than core beliefs. This stability within sub-systems is reinforced by 'relatively stable parameters', or wider features of the policy system, exogenous to the subsystem, that are unlikely to change over one cycle. These parameters include relatively easy-to-identify factors such as the rules and constitutional structures of a political system (which provide incentives for action) and the fundamental social structures and values of the wider polity (e.g. 'Large-scale nationalization of the means of production is a viable policy option in many European countries, but not the US' – Sabatier, 1988: 135). They also include the 'basic attributes of a problem area' (Weible *et al.*, 2009: 135). For example, Sabatier (2007b: 193) highlights the properties of natural resources relevant to many environmental policies.

Instability tends to come from 'external (system) events' or exogenous 'shocks' to the sub-system. Examples include the election of a new government with different policy ideas, a sudden change in public opinion (see Jones and Jenkins-Smith, 2009) that affects the positions of competing coalitions (such as a surge of environmental concern), a sudden change in socio-economic conditions (such as a global recession), and the effect of policies made in other sub-systems. Although less powerful coalitions can enhance their positions through learning and seeking new allies, they are unlikely to challenge a dominant coalition without the help of an external event (Sabatier, 1993: 35). These shocks 'can foster change in a subsystem by shifting and augmenting resources, tipping the power of coalitions, and changing beliefs' (Weible *et al.*, 2009: 124).

Overall, we have stable and dynamic elements. Stability comes from the fixed parameters of policy, such as fundamental social values that represent more of a resource for some coalitions than others (compare with Bachrach and Baratz's 1970 discussion of non-decision-making barriers in Chapter 3). It also comes from the tendency towards incrementalism produced by a brokered compromise between established advocacy coalitions. Change takes two main forms when produced by two different sources. First, incremental change follows policy learning by coalitions studying and learning from the impact of policy. It is apparent even if one coalition dominates proceedings for long periods, since coalitions are always learning from policy evaluation and reacting to external events (learning and adaptation may also follow debates between competing coalitions). In this case, policy change is minor because it concerns only the secondary aspects of coalition beliefs and public policy. Second, non-incremental change may follow a shift in power following a 'shock' to the political system that helps some and constrains others. It may lead to the replacement of one coalition by another or a new balance of power between the coalitions, forged by a policy broker. In this case, change may be major if it concerns the policy core aspects of coalition beliefs and public policy, but this relies on the ability of a competing coalition to push for (for example) legislative change (perhaps by exploiting a 'window of opportunity' to gather short term support from allies elsewhere – Sabatier, 1998: 119). In either case, policy learning and the judgement of new evidence is not straightforward. Rather, it is shaped by the existing beliefs holding coalitions together. Coalition beliefs influence the slant put on new evidence and the importance of that new evidence compared to other issues. Thus, one basic premise of the ACF is that the visible jostling that we see, regarding competing policy positions and different takes on the best way to deliver policy, is underpinned by deeper beliefs that shape the interpretation of evidence.

Applications and revisions

The ACF has undergone continuous revision since its introduction and application (Box 10.1). The first revision followed Sabatier and Jenkins-Smith's (1993) review. First, it identified the need to clarify the role of policymakers. They found that, although administrative agencies were often members of coalitions, they took 'more centrist positions than their interest-group allies' and could even 'switch sides' following 'major exogenous events' such as elections (1993: 213–14). They also suggest that 'that a 'hierarchically superior jurisdiction' may, in rare cases, override sub-system policy in the face of opposition from the dominant coalition (1993: 217; compare with Radaelli 1999: 665), although the implementation literature suggests that this is not the end of the story (Sabatier, 1998: 119). Second, technical information can have 'important impacts on policy' by influencing policy brokers even when it does not change the views of the dominant coalition (Sabatier and Jenkins-Smith, 1993: 219). Third, it sought to make clear the difference, within policy core beliefs, between 'normative precepts' that are unlikely to change, and 'precepts with a substantial empirical content' that are more likely to change in the light of new evidence (1993: 220–1). Fourth, it clarifies the role of exogenous shocks. While these are *necessary* conditions for major policy change, they are not *sufficient*; a competing coalition must also have the skill to exploit its new opportunity (1993: 222).

A further revision was prompted partly by the rise in ACF applications to countries other than the US (below). Sabatier (1998: 110–14; Sabatier and Weible, 2007: 192) makes a distinction between 'nascent' and 'mature' sub-systems, suggesting that, in the latter, there are 'specialized subunits within agencies at all relevant levels of government to deal with the topic', while participants 'regard themselves as a semi-autonomous community who share a domain of expertise' and identify the issue as a 'major policy topic'. Further, it is only in mature systems that we see the degree of sub-system stability; relationships may be more fluid in nascent sub-systems when issues are still emerging, the problem is still being defined, and the costs of action are unclear (note that Radaelli's 1999: 665; 676 analysis of the EU shows how difficult it is to decide if a sub-system is mature or not).

Box 10.1 ACF case studies

Weible *et al.* (2009) analyse 80 ACF studies conducted from 1987 to 2006. These are best described as ACF-inspired case studies because 55 per cent 'do not explicitly test any of the hypotheses' (2009: 128). There is also a tendency to focus on particular hypotheses:

- The most researched hypothesis (18 case studies) regards an external shock as a 'necessary, but not sufficient, cause of change in the policy core attributes of a governmental program'. The evidence suggests that external shocks lead to major policy change in some areas but not others. This confirms the idea that, to understand the effect of factors such as socio-economic pressures, we must identify how they are mediated by actors within subsystems (2009: 128).
- The second most researched (13) hypothesis is that coalitions exhibit long term stability when there are 'major controversies' and 'policy core beliefs are in dispute'. The evidence suggests that coalition membership 'can be stable over time' but that 'defection is also common' (2009: 128–30; 135). Many studies identify defection following: external events such as elections; corporatist structures that may reduce the opportunities for access and increase incentives to flit between coalitions to seek influence; and, relatively unstable 'sub coalitions', when members 'are glued together by some of their policy core beliefs against a common opponent but who are also internally divided in other policy core or secondary beliefs' (2009: 130; compare with Hann, 1995: 23–4, and Cairney, 1997: 892, on coalitions of convenience; there may also be a second type of 'coalition of convenience' – when an individual remains as part of an advocacy coalition until another coalition, closer to her or his beliefs, emerges as a serious political force).
- The third and fourth (11 and 9 case studies) regard the increased likelihood of policy learning across coalitions when the debate focuses on secondary aspects (lower stakes issues with a strong empirical element) in a forum that encourages technical, not normative, debates. The evidence is mixed, with learning across coalitions also identified at the policy core level. Professional fora also do not guarantee success because the surrounding 'high political conflict' often limits their effectiveness (2009: 130).

Most ACF case studies 'remain within environmental and energy policies', with relatively few studies exploring areas that primarily affect people rather than natural resources (Weible *et al.*, 2009: 125). Further, some of those studies are restricted to very specific issues rather than sub-systems as such (e.g. Larsen,Vrangbaek and Traulsen, 2006, on over-the-counter medicines). Case studies in other areas may prove to be as important as studies in other countries. The bias towards environmental policy may, for example, exaggerate the role of the EU in domestic policy networks (it is the most 'Europeanized' policy area) and the extent of wider international cooperation (Litfin, 2000).

Sabatier (1998: 121) revises the ACF diagram to reflect institutional differences and the 'degree of consensus needed to institute a major policy change'. Drawing on Lijphart (1999), Sabatier and Weible (2007: 200) argue that the 'norms of consensus and compromise' vary markedly across political systems. In Westminster systems, a political majority can be commanded relatively easily and there is less incentive to seek broad support for policy measures. This contrasts with consensus democracies with strong incentives to form coalitions. In turn, the incentives for coalitions to cooperate with each other and share information are lower in Westminster systems and higher in consensus democracies (2007: 200; but compare with Chapter 4 on policy styles). Political systems may also vary in their openness, which refers to, '(1) the number of decision making venues that any major policy proposal must go through and (2) the accessibility of each venue' (2007: 200). For example, the US tradition of multiple, open venues may contrast with 'corporatist' systems characterized by centralized decision making, restricted to a small number of leaders of business groups and unions. In the latter we may find that coalitions have fewer active members and that more actors may take on the role of policy broker. Both factors combine to produce the 'long-term coalition opportunity structures' box now found in Figure 10.1.

A major revision by Sabatier and Weible (2007: 204–7) identifies two further sources of policy change. The first involves a new distinction between external and internal shocks. While the former may be exploited by a minority coalition to advance its position within the sub-system, the latter is a crisis of confidence within the dominant coalition. In both cases a 'focusing event' may shift the balance between coalitions if heightened attention, particularly from new audiences, prompts new ways to solve policy problems and provides further resources (e.g. public or financial support) for minority coalitions to exploit (compare with Chapter 9 on problem definition). An internal shock occurs when the event prompts a dominant coalition to revisit its policy core beliefs, perhaps following a realization that existing policies have failed monumentally (this process is central to Hall's 1993 work in Chapter 11).

The second draws on the 'alternative dispute resolution' literature to identify the conditions in which major policy change can result from negotiated agreements between 'previously warring coalitions' (Sabatier and Weible, 2007: 205–7): a previous 'stalemate' that suits no-one; a negotiating process that builds trust, involves frequent meetings and minimal turnover of staff, gives 'all relevant groups of stakeholders' the power of veto and is chaired by a 'respected "neutral"'; and a realization that there is no better alternative. The issue also has to be amenable to resolution though empirical research, rather than issues such as abortion that are too mired in normative beliefs to allow participants to engage with each other in a meaningful way.

Applications outside the US

The ACF was based on the US political system, but it is 'intended to apply to all policy areas' in most developed countries (Jenkins-Smith and Sabatier, 1993: 225) and many studies have been conducted in other systems. Its themes have proven to be readily transferable to the study of the EU and its member states, while attempts have been made to apply the analysis to countries such as Canada, Australia, Sweden and Japan and, in a few cases, Africa, South America and Asia (Sabatier and Weible, 2007: 217–20; Weible *et al.*, 2009: 125). This need to adapt a framework developed in the US to other political systems has perhaps accelerated the desire of its authors to revise the ACF in light of empirical investigation:

> One of the most frequent criticisms of the ACF is that it is too much of a product of its empirical origins in American pluralism. It makes largely tacit assumptions about well-organized interest groups, mission-oriented agencies, weak political parties, multiple decision making venues, and the need for supermajorities to enact and implement major policy change. (Sabatier and Weible, 2007: 199)

First, for example, coalitions seeking stability in 'separation-of-power systems' may pursue legislative change because laws, once enacted, are difficult to change; in 'Westminster-style' systems, where laws are easier to change, coalitions may 'rely upon a variety of more informal, and longer-lasting, arrangements' (Sabatier, 1998: 103). Second, policy-oriented learning may be 'more difficult in Britain than in many other countries because of the norms of secrecy so ingrained in the civil service' (1998: 103). Third, a change in the 'systemic governing coalition' (Figure 10.1) may be difficult to define. In separation-of-powers systems, it refers to 'the replacement of one coalition by another in both houses of the legislature and in the chief executive' (1998: 120). In a two-party parliamentary system it may merely refer to the replacement of one party by another. In a multi-party system there may be changes only at the margins, perhaps with the largest party remaining in government and forming a coalition with another party. Sabatier (1998: 120) suggests that a change may only be deemed to occur if there is a 60–70 per cent turnover in the coalition.

However, not all applications produce the need for revision. For example, the argument that administrative agencies are often part of coalitions is based on the idea that civil servants are not neutral; they have a policy bent. This has academic support 'even in European countries with a strong tradition of elitist – and supposedly neutral – civil servants' (Sabatier and Jenkins-Smith, 1993: 214). Indeed, the UK, as the archetypal neutral service, displays a tendency towards 'clientelism', or defending the position and interests of one's clients within government (Richardson and Jordan, 1983: 258; although this action may not be driven by *beliefs* – Cairney 1997: 891; Sabatier, 1988: 141, also suggests that 'high' civil servants in the UK may be brokers).

We may also identify differences that might be linked to political systems, but which have already been considered within the US. In particular, intergovernmental relations varies markedly by political system. For example, the UK has asymmetric devolution in which policymaking autonomy for some issues (including health and education) has been devolved to 16 per cent of the population (in Scotland, Wales and Northern Ireland) and the UK government represents England in UK-wide negotiations. There are examples of multi-level policymaking when the devolved, member state and EU policymaking processes are intertwined, but also examples where the division of responsibilities is clear and there is a case for analysing the advocacy coalition process within separate sub-systems. This setup differs from a federal structure where states have roughly equal powers and the federal role is relatively well defined.

Yet, this issue has been addressed to some extent in US case studies. The key question is whether to analyse one sub-system containing actors from all levels of government, or to identify a separate sub-system at each major territorial or governmental level. Sabatier (1998: 115) suggests that different case studies have taken different approaches based on 'empirical considerations regarding the degree of (a) legal autonomy of each level and (b) actor integration among levels'. To this we can add: (c) the extent of policy convergence between the EU and member states (that we expect to occur eventually in a stable, well integrated sub-system dominated by one coalition). For example, EU environmental policy may be best viewed as multi-level because the agenda is set by the EU and implemented by member states and devolved governments, while compulsory education may be best studied at a territorial level to reflect devolution within the UK and the lack of EU involvement. Sabatier (1998: 121) also suggests that a 'relatively minor change at the European level may nevertheless entail a policy core change in specific countries'. This issue may prompt us to analyse their respective sub-systems separately until the differences disappear (unless we want to examine *perceptions* of policy change from the perspectives of different actors, such as when EU member states consider not only the nature of policy but also its effect on their autonomy).

Similar issues regarding analytical boundaries arise when we consider how to separate overlapping sub-systems which share policy interests. This is an empirical question supplemented by a degree of judgement regarding the activities of groups and institutions (Sabatier and Weible, 2007: 193; Jones and Jenkins-Smith, 2009: 52).

The ACF and the public policy literature

The ACF is perhaps unusual in that one of its co-authors makes it very explicit not only how his work relates to the literature, but also how the literature should progress. It is an ambitious attempt to bring together a disparate policy literature into a single framework, but also to reject much of what came before. For example, see Sabatier (1993: 36–7; 1991) on the links between the ACF and multiple streams analysis, pluralism, new institutionalism, institutional rational choice and Hofferbert's 'funnel of causality'.

Beyond stages

The ACF reserves particular criticism for the 'stages heuristic', or the study of public policy that breaks the process down into discrete stages such as agenda setting, policy formulation and implementation. It is based in part on Sabatier's (1986) earlier attempts to get beyond the debate between top-down and bottom-up approaches to implementation (see Chapter 2). Alternatively, it focuses on policy change 'over a decade or more' within sub-systems that include actors involved at all stages. Although there is still a focus on a full policy cycle, the ACF rejects the need to divide that process into clearly separated phases of policy development (although see Weible *et al.*, 2009: 136, on combining the ACF with cycles).

Beliefs versus interests?

The selection of beliefs as the driver of individual behaviour, rather than instrumental rationality or a focus on material interest, is something that sets the ACF apart from most theories of public policy (although Sabatier, 1988: 142, suggests that 'belief systems are normally highly correlated with self-interest and the causation is reciprocal'; see also Weible and Sabatier's (2005: 182) comparison of networks based on beliefs or the pursuit of power). It is described by Sabatier (1998: 122) as 'an alternative to the institutional rational choice models currently dominating much of policy scholarship'. The choice is based partly on practical grounds: 'I personally have great difficulty in specifying *a priori* a clear and falsifiable set of interests for most actors in policy conflicts' (Sabatier, 1993: 28). In contrast, beliefs can be established via questionnaires and documentary content analysis (Jenkins-Smith and Sabatier, 1993c; Sabatier and Weible, 2007: 196; see also Weible *et al.*, 2009: 127, on the methods used in 80 studies; compare with critiques by Hann, 1995: 24–5, and Fischer, 2003: 100–1). Further, the practical means to achieve interests – or 'a set of means and performance indicators necessary for goal attainment' – can be incorporated within belief systems. However, its exponents do not always agree on how best to describe interests within belief systems. This debate arises when one of their case studies suggests that 'material groups' representing business or trade associations are more likely to adjust their beliefs than 'purposive' or cause groups (Sabatier and Jenkins-Smith, 1993: 224–5). For Sabatier, it suggests that the difference can be incorporated into the material group's policy core beliefs (the belief is perhaps that material groups are entitled to pursue profit). For Jenkins-Smith, the profits motive suggests that material groups are willing to 'say almost anything to obtain them' and, therefore, to form 'coalitions of convenience' with other groups that may have 'very different beliefs' (compare with Cairney's, 2007a: 58, description of the British Beer and Pub Association, whose 'interests were served at different times by different coalitions').

The focus on beliefs also reflects a disciplinary bent, drawing 'more heavily on work in cognitive and social psychology than in economics' (Sabatier, 1998: 109). The ACF assumes that actors are 'instrumentally rational – i.e. they seek to use information and other resources to achieve their goals' but rejects the rational choice assumptions of perfect cognition and information that allow individuals to rank their preferences (is this a caricature of RCT? See Chapter 7). Instead, preferences or goals 'should be ascertained empirically' and the ACF focuses on the 'cognitive biases and constraints' that determine how they perceive their world and process information (1998: 109). Boundedly rational individuals use short-cuts to decide which information to pay attention to, and how to interpret its meaning and significance. The main short-cut or heuristic is the set of policy core beliefs: 'actors always perceive the world through a lens consisting of their pre-existing beliefs' (1998: 109).

Do beliefs prompt collective action?

Sabatier (1998: 116) recognizes that a common set of beliefs may not inevitably produce collective action. As we found in Chapter 7, individuals with the same beliefs, aims and interests may not cooperate if each individual feels that s/he can benefit from the outcome of collective action without making a contribution ('free ride'). This is a concern for the ACF because various case studies demonstrate that coalition members 'express similar policy beliefs' but not that 'members have engaged in collective action to realize policy goals' (Schlager, 1995: 248). Sabatier (1998: 116) suggests that the incentive to pursue one's self-interest is highest in 'material' groups, but 'cause' groups also have to consider how best to maintain their revenue and membership numbers by competing with similar groups for grants and visible policy successes. Further, there are 'transactions costs' involved in collective action; members of different institutions, with different rules and incentives, may find it difficult to work with other people even if they share the same beliefs (1998: 115–16).

So, policy core beliefs may act as the glue that bind participants together, but the strength of the glue (perhaps the range is from superglue to the Pritt stick) depends on factors that would not look out of place in rational choice analysis: the frequency that coalition members interact, the costs they bear when sharing information and their ability to produce policies that each group perceives to be fair (Sabatier, 1998: 116; Schlager; 1995: 262; see also Sabatier and Weible, 2007: 195, on 'policy core policy preferences' as the 'stickiest glue'). In other words, the ACF (following the Institutional Analysis and Development framework developed by Ostrom) identifies *trust* as a key source of collective action (Schlager; 1995: 248; Zafonte and Sabatier, 2004: 78; Leach and Sabatier, 2005).

Sabatier and Weible (2007: 197; Sabatier, 1998: 110; Weible *et al.*, 2009: 122) provide two further reasons to expect collective action in coalitions: (1) the 'devil shift', when coalitions distrust and fear the power of their competitors, may exaggerate the benefits of participation and reduce the perception that free riding is possible; and (2) there are fairly low costs to 'weak participation' which involves being aware of the strategies of one's allies and pursuing 'complementary strategies' (this is the approach taken by Princen, 2007: 21 to identify tobacco and alcohol coalitions in the EU). The latter suggests that many individuals would act this way anyway in the pursuit of their policy goals, perhaps undermining the idea that coalition activity involves a 'non-trivial degree of coordinated activity over time' (Sabatier, 1988: 139).

Institutions and institutionalism

A further way to encourage cooperation is to create and enforce rules for individuals to follow. Sabatier and Weible (2007: 194) acknowledge the importance of institutions as rules (but not a focus on discrete *organizations* when 'there are at least fifty to a hundred organizations at various levels of government that are active over time' – Sabatier, 1993: 25). In particular, they follow the normative institutionalist suggestion that 'Rules are followed because they are seen as natural, rightful, expected and legitimate' (March and Olsen, 2006b: 689). These rules are created by coalitions or 'the product of strategies by advocacy coalitions over time' (Sabatier, 1993: 37). Yet, perhaps more could be said about what leads members to follow some rules but not others. As Chapter 4 suggests, institutions provide the 'rules of appropriateness', but 'individuals must pick and choose among influences and interpret the meaning of their institutional commitments' (March and Olsen, 2006a: 9; Peters, 2005: 26). We can perhaps say that coalition members follow coalition rules, but know less about why they do so and, perhaps more importantly, why members cease to follow those rules. People may enter the political system to pursue their beliefs, and they may follow many norms, but they also have their own preferences and expectations about how they should behave.

Conclusion

The ACF presents a novel discussion of at least four key aspects of the policy process. First, it goes beyond the iron triangle image of policy sub-systems in which a small number of groups and government actors control the process by excluding most participants. It identifies a wider variety of players, including journalists and academics (to highlight their long-term 'enlightenment function' and the importance of technical information or knowledge) and actors across various levels of government (to reflect the need to study policy change during a full policy cycle). In this sense, the focus is less on competition and exclusion *within* insulated policy communities towards competition *between* different coalitions sharing different beliefs within a wider sub-system. Second, it pursues a distinctive approach to the policy cycle and implementation. It rejects the analytical distinctions between stages in the policy cycle and seeks to go beyond the implementation literature that became bogged down in an intractable debate between 'top-down' and 'bottom-up' approaches. Instead, it focuses on policy change 'over a decade or more' within sub-systems that include actors involved at all stages. Third, it builds on models that identify the importance of 'external' or 'structural' factors, such as socio-economics pressure, by exploring how they affect the beliefs and strategies of members of advocacy coalitions. For example, the values of the population are framed and exploited better by some coalitions than others, while the nature of the constitution and the basic rules of political systems provide opportunities for coalitions to protect existing policy positions or seek audiences sympathetic to change. Further, while external 'shocks' provide the impetus for major policy changes within sub-systems, they do not do so inevitably. Rather, this also requires a major rethink by a dominant coalition suffering a crisis of confidence, or the skilful manipulation of the situation by a minority coalition. Last, but not least, it outlines the importance of ideas, including the role of beliefs and the importance of technical information (Weible *et al.*, 2009: 122). Much of the ACF's value comes from its ability to theorize convincingly the relationship between power and the ideas – a relationship that we continue to study in Chapter 11.

The policy process is populated by a huge number of actors who try to influence events by engaging in both the technical and highly politicized aspects of policymaking. Advocacy coalitions exercise power to compete for dominance, or the chance to translate their beliefs into policy positions adopted by government authorities. There may be long periods of policy continuity, when one coalition dominates the sub-system, and less frequent periods of major change as its position is threatened by external 'shocks' (such as changes in socio-economic conditions or the effects of electoral upheaval). We can link this process to at least three types of policy learning. First, the dominant coalition engages in learning that affects secondary aspects of its beliefs. In turn, it accepts or encourages minor policy changes that do not challenge its more fundamental beliefs. Second, an internal shock prompts it to engage in a more radical examination of its policy core beliefs (in other words, individual members revisit their own beliefs and encourage others to do the same) which may lead to its acceptance of major policy changes. Third, an external shock provides a minority coalition with a window of opportunity to adapt to the new situation and persuade governmental authorities to revisit the nature, cause of, and solution to the policy problem. If successful, this leads to major policy change. Overall, we have a framework that helps explain both continuity and change, and sub-system stability and instability, across a full policy cycle of a 'decade or so'.

Although the ACF was conceived in the US, it has proved a useful framework for the analysis of policy in the EU and many other systems. There have been over 80 case-study applications of the ACF since 1987. Some mixed results, combined with further theoretical reflection (often in response to criticism), have produced various revisions, with new sources of policy change identified and many aspects of the framework clarified (including the role of the individual and the likelihood, and meaning, of collective action). In this sense, the ACF resembles one of its coalitions; its authors engage in learning to refine the ACF's secondary aspects while protecting the core argument. This is no accident. Rather, it reflects a 'Lakatosian' approach to science that may be relevant to the overall study of public policy (Chalmers, 1999, and Majone, 1980, are good starting points for the study of Lakatos).

Chapter 11

The Role of Ideas

This chapter examines:

* How we define and identify ideas.
* The literature which treats ideas as independent variables – viruses, norms, ideologies and world views.
* The use of multiple streams analysis to bring together a focus on powerful ideas and the receptivity to them.
* The applicability of multiple streams analysis to the US and other political systems.

The role of ideas is central to our understanding of public policy. It has arisen in most chapters so far, including the manipulation of beliefs to exercise power (Chapter 3), the institutionalization of ideas (Chapter 4), the selective use of information to frame policy problems (Chapter 9) and the identification of beliefs as the driver for policy action and the glue that binds coalitions together (Chapter 10). Each discussion suggests that, while a theory of power relations is a central theme in the literature, it is only one part of the story. When we seek to explain how actors exercise power, we also need to examine how they treat ideas, or the knowledge, beliefs, **world views** or **ideologies** shared and promoted by policy participants. Power is often exercised under conditions in which most people accept the same ideas (Box 11.l). For example, participants in many countries treat concepts such as democracy, free speech and capitalism as a given when engaging politically; scientists may share the same standards of proof when producing knowledge; countries may share common **norms** of behaviour; while members of the same political party may take for granted their ideological beliefs on the role of the state. In other cases, these ideas are a bone of contention. For example, there may be competition to establish 'how the world works' and what policy solutions are appropriate in these circumstances. Or, the basis for shared beliefs may change over time as

World view – a fundamental set of beliefs about how the world works and how we should engage with it.

Ideology – a comprehensive set of political beliefs and values held by an individual or social group.

Norm – a rule or standard of behaviour considered to be normal and therefore acceptable.

people come to challenge them (see Axelrod, 1986: 1096, for examples). Our aim is to conceptualize this relationship between power and ideas: how do we balance a study of ideas and interests, or knowledge and power? Where does one concept end and another begin? How can we use the concept of ideas to explain behaviour? This is no easy task because the term 'idea', like power, has multiple meanings.

There are two main ways to explore these questions. First, we explore a variety of discussions that conceptualise ideas and power in different ways. They treat ideas as more or less important to the overall explanation. In some discussions, the role of ideas is the **independent variable**, or the source of explanation, which makes, 'history a contest of ideas rather than interests' (John, 2003: 487; 1998: 149). The 'power of ideas' suggests that, 'ideas have a force of their own' and that 'the power of the idea itself explains its acceptance' (Jacobsen, 1995: 285). Ideas are often associated with metaphors used to describe an irresistible force – viruses infecting political systems or high tides sweeping all obstacles aside to cause profound change. Or, norms and world views place limits on the ways in which individuals, groups or institutions operate. They may be treated as structures which constrain agents, particularly if we are talking about the big ideas – such as capitalism, socialism or religious ideas – which may be impervious to change for decades (Parsons, 1938: 659). Or, the importance of ideas shifts our focus from the power of a small band of elites, towards a much wider range of experts and commentators engaged in the manipulation of ideas (John, 1998: 156; Majone, 1989). In other discussions, the role of ideas is the **dependent variable**, or the phenomenon to be explained. Ideas are produced and promoted by political actors and considered by decision makers. In this case, the main focus is on *receptivity* to ideas: if there is an almost infinite number of ideas, then how and why do decision makers choose one at the expense of others (Cairney, 2009c; John, 1999)?

> **Independent variable** – the object one expects will cause a change in another object.

> **Dependent variable** – the object of study whose change is caused by another.

Second, we explore theories that incorporate the role of ideas into complete explanations of the policy process, exploring how a combination of concepts – such as ideas, power, institutions, socio-economic factors and policy networks – can be used to form policy theories. Punctuated equilibrium and the ACF are prime examples of such 'synthetic' theories (John, 2003) and this chapter considers their links to Hall's highly influential 'institutionalist' account of 'social learning'. It then describes Kingdon's (1984; 1995) model of agenda setting. Kingdon identifies popular conceptions about ideas as the main source of explanation. The phrase 'an idea whose time has come' highlights its role

Box 11.1 Ideas and interests

These quotations give a flavour of the importance of ideas in explanations of policymaking. Most present the argument that policymaking is not just about power. Instead, we must identify how power and ideas combine to produce a more convincing explanation of policy processes and outcomes:

> To 'take ideas seriously' is to recognise the symbiotic relationship between power and the role of ideas, rather than explain policy primarily in terms of influence and material interest. (Kettell and Cairney, 2010: 301; Box 11.4 on p. 238)

> We miss a great deal if we try to understand policy-making solely in terms of power, influence and bargaining, to the exclusion of debate and argument. Argumentation is the key process through which citizens and policymakers arrive at moral judgements and policy choices. (Majone, 1989: 2)

> Lobbyists marshal their arguments as well as their number ... The content of the ideas themselves, far from being mere smokescreens or rationalizations, are integral parts of decision making in and around government ... in our preoccupation with power and influence, political scientists sometimes neglect the importance of content. (Kingdon, 1984: 133; 131)

> Decision makers need ideas, or a consistent political message that will command popular support and motivate those who carry out policy ... [However, the use of ideas underpinning political messages will] recognize some social interests as more legitimate than others and privilege some lines of policy over others. (Hall, 1993: 291–2)

> Raw political power may carry the day against superior evidence, but the costs to one's credibility in a democratic society can be considerable. Moreover, resources expended – particularly in the form of favors called in – are not available for future use. Thus those who can most effectively marshal persuasive evidence, thereby conserving their political resources, are more likely to win in the long run than those who ignore technical arguments. (Jenkins-Smith and Sabatier, 1993b: 44–5).

as 'an irresistible movement that sweeps over our politics and our society, pushing aside everything that might stand in its path' (Kingdon, 1984: 1). Kingdon suggests that such explanations are incomplete since they ignore the conditions that have to be satisfied before a policy will change. This approach is often called 'multiple streams analysis' because policy does not change unless three separate streams come together at the same time: a policy problem is highlighted and framed in a certain way, a solution to that problem is available and the political conditions are conducive to action (Kingdon, 1984: 174). In other words, the promotion of a new idea will not be successful unless decision makers have the motive and opportunity to adopt it and 'translate it into policy' (Lieberman, 2002: 709). This 'window of opportunity' for policy change only stays open for a limited period. In effect, we are invited to consider not only the power of an idea, but also the receptivity of decision makers to the idea.

Defining ideas

Ideas can be defined broadly as beliefs, thoughts or opinions. They are used to help us understand and give meaning to policy problems and help us frame what we believe to be the most appropriate solutions. Yet, things become more difficult when we try to go beyond this broad definition towards something more concrete. Within the literature we find a range of approaches which treat ideas as more or less important. Ideas can be:

- 'viruses' which 'mutate', take on a life of their own and infect political systems;
- world views or ideologies which are taken for granted and place limits on policy debate;
- norms which determine broad attitudes to the regulation of behaviour;
- institutions or paradigms which influence how people understand their environment;
- new ideas used to reframe policy problems to justify policy decisions;
- scientific knowledge or expertise which (if accepted) alters the conditions in which policy actors operate;
- beliefs shared by interest groups and civil servants within policy (or epistemic) communities;
- core beliefs shared by advocacy coalitions that shape policy learning and action;
- traditions, or sets of understandings received through socialization;
- understandings of the world used to articulate our interests;
- forms of knowledge or language used to dominate the policy process;
- visions employed by political leaders to encourage people to act in the public rather than self-interest;
- policy proposals which survive by adapting and evolving to political circumstances. (Béland, 2010; Béland and Cox, 2010; Blyth, 2002; Cairney, 2009c; Campbell, 2002; Fischer and Forester, 1993; Goodin and Tilly, 2006; Haas, 1992; Hay, 2006a: 65; John, 1998; 1999; 2003; Majone, 1989: 25; Radaelli, 1995; Reich, 1988: 4; Rhodes, 2006a: 91; Richardson, 2000)

As John (2003: 487; 1998: 144) suggests, 'it is not clear exactly what ideas are. Depending on the author, they are sometimes policy proposals, new techniques or solutions, systems of ideas, or discourse and language'. Similarly, Campbell (2002) identifies: cognitive paradigms and world views, normative frameworks, world culture, frames, and programmatic ideas. The key factor is the extent to which ideas are beliefs shared by others. Yet, this could refer to normative or principled beliefs, regarding what is right and wrong, or empirical and causal beliefs regarding what factors cause others to change (see Parsons, 1938: 653; Jacobsen, 1995: 291). Shared beliefs may be visible or widely taken for granted. They may also be given more or less prominence in explanations of policy outcomes.

Ideas as the primary source of explanation: viruses and norms

The attempt to marry the concepts of power and ideas, without privileging one or the other, is a key feature of the literature on ideas – even when ideas seem to be presented as the main source of explanation. Some authors employ metaphors to describe ideas as viruses infecting political systems or as irresistible forces sweeping all obstacles aside to cause profound change. For example, Richardson's (2000: 1019) study, of the breakdown of closed policy communities in Western Europe from the 1980s, uses the analogy of viruses to describe the devastating effect that ideas can have on the policy process: 'Our resort to the virus analogy is meant to convey the importance of exogenously generated ideas as a shock to both existing institutional arrangements and the actors that benefit from them'. The preferences of actors, such as the public, are changed by ideas and knowledge which reside in the political community in much the same way that 'viruses present in the atmosphere we breathe'. Similarly, 'exogenous changes in policy fashion, ideas or policy frames' cause major changes to previously stable policy communities.

Similarly, 'exogenous changes in policy fashion, ideas or policy frames' cause major changes to previously stable policy communities. 'New ideas have a virus-like quality and have an ability to disrupt existing policy systems, power relationships and policies' (for example, massive post-war high rise housing and road construction schemes were introduced quickly and before decision-makers realised their damaging effects, while post-1979 ideas such as deregulation and marketization infected a range of policy sectors). Extending the analogy to viruses such as SARS, policy viruses often spread through international travel, with stakeholders and decision makers increasingly able to meet their international counterparts and 'bring new ideas and policy frames back home' (Richardson, 2000: 1018).

When viruses infect the policy process, they set the agenda for policy making and limit the scope of public debate (2000: 1018–19). If this new agenda conflicts with the old, then policy communities become unbalanced and may break down. While this presents ideas as devastating, it may actually refer to the introduction of knowledge which now seems innocuous and which we take for granted (such as the effects of smoking, diet and exhaust fumes on health – 2000: 1020). Yet, the effect of new knowledge can be profound, particularly when it spreads across a range of countries to produce major policy transfers (2000: 1020; Chapter 12).

Baumgartner and Jones (1993: 237) present a similar account of 'powerful forces of change that sweep through the entire system'. While they are linked to the actions of interest groups, decision makers and the 'national mood', Baumgartner and Jones portray the image of an almost uncontrollable process which is independent of any one actor. Since political leaders cannot 'reverse the tides', their most advantageous course of action is to harness the energy that these ideas create and use them to promote sympathetic policy proposals. Yet, the problem with viewing ideas as irresistible forces is that they generally appear to be resisted (for example, see Box 11.2). Therefore, these metaphors are also accompanied by discussions about how ideas are *accepted* within political communities. For example, for Richardson (2000: 1018) new ideas may originate within existing policy networks. If not, they are still only a '*potential* threat' and this potential is only realized if such new ways of thinking cannot be accommodated within the existing frames of reference. Actors within policy communities survive by 'mutating' the virus or themselves (that is, changing their behaviour to embrace or at least cope with a new frame of reference). Similarly, for Baumgartner and Jones (1993) the ability of some ideas or issues to 'catch fire' is very unusual. The consequence of intense levels of attention to one idea is that most ideas with the potential to destabilize existing policy arrangements are ignored (Cairney, 2009c). Overall, ideas are rarely portrayed as the strong and independent forces that the terms 'virus' and 'sweeping tide' suggest.

Perhaps a stronger treatment of ideas as independent variables can be found in discussions of norms as determinants of behaviour. Axelrod (1986: 1095) suggests that when we see many people or nations displaying 'a great deal of coordinated behaviour that serves to regulate conflict', we tend to attribute this behaviour to norms (in the absence of a central policing authority). Further, 'an established norm can have tremendous power' as a 'mechanism for regulating conflict in groups' (1986: 1095). For example, the norms of duelling once explained why people appeared willing to risk death to settle disputes, while international norms 'have virtually wiped out colonialism, inhibited the use of chem-

Box 11.2   Ideas and the case study of tobacco

Tobacco control policy is a good candidate for the phrase 'an idea whose time has come'. Post-war policy in most countries was controlled by a strong policy community of tobacco companies and policymakers in finance, trade and industry departments. A policy monopoly was maintained by establishing a dominant image of tobacco related to its economic benefits. It helped exclude doctors and public health groups with stronger links to health departments (Cairney, Studlar and Mamudu, 2012; Cairney, 2007a).

However, from the 1990s, the virus-like spread of new ideas infected policy communities and contributed to their collapse, with the balance of power shifting to public health actors. The new ideas related to the scientific evidence which established increasingly strong links between smoking and ill health. The policy image of tobacco as an economic and civil liberties issue was replaced by a focus on public health and the need to intervene (Cairney, 2009c). Smoking prevalence has fallen, smoking behaviour has become 'denormalised' (Studlar, 2007a: 1) and many countries have used similar policy instruments to control tobacco (Studlar, 2004). The driver for convergence has been increased acceptance of the scientific evidence on smoking and passive smoking (Feldman and Bayer, 2004: 1). The post-war debate on the 'facts' was replaced by government acceptance of the scientific evidence and the debate has shifted to the question: 'what form of tobacco control works best' (Cairney, 2009c)? It suggests that tobacco control based on public health knowledge is an idea 'whose time has come' (at least in developed countries) and that the spread of the 'virus' explains significant policy changes. However, there are two main limitations to this explanation. First, the response to this idea has varied markedly according to the 'vested economic interests, cultural practices, and political factors' of each country (Studlar, 2004). Second, there have been significant time-lags (20–30 years) between the proposal and acceptance of scientific knowledge and then the introduction of concrete policies to address the problem (Studlar, 2007b). The spread of the ideas virus depends on levels of resistance by the host. When we assess the strength of ideas we must also consider how successfully they are promoted and how receptive decision makers are to them.

ical warfare, and retarded the spread of nuclear weapons' (1986: 1096). As we saw in Chapter 4, norms may also be used to explain why people follow and reproduce the rules of institutions. Yet, there are two main qualifications to Axelrod's picture of norms as strong forces influencing behaviour. First, Axelrod is really describing two forms of observable behaviour: the use of sanctions to punish a departure from a norm, or 'metanorms' – the punishment of someone who *doesn't* punish the departure from a norm (historical examples include white men punished for not lynching black men, the communist culture of calling on society to denounce others, and the US sanctions on foreign companies unwilling to boycott the Soviet Union); and political actors choosing to adhere to norms, rather than challenge them, for fear of sanctions (1986: 1097).

Second, there is plenty of evidence to suggest that norms *are* challenged frequently and that, when successful, 'the standing of a norm can change in a surprisingly short time' (1986: 1096). In other words, norms can be taken more or less seriously according to the levels of collective adherence to them, the likely scale of sanctions, and the motivation of individuals (or how 'bold' or 'vengeful' they are). Axelrod (1986: 1087) takes an evolutionary game theory approach to norms, modelling likely behaviour according to trial and error strategies (see Chapter 7). The simulations suggest that some fairly traditional factors explain why people adhere to norms, including: the exercise of power to enforce sanctions; the use of disproportionate sanctions to head off future challenges; socialization, to ensure that people are uncomfortable with the idea of violating norms; and, the formalization of norms into laws. The common theme is dominance: 'it is easier to get a norm started if it serves the interests of the powerful few' (1986: 1108). Otherwise, it would be difficult to explain why certain norms take hold and why decision makers pay more or less attention to them over time, particularly since 'world culture' is 'rife' with contradictions and competing norms (Campbell, 2002: 25–6).

Therefore, the general theme of the ideas literature is that although many accounts *appear* to cite ideas as the main source of explanation – as entities which act to regulate behaviour or cause policy change – they are supplemented by references to power. The appearance of an empirically independent effect of ideas is largely the result of the limitations to the language we can use to express social and political relationships. If there is a symbiotic relationship between ideas and interests, or if the concepts of power and ideas are inextricably linked, then a degree of confusion will always arise when we attempt to separate the two analytically to explore their effects independently of each other (Jacobsen, 1995: 309). This analytical problem applies to all concepts in the social sciences. The problem is often compounded by the polemical nature of studies which try to 'bring ideas back in'. Many accounts react against the argument that ideas are merely 'hooks' or 'intellectual rationales for material interests', legitimizing political practices that were already established. They make untenable claims about the strength of ideas independent of the interests that accept and reproduce them (1995: 285–6). The ACF has the same problem if treating policies primarily as the 'translations of beliefs' (Weible *et al.*, 2009: 122). This translation requires the exercise of power and we need some knowledge of who is most powerful within advocacy coalitions and sub-systems (Hoberg, 1996: 137; Sabatier, 1988: 161 note 11; Kim and Roh, 2008: 669; 675, drawing on Maloney *et al.*, 1994; see also Cairney, 1997: 893; Fenger and Klok, 2001).

Coalitions, punctuations and paradigms

The alternative is to identify the importance of ideas and power within a wider policymaking context – in fact, this is our main aim. For example, the ACF (Chapter 10) conceptualizes the powerful effects of external shocks and socio-economic conditions by considering how they are *identified* as important; how perceived constraints are interpreted by members of advocacy coalitions (within reason – Sabatier and Weible's (2007: 193) suggestion that the structures of a political system establish 'the resources and constraints within which subsystem actors must operate' is not a million miles from Ward's (1987) discussion of structural power). While the external effect may provide a key impetus for major policy change, this change only occurs when it is mediated by actors exercising power (compare with John, 1998: 172; Hay, 2006b: 587; see also Stolfi's 2010 case study using structural and ideational factors to explain budget reform in Italy). In turn, the process of mediation is guided by coalition beliefs that act as cognitive filters when actors consider the magnitude of, and the best way to respond to, the problem.

Chapter 4 explores the ability of actors to 'institutionalize' ideas, or incorporate shared beliefs into decision making structures. Chapter 9 identifies a similar process: the widespread acceptance within government of a particular definition of a policy problem ensures one particular solution, and often a new organization is set up to implement this solution. Punctuated equilibrium suggests that such organizations endure when the way of thinking about and solving policy remains constant for long periods. In effect, the language of policy excludes most participants: a wave of enthusiasm legitimizes the conduct of the new organization and attention to its activities is minimized because policy is taken for granted and the language used (to frame policy as solved, humdrum or technical) minimizes external attention.

A combination of accounts takes us to studies portraying ideas as 'paradigms', or overarching views of reality which limit the terms of discussion and action. Most notably, Hall's (1993) study of economic policymaking gauges the ability of ideas, or the process of 'social learning', to *cause* or *inhibit* first, second and third order changes in policy (see also Campbell, 2002: 23). First order change is incremental, with current policy based on the lessons of past policy decisions. It refers to a change in policy instrument settings (such as the minimum lending rate) while maintaining the instruments themselves and the government's overall goals. The process of learning is generally internalized, with civil servants and experts resisting pressure (or receiving minimal attention) from most ministers and interest groups. Second order change is also based on adapting to past experience while maintaining overall goals, but with more wholesale changes to policy instruments (such as new systems of monetary and public spending control). While outside interests are more involved, their views are merely used by officials to promote changes sanctioned from within. Third order change refers to a radical shift in policy involving changes to the 'hierarchy of goals behind policy' (such the replacement of unemployment by inflation as the key concern). Third order change is rare and can be compared to **Kuhn's** 'paradigm shift' (compare with Genieys and Smyrl, 2008a: 6). Policy instruments are underpinned by policy goals which, in turn, are underpinned by a 'policy paradigm', or a wider understanding of the world:

Kuhn's (1970) model of scientific progress suggests that advances have not been incremental or based on the linear accumulation of knowledge. Rather, science is conducted and evaluated by communities who share a common paradigm or view of the world (and therefore do not question their own assumptions). When these communities of experts fail to provide further advance (or cannot explain why the world does not work in the way they think it does) they are replaced by other communities with different ideas and ways of thinking.

> Policymakers customarily work within a framework of ideas and standards that specifies not only the goals of policy and the kind of instruments that can be used to attain them, but also the very nature of the problems they are meant to be addressing ... this framework is embedded in the very terminology through which policymakers communicate about their work, and it is influential precisely because so much of it is taken for granted and unamenable to scrutiny. (Hall, 1993: 279)

First and second order change can be called 'normal policymaking' because they refer to adjustments made within an existing paradigm. Third order change is more radical and requires a major departure from the way that policymakers would normally think and act. It follows significant policy failures which command the attention of the wider political world, call into question current thinking and undermine its advocates. It produces a shift of power within government, with new governments taking over and introducing radically different policies or existing policymakers rejecting the advice of one set of experts in favour of another. In other words, those closest to the existing paradigm are only likely to make incremental changes, adapting and 'stretching' their theories to accommodate new information. At the brink of third order change, their concepts are so stretched that they cannot meaningfully explain and address policy problems. This prompts a 'first principles' battle of ideas (in which current assumptions are challenged and much less is taken for granted) which only ends 'when the supporters of a new paradigm secure positions of authority over policymaking and are able to rearrange the organization and standard operating procedures of the policy process so as to institutionalize the new para-digm' (Hall, 1993: 281).

From the approaches of Hall and punctuated equilibrium theory (Chapter 9) we can ascribe two main roles to ideas (but note that Hall uses the term 'punctuated equilibrium' to refer to the different, institu-tionalist, literature outlined in Chapter 4). First, ideas – as paradigms – undermine policy change. Policymakers establish a language and set of policy assumptions that excludes most policy participants. For Hall (1993), first or second order changes are characterized by the insulation of civil servants and experts by knowledge and ideas. Third order change is rare and only occurs when policy failures are so significant that they produce shifts in power that displace existing policymakers and cause current experts to fall out of favour. Second, when new idea are adopted, they sweep aside existing policy monopolies (Baumgartner and Jones, 1993: 237) and cause a complete shift in the way that policy is under-stood and made within government (Hall, 1993: 287). The choice of a new policy paradigm follows a shift in media, interest group and polit-ical attention that undermines the ability of public officials to maintain a policy monopoly.

A combination of Hall and the ACF suggests that, while first order learning to modify secondary aspects is commonplace, third order learning to modify core or policy core beliefs is rare and only follows a profound failure of existing theories to accommodate new information. The ACF argument that powerful ideas are subject to challenge fol-lowing an external shock to the sub-system, which either forces coali-tions to question their beliefs or gives competing coalitions the upper hand, is similar to Hall's focus on policy failure as a source of 'third order' change, when experts are forced to revisit their theories or forced out by policymakers more convinced of the value of new theories.

A key theme in Hall (1993) is that such change is rare or exceptional. In the ACF this appears to be a more open-ended empirical question; shocks appear to be much more common than the complete systemic failures necessary for paradigm shift (but compare my account with Fischer, 2003: 96). Yet, Hall also suggests that it happens more often than it used to; the 'outside marketplace' for ideas has expanded and opportunities are more likely to 'spring up' to 'provide outsiders with influence over a formerly closed process' (1993: 289; see also Baumgartner and Jones, 1993: 42–3). Politics is therefore not just about policymakers exerting power, but also outside interests acquiring power 'by trying to influence the political discourses of the day' (Hall, 1993: 290). This ability to influence policy increases as policy is seen to fail, and the current policy paradigm breaks down if it cannot adapt to the problems it faces. It prompts political actors to provide a new way to understand and solve policy problems. The policy process is therefore

---

Box 11.3   Elites, ideas and the evolution of public policy

Genieys and Smyrl's edited volume supplements the punctuated equilibrium-style accounts of policymaking in which long periods of policy stability are punctuated by profound change (2008a: 6–7). They identify the 'creative destruction of political competition', which describes a process in which many actors (parties, elected policymakers, civil servants, unions, interest groups, etc.) compete for 'cognitive control' (2008a: 10–11). In other words, this is a partial return to Chapter 9's agenda setting in which actors compete to define the nature of the policy problem to ensure that a particular actor or organization can claim to be the authoritative decision maker. Success ensures that one venue may control policymaking, but only temporarily because no-one can impose their beliefs to the extent that they become hegemonic or unquestioned.

Genieys and Smyrl (2008b: 23) discuss the famous phrase 'le référentiel' (Jobert and Muller, 1987) which represents a fundamental set of ideas, imposed by powerful elites (but often by using benign terms such as 'efficiency' or 'modernization'), which determines how policy problems are understood and solved. They reject the argument that a small, unified, 'power elite' can control the policy process in this way. Rather, people with different ideas compete to have them accepted and perhaps institutionalized within particular sectors of government. Such institutions do not become fixed 'structures' because: 'A given set of institutions, just like a given ideology, can be used in the service of a variety of policy programs' (2008b: 44–5) (compare with constructivist institutionalism in Chapter 4). Yet, they also suggest that elites play a stronger part in the institutionalization of ideas than in the ACF (Genieys and Smyrl, 2008c: 174). They draw on a wide range of case studies – on sub-national, national and supranational policymaking in France, Spain, the EU, Canada and the US – to produce some interesting conclusions about the importance of ideas to discussions of elite power. The dominance of particular policy domains by elites is often significant and it explains why policy may not change for long periods. However, change may not necessarily occur merely because those elites are displaced or a crisis forces a fundamental rethink. *It can also change when elites rethink their interests.* In other words, interests are not fixed and they are not obvious. Rather, elites can reinterpret their interests, or reconsider their motivation to engage in policymaking, when they pay attention to different things, draw on different information or otherwise engage in different ways of thinking (2008c; compare with Blyth in Chapter 4, Lindblom in Chapter 5 and agenda-setting in Chapter 9).

---

characterized by 'the presence of a policy paradigm [generating] long periods of continuity punctuated occasionally by the disjunctive experience of a paradigm shift' (Hall, 1993: 291). In effect, the privileged status of a paradigmatic set of ideas ensures that most ideas are ignored or rejected, only to be revisited in rare cases of third order change (following policy failure), policy punctuations (following intense levels of 'external' attention and positive feedback), or internal/external shocks (compare with Box 11.3).

Policy windows, multiple streams and garbage cans

Kingdon's (1984; 1995) multiple streams analysis provides a further way to incorporate an understanding of ideas within a wider theory of policy-making. As Chapter 9 discusses, there is an almost unlimited amount of policy problems and solutions (or ideas) that could be considered – yet very few issues reach the top of the agenda and very few policy solutions are considered. But what determines which problems and solutions are discussed? What determines whether an idea is accepted or not? Kingdon's (1984) model suggests that ideas are not accepted, and policy does not change significantly unless three separate streams – problems, policies, politics – come together at the same time. It is inspired by the 'garbage can model' (Cohen *et al.*, 1972) which questions the assumption of comprehensive rationality in decision-making organizations (Chapter 5).

A garbage can model of organizational choice

Cohen *et al.*'s (1972) concept of 'organized anarchy' may be comprehensive rationality's polar opposite since organizations do not make choices based on clearly defined and shared aims. When organizations make decisions:

- There is no clear process in which: policy aims are identified in terms of the values of the policymaker, the organization identifies systematically all the means to achieve those aims and then selects the best. Rather, the organization hosts a set of contradictory preferences which are difficult to define and rank because it has an unclear decision-making process (or people fudge their objectives to avoid confronting their inconsistencies).
- Analysis of the decision-making context is never comprehensive and not all relevant factors/possibilities have been considered. Rather, time is limited, the attention of participants to each possibility is uneven, the identification of preferences is based on 'trial and error' and decisions to act are based on 'learning from the accidents of past experience' (1972: 1).
- Or, 'rationality' can mean more than one thing in politics. While the ideal of comprehensive rationality suggests that organizations identify problems and then find solutions, the conception of rationality as self-

interest suggests that organizations seek ways to protect or enhance their position by justifying their own existence.

Such is the departure from comprehensively rational decision making (in the garbage can model) that solutions appear to be formulated before problems are identified or articulated clearly. Organizations represent, 'collections of choices looking for problems, issues and feelings looking for decision situations in which they might be aired, solutions looking for issues to which they might be an answer, and decision makers looking for work' (Cohen *et al.*, 1972: 1). The garbage can is a receptacle into which a volatile mix of problems and solutions are dumped. Comprehensive rationality suggests a linear process involving the identification of a problem, the production of solutions and the choice of a solution which solves the problem. Organized anarchy suggests that the organization consists of a number of '*relatively independent streams*' which enjoy a much more complicated and unpredictable relationship. While problems are identified, solutions proposed and choices made, it is by no means inevitable that the process is chronological or that these streams will come together in any meaningful way (1972: 3). Problems are poorly understood, goals are ambiguous, conflict is commonplace and decision makers 'may have other things on their mind' (1972: 16). Therefore, outcomes often depend not on 'organizational goals' but on which participants within the organization become most involved.

While Cohen *et al.*'s (1972) exemplar of garbage can policymaking is a university, Kingdon (1984; 82–3) extends these themes to the policy process in the US federal government, highlighting the elusiveness of comprehensive rationality when: people and organizations have limited cognitive abilities; people move in and out of the policy process; coalitions are built of people with different goals; and people appear to be creating problems to justify their policy desires. As a result the policy process is as much accidental as rational. As the size of the organization increases (from a university to a government) so too does organizational fragmentation, variations in participation/interest and the inability to define precise goals (for example, what exactly do we mean when we say we want to solve poverty?). In other words, the three 'relatively independent' streams – problems, policies, politics – often come together in rather unpredictable ways and the acceptance of new policy ideas within government is not straightforward.

Multiple streams 1: problems

Problems are policy issues which are deemed to require attention. As Chapter 9 discusses, there are no objective indicators to determine which problems are the most deserving of our attention (Majone, 1989: 24).

Rather, problems receive attention based on how they are defined by policy participants. It involves a process of issue framing, assigning causal responsibility, and competition to choose one indicator of policy problems over others (Kingdon, 1984: 98–9). A key distinction can be made in problem definition between mere *uncertainty*, in which there is imprecision or a lack of information, and *ambiguity*, in which perceptions of problems can change and the ambivalence of audiences can be manipulated (Zahariadis, 2007: 66). In a political environment where the evidence is rarely conclusive enough to remove uncertainty, persuasion and argument (not 'facts') are the tools used by policy participants to address ambiguity (Majone, 1989: 8; 21).

In some cases, problems receive attention because of a crisis or focusing event (Birkland, 1997). In others, a change in the scale of the problem will draw attention. However, a focusing event on its own may not be sufficient. Rather, it may need to reinforce a problem 'already in the back of people's minds' (Kingdon, 1984: 103). Further, and perhaps more importantly, most problems do *not* receive attention by decision makers. Policymakers 'could attend to a long list of problems' but they 'pay serious attention to only a fraction of them' (1984: 95; 120). The policy agenda is congested (with attention often focused on solving the problems of previous policies) (1984: 106; 196), while the perceived intractability or excessive costs of problems may undermine serious consideration. Therefore, raising an issue to the top of the policy agenda, and getting people to see new problems (or old problems in a new way), is a major accomplishment (1984: 121), and one which must be acted upon quickly, before attention shifts elsewhere. In part, this can be achieved by demonstrating that a well thought out solution already exists.

Multiple streams 2: policies

Policies are ideas/solutions proposed by pressure participants but they should be considered as 'relatively independent' of the problem stream for two main reasons. First, 'solutions' may actually be strategies to address a separate aim (such as protecting an organization or getting elected) (Kingdon, 1984: 129–30). Second, problems rise and fall on the agenda relatively quickly, while solutions take much more time to develop and refine. Kingdon employs an evolutionary metaphor to describe the time and effort it takes for feasible policy solutions to develop; they whirl around in the 'policy primeval soup', evolving and mutating as they are proposed by one actor but then reconsidered and modified by a large number of policy participants (compare with Durant and Diehl, 1989: 201–3). The development of new ideas generally takes place within communities of 'researchers, congressional staffers, people in planning and evaluation offices and in budget offices, academics, interest group analysts' (Kingdon, 1984: 18; note the potential for terminological confusion – Kingdon's policy community is not the same as Jordan and Richardson's, which is more like an iron or cozy triangle – Chapter 9)

There are three common elements to the process. First, there is no reliable way to track the source behind the production of ideas. Ideas 'come from anywhere' and tracing the dominant players behind the promotion of ideas is futile since 'nobody really controls the information system' (Kingdon, 1984: 78; 81). Second, the process of proposing new ideas and having them accepted usually takes a long time. Policy specialists with established views have to be 'softened up' to new ideas (1984: 134–6; compare with 1984: 18 and Zahariadis, 2007: 72, on the rapid adoption of some ideas). Third, while there many ideas floating around in the 'policy primeval soup' – i.e. far more than are considered by policymakers at decision time – only some 'survive and prosper' by adapting to meet certain criteria (1984: 131; 123). This includes: 'technical feasibility' (will it work if implemented?); 'value acceptability within the policy community' (for example, in the US there is a culture against the socialization of public services); tolerable anticipated costs (often producing 'slimmed down' versions of ideas); public acceptability (or an important sub-set of the public); and, a 'reasonable chance for receptivity among elected decision makers' (1984: 138–46).

On the basis of these criteria, the 'policy community produces a short list of ideas' and begins to accentuate some policy problems over others, to maximise the chance that an idea will be accepted (Kingdon, 1984: 146). In other words, to deal with this disconnect between lurches of attention and the time it takes to produce solutions, communities of policy specialists develop proposals *in anticipation of future problems*: 'They try out their ideas on others by going to lunch, circulating papers, publishing articles, holding hearings, presenting testimony, and drafting and pushing legislative proposals' (1984: 122–4). Then, proponents of those solutions either chase or create policy problems.

There are numerous instances of solutions chasing problems in politics. For example, the solution of mass public transport addressed the problems of congestion in the 1950s, pollution in the 1960s and oil shortages in the 1970s in the US (1984: 181) while it may now be linked to excessive fuel prices. Health Maintenance Organizations (HMOs) were initially framed in the US as a means to extend health care delivery to the poor. Then they were advanced as a means to reduce health care costs in general (Stone, 1989: 298). In the UK, the practice of 'harm reduction' to make drug use safer was adopted following the identification of HIV/AIDS (Cairney, 2002). The use of private health care was framed by the Conservative government as 'rolling back the state', while under Labour it was a means to reduce surgical waiting lists. In many Western countries, major public health reforms became attached to the agenda set by 9/11 and the threat of bio-terrorism (Avery, 2004).

Multiple streams 3: politics

The politics stream regards how receptive people are to certain solutions at particular times. Changes in the political system often cause attention, and receptivity, to a particular problem and its solution to rise. They include: 'Swings of national mood, vagaries of public opinion, election results, changes of administration … turnover in Congress … and interest group pressure campaigns' (Kingdon, 1984: 19). Each change may affect the receptivity of policymakers to ideas depending, for example, on the need to 'build electoral coalitions' or become re-elected (1984: 19). Major political events, such as the election of a new President, make 'some things possible that were impossible before', make 'other things out of the question' and create 'a receptivity to some ideas but not to others' (1984: 152). Similarly, decision makers and policy specialists make judgements about how receptive the public is to government policy (for example when the 'national mood' appears to be against 'big government' and higher taxes – 1984: 154). They also weigh up the balance of interest group opinion and assess the political costs of going against the tide (1984: 157–8). On the one hand, this process is an important source of inertia: existing government programmes have an established clientele with much to lose from policy change, while many equally worthy policy alternatives may suffer from a lack of organised advocacy (1984: 159). On the other hand, swings in national mood and changes in government can be enough to overcome these obstacles, while some policymakers thrive on a challenge to vested interests (1984: 160). Or, if there are a number of venues that could introduce policy changes, the competition between them could either *constrain* or *accelerate* the promotion of issues to the top of the agenda (depending on the perceived popularity of the issue and the political benefits to be had from jumping on the bandwagon – 1984: 165).

Why are the three streams separate and how do they come together?

The policy process is broken down into different sectors and processes. While there is no clear line between them, different participants play different roles in each process. For example, in the US, the President may dominate the agenda, but s/he is 'unable to determine the alternatives that are seriously considered, and is unable to determine the final outcome' (Kingdon, 1984: 26–7). Interest groups may get enough people to pay attention to an issue, but cannot then determine what solutions are considered or chosen within the specialist community (1984: 53). While public and media attention may cause decision makers to focus on certain issues, it may not last long enough to influence the lengthy consideration of solutions (1984: 62). While elected politicians and senior officials may have a strong affect on the definition of problems, and the final decisions, civil servants and other policy specialists play a larger part in the coordination, selection and presentation of solutions. Since policymakers do not have the time to devote to detailed policy work, they delegate it to civil servants who consult with interest groups, think tanks and other policy specialists to consider ideas and produce policy solutions.

In turn, policymakers decide which problems they deem most worthy of their attention. They do not 'discover issues', they 'elevate issues' – particularly when responding to relatively fleeting public and media opinion (1984: 31; 40). Therefore, the strategy of interest groups or policy proponents is either to create enough interest in policy problems to lobby for a solution, or to wait for the right moment in politics that gives them the best chance to promote their solution. This emphasis on 'solutions chasing problems', often with the help of 'policy entrepreneurs' who frame issues and promote their 'pet' solutions to policymakers, is central to the acceptance of new ideas within a 'window of opportunity'. If the motive and opportunity of decision makers to translate ideas into action is temporary, then it limits the time to find policy solutions when a new policy problem has been identified: 'When the time for action arrives, when the policy window ... opens, it is too late to develop a new proposal from scratch. It must have already gone through this process of consideration, floating up, discussion, revision and trying out again' (1984: 149). Therefore, 'advocates lie in wait in and around government with their solutions at hand, waiting for problems to float by to which they can attach their solutions, waiting for a development in the political stream they can use to their advantage' (Kingdon, 1984: 165–6). This window of opportunity for major policy changes opens when:

> Separate streams come together at critical times. A problem is recognized, a solution is developed and available in the policy community, a political change makes it the right time for policy change, and potential constraints are not severe ... these policy windows, the opportunities for action on given initiatives, present themselves and stay open for only short periods. (Kingdon, 1984: 174)

The policy window can be initially opened by any one stream. For example, a policy problem may suddenly appear to be a crisis requiring immediate resolution, a policy advance could make a problem solvable and therefore more worthy of attention, or a change of government could open up avenues of influence for policy entrepreneurs (1984: 21; 204;

Box 11.4   'Taking the power of ideas seriously'

Kettell and Cairney (2010) 'take ideas seriously' by considering idea- and power-based explanations for UK embryology policy. The ability of scientists to use human embryos for research is always controversial, involving a 'battle of ideas' between advocates highlighting the medical benefits ('hope') and opponents highlighting the 'dangers of unregulated scientific advances' ('fear') (2010: 307). The case study informs most of our discussions of ideas in public policy. First, the ideas themselves were not enough to 'infect' political systems; the exercise of power in key institutional arenas was necessary to secure policy outcomes. Second, a new paradigm has developed without the crisis we associate with Hall's third order change. Rather, the existing medical paradigm has extended into this new sphere of policy. Third, rather unusually, this extension involved the breakdown of a policy monopoly from within to foster a new monopoly in the future. In other words, the medical-scientific profession encouraged widespread debate to ensure the necessary public and governmental support for an extension of its work. Fourth, the ability of groups to open up multiple 'windows of opportunity' for policy change can be linked to consistent governmental receptivity to the idea of medical advance through embryonic research. Fifth, the identification of debates based on 'hope' and 'fear' confirms the ideas of advocacy coalitions based on core beliefs, while the dominance of the medical-scientific advocacy coalition for several decades shows how impervious to change policy can be when driven by core beliefs.

---

see Chapter 13 for a discussion of entrepreneurs). Then, if the three streams come together, each factor acts as an impetus to policy change – a policy problem is reframed, a new solution is identified and the conditions are right for policy change. However, if they do not, then each factor can act as a constraint to further action (1984: 19). For example, a problem as currently defined, or the ideological stance of governing parties, may preclude certain solutions (see Chapter 3 on problems being 'organized out' of politics). Or, the problem may appear intractable, with solutions deemed ineffective or too expensive.

The point is that the use of particular ideas to define and solve policy problems is far from a straightforward process. Therefore, to explain the adoption of ideas we must explore the particular circumstances in which policy change takes place. It involves a clumsy combination of metaphors: the policy window opens to allow the three streams to couple, and each stream is dumped into a garbage can, with policy outcomes depending on the strength of each stream, 'the mix of elements present and how the various elements are coupled' (Kingdon, 1984: 174). In other words, even when major policy change is likely to take place, the final outcome is rather unpredictable. It depends on factors such as the ability of the public to remain involved, the ideas available to solve the problem, and the spirit of compromise in the political stream (1984: 186). The image of organized anarchy is furthered by the unpredictability of many windows of opportunity and the short period of time in which the window stays open (because, for example, focusing events do not command attention for long, new governments only enjoy short honeymoons, and/or no feasible policy solutions appear to exist – 1984: 177–8). The infrequency of policy windows also suggests that when new legislation looks likely to be adopted, there is a deluge of interest and a range of participants keen to jump on an idea's bandwagon: 'the submission of a legislative proposal becomes a garbage can into which modifications, amendments, wholly new directions, and even extraneous items can be dumped as the bill wends its way through the legislative process' (1984: 186). Overall, the image of messy politics portrayed by multiple streams reflects the ambiguity inherent in the policy process and a 'partially comprehensible' world. People may not know what they want and governments may make promises to solve problems they do not fully understand: 'Yet, choices are made, problems are defined and solutions are implemented' (Zahariadis, 2003: 1).

Multiple streams analysis therefore combines two main views of ideas. An 'idea whose time has come' suggests *inevitability* and that the idea is the main source of explanation. The policy window suggests *uncertainty*, with the receptivity to an idea more important than the idea itself (Kingdon, 1984: 76; 101–3). A combination of these views suggests that:

> An idea's time arrives not simply because the idea is compelling on its own terms, but because opportune political circumstances favour it. At those moments when a political idea finds persuasive expression among actors whose institutional position gives them both the motive and the opportunity to translate it into policy – then, and only then, can we say that an idea has found a time. (Lieberman, 2002: 709)

Further, since a policy window does not stay open very long, an 'idea's time comes, but it also passes', particularly if the reasons for a particular level of attention to the policy problem fade before a coalition behind policy change can be mobilized (Kingdon, 1995: 169). There is an almost infinite number of ideas which could rise to the top of the political agenda, producing competition to dedicate political time to one idea at the expense of the rest.

The Generalizability of multiple streams analysis: case studies in Europe

How relevant is this theory, based on the US political system, to other countries? On the one hand, the focus on a messy political process –

linked strongly to the US' separation of powers – seems increasingly relevant to an EU process characterized by power diffusion between EU organizations, member states and sub-national authorities (Richardson, 2008; Cairney, 2009c). On the other, some aspects of the US system may seem alien to students of relatively centralized parliamentary systems. For example, Kingdon's (1984: 186) picture of a legislative proposal as a garbage can 'into which modifications, amendments, wholly new directions, and even extraneous items can be dumped' only holds when multiple participants can amend legislation. This is unlikely to occur in a parliamentary system in which one party of government dominates proceedings (Page, 2006: 208). Further, in these relatively centralized countries, the policy environment *may* be less crowded, access to decision makers may be more controlled, the turnover of politically appointed civil servants is less significant and the agenda setting process may be more straightforward (Zahariadis, 2003: 16–17; 2007: 77).

Yet, the concept of 'organized anarchy' was originally developed to apply to decision making within large institutions such as universities. Therefore, the model's focus on bounded rationality and a separation between problems, solutions and politics should apply to all large and complex governments (see Cairney 2009c on the UK). The common aim of multiple streams studies is to identify the successful adoption of one particular idea at the expense of many others within a political process characterized by:

- Ambiguity (there are many ways to frame any policy problem);
- Competition for attention (few problems reach the top of the agenda);
- An imperfect selection process (new information is difficult to gather and subject to manipulation);
- Limited time (which forces people to make choices before their preferences are clear); and
- A departure from comprehensive rationality (a linear decision-making process – identifying problems, formulating solutions and making a choice). (Zahariadis, 2003: 2–15)

For example, Zahariadis (2003) presents a range of comparative case studies, confirming the explanatory power of multiple streams analysis in political systems with different cultures and institutional arrangements. Using privatization as a key example of policy change, Zahariadis shows the relatively high receptivity to this idea in the UK following the election of Margaret Thatcher's Conservative Government in 1979. The ideology behind 'rolling back the state' preceded any serious problem identified in the wider political community and the idea of privatization subsequently became a solution in search of a problem, opening up a series of policy windows for the sale of individual companies (2003: 59).

For example, the coupling of problems, policies and solutions took place for the privatization of BT, the British telecommunications monopoly, when the government created its own problem by refusing to fund the development of nationalized industries through taxation. When BT needed to secure funds for expansion, the two alternative ideas to privatization were effectively rejected, by BT (raising funds internally would cause a hike in prices) and the Treasury (unwilling to loan or provide the sums required), while the technical feasibility of BT's privatization increased when it became an organization separated from the post office (2003: 32–3). This move in 1984 created a strong precedent for the idea of privatization which provided political rewards to a government keen to reduce public sector spending, encourage popular capitalism (through shareholding) and challenge public sector unions (2003: 34).

In turn, the focus on serendipitous reasons for policy change can be reinforced by showing the obstacles to other policy changes in similar circumstances. For example, the sale of British Rail took place almost a decade later because the couplings which took place in a series of policy windows produced different results: in 1979 it produced a more limited solution (the sale of subsidiary companies) when the idea of privatization was not fully developed; in 1982 the problem of union strike action (and the effect this would have on any share issue) replaced the problem of public subsidy; and in 1987 the government no longer had the same need to raise money (Zahariadis, 2003: 79). When the problem became redefined – as the need to encourage popular shareholding – to justify the ideology, the sale of BR still looked unlikely because of the unattractive state of BR's finances and the technical infeasibility of breaking up the network. Then a series of major accidents in the late 1980s shifted attention to rail maintenance and safety (which privatization could not solve). Indeed, more limited policy change – involving the contracting out of services – was only made possible following a new window opened by a Conservative party election victory in 1992 (2003: 84).

Zahariadis (2003) shows how problems, solutions and politics are coupled in different ways in different countries. For example, in the case of French telecoms, the problem was different: there were no equivalent budget problems (indeed, French telecoms were seen largely as a success), no equivalent split from post office, and no drive to challenge the industrial opposition to telecoms privatization. While a window for privatization was opened up by the political stream following the appointment of Jacques Chirac as Prime Minister in 1986, telecommunications did not join the list of 65 businesses sold. The French government was receptive to different ideas on the benefits of privatization, as a way to ensure the state is not overstretched (and not engaging in excessive subsidies for failing businesses) rather than as a way to roll it back (2003: 38). Instead, the French government liberalized the industry as a way to encourage competition. In Germany, the problem and political streams were systematically different. The legacy of Nazi abuses of the state produced a lower propensity to nationalize industries, with successive German governments preferring to maintain a minority stake in a range of companies. Further, previous pushes to promote popular capitalism (in the 1960s) were unsuccessful, while attempts in the 1980s (following the election of Helmut Kohl's Christian Democrats) to follow international trends were undermined by more dominant images of the policy problem – including the value of certain industries to regional populations and the centrality of government influenced industries to Germany's international competitiveness (2003: 62). As a result, major privatizations only took place in the 1990s following the window opened by German reunification and the perceived need to dispose of much of East Germany's industrial ownership (2003: 62).

Conclusion

The role of ideas is important and its discussion within political science undoubtedly improves our ability to explain complex policy events and outcomes. However, the ideas literature has the potential to confuse, for four main reasons.

First, the term 'idea' can relate to a wide spectrum of concepts, including very broad world views at one end to very specific policy proposals on the other. While an idea may be defined as a shared belief, in practice we find that the ideas literature describes a wide range of social practices. Therefore, for our purposes it is important to identify common themes, such as the extent to which ideas explain political behaviour and the links between ideas and power.

Second, ideas can represent independent or dependent variables; the main source of explanation or the object to be explained. Yet, in practice the links between ideas and interests are impossible to separate completely. As a consequence, attempts to separate analytically the explanatory power of ideas, and identify the causal processes involved, may paint a misleading picture. Descriptions of the role of ideas in public policy do not make sense unless they are accompanied by descriptions of the ways in which political actors accept, reproduce or make use of them. Therefore, even when the literature appears to describe ideas mainly as independent variables – as viruses, tides, norms and paradigms shaping or limiting behaviour – the discussions generally complement theories of power and behaviour.

Third, in our discussion of coalitions, paradigms and punctuations we have encountered two main types of explanatory power for ideas. On the one hand, ideas command considerable explanatory power: a paradigm which becomes institutionalized can constrain and facilitate political behaviour for decades. On the other, the political system often seems resistant to new ideas. Indeed, the consequence of the dominance of one idea is that the vast majority of ideas are rejected or receive no attention. This gives us a dual picture of ideas: as important, sweeping everything aside and then setting the policy direction for decades, or as unimportant, since a very small number act in this way at the expense of the rest. Most ideas are as likely to reach their final destination as sperm in the fallopian tubes, but the acceptance of a small number of ideas may have a profound effect on public policy.

Fourth, our discussion of ideas may highlight different links to power. On the one hand, a focus on ideas signals a shift of focus from elitism to pluralism; from the power of a small band of elites towards a much wider range of experts and commentators engaged in the production of, and argumentation about, ideas (John, 1998: 156). Public policy decisions are underpinned by societal values and moral judgements determined through a wider process of argumentation and reciprocal 'persuasion' within society rather than merely the exercise of interests (Majone, 1989: 2) On the other, ideas in the form of language or paradigms *limit* wider debate and provide fertile conditions for the maintenance of power by elites. Elected policymakers may not monopolize power because they are influenced by wider ideas which are outside of their control and prompt them to justify their behaviour in terms of discourse acceptable to the public. However, this does not necessarily mean that power is dispersed. The use of ideas to establish policy monopolies suggests that *other*, unelected, elites operate under a cloak of anonymity for long periods.

In this light, it is not surprising that multiple streams analysis emphasizes the messy and often random nature of agenda setting and decision making. The phrase 'an idea whose time has come' usefully describes the notion that certain policy solutions and ways of thinking have profound effects on public policy. Yet, major policy changes may not take place until these ideas 'couple' with newly framed policy problems and opportune political circumstances during a 'window of opportunity'. In other words, an idea's time only arrives when decision makers have the motive and opportunity to translate ideas into policy. This is something to bear in mind when, in Chapter 12, we extend our analysis to the transfer of ideas across political systems and sub-systems. While the concept of policy transfer suggests that the same ideas may prompt similar actions across a range of countries, the 'window of opportunity' suggests that policy change often results from idiosyncratic elements linked to the particular circumstances of individual political systems.

Policy Transfer

This chapter examines:

- What is policy transfer and how do we distinguish it from other terms such as lesson-drawing, diffusion and convergence?
- Who does it?
- Where do they transfer from?
- Why do they do it?
- What do they transfer?
- How much do they transfer?
- How 'rational' and how successful is the process of transfer?

There is now a strong focus in political science on policy learning and transfer. Policy learning is a rather vague term employed to describe the use of knowledge to inform policy decisions. That knowledge can be based on information regarding the current problem, lessons from the past or lessons from the experience of others (although bear in mind that this is a political, not technical or objective, process). Policy transfer is also a rather vague term to describe the transfer of policy solutions or ideas from one place to another. Although they can be very closely related (one would *hope* that a government learns from the experiences of another before transferring policy) they can also operate relatively independently. For example, a government may decide *not* to transfer policy after learning from the experience of another, or it may transfer without really understanding why the exporting country had a successful experience. This chapter focuses specifically on policy transfer (see Chapter 10 for various discussions of learning).

Policy transfer is not the only term to describe the transfer of policies and ideas. *Lesson-drawing* brings together the study of learning from the past as well as other countries (Rose, 1993). *Policy diffusion* describes a large body of work on the spread of policy solutions among US states (Walker, 1969). *Policy convergence* refers in a much broader way to the evidence for similarities in policy across countries (I use 'country' as a shorthand; some use the term 'region' because these processes can be observed within as well as across countries, or in multiple countries). The literature invites us to consider what causes this convergence and who pursues such similarities (Bennett, 1991a). In some cases it involves the deliberate transfer of policy from one country to another (in others, governments just make similar decisions based on similar problems and ways of thinking). If so, we may ask a further series of questions, including: is the transfer of policy voluntary; which actors are involved; how much policy is transferred; and how do we explain variations in levels of transfer (Dolowitz and Marsh, 1996)? The literature identifies wide variations in results. For example, the levels of coercion involved can vary from completely voluntary transfer, in which one country merely observes and emulates another, to coercive transfer, in which one country is obliged to emulate the example of others (Dolowitz and Marsh, 1996). Transfer can involve a wide range of international actors, or merely a small professional network exchanging ideas. It can relate to the wholesale transfer of policy programmes, broad ideas, minor administrative changes or even the decision to learn negative lessons and *not* to follow another country. The scale of transfer and likelihood of success also varies markedly and is affected by factors such as the simplicity of policy and whether or not the values and political structures of the borrower and lender coincide.

The value of a focus on policy transfer is that it helps us explain why policy changes and gauge the extent to which that change is common throughout the world (Box 12.1). Yet, it is also easy to overestimate its value by *assuming* that transfer has taken place, rather than countries just making similar judgements on similar problems. There is also potential to exaggerate policy similarities, by focusing on the decisions made rather than the implementation, or by assuming that policy will mean the same thing in all countries (for example, 'new public management', or the application of private sector business methods to the public sector, can have different meanings in Japan and the US – James, 2001). Further, we may ask if policy transfer is a theory of political behaviour or merely an umbrella term used to describe a wide range of practices (James and Lodge, 2003; Berry and Berry, 2007: 247).

Lesson-drawing, diffusion, convergence and policy transfer: what do they mean?

Lesson-drawing

Lesson-drawing is the focus of Rose (1991: 4; 1993; 2005) who posits the basic question: 'Under what circumstances and to what extent would a programme now in effect elsewhere also work here'? The focus is on policymakers seeking to learn lessons from successful countries (perhaps after they have considered their own past experiences) and then calculating what it would require to take that success home. It produces a series of questions about the nature and extent of lesson-drawing, such

---

Box 12.1   Examples of widespread policy convergence or transfer

Policy convergence or transfer seems most impressive when the same basic idea or policy solution is adopted across the globe:

* The privatization of 8500 state-owned enterprises took place in over 80 countries from 1980–92 (Kikeri, Nellis and Shirley, 1992).
* The broad principles of 'new public management' (the application of private sector business methods to the public sector) are just as widespread (OECD, 1995; Ormond and Löffler, 1998). Hood (1995: 94) describes the process as an 'alleged paradigm shift'. While the 'Anglo-American model' can be found in the UK, USA, Canada, Australia, New Zealand, Netherlands and Sweden (Common, 1998: 442), other variants (based on different ways of doing business) can be found in Japan and Germany (James, 2001). Recent discussion in countries such as Australia and New Zealand consider if recent reforms are 'post NPM' (Ramia and Carney, 2010; Lodge and Gill, 2011). However, Goldfinch and Wallis (2010) describe the idea of global NPM followed by a post-NPM agenda as a 'myth'.
* Policies to address money laundering have been adopted by 170 countries in less than 20 years (Sharman, 2008).
* At least 140 countries now have a 'national environmental strategy' (Busch and Jörgens, 2005: 868).
* A majority of countries have central banks and most have introduced reforms to make them legally independent since the 1990s (Marcussen, 2005: 903).
* The World Health Organizations' Framework Convention on Tobacco Control (FCTC) has been signed by 172 countries, 'which makes it the most widely embraced treaty in UN history' (WHO, 2008).
* Most newly democratized countries imported electoral systems from other countries (Norris, 1997).

---

as: from where are countries most likely to learn; how much of a policy programme is imported; and, how easy will it be to adapt the programme, given the importing country's social, economic and political conditions? This is a research agenda that flows throughout much of the transfer literature. Note that the term 'programme', not policy, is used deliberately to suggest that 'policy' is vague, while programmes 'are the stuff of public policy; they are concrete measures for doing such things as delivering hospital care' (2005: 17). Similarly, a 'lesson' is 'much more than a politician's prescription of goals and priorities' or a 'simple exhortation to "be like America"'; it also denotes 'the laws, appropriations and personnel and organizational requirements needed for a programme to be put into effect' (2005: 22).

Policy diffusion

The diffusion literature began as a study of policy innovation and emulation within the United States (but see Box 12.2 on p. 250 for an application to the EU). Walker (1969: 881) defines innovation as 'policy which is new to the states adopting it' and examines why some states lead the way and others often choose to follow. Walker (1969: 884–7) offers a wide range of explanations for innovation. It may be most likely within:

- The 'larger, wealthier, more industrialized states';
- States with high competition between candidates (producing a demand for new ideas);
- States with high turnover (with most innovation taking place at the beginning of a new administration);
- States with the most extensive policy and research staffs;
- Urban states with more 'cosmopolitan' populations more tolerant of change or experiencing more planning and infrastructure-based problems that require innovation. (See also Grey, 1973: 1182.)

Walker also offers several reasons for emulation:

- The policy may be viewed widely as a success;
- The federal government may encourage (or states may otherwise feel obliged to follow) policy uniformity and national norms;
- Interest groups promote best practice from the innovating states;
- States have close policy ties because they have something in common (such as geography or ideology);
- Boundedly rational decision makers use learning from other states as a short cut or rule of thumb;
- The innovation in one state may have a knock-on effect obliging other states to follow (or lose out, because they compete with each other economically). (See also Berry and Berry, 2007: 225–6.)

In many cases, policies are 'virtually copied' and diffusion may increase as the ability to communicate increases (Walker, 1969: 881; 898). However, the differences in policy conditions across different states, combined with varying degrees of willingness to follow the leader (according to the type of innovation and the values of policymakers in each state), creates uneven diffusion and conjures up a picture of ink diffusion in water (the spread is often uneven and unpredictable). The literature focuses not only on the process but also the patterns of diffusion; the overall spread and the speed of adoption.

To some extent, the early literature's focus on the US limits its geographical coverage and its ability to explain adoptions across countries with more significant differences in culture and political systems. However, the themes discussed have a much wider resonance. First, we can see this pattern of regular borrowing and lending (some innovate, others emulate) in the international policy community (below). Second, the explanations for emulation, such as shared geography, shared ideology and knock-on effects ('externalities') are used extensively in the literature (e.g. Rose, 1993). Third, it highlights a key concern in the literature when we try to pin down the causes of emulation: does the impetus to transfer policy come from within or outside the importing region (Eyestone, 1977: 441)? Fourth, it highlights the importance of the formulation/implementation distinction, particularly when problems with implementation lead to 'disinnovations' (1977: 445). Finally, the diffusion literature alerts us to the possibility that policy similarities result from independent decisions based on similar domestic policy conditions rather than emulation (1977: 441). US states are increasingly likely to know about each other's innovations in the communication age (Berry and Berry, 2007: 232), but countries with similar policy problems could address them in similar ways without knowledge of each other and without there being policy transfer (Holzinger and Knill, 2005: 786; Hoberg, 2001: 127).

Policy convergence

Policy convergence describes a movement, over time, towards policy similarities among different countries (a related term in organizational research is 'isomorphism' which means to become more alike). Bennett's (1991a: 216) review suggests that the focus on convergence was preceded by studies of 'societal convergence' that arose from the comparative politics literature. They sought to explain broad similarities with reference to worldwide industrialization: a common socio-economic project explains movement towards similarities, while political and cultural differences become much less important to explain change. The more popular (but also more vague) term is 'globalization' which produces common policy problems and pressures to converge without necessarily learning or transferring from other systems (Chapter 6).

A focus on this broader picture of convergence without emulation could lead to some confusion because the focus on this chapter is the more specific question of policy transfer. We need to know if convergence just means 'becoming more alike' or if ir refers specifically to transfer. Bennett (1991a: 217) selects the latter. He argues that the policy convergence literature should go beyond the broad argument that 'comparable conditions produce comparable problems which produce comparable policies'. In doing so, the key focus moves from an overall consideration of convergence to 'single convergence mechanisms'

(Holzinger and Knill, 2005: 777). In other words, we examine the political processes involved rather than assume a 'black box' between socioeconomic forces at one end, and outcomes at the other. The more focused study of policy convergence contrasts with studies of globalization. It identifies the decisions of policymakers when they weigh up both external constraints to converge, and domestic pressures to diverge or stay different (Hoberg, 2001: 127).

Bennett (1991a: 231) argues that we should not assume that emulation has taken place simply because policy convergence has taken place. Rather, we need to highlight the explanatory processes at work. Bennett (1991a) identifies four main causes from the literature:

- Emulation, in which the model adopted by one country 'serves as a blueprint that pushes a general idea on to the political agenda' of another (1991a: 221–2);
- The exchange of ideas between international policy networks (1991a: 224);
- Interdependence and the transnational nature of many policies. It prompts governments to search for ways to cooperate and 'mitigate the unintended external consequences of domestic policy'. Such harmonization may be facilitated by supra-national organizations such as the EU (1991a: 226);
- Penetration, in which the actions of one or more countries (or organizations) puts pressure on others to follow.

More recent reviews of the literature are more sceptical about our ability to find a common thread in what is a heterogeneous field of study (Heichel, Pape and Sommerer, 2005). Yet, while different studies have produced a shopping list of causes, they are actually different terms describing the same thing (the 'new' terms are in brackets): independent decision making without emulation (parallel domestic problem pressures); emulation (social emulation or mimetic processes); the exchange of ideas (informational networks); and, interdependence and penetration (international legal constraints, normative pressures, direct economic competition or coercion, international economic integration) (see Holzinger and Knill, 2005: 779).

Policy transfer: all together now

Dolowitz and Marsh (1996: 344) claim that the terminological differences are not 'overly significant' when they try to bring together this literature under the policy transfer umbrella. Yet, the breadth of study is betrayed by the unwieldy definition they are forced to produce. Policy transfer is: 'the process by which knowledge about policies, administra-

> ## Box 12.2   The diffusion of environmental policies
>
> Busch and Jörgens (2005) use the concept of diffusion to explain the international adoption of 'environmental policy innovations'. They follow Bennett's (1991a) recommendation to go beyond broad explanations of convergence based on globalization, and identify three main methods of policy adoption: harmonization, in which countries sign international legal agreements and supranational organizations coordinate policy; imposition by 'economic, political or even military threat'; or, diffusion 'by means of cross-national imitation, emulation or learning' (2005: 862). They suggest that diffusion largely explains the international spread of 'national environmental strategies', the widespread creation of environmental ministries and dedicated agencies, and the adoption of (often German inspired) 'feed-in tariffs' (which encourage energy producers to produce some renewable energy), while harmonization by the European Commission helps explain why many EU countries adopted renewable energy quotas.

tive arrangements, institutions and ideas in one political system (past or present) is used in the development of policies, administrative arrangements, institutions and ideas in another political system' (Dolowitz and Marsh, 2000: 5; 1996: 344). Dolowitz (2010) has offered a more recent definition: 'the processes by which agents become aware of information relating to the policy domain of one political system and subsequently transfer this into another policymaking system – where it is used or stored for potential use'. In both cases, a parsimonious definition is elusive, with greater definitional coverage succeeding at the expense of clarity (as with most definitions). Further, the definition does not capture the focus of much of the broader convergence literature, which may be to confirm the phenomenon of convergence rather than detail the particular processes of transfer which might aid convergence (Heichel *et al.*, 2005: 818). In other words, while it is legitimate to consider this to be a family of concepts – which have broadly similar practical questions surrounding the process of transfer – we should always be mindful of the variations in approach.

Who does it and from where are lessons drawn?

Some countries tend to innovate while others emulate, so it is important to recognize a distinction between those involved in the selling of ideas and those most involved in importing them (although transfer is rarely in one direction only). It may be particularly important when we discuss the nature of transfer; the extent to which it is voluntary or coercive (i.e. do some countries innovate then encourage others to emulate?).

Countries

Which countries tend to borrow and which lend? In some cases there are systematic leaders. Sweden has long been a beacon for the social democratic state, Germany has a history of effective inflation control, and Japan has become known for innovation in a range of areas (Rose, 1993: 107–8). Further, the decision to transfer once can establish a longer term borrowing and lending relationship. For example, Japan borrowed Germany's police system because it had already borrowed related aspects in law and local government (Page, 2000: 6). Most importantly, the US has become known not only as a source of ideas to borrow but also the main source of influence behind coercive forms of policy transfer (see below). However, while countries like Canada and the UK tend to borrow from the US they also lend some polices in return (Dolowitz, Greenwold and Marsh, 1999; Hoberg, 1991; Dolowitz and Marsh, 2000: 10). Relationships between other countries also demonstrate these phases or issue-specific patterns. While Germany exported unemployment policies to Sweden and the UK in the early twentieth century, Sweden exported data protection laws to many countries from the 1970s (Dolowitz and Marsh, 1996: 352) and the UK was one of the frontrunners in privatization from the 1980s. Further, while New Zealand initially borrowed certain aspects of 'new public management' it then became a beacon for subsequent lending (Armstrong 1998; Common, 1998).

To a large extent, the evidence suggests that importing countries are attracted to different programmes from different countries at different times. Rose (1993: 98–9) suggests that countries are more likely to learn lessons from others if they share similar policy conditions, geography and ideology. Yet, in practice this commonality is likely to vary. For example, while US states may, in the past, have been most likely to learn from other states on their borders, advances in communications have reduced the constraints to looking elsewhere. It suggests that 'geographical propinquity' now means something else, referring to a perception of shared policy concerns (1993: 99–102). In some cases, it may refer to geographical similarities (explaining connections between rural states or urban conurbations of similar size). However, it can also refer to ideology, or the ways in which each government frames and attempts to solve policy problems (Chapters 9 and 11). For example, ideology may explain why the UK became so focused on the US for ideas during the Thatcher and Reagan eras (Dolowitz and Marsh, 1996: 350). Overall, physical constraints to transfer are less important as global economic forces and the rapid growth of technology and communication, transport and the role of supranational organizations pushes regions towards more and more transfer 'across diverse countries' (Dolowitz and Marsh, 2000: 7).

Actors

Most of the actors involved in transfer are merely the regular and most powerful participants within the domestic policy process: 'elected officials, political parties, bureaucrats/ civil servants [and] pressure groups' (Dolowitz and Marsh, 1996: 345). However, other actors and organizations are involved and policy transfer extends our focus from domestic to international political processes:

1. *Supranational institutions*. These include broad organizations such as the European Union (EU), Organisation for Economic Co-operation and Development (OECD), World Bank and United Nations (UN), as well as their particular institutions, such as the European Commission and the World Health Organization (within the UN).
2. *Policy entrepreneurs*. The term 'policy entrepreneur' means different things in different contexts, but broadly refers to actors who sell policies (Chapter 13). In policy transfer, entrepreneurs can be prominent individuals or consultants who use their experience in one country to sell that policy to another (for examples, see O'Neill, 2000: 63; Common, 1998: 440; Dolowitz and Marsh, 1996: 345). They can be NGOs (non-governmental organizations) such as think tanks which promote best practice internationally (Stone 2000). International entrepreneurs often have particular credentials, either from an exporting country or a supranational institution that ties its cooperation to the use of a particular expert (Dolowitz and Marsh, 2000: 10). The classic case is the Harvard Business School professor who travelled the world selling new public management, backed notionally by the US government keen for other countries to follow its lead.
3. *International policy communities*. An 'epistemic community' is an international 'network of professionals with recognized expertise and competence in a particular domain and an authoritative claim to policy-relevant knowledge within that domain or issue-area' (Haas, 1992: 3; see also Holzinger and Knill, 2005: 784; Rose, 1991: 6; Campbell, 2002: 25). Epistemic communities contain actors with shared beliefs and a 'common policy enterprise' which is coordinated and presented in a range of countries. In effect, they operate like a series of domestic policy networks which are connected through international professional organizations (Bennett, 1991a: 224). Members of these networks then promote the widely shared ideas within their own countries.
4. *Multinational or transnational corporations*. According to Dolowitz and Marsh (1996: 348), MNCs 'hold a trump card' because they can 'threaten to take their business elsewhere' if governments do not

minimize their regulations on companies. However, the effect of such demands on individual countries varies considerably (see Chapter 6 on the 'race to the bottom'; Bennett, 1991a: 228–9).

5. *Other countries.* Policy transfer often follows pressure from other countries, either directly (through encouragement or coercion) or indirectly (by establishing new norms, inspiring others to follow or causing unintended consequences for the importing country). Holzinger and Knill (2005: 785) suggest that the innovating country benefits from the decision by others to follow, because this reduces its costs when dealing with them (much like the adoption of a common currency, such as the Euro or perhaps the US Dollar which is often used as a proxy currency in other countries).

The role of these transfer agents will vary by issue, and transfer may follow a combination of efforts. For example, in high profile cases, one or more countries may put pressure on another via a supranational organization. Alternatively, policy may change quietly as epistemic communities frame issues as humdrum and technical, and pursue policy change below the radar.

Why transfer? Is transfer voluntary?

To identify the reason for transfer we must decide if the process was voluntary or coercive. In other words, who decides that the importing country should transfer: the importing country itself or external agents? In many cases the answer is 'both' and the process contains a mix of voluntary and coercive elements. This prompted Dolowitz and Marsh (2000: 13) to produce a policy transfer continuum, as seen in Figure 12.1.

At one end (the left hand side of Figure 12.1) we find voluntary transfer, which Dolowitz and Marsh (1996: 346) associate with Rose's (1993) lesson-drawing. In such cases, transfer is by no means inevitable. Rather, it follows some level of internal dissatisfaction with existing policy that cannot be addressed adequately by the ideas floating around the domestic political process. Only then do decision makers widen their search for ideas elsewhere (1996: 347). Or, Bennett (1991a: 200) suggests that there is a 'natural tendency to look abroad' to see how others have reacted to similar policy problems and to seek ideas when innovation is required. Alternatively, governments may merely look abroad for ideas and evidence to legitimize their existing aims. In all three cases there is no external pressure to examine policy change.

At the other end, we find direct coercive transfer. This refers to the influence exerted by an organization, country or supranational body to make another country adopt a certain policy. For Dolowitz and Marsh

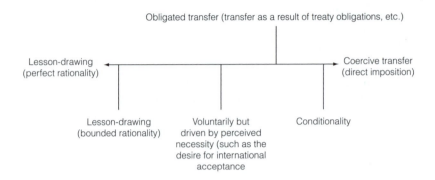

Figure 12.1   *The Dolowitz and Marsh policy transfer continuum*

Source: Dolowitz and Marsh (2000: 13).

(1996: 348; 2000: 10–11) direct imposition by another country is rare. Indeed, extreme examples such as regime change in Iraq may represent a process that is qualitatively different from other forms of coercive transfer that are very high up the scale (although see Holzinger and Knill, 2005: 781). Rather, in most cases there is still some degree of (albeit limited) choice within the importing country. Coercion therefore refers to the agenda for transfer being set elsewhere and the adverse consequences if the importing country does not cooperate. In this context, the most significant example is conditionality: when developing countries seek loans from the International Monetary Fund or World Bank in critical circumstances they are effectively obliged to undertake 'good governance' (Chapter 8) reforms in return. In most cases, new public management reforms and a reduction of the role of the state in the economy are also 'encouraged' (Biersteker, 1990; Hopkins, Powell, Roy and Gilbert, 1997). In turn, the agenda of the IMF or World Bank is influenced by other countries, most notably the US (Wade, 2002).

While 'obligated transfer' may seem more coercive than conditionality, it is more to the left on the spectrum because the original decision to become subject to treaties is often voluntary, while most countries should have the ability to influence international policies. As Bennett (1991a: 226) suggests, supranational organizations are created to deal with interdependence, which prompts governments to cooperate. Similarly, while Dolowitz and Marsh (2000: 15) point out that the Court of Justice can 'force member states to comply with European policy', they ask: 'since individual nations voluntarily joined the Union, can any act of the EU be considered coercive in terms of policy transfer'?

The third main category – indirect coercive transfer – demonstrates the difficulty of separating voluntary and coercive elements. It refers to a process of voluntary transfer in which the importing country *perceives* the need to change. In other words, while there are still coercive elements involved (the policy agenda may still be driven elsewhere and there may still be consequences if the country does not emulate another), the driver for change comes more clearly from the importing country. For Dolowitz and Marsh (1996: 348–9) this refers

Externality – a term in economics referring to the (often unintended) effects of the actions of one agent on another (negative or positive).

mostly to the role of **externalities**. For example, countries react to a range of external pressures in the shape of norms (when countries adopt the same behaviour and expect others to follow suit), embarrassment (a feeling of being left behind) and economics (when countries react to the decisions made in competitor countries). Externalities are

often felt most by small states which share a border with larger states (Hoberg, 1991). For example, Canada is affected disproportionately by economic and regulatory decisions made in the US (as its main market for many goods and services), while its attention to the US media and reliance on US expertise act as further sources of emulation (1991: 110). These effects can also be seen in sub-national authorities. For example, the decision by the UK government to increase university tuition fees in England puts immense pressure on the devolved governments to follow (since lower fees would lead to an inflow of English students searching for a cheaper education and an outflow of staff looking for better conditions – Cairney, 2008: 12).

This notion of perceived necessity explains the distinction between two forms of lesson-drawing: 'perfect' (*comprehensive*) and bounded rationality. The more an importing country feels compelled to act quickly, then the more bounded its decision-making process. Conversely, the less pressure on a government to transfer, then the more we travel towards the 'perfect' end of the Dolowitz and Marsh continuum.

Coercive transfer – how is it measured, demonstrated and justified?

When we examine most cases of transfer, it becomes clear that there is considerable debate and confusion regarding the level of coercion. For example, the use of conditionality to coerce developing countries attracts different views. Cammack (2004) argues that the World Banks's putative aims to reduce world poverty mask its main goal of capitalist hegemony. It can then be linked to the 'unipolar' role of the US and its attempts to dominate world politics (Wade, 2006). Indeed, the power of the US in world politics is a key theme of the transfer literature. Yet, Wade (2002) also argues that while the US may seek to

Hegemonic project – the pursuit of dominance in terms of the way we think about and address policy problems.

influence directly the economic policies of other countries through the World Bank and IMF, its use of free-market *ideas* as part of a wider **hegemonic project** may be as important. Stone (2004: 554) has a similar discussion of knowledge and the dissemination of 'best practice' by the World Bank. Hopkins *et al.* (1997: 513) also question the assumption of coercion. Rather, the effect may be more modest, suggesting merely that the importing country would not otherwise have reformed without being bribed, induced or rewarded (see also Meseguer, 2003: 24). Holzinger and Knill (2005: 781) caution against the assumption of high levels of coercion; there is a difference between a government being resistant to a policy transfer and a government which just sees the policy as not high on its list of priorities. Finally, Stone (2004: 554) suggests that since economic sanctions or inducements are often ineffective, it is often difficult to identify *successful* coercion (see the discussion of implementation below).

Humanitarian interventions are similarly difficult to place on the continuum for two main reasons. First, the level of imposition relates to international rules and norms of legitimacy which shift over time. Wheeler (2000: 8) argues that 'humanitarian claims were not accepted as a legitimate basis for the use of force in the 1970s but ... a new norm of UN-authorized humanitarian intervention developed in the 1990s'. Second, humanitarian intervention may be more or less coercive depending on the perceptions of its audience. In other words, is it imposed if it is welcomed by a country's population but not its state? Or, in the case of the FCTC (Box 12.1), is it inappropriate to oblige a range of countries to sign up when this may help the population's health and guard against the unethical practices of MNCs? These issues are broached in a different form in developed countries. For example, Bennett (1991a: 228) suggests that the actions of foreign governments, supranational organizations or MNCs can have a 'coercive effect on states that have been *slow to act*' (emphasis added). It suggests that some forms of penetration are considered to be acceptable, or a natural part of international politics. Much 'coercion' also relates to exclusions from an international 'club' and its associated benefits, rather than the more severe sanctions associated with international relations (Bennett, 1991a: 228). A study of the perceptions of the borrower are often no clearer, particularly since the *appearance* of coercion may help governments introduce policy 'not favoured by its citizens' (Holzinger and Knill, 2005: 781). Overall, these issues further complicate the question of power and responsibility when we seek to balance external and domestic reasons for the adoption of policy ideas.

What is transferred? How much is transferred?

There is considerable variation in the type and extent of borrowing and lending. Effectively, policy transfer can range from the decision to completely duplicate the substantive aims and institutions associated with a major policy change, taking decades to complete, to the very quick decision *not to emulate* and, instead, to learn 'negative lessons' (although the latter may seem like a conceptual stretch too far). Bennett (1991a) identifies five key measures to determine policy convergence: policy goals, content, instruments, outcomes and/or styles. Dolowitz and Marsh (1996: 349–50) list seven: 'policy goals, structure and content; policy instruments or administrative techniques; institutions; ideology; ideas; attitudes and concepts; and negative lessons' (compare with Rose, 2005: 22).

With the exception of negative lessons (Box 12.3), the main difference is that Bennett (1991a: 221–3) is keen to distance his focus from the wider convergence agenda which identifies similarities without demonstrating a convincing link to emulation. In other words, we need evidence not only of one country studying another, but also that this translated into concrete results in the form of policy content. Alternatively, Dolowitz and Marsh (1996: 350) point to exemplar countries as a broad source of ideas and knowledge, while in some cases countries have loaned or borrowed ideological *rhetoric* to sell a range of policy programmes. In other cases, this process may be clouded by the transfer of policy content between countries with different ideological approaches (see the discussion of 'Patient Choice' in England and Wales – Cairney, 2009a – or the adoption of 'Reaganite' ideas by a left-wing

---

Box 12.3   Learning negative lessons

For the term 'negative lessons' to mean anything, we must demonstrate that the 'importing' country drew lessons from, and then acted on, the 'exporting' country's bad experiences. Otherwise, policy transfer would include the notional study of another country which leads to nothing, such as 'fact finding' missions by politicians to hot countries during the summer holidays. For example, many countries may have learned from the UK how not to tackle BSE (Stone, 1999: 52). A more local example can be found in Scottish drugs and HIV policy. When the Greater Glasgow Health board studied Lothian it found that the prescribing of methadone to reduce HIV and heroin-related deaths led to deaths caused by methadone ingestion (when patients sold their methadone to others). It therefore introduced methadone prescribing, but on a daily (rather than weekly) basis under pharmacist supervision (interview, Lothian Health Board, 1998). In turn, Lothian emulated Greater Glasgow's modified strategy.

New Zealand government – Clancy, 1996). Or, the same policy outcomes may result from different political processes (Bennett, 1991a:
229).

The extent of borrowing also varies. Rose (1993: 30–2) provides five
main categories along a continuum from duplication to inspiration (it is
possible for several elements to be apparent in complex areas such as tax
policy). The first is *complete duplication*. This may be possible only
within political systems, such as the US, because of the 'close similarity
of institutions and laws'. One way to prove duplication is to find identical wording in the legislation. Yet, even within the UK this is difficult
since some Scottish legislation which is effectively 'cut-and-pasted' from
the UK still has to account for differences in Scots law (Keating *et al.*,
2003). Two more likely strategies are: *adaptation,* when an importing
country tailors the imported policy to domestic circumstances; or making
a *hybrid* policy from the exporting and importing region (common when
policy is transferred from a federal to unitary state, but existing administrative arrangements are maintained). The fourth and fifth categories
suggest that lessons come from more than one country: a country may
create *synthesis* by extracting some aspects of one or more exporting
programmes (such as when new democracies borrow elements of electoral systems and legislative models to make a complete system); or
merely use lessons from others as a broad inspiration. The latter would
not satisfy Bennett (1991a). The example of devolution in Scotland also
demonstrates the difficulties in *proving* transfer using the rhetoric of
importing countries. Although the architects of devolution paid much lip
service to the Nordic 'consensus democracies' as an inspiration, and
claimed to learn negative lessons from Westminster, Scotland's political
system still resembles closely the politics of the UK (McGarvey and
Cairney, 2008). Perhaps a sixth category is the use of information gathered elsewhere to merely package decisions already made. For example,
UK Government ministers were attracted to US policies on child support
because it helped them 'punish absent parents' and reduce public
spending on single parents (Dolowitz, 2003: 103).

What determines the likelihood and success of policy transfer?

The discussion so far highlights many factors which affect the likelihood
of transfer, including: geopolitical (coercion, externalities, interdependence); 'geographical propinquity'; and the similarities between the
importer and exporter (be it their values or their political structures or
administrative arrangements). To this we can add some practical considerations which may enhance the success of transfer:

1 The policy is not unique or dependent on inimitable organizations.
2 There are few resource constraints to implement policy.
3 The policy is simple with a clear cause-and-effect.
4 There is adequate information available about what the policy is and how it works.
5 The new policy does not mark a radical departure from the importer's original policy. (Rose, 1993: 132)

This is largely an extension of a series of questions central to the implementation literature (Chapter 2; see also McConnell, 2010: 136–8). Two of the top-down conditions for successful implementation are that: there is an understanding of clear and consistent policy objectives; and, the policy will work as intended when implemented. In the case of transfer, the importer must ask if the original policy worked as intended in part because of the wider political structure, values or administrative arrangements in the exporting country (or, if it did not work, will it work better in a different setting?). For example, it may be difficult to transfer policy from the federal US to unitary UK. Dolowitz's (2003: 106) study of welfare policy shows that US federal policy is pursued on the assumption of supportive welfare services and a systematic involvement of the courts at state and local levels (not a feature in the UK). Similarly, the application of 'new public management' may be difficult in developing countries with an immature private sector or cultural differences from developed countries (Page, 2000: 10; Massey, 2010).

This extension of the discussion of transfer to success and failure presents us with two separate but related studies: transfer success and implementation success. For Dolowitz and Marsh (2000: 17) transfer success refers to the extent to which a policy was adapted properly. In turn, failure can relate to one (or a combination) of three factors:

1. Uninformed transfer – when the borrowing country has incomplete information about the crucial elements that made the policy a success in the lending country;
2. Incomplete transfer – when those crucial elements of policy are not transferred;
3. Inappropriate transfer – when not enough attention is paid to adaptation, or the differences in policy conditions, structures and aims of the lending country.

For example, let us compare an example of unsuccessful and successful transfer. Dolowitz's (2003) case study of the Child Support Agency in the UK shows that problems of adaptation were compounded by different aims. In the UK the driver was to raise revenue (focusing on a small number of absent parents) even though the policy in the US was geared towards wider coverage regardless of ability to pay (see also Sharman, 2010 on 'dysfunctional policy transfer in national tax blacklists'). It compares badly to Dolowitz and Marsh's (2000: 16) claim that the transfer of the US *Earned Income Tax Credit* to the UK (*Working Families Tax Credit*) 'falls as close to the purely rational end of the continuum as policy is ever likely to' (based on the time that the UK government had to study the issue and the relative lack of pressure to change policy). Yet, the latter context does not mean that the policy will be an *implementation* success. As Chapter 2 suggests, it depends on wider issues of implementation, such as compliance, support from interest groups, political will and the effects of wider socio-economic factors.

The wider role of implementation is also crucial to other aspects of transfer. We are likely to get a significantly different impression about the levels of policy convergence if we focus on the broad policy choices made (see Holzinger and Knill, 2005: 777) rather than their long term effects. Issues of implementation also qualify our earlier conclusions on coercive transfer. While some countries may be forced to make policy choices, there is less evidence to suggest that these are followed through. For example, the EU may force member states to adopt harmonizing directives, but its role in implementation often stops as soon as EU-wide policies are translated into member state legislation. The EU is notoriously weak to implement in many policy areas – it is under resourced and the penalties for non-compliance may not be particularly serious (with the notable exception of environmental regulation in which it has had a strong, long-term role). Or, its power is exercised to force the implementation of very broad laws which leave a lot of discretion in the implementation (Duina, 1997; Mastenbroek, 2005; Falkner, Hartlapp, Leiber and Treib, 2004). There is similar evidence of the failed implementation of agreements linked to conditionality in developing countries. For example, Hopkins *et al.* (1997: 512) link the implementation gap to a lack of 'ownership' (or commitment to follow things through) felt in the importing country, while Meseguer (2003: 24) describes overall implementation levels as 'dismal' (when only 6 of 30 countries implemented conditional policies tied to IMF Extended Fund Facility loans).

Links to the wider literature: is the transfer process 'rational'?

As Chapter 5 suggests, policy transfer is one of many concepts – also including incrementalism, punctuated equilibrium, multiple streams analysis and multi-level governance – that uses the ideal of comprehensive rationality as an ideal-type to be rejected. In this case, 'perfect' rationality represents an ideal on the policy transfer continuum, signifying a complete lack of pressure to engage in transfer and therefore in a position to learn lessons comprehensively. However, while the aim is to suggest that the lesson-drawing process can never be comprehensively rational (Dolowitz and Marsh, 2000: 22; compare with Bennett, 1991b: 37), there is a danger that we cause confusion in the process by effectively linking rationality to coercion. In other words, being forced into policy change by another country or supranational authority is not best described as a problem of bounded rationality. Certainly, in cases of indirect coercive transfer, the more pressure there is to transfer, then the less time there is to devote to the policy analysis required for significant decisions. Yet, as with our discussion of implementation, the pressure to act and make choices in a limited time is only one consideration involved in discussions of rationality. Therefore, removing the pressure to act will not solve other problems related to the identification of policy aims, the separation of facts from values and the analysis of policy solutions (and their consequences) with limited staff, cognitive and predictive resources.

If we put this problem of ambiguity to one side, it is still useful for us to combine the insights from the transfer literature with those gleaned from other chapters. For example, a combination of *incrementalism* and policy transfer may produce two diverging conclusions. On the one hand, governments learn from their own mistakes and a large preoccupation of decision makers is solving problems caused by previous policies. At the very least the search for outside experience is not automatic; it requires 'policy failure' or a level of dissatisfaction with existing policy (Rose, 1993: 5; Dolowitz and Marsh, 1996: 348). Further, the search for ideas from countries with different starting points (including political structures and values) may be unrealistic given the limited scope for radical change. Subsequent lesson-drawing may then exhibit path dependence as the lender imports a range of policies related to the original import (Page, 2000: 6). On the other hand, Berry and Berry's (2007: 225) discussion of diffusion suggests that non-incremental change is consistent with Lindblom's model. Boundedly rational states use emulation as a rule of thumb or short-cut to decision making when resources are limited (Walker, 1969: 889). In such cases, radical changes may result from limited policy analysis.

A combination of *multi-level governance* and policy transfer suggests that we may no longer witness the straightforward adoption of policies from one country to another. Rather, the importation of policy can take place at various levels – local, regional, national and supranational. This introduction of complexity produces uncertain effects. On the one hand, MLG may encourage more innovation as regions compete with each other and are given more scope to try out new ideas (Hooghe and Marks, 2003). In turn, it may produce more emulation as regions follow best practice, or the success of policies adopted by devolved governments puts pressure on the national government (or vice versa) to follow. MLG may also increase the demand for policy transfer since it introduces a range of new audiences for ideas and new ways for epistemic communities or entrepreneurs to venue-shop. On the other hand, the adoption of policy transfer at one level may be undermined by interdependence and a lack of cooperation at others. In this sense, MLG further exacerbates the implementation gap and qualifies the significance of policy transfer (if we focus on outcomes rather than policy choices).

Finally, a combination of *agenda-setting* and policy transfer suggests that policy failure is a contentious rather than a technical issue, while lessons from other countries are not just 'there'. Rather, they are subject to framing and evaluation as they are reported. As Page (2000: 4) suggests, 'the perception of how the policy operated in the exporter jurisdiction might be crucially shaped by the observer from outside who seeks to import it'. Further, in many cases, foreign experience may be merely framed as a way to legitimize existing practices. *Punctuated equilibrium* suggests that this process will involve positive and negative feedback. In periods of policy monopoly and limited government attention, policymakers will be resistant to new information gathered from the experience of other countries. In periods of positive feedback, those lessons may be given disproportionate attention by policymakers focused acutely on one issue at the expense of most others. *Multiple streams analysis* suggests that policy transfer will not take place unless a range of conditions are met: the problem is redefined in a certain way (perhaps because of rising attention to the lead taken by another country), a solution (derived from international experience) exists, and policymakers are receptive to this new information. For Berry and Berry (2007: 237) this scope for emulation is a 'rare political opportunity'. In other words, lesson-drawing merely forms one part of a much larger set of ideas or solutions which compete for the attention of governments. Further, receptivity to these new ideas (perhaps following the election of a new government) may be more important than the ideas themselves. The *advocacy coalition framework* suggests that the pressure on a policy broker to change policy comes from competition between domestic coalitions rather than coercion from another country.

We discuss these issues in greater depth in Chapter 13. The key point is that a wider discussion of ideas gives us useful perspective on the nature of the transfer of ideas. Yet, there is an important cultural difference to note in many of these discussions. It is significant that many of these theories of ideas were developed from studies of the US in which coercive transfer is much less likely than in most other countries. What happens if we shift our attention to countries more subject to coercion? Levels of 'positive feedback', 'receptivity' and competition may be less important than the pressure exerted from outside the system. Or, coercion (direct or indirect) will at least be a key determinant of the demand for new ideas.

Conclusion

There is some scope for confusion when we discuss policy transfer. It is not the same as learning because countries can emulate countries without learning from them, or learn not to emulate. It is also not exactly the same as convergence which can refer more broadly to the evidence for policy similarities across regions. Policy transfer explores the more specific process of policy importation and exportation. This is a complex and variable process. The actors involved are a combination of the 'usual suspects' as well as policy entrepreneurs, supranational organizations, international policy communities, MNCs and other countries. The extent of transfer ranges from the complete adoption of ideologies and wholesale programmes, to particular policy instruments, broad ideas or even negative lessons. When transfer is voluntary it is more likely to take place (or perhaps be successful) when the borrower and lender share factors such as policy conditions, 'nearness', values and political structures. However, there are also examples of transfer between countries which do not seem to have that much in common (or their shared experience is subject to much interpretation and debate).

A key problem, when we try to theorize the relationship between policy transfer and change, is that it is difficult to pin down the independent variable. In other words: who or what is the main driving force behind transfer? Of course, the issues discussed in this chapter suggest that the answer to this question varies quite dramatically. It ranges from direct coercion by powerful countries or organizations to a relatively benign process often driven by importing countries or epistemic communities. Or, we may have to weigh up explanations between the selling power of entrepreneurs and the receptivity of a domestic audience to new ideas. In other words, the nature of the idea itself is not a sufficient explanation for transfer.

Yet, policy transfer analysis is still important as a description of policy change. It highlights a range of practices which aid explanation and guards against assuming that policy ideas originate from within a political system. It helps us explain why countries adopt some ideas over others and why some ideas may be more successful in some countries than others. It is increasingly relevant to an international political system which seems to be increasingly interdependent (economically, politically and socially) and connected by advances in communication technologies.

James and Lodge (2003) question the distinctiveness of policy transfer research when many of the questions involved are covered in the existing literature on policy change. Further, it is difficult to *establish* that policy transfer has risen in scope and significance if it is part of a broader process of public policy and learning rather than a distinct practice (see also Evans and Davies, 1999). The transfer of policy is difficult to demonstrate, while much learning may refer to the 'transfer of policy knowledge but not a transfer of policy practice' (Stone, 2004: 549). Yet, while the absence of proof of transfer is a key problem for Bennett (1991a: 223) and a source of concern for Holzinger and Knill (2005: 775), for Page (2000: 4) it is more of a distraction from an interesting new avenue of research. Therefore, while we could treat these problems as killer blows, for our purposes it is better to see how transfer can be combined with other approaches as we develop multiple theories. Transfer has much to add to the existing literature: implementation failure can derive from misunderstandings of international policy evidence; the external pressure to act may further undermine the notion of comprehensive rationality; emulation as a rule of thumb may produce non-incremental change; and, a focus on coercion may qualify major models of policy change (punctuated equilibrium, multiple streams, advocacy coalition framework) which ignore the kinds of political constraints that are least likely to be experienced in the US. Overall, it is a useful addition to the policy literature.

Chapter 13

Conclusion

The aim of this chapter is to consider:

• The scope for synthesis when we combine several theories.
• The extent to which theories of public policy are complementary or contradictory, exploring the idea of a 'policy shoot-out'.
• The value of multiple, independent perspectives.

We have good reason to think that we can use the literature described so far to accumulate knowledge of the policy process. Although there is a proliferation of approaches and concepts, they display an impressive degree of unity and a common research agenda. Most theories of public policy identify the same key empirical themes and conceptual issues. They ask similar questions and identify similar causal processes. At the conceptual level, most explore the relationship between structure and agency and the interplay between individuals, institutions and their policy environment. While a small number of discussions downplay the role of agency, most present an understanding of how individuals deliberate and make choices within the context of institutional and structural constraint, and generally draw on the idea of bounded rationality. Most consider the interplay between the exercise of power and the role of ideas, and seek to theorize the relationship between sources of stability or instability and policy continuity or change. At the empirical level, many theories consider the pervasiveness of policy specialization and sub-systems, and seek to account for a shift from the centralization of power within government towards power diffusion, or from the 'clubby days' of post-war policymaking towards a more open and competitive group-government process.

The aim of this chapter is to explore the main ways in which we can combine the insights of these theories. Sabatier (2007b: 330) highlights three advantages to the use of multiple theories: it provides 'some guarantee against assuming that a particular theory is the valid one'; it shows us that 'different theories may have comparative advantages in different settings'; and, the knowledge of other theories 'should make one much more sensitive to some of the implicit assumptions in one's favoured theory'. Indeed, combining the merits of theories represents 'standard advice' in the literature (2007a: 330).

Yet, the literature is less clear about *how* we combine theories. One option is to assume that theories are broadly complementary and that we can combine their insights in a relatively straightforward manner (John, 1998: 18). It can be achieved in two main ways. First, we can produce a single theory that combines key insights from a range of theories. For example, John (1998) considers the role of evolutionary theory, while I set out the 'policy transfer window' that applies Kingdon's (1995) theory to the transfer of policy ideas. Second, we can maintain a separation between theories to provide multiple, complementary, perspectives. For example, we can identify bounded rationality as our starting point, but use different theories to explore its consequences (Box 13.1).

The alternative option is to suggest that theories provide competing or contradictory explanations and that one is better than another. This approach is summed up in the 'policy shootout' which promotes the most promising theories based on the 'basic tenets of science' (Eller and Krutz, 2009: 1). However, it is problematic without a universal understanding of, or agreement on, scientific method. Further, policy change is open to interpretation and we have the ability to produce competing, and equally convincing, empirical narratives. Consequently, the most valuable theory in each case may depend on the narrative of policy change that we select rather than just the scientific nature of the theory. We can therefore highlight instances in which theories provide competing assumptions or predictions, but be less certain about how to choose between them.

Synthesis

Our first option is to produce a single theory that combines key insights from a range of theories. This is what many theories of public policy – such as multiple streams analysis, punctuated equilibrium and the advocacy coalition framework – do already. They are 'synthetic' because they combine a discussion of many concepts to theorize 'the relationship between the five core causal processes … institutions, networks, socioeconomic process, choices, and ideas' (John, 2003: 488; 1998: 173). For John (2003: 495), although each theory has its limitations, public policy research still follows their agenda. The challenge is to improve established approaches.

Evolutionary theory

For example, John (2003: 495, extending the work of Kingdon, Baumgartner and Jones) proposes evolutionary theory to capture the 'five core causal processes'. Each factor interacts with the other to

Box 13.1 Multiple theories and the banking 'bail out'

How do these discussions apply to our example of the banking 'bail out' (Chapter 1)? A 'complementary approach' may produce a range of explanations based on the most widely used concepts and theories. Many begin by considering the consequences of bounded rationality. One type of consequence is incrementalism and inertia when governments form close and stable relationships with powerful groups, such as business groups and the banking sector, and produce policies that satisfy their common aims (including the maintenance of economic growth in a capitalist system). These arrangements endure because there are good reasons to devolve decisions and consult with certain interests, and because new governments inherit the commitments of their predecessors. So, the rules on banking that contributed to the financial crisis were based on long-standing agreements produced by policy participants and government officials, then accepted and reinforced by successive governments.

We can compare this account with accounts of non-incremental change. For example, punctuated equilibrium theory and multiple streams analysis link bounded rationality to lurches of policymaker attention, often during crises, that produce calls for new ways of thinking about and solving policy problems. So, the rules on banking may be changed radically following heightened attention and the involvement of new actors, perhaps during a brief window of opportunity. Such explanations can be complementary because they can be used to construct an overall account of policymaking that explains periods of stability/continuity and instability/change. The alternative is to treat theories as competing accounts; to suggest that an account based on, say, rational choice or the ACF is explained more convincingly and/or better supported by the evidence. One aspect of this approach is to say that some factors are more important than others to explanation. For example, we might say that the pressures of the capitalist system play more of a part in explanation than the ability of policymakers to make choices. The other aspect is an appeal to scientific methods to demonstrate why some accounts are more reliable than others. It takes us beyond the evidence itself to focus on how we gather and explain it. This aspect may be particularly important when we compare theories that contain opposing arguments (e.g. people are driven by their beliefs, not interests).

produce outcomes: institutions constrain actors but actors can challenge or reconstitute rules; 'economic power structures' give actors resources to pursue their interests through networks; policies are 'ideas concretized by political action (i.e. interests)', and so on (John, 1998: 183). John (1999: 43) compares the transmission of ideas within politics to the transmission of **memes** within society. Memes are reproduced because they are the most adaptable to their environment or most attractive to the 'selection mechanism' at hand. Ideas which were unacceptable in the

Meme – the social equivalent of a gene: 'an information pattern, held in an individual's memory, which is capable of being copied to another' (John, 2003: 493). It is used by Dawkins (1976) to explain why types of information – common sense, cultural references, phrases, technology, traditions, theories – 'survive' and are reproduced across generations.

past often gain favour following shifts in government, public and media opinion (or venue shift – 1999: 46; Walsh, 2000: 487). The focus on evolution does not suggest that certain policies will inevitably succeed (be selected) because they are fitter than the others. As in Kingdon's account, there is an element of chance. Ideas are adopted as policies because a number of things come together at a particular time: 'there is a coalition behind it'; it 'solves the public problem' and it 'is an idea that works' (1998: 183; 1999: 48–9). We have a large set of ideas that may already exist and be promoted by certain actors, but only some become policy when they receive support from enough people. Further, ideas are evolving constantly as different actors adapt them to suit particular problems at particular times.

The same process of evolution can be identified in decision making. Drawing on rational choice theory, John (1998: 184) suggests that the strategies of actors evolve over time as individuals learn to cooperate with each other and adapt to their environments. They also learn, and their preferences change, when they formulate and adapt ideas. John (1998: 185) draws on studies of implementation to argue that evolution does not end when policies are selected at the formulation stage. Rather, policy evolves further as new actors (or actors more powerful at the point of delivery) influence the progress of policy. Finally, drawing on accounts of institutions and structures, John (1998: 186) describes this process as 'structured evolution' since the institutions, networks and socio-economic constraints that affect behaviour are more static than strategies and ideas.

John (1998: 187) expresses concern about his own theory by noting that it may not be parsimonious or clear on the causal mechanisms involved. What exactly is a meme (John, 2003: 495)? Memes appear to be entities which are adopted (and need a carrier) and which (somehow) act to ensure their adoption. Therefore, it is not clear what causes policy change. The discussion resembles complexity theory in which it is difficult to identify the effect of human agency; there is a lot of interaction between a lot of elements, producing an outcome that is beyond the control of individuals.

Further, the term 'evolution' is so loaded that evolutionary theory becomes bound up in assumptions about the survival of the fittest and evolution-as-progress. For example, John (1998: 185) describes his theory as 'Lamarckian' rather than 'Darwinian' to focus our attention on how actors adapt and 'learn strategies to evolve'. Yet, for Sementelli

(2007: 743–5), 'Lamarckian' typifies a belief in progress towards perfection through evolution, rather than the alternative conception in which 'things evolve in every direction' and evolution can mark regress as well as progress. Dowding (2000) also identifies a tendency to conflate processes of learning with processes of 'natural selection' within evolutionary accounts. These problems may distract us from what seem to be rather conventional questions that arise from evolutionary theory (such as 'What is the role of powerful elites in selecting policies?)

A further disadvantage is that the theory is not distinct enough from other accounts. John's (1998: 186) suggestion that ideas and interests play out within a structured environment seems like the ACF. Further, in John's (1998: 188–94) example of the UK poll tax, Kingdon's model explains why the policy was adopted, while a straightforward discussion of implementation may explain why it failed (see also McConnell, 2000, for a socio-economic explanation). In short, we may favour new theories only when we can demonstrate a useful degree of novelty (John, 2003: 495). Do we need more evolutionary theories merely to account for the role of serendipity and chance in the policy process?

John (1999: 47) argues that such problems can be overcome if we can identify the selection mechanism which causes some ideas to be successful while most fail. Evolutionary theory requires the identification of: competing memes; selection (and de-selection) processes; changes to policy memes by political actors seeking to adapt their aims to current circumstances; and, the 'random mutation of ideas and their fortuitous success in particular environments'. John (1999: 48–9; 2000) invites us to explain policy changes with evolutionary theory and then compare such accounts with other theories to see which one is the most convincing (compare with Kay, 2006: 54).

The policy transfer window

We can also produce synthetic accounts which focus on particular aspects of the policy process. For example, we can combine the insights of two literatures: the role of ideas and policy transfer. First, we can draw on approaches used to explain the promotion and adoption of ideas to demonstrate how and why transfer takes place. Then, the transfer literature can help us explore the extent to which the adoption of ideas is voluntary.

Metaphors to describe the profound effect of ideas are generally accompanied by discussions about how ideas are accepted within political communities. We may treat ideas as 'viruses' but also consider the role of the 'host' and the ability of policymakers, with established beliefs, to resist 'infection'. Our focus moves from the power of the ideas themselves to their successful promotion within the political system as part of a wider process of agenda setting. An idea's time may come, but it 'also passes' (Kingdon, 1995: 169). Much depends on the receptivity to ideas within government. Receptivity is influenced by the presence of existing ideas within a political system that, in many cases, undermine policy change. For example, policymakers establish a language describing the nature of policy problems that can be used to exclude participants with different views.

Major policy change may only occur when established ideas – as paradigms, belief systems, monopolies or institutions – are challenged. In some cases, major change follows an event. A significant policy failure may prompt a shift in power when existing policymakers are displaced or experts fall out of favour. 'Shocks' to the policy sub-system may prompt dominant advocacy coalitions to revisit their beliefs or allow the leaders of minority coalitions to exploit the opportunity to gain more favour within sub-systems. An established policy monopoly may break down completely when pressure participants, dissatisfied with current policy ideas in one venue, seek more sympathetic audiences elsewhere and attract attention from powerful actors more willing to consider radically new solutions to problems. In other cases, institutional change may be more gradual as ideas are challenged and reinterpreted, or when the ways in which elites understand policy problems evolves.

These theories suggest that major policy transfers are unusual. Transfer using radically new ideas from other regions may happen occasionally, but external ideas generally compete with many others for the attention of governments. Further, receptivity may be more important than the ideas themselves. There is much in the transfer literature to acknowledge these limitations: the emulation of radically new policies is rare; the search for new ideas may only follow policy failure; and foreign experience may often be used to legitimize existing practices (Chapter 12). The concept of policy transfer also adds to the literature on ideas. Its value is demonstrated by the policy transfer continuum which contains two ideal types. At one end, voluntary transfer involves decision makers widening their search for ideas on their own initiative; at the other, direct coercive transfer regards the influence exerted by an organization, region or supranational body to make another region adopt a policy. In between, we have indirect coercive transfer in which the importing country *perceives* the need to change or follow the lead of another region (Chapter 12). The focus on coercion challenges the assumption of voluntarism in theories that examine US policymaking. The US tends to innovate rather than emulate; it applies pressure on other countries but is less subject to pressure. If we shift our attention to countries more subject to external influence, direct or indirect coercion will be a key influence on the supply of and demand for new ideas.

The 'policy transfer window' represents one way to combine a focus on policy transfer and the adoption of ideas within political systems. It is based on Kingdon's (1984) identification of the role of problems (how is the policy problem defined?), policies (which ideas or solutions are available?) and politics (how receptive are policymakers to these ideas?) In Kingdon's model, while multiple streams come together to produce change, policymaker receptivity is the most important stream. In the policy transfer window, our attention shifts to the power of an external actor to oblige importing governments to consider particular solutions. The window of opportunity now depends on the ability of external actors to set the agenda, the applicability of their ideas, and a combination of (a) the level of domestic actor receptivity to those ideas and (b) their ability to resist transfer. The window may still open rarely and with unpredictable results, but the process is not influenced solely by domestic actors (for an application see Cairney *et al.*, 2012).

Combined literatures, but different meanings?

A combination of theories, or the insights from those theories, requires that we talk about the same thing. Yet, our search for a common language is often hindered by the use of the same term to mean different things in different theories. This issue is important because it is easy to identify common issues and terms in public policy theories but hard to determine the implications.

What is a policy entrepreneur?

For example, 'policy entrepreneur' is used by Kingdon (1984: 21; 104) to describe actors who use their knowledge of the process to further their own policy ends. They 'lie in wait in and around government with their solutions at hand, waiting for problems to float by to which they can attach their solutions, waiting for a development in the political stream they can use to their advantage' (Kingdon, 1984: 165–6). Entrepreneurs may be elected politicians, leaders of interest groups or merely unofficial spokespeople for particular causes. They are people with the knowledge, power, tenacity and luck to be able to exploit windows of opportunity and heightened levels of attention to policy problems to promote their 'pet solutions' to policymakers (see also Jones, 1994: 196 on their ability to reframe issues). John's (1999) treatment of entrepreneurs is similar, but he perhaps replaces the image of a surefooted calculating individual with someone that follows a trial and error strategy; entrepreneurs try out combinations of ideas, 'to find the one that replicates' (1999: 45).

In policy transfer, entrepreneurs can be consultants, NGOs or think tanks which promote best practice internationally. International entrepreneurs often have added credentials, either from the exporting country or from a supranational institution such as the World Bank that ties its cooperation to the use of a particular expert (Dolowitz and Marsh, 2000: 10). The classic case is the Harvard professor who travelled the world selling new public management, backed notionally by the US government (Common, 1998: 441). In this case the entrepreneur is perhaps guaranteed some level of success and is always on the road and looking for business rather than waiting for the right opportunity to act.

'Entrepreneur' is used in rational choice to explain why some individuals seek to provide public services or form political parties or interest groups when we assume that most free ride (McLean, 1987: 29). In business, entrepreneurs are innovative actors who provide a good or service that otherwise may not be provided; in return for their services they take a profit. The amount of profit depends partly on the level of competition by different entrepreneurs (1987: 28). In politics, it may be more difficult to sell goods, particularly when they are non-excludable (Chapter 7). Political entrepreneurs may profit through other means: when people make voluntary donations; when organizations pay politicians to try to secure contracts or other favours; and, through taxation. Again, the amount of profit depends in part on the level of competition: a high taxing, corrupt politician might be replaced by a cleaner and cheaper opponent (1987: 29). In other cases, politicians pursue measures simply because they believe that there will be an electoral payoff (Mclean, 2002: 541). In the case of organizations, there are people who value a good or service so much that they pay for it regardless of the ability of others to free ride. Or, there are entrepreneurs, driven partly by ideology, who provide a cheap solution to a problem shared by many in exchange for a donation to pursue further initiatives (McLean, 1987: 32). Mintrom and Vergari (1996: 431; see also Mintrom and Norman, 2009) use 'entrepreneur' in a similar way to Kingdon (someone selling ideas) and to rational choice (someone solving a collective action problem) to explain change within the ACF. For example, coalitions are born when entrepreneurs frame issues to encourage members with common beliefs to coalesce around an issue.

Overall, while 'entrepreneur' may be a key concept used to explain the timing and degree of policy innovations, we need to be clear about how we use the term. Who are the entrepreneurs? What is their role? What skills do they posses? Do entrepreneurs sell ideas or services? Do they benefit from policy outcomes that favour their beliefs, or material outcomes? Is an entrepreneur a domestic actor joining streams from within, or an external actor applying pressure (or both)?

Punctuated equilibrium

Punctuated equilibrium describes long periods of stability punctuated by rapid and profound change. The same term is used to identify the same basic process in two separate literatures without much recognition by one of the other (mostly because it was imported by both from natural science studies of evolution). It is increasingly challenged within institutionalism as an explanation for change; described as a catch-all metaphor to explain radical change without sufficient reference to agents or instability (Peters, 2005: 77–8; Sanders, 2006: 41). Yet, it is used in a more accepted way within the agenda-setting literature. It denotes instability, or the ever-present potential for change within particular policy areas, cloaked by an overall picture of public policy stability and continuity. Stability is associated with low levels of attention to a policy issue when policy communities maintain a policy monopoly (dominate the way that we understand and address a policy issue). Punctuations occur when other actors successfully challenge that monopoly, prompting previously excluded groups or uninvolved actors to pay attention, and often reconsider their attitude, to that issue.

The meaning of instability

The issue of instability provides further conceptual challenges. In many chapters we identify the appearance of stable behaviour in the context of the ever-present potential for change – but does each theory conceptualize instability in the same way? Rational choice identifies the problem of intransitive policy decisions and 'cycling' when one policy has a majority preference against it and is replaced by another, only for us to find a majority against the new policy. So what stops policymaking becoming completely unstable? For Riker (1980: 445), individual preferences represent one of three factors that determine social choice. We must also consider: (a) institutions – how they provide incentives to vote and encourage relationships between voters and parties (Dewan *et al.*, 2009: xxvi); and (b) agenda-setting – the 'political skill and artistry of those who manipulate agenda … to exploit the disequilibrium of tastes for their own advantage' (Riker, 1980: 445). Both may be used to minimize majority preference issues. For example, individuals vote once every four years and leave most decisions to politicians, and/or power is exerted to ensure that social choices are made in a particular order and a limited number of issues are considered (Majone, 2006).

Similar discussions appear in punctuated equilibrium theory, while constructivist institutionalism (Chapter 4) has similar intentions when it treats institutions as paradigmatic sets of ideas that can be challenged and replaced. In each case, we identify the appearance of stable behaviour but in the context of the ever-present potential for change. Or, we examine the difference between the constant *potential* for disequilibrium and the small extent to which non-incremental change actually *occurs* (Green and Shapiro, 1994: 114). But are we really talking about the same thing, beyond the rather bland statement that anything can happen but only some things do? The short and unsatisfactory answer is that it is difficult for us to tell.

Combining theories: commonalities and contradictions

In summary, we can say that, while synthesis may be possible, it is also problematic. In this section we consider if a combination of theories also masks serious contradictions:

- Theories may contain different assumptions regarding key conceptual issues – for example, are people driven primarily by their beliefs or self interest; are they comprehensively or boundedly rational?
- They may place weight on some causal factors at the expense of others – such as structures over agents or vice versa.
- They may use different methods, perhaps based on different ideas about our knowledge of the world and how we can gather it.

An uncritical combination of theories may mask these contradictions. On the other hand, the commonalities of theories are often masked by debates, based on a limited understanding of theories, which often produce more heat than light when they assume that these contradictions exist. We should therefore consider more closely if theories are contradictory or complementary: does acceptance of one necessitate rejection of another? In this section we consider three types of issue related to the use of particular methods, the role of science and the 'commensurability' of particular theories.

Rational choice: appearances can be deceptive

Rational choice theory raises a fundamental question about what assumptions we should make and what scientific approach we should take. 'First principles' rational choice is based on deduction, not induction. We make a small number of simple assumptions and produce a model that explores their logical implications. For example, game theory examines the choices that actors make when situated within their decision-making environment and faced with a particular set of incentives and the need to anticipate the choice of other actors. This approach prompts criticism because the assumptions are unrealistic – people do not have the ability to behave in the manner we assume. More importantly, it prompts different views about what to do next. For critics, the better approach is to consider bounded rationality – making more realistic assumptions and using them to guide empirical research. For proponents, we explore the extent to which our models raise interesting conclusions that are worthy of further study. This is what makes RCT valuable to studies of public policy: it raises fundamental questions about collective action problems, how policymakers create institutions to address them, and what the consequences are when we face collective action problems within institutions. Or, we explore the extent to which RCT explains political behaviour. The aim of substantive rational choice is to establish what proportion of political outcomes one can explain with simple models exploring the choices of individuals under particular conditions.

RCT prompts us to consider public policy in new ways, but the links between RCT and other theories are difficult to identify because it attracts so much critical attention that misrepresents the issues. Take, as a first example, the adoption of methodological individualism – which appears to set RCT apart from explanations based on structural factors (Chapter 6). Many accounts suggest that RCT privileges 'the role of actors over and beyond that of social structures' (Griggs, 2007: 175; compare with Hindmoor, 2006a: 1; Marsh *et al.*, 2000: 481; MacDonald, 2003: 558). Yet, the explanatory power of rational choice theory comes as much from structures as individual agents (Dowding and King, 1995: 1; Hindess, 1988: 26–8, 38, 95; Hampsher-Monk and Hindmoor, 2010: 52; Ward, 2002: 75–7; Tsebelis, 1990: 40; Hay, 2004a: 51; 2002: 110; see Marsh and Smith, 2000: 5–6; 10–11; Dowding, 1995b; 2001 for an application of this debate to policy networks analysis).

The rationality assumption may be used to explore the outcomes to which structures and institutions contribute. The aim is to demonstrate: (a) that if individuals act rationally in this situation then this is how they will behave (or what their best choice will be); and (b) those same individuals acting rationally will behave differently in a different situation. For example, consider the behaviour of the same individuals in the prisoner's dilemma, chicken and assurance games (although tread carefully here – part of the 'structure' of the game regards whether or not the players are cooperative). It shifts our attention from the assumptions we make about individual behaviour to the effect that the decision-making environment has on incentives and therefore action (Hay, 2004a: 52–4; Hindess, 1988: 39–43). Or, structural factors can be incorporated into rational choice models – for example, a strong and demonstrable attachment to a social group or the drive to follow institutional or normative rules can be included in the preferences of individuals (Ward, 2002: 78). In this sense, 'methodological individualism' may seem like false advertising because it can prompt studies to focus on the significance of *interactions between individuals* in *structured conditions* that affect their behaviour. There are three main causes of confusion regarding structure and agency in this context. The first regards the assumptions we make about the homogeneity of individuals. If, as in the prisoner's dilemma, all individuals would make the same choice (there is only one best choice) then it is the structure of the game that provides the explanation. If, in more detailed accounts, individuals have different beliefs and desires then the explanation comes from how they make choices *and* how those choices might change in different environments. The second regards our definition of methodological individualism. Consider the difference between the insistence that 'explanations of social phenomena must be given in terms' that are *reduced* or *reducible* 'to propositions which contain reference to individuals alone and not social wholes' (Dowding, 1991: 10). The former may suggest an inability to treat groups and organizations as rational in the same way as individuals since they do not have beliefs and therefore cannot satisfy their preferences (if indeed a group can generate a group preference) according to their beliefs. Yet, microeconomics is rife with discussions of the actions of groups such as firms (Parsons, 2005: 68). This may suggest that organizations such as groups can act if we impute the same preferences to all members of the group. Or, we refer to organizational action as a shorthand and understand that this concept can be unpacked (Dowding and King, 1995: 1; compare with Allison, 1971 on state rationality and Hindess, 1988: 5, 46 on social actors).

Take, as a second example, the notion that RCT is incomplete because it assumes that people's preferences are fixed when we know, instead, that they depend on people's beliefs and understanding of the world: 'what actors believe may be just as important as what they want' (Campbell, 2002: 22; see also Jacobsen, 1995: 284). Their beliefs inform their preferences and how they think they should pursue them. Yet, the assumption of preferences in some models does not preclude our ability to explore their origins in others. For example, Hay (2004a: 58) suggests that the power of ideas can be incorporated if RCT draws on constructivism or interpretivism to explain 'individuals' motivations, values and expectations' (although Hampsher-Monk and Hindmoor, 2010 suggest that not much of it does). Further, the broader role of ideas *is* a feature of rational choice analysis – such as when Riker highlights the use of ideas to manipulate agendas, or when we suggest that 'rationally ignorant' individuals use ideology or cues from 'opinion leaders' with similar beliefs as a shortcut to information gathering (Ward, 2002: 77, 85; compare with Hindess, 1988: 22).

Further, rational choice analysis can inform how the role of ideas works. For example, the explanatory force of norms derives in large part from the extent to which people are punished when they do not follow them (for example, the mafia may punish those who do not follow the norm of *omertà* in the prisoner's dilemma). Such activity entails 'an enforcement cost without any direct return to the individual' (Axelrod, 1986: 1100). It introduces the importance of 'metanorms', or the punishment for those who do not punish people who defect from a norm. In both norms and metanorms there is still a cost that a self-interested individual would not incur without some other explanatory factor (such as high levels of 'vengefulness' – 1986: 1109). Norms are more likely to be followed when the matter is not contentious (e.g. which side of the road to drive on), it is not costly to do so (e.g. the norm of voting), when the costs of enforcement are low (e.g. looks of disapproval) (Ward, 2002: 76) and when individuals are unable to pursue their self-interest under the 'cover' of more acceptable behaviour (Hindmoor, 2006b: 95).

Take, as a final example, criticisms of rational choice based on confusion between preferences/interests within discussions of institutionalism. For example, normative institutionalism focuses on behaviour that goes against the *interests* of the individual because it is the role they are expected to perform (Peters, 2005: 30 gives the examples of soldiers and firefighters), while historical may focus on how class positions inform class interests (Thelen and Steinmo, 1992: 8). Yet, neither contradict rational choice; if institutional and class identities are central to behaviour then they, rather than narrowly defined self-interest, will be reflected in their preferences (see Dowding, 1994: 107; Immergut, 1998: 25).

Such artificial debates generally reflect a tendency within the literature to caricature each approach; in the absence of this process we can reach different conclusions. For instance, rational choice does not suggest that individuals are calculating automatons whose actions are effectively determined by their structural positions. Rather, 'first principles' rational choice explores what such a model of behaviour would look like and how the insights gained from that model could be used to inform research into the real world. It is not the same as institutional rational choice which often makes more realistic assumptions about the role of individuals and, therefore, the extent to which they are influenced by structures (Dowding, 1994: 107–8; 110; see Ostrom, 2007: 30–1, 37, for an example of models based on the 'fallible learner', bounded rationality and unpredictable rule following). Similarly, sociological institutionalism need not assume that individuals merely reproduce the rules they follow. Indeed, Hall and Taylor (1996: 956) acknowledge that the 'calculus' and 'cultural' approaches are not necessarily polar opposites since proponents of each could acknowledge that 'a good deal of behaviour is goal-oriented or strategic but that the range of options canvassed by a strategic actor is likely to be circumscribed by a culturally-specific sense of appropriate action'.

This suggests that there is not a stark ontological division between each approach. Rather, each approach often asks different questions and focuses on different aspects of political behaviour – but these questions can be complementary rather than contradictory (Dowding, 1994: 105) and 'problem-oriented scholars mix approaches all the time' (Schmidt 2006: 177). The same can be said for mixed methods. Sanders (2006: 42) notes that historical research is based on thick description and 'inductive reasoning' while rational choice employs abstract, deductive analysis. Lowndes (2010: 74) also lists mathematical modelling, game theory, laboratory studies, ethnography and case studies as the methods on offer for different studies. If we remove the ontological divide between each approach we can also remove any limitation on which approach we are obliged to follow in each tradition (Della Porta and Keating, 2008a; 2008b).

The shootout

A 'policy shootout' (Eller and Krutz, 2009: 1) may help us decide which approach is most appropriate. It is based on the idea that we can use scientific principles to decide which theories are most worthy of our attention:

1. A theory's methods should be explained so that they can be replicated by others.
2. Its concepts should be clearly defined, logically consistent and give rise to empirically falsifiable hypotheses.
3. Its propositions should be as general as possible.
4. It should set out clearly what the causal processes are.
5. It should be subject to empirical testing and revision. (2009: 1; Sabatier 2007a: 5; 2007b: 326–31)

There are at least two factors that make this process more complicated. First, the extent to which theories adhere to these principles is debatable. For example, Sabatier (2007b: 327) lauds the Institutional Analysis and Development Framework (IAD) and ACF frameworks because they meet these principles and have been subject to extensive testing by their primary authors and other researchers (Sabatier rejects policy cycles and multiple streams analysis on this basis). Yet, rational choice may not always live up to his principles. For example, first principles rational choice often produces paradoxes rather than hypotheses. In cases such as the collective action problem and the paradox of non-voting, we are invited to consider why people do *not* behave in the way we would expect. Rational choice is also, like all theories, ambiguous about causal processes: are outcomes caused by intentional behaviour or the structure of the decision-making environment? Perhaps most importantly, Green and Shapiro (1994: 179) argue that the 'empirical contributions of rational choice theory' are 'few' and 'far between' – a charge that has become rather popular within political science (Hindmoor, 2006a). The same problem holds for the ACF: most ACF-inspired case studies 'do not explicitly test any of the hypotheses' (Weible *et al.*, 2009: 128). Yet, both approaches still survive (see the special issue on the IAD in *Policy Studies Journal*, 39, 1, 2011).

Second, the principles give a misleading impression of social scientific research or present an artificial standard. Researchers may explain their methods and, in some cases such as documentary analysis, build ways to verify the validity and reliability of codes into the research design. Yet, in most studies, the results are accepted on trust; they are not replicated directly. For example, a theory's main method may be the (well respected) elite interview, but it would be absurd to expect one researcher's interview data to be replicated by another (especially when interviews are anonymized). Further, very little policy research involves making a prediction in the form of a prophesy that is then checked in the same way as one's horoscope. Rather, we tend to examine the evidence and assess the extent to which it is consistent with the logic of a theory after the fact (I am paraphrasing Dowding here). It would be disingenuous to suggest otherwise.

Finally, the idea of subjecting 'empirically falsifiable' hypotheses to testing is misleading. Policy change is open to interpretation and we can produce competing, and equally convincing, empirical narratives. Narratives of policy change are as open to debate as theories; if we can't resolve what the evidence is, then we may struggle to choose decisively between theories. Indeed, the most valuable theory in each case may depend on the narrative of policy change that we select rather than just the nature of the theory. We can highlight instances in which theories provide competing assumptions or predictions, but be less certain about how to choose between them (see also Box 13.2).

Overall, there is not a universal understanding of science and how we should decide between scientific accounts. These principles do not provide a convincing way to choose one theory and reject others. There is little evidence to suggest that the most prominent theories are selected on this basis (indeed, Meier, 2009 suggests, provocatively, that the popularity of theories depends on the academic abilities and standing of their proponents). Similarly, there has been no resolution to the 'methodological wars' prompted by rational choice. Instead, we have a form of methodological pluralism in which different studies take different approaches. While there are practical limits to the variety of acceptable methods (based on professional views expressed through the peer review process of journal publication and grant distribution), there is enough tolerance of variety and enough defences of methodological pluralism (Della Porta and Keating, 2008a; 2008b) to ensure that we do not have to select 'one best way'.

Box 13.2 'Incommensurability'

A further complication to our comparison of theories, and the selection of one at the expense of another, is that theories may be 'incommensurable' (for a concise summary, see Hindess, 1988: 73–5). The same words might be used in each theory, but they may mean something else according to the paradigm from which they were derived. Researchers may look at the same object but view and interpret it differently. They may 'not share a common set of perceptions which would allow scientists to choose between one paradigm and the other … there will be disputes between them that cannot all be settled by an appeal to the facts' (1988: 74). Of course, this argument is problematic because it points to the inevitability of 'relativism' in which all theories are of equal value because we cannot demonstrate that some statements are more accurate than others (1988: 75). This would be a disingenuous position for me to take when I have decided that only a small number of theories deserve consideration within this book (and, in empirical work, I trust some measures and sources more than others). A useful compromise is that we present narratives of policy change, based on analysis of particular policy instruments and types, but be open to competing narratives based on other measures. We appeal to the 'facts' but recognize that the evidence may be sought using other measures and subject to different interpretations. Some theories may be most useful in certain circumstances, but this is conditional on the acceptance of a particular narrative (which in turn may be guided by an agenda set by a particular theory). This process may be more of an art, and less of a science, than many of us are willing to admit.

Are some theories better matched than others? Is it easy to tell?

Many theories, when compared, appear to contain complementary *and* contradictory elements (see Sabatier, 2007b: 330, on the IAD and ACF). This may be caused more by the difficulties we face when trying to translate their language than a fundamental disagreement about how political systems work. For example, in the field of group-government relations we can combine the insights from multi-level governance, punctuated equilibrium and the advocacy coalition framework. Indeed, the use of PE and ACF may provide much needed insights on the causal processes involved in MLG (given the tendency of much of the MLG literature to be vague on what causes policy change). Each account shares a common understanding of the research problem: the importance of group-government relations and the need to capture a shift from 'iron triangles' to a more open, complex and competitive policymaking environment containing multiple venues and levels of government. Yet, there are also two conceptual barriers to synthesis.

First, the ACF suggests that a political system's 'basic constitutional structure' provides a source of stability within sub-systems, while MLG and PE stress the fluid nature of constitutional arrangements. The constitutional structure may always appear to be in flux because jurisdictional boundaries are constantly shifting and many actors enter and leave the policymaking process in an unpredictable way. MLG identifies blurry boundaries between state/non-state action and the formal/informal powers enjoyed by governing institutions at various levels. PE highlights a tendency for overlaps of governing responsibility both horizontally (executive, legislature, and judicial) and vertically (between institutions or between federal, state and local government). There is often no natural jurisdiction for policy problems and it is common for decision-making responsibility to shift over time and for an issue to become the jurisdiction of more than one institution at the same time. Yet, the differences may be exaggerated because the ACF also contains similar elements. Sub-systems include a range of actors at all levels of government to account for this tendency for policy to be considered by different levels, and the ACF shares with PE a focus on venue shopping. Further, 'constitutional structure' may refer merely to the basic make-up of a political system (such as a federal versus unitary state), to aid comparisons between political systems and our analysis of the effects of formal rules on behaviour. Therefore, the differences may be caused by conceptual confusion, not contradiction.

Second, the role of beliefs makes things more difficult. The ACF suggests that a sub-system's structure of belief systems acts as a source of stability. People act on their beliefs rather than self-interest; they are driven by the desire to articulate beliefs and pursue them within coalitions of like-minded people. Further, beliefs can be ranked and are relatively fixed. With PE, actors have a variety of multiple, often conflicting, interests that are difficult to rank. Much depends on problem definition: while their beliefs may not change, their attention may lurch, causing them to act in a different way when they pay attention to a different aspect of the same problem. The emphasis in the ACF is that beliefs influence action because they inform how people view policy problems. With PE, we focus on the ability of events, persuasion and shifting agendas to influence how people process information, weigh up their interests and act accordingly. The driving force of explanation is the level of attention to one issue at the expense of another. When one belief receives disproportionate attention, most others are ignored and not acted upon. Yet, in the next time period a different belief may receive disproportionate attention and become subject to an intense period of activity. Again, these differences may be exaggerated because an individual can shift her attention without ignoring her basic beliefs. Or, her beliefs may limit the extent to which her attention will shift. However, the focus of explanation seems to be different, which makes the theories difficult to reconcile. Put simply, the explanatory focus of ACF is the belief system as a filter for information and driver for action; for PE it is the decision-making context and the shift in levels of attention to explain action. This divide seems to makes it difficult to combine their insights in a straight-forward way.

Multiple theories, multiple perspectives

There is no single theory applicable to public policy as a whole. The world is too complex to allow for parsimonious and universal explana-tions. Our choice is to produce a single theory that is so complicated it defeats the purpose of parsimonious explanation, or simpler theories that explain parts of the story in different ways. In this section we consider how to combine the insights of theories without seeking synthesis or a policy shootout. We assume that the only sense of competition between theories is for our attention. Students of public policy face the same problems as boundedly rational decision makers: an infinite wealth of potentially relevant information to choose from, but finite resources with which to choose. As a result they are forced to focus their attention on one particular aspect of research and a small number of possible explana-tions. It is often in this sense that theories of public policy are presented as competing accounts; more attention to one means less attention to the other. Yet, they need not be treated as competitors in a wider sense. The alternative is to portray them as a collection of lenses through which to view public policy. A multiple lenses approach does not ask you to choose from conflicting accounts of the policy process, but to explore a range of aspects of the same policy issue, asking for example: was there policy transfer? What is the role of institutions? Which venues or levels of government were most active? This allows the researcher to develop a 'checklist' of questions and ways to address the same issue.

We can approach this task in two complementary ways. The first is to consider these issues at a theoretical level, exploring a range of insights based on the same conceptual starting point (for example, bounded rationality), or examining the same insight from multiple literatures (for example, the insulation of institutions). The second is to consider how to combine multiple theories in empirical studies.

What is the implication of bounded rationality?

Comprehensive rationality represents an 'ideal' description of the power of a central decision maker to articulate a series of consistent policy aims and make sure they are carried out. The point is that the assumptions necessary to demonstrate this power are unrealistic. Therefore, many theories describe what happens when they are relaxed: the search for knowledge is limited by capacity and ideology; problem definition is determined by facts and values; policy makers have multiple objectives which are difficult to rank; and, the policy process is difficult to separate into stages. Most adopt Simon's (1976) term 'bounded rationality' (Schlager, 2007: 299–302).

Much of the modern literature extends Lindblom's focus on incremental change. Lindblom (1959; 1979) combines a discussion of the limits to comprehensive rationality with the argument that policymakers rarely pursue non-incremental change, because: (a) they need to build on past policies; and (b) considerable effort has been invested in seeking an agreed position among a wide range of interests. Lindblom's analysis was based on the assumption of a pluralist US, but policy communities analysis suggests that incrementalism is pervasive in most political systems, including the 'majoritarian' UK. Regular changes of government do not necessarily cause wholesale shifts in policy. In part, this is because most decisions are effectively beyond the reach of policymakers. The size of government necessitates breaking policy down into a large number of more manageable issues; policymakers can only pay attention to a small number. The pervasiveness of 'inheritance before choice' and 'policy succession' extends the discussion of incrementalism to inertia. The effect of decades of cumulative policies is that newly elected policymakers inherit a huge government with massive commitments. Policymaking may be more about dealing with the legacies of past decisions than policy innovation.

Yet, many theories use the same starting point, bounded rationality, to predict the greater likelihood of non-incremental change. Punctuated equilibrium suggests that bounded rationality produces incremental and radical change. Policymakers must ignore most issues and promote a few to the top of their agenda. Major policy change occurs when they (and often other actors in different venues) shift their attention to an issue that was previously insulated by a policy monopoly and received minimal involvement from other actors. Multiple streams analysis combines an overall assumption of policy continuity with the identification of non-incremental change when three streams (problems, policies, politics) come together during a window of opportunity. Theories of policy diffusion demonstrate that one rule of thumb of boundedly rational decision makers is policy transfer. In some cases, states emulate others, on the assumption that the innovating state was successful. Overall, the benefit of a multiple theories approach in this context is that a wide range of approaches can produce different conclusions from a common position or the same basic understanding of public policy.

The insulation of institutions

Or, we can identify the same basic understanding of public policy by a wide range of approaches with different theoretical starting points. For example, the institutionalist literature highlights the ability of organizations to live on after their aims have been met or they no longer serve a useful purpose. Organizations may be able to maintain their standard operating procedures in the face of changing environments and the decisions of higher level policymakers (Peters, 2005: 110; Hall and Taylor, 1996: 947; DiMaggio and Powell, 1983; March and Olsen, 1996: 256). This argument is pervasive in the literature, with many studies suggesting that participants follow rules designed to protect organizational routines or interests rather than solve the problem at hand. Lipsky (1980) argues that street-level bureaucrats establish routines and use rules of thumb to satisfy a proportion of central government objectives while preserving a sense of professional autonomy necessary to maintain morale. Instructions from the top are to some extent replaced, as the source of explanation for policy change, by standard operating procedures, cultures and practices at the bottom. Baumgartner and Jones (1993) argue that organizations are often set up to solve problems that receive heightened public attention, but that they endure long after that attention has faded. This is particularly the case when an organization creates a policy monopoly, based on a public perception that the problem has been solved and that the issues are technical, that helps minimize external attention and insulate a small number of participants within a policy community.

From theories to research: where do we go from here?

Few researchers are in the position to explore each theory exhaustively when they engage in empirical research. Indeed, few are able to explore more than one. For example, imagine the resources required to replicate Baumgartner and Jones' (2009) study of policy agendas (including tracking the long term direction of problem definition in media reports and governmental and congressional inquiries and debates) *and* to adopt the methods set out by Jenkins-Smith and Sabatier (1993c, including documentary analysis and questionnaires probing the beliefs of participants). Such problems are magnified when we adopt a wider range of theories, producing the need to make rather pragmatic decisions about research designs. Most of us will be wondering what it means, in practice, to combine multiple theories in empirical studies when resources are limited.

One option, captured by the term 'meta-analysis' (the analysis of analysis), is to develop a model to draw systematic lessons from the literature. For example, Exadaktylos and Radaelli (2009) analyse a sample of the literature on 'Europeanization'. The advantage of meta-analysis is that it furthers the accumulation of knowledge derived from a range of sources with different perspectives. We can identify a small number of causal processes and extract from each study a finding that can be compared with findings from other studies. In some cases, it involves identifying a key argument and exploring the extent to which the literature supports it. Examples include: 'Participation of non-state actors leads to more ecologically rational decisions than in top-down modes of governance' (Newig and Fritsch, 2009: 200); and, 'sources of potential environmental risk may be concentrated among racial and ethnic minorities and the poor' (Ringquist, 2005: 223). It may also address issues that have arisen throughout this book, such as: the qualitative/quantitative distinction in which we consider if we want to identify all causes in a particular case study, or explore the effects of one cause in all cases; and, how we conceptualize factors such as time (simply as a number of years or as a way to describe cause and effect?) (Newig and Fritsch, 2009: 512–14; see also Kay, 2006: 3). Meta-analysis may guide us when we seek to combine the insights of studies that were not really designed to be compared.

A second option involves combining the merits of multiple theories to identify key factors and produce questions to be answered by new empirical research. In this instance we break theories down into their component parts to focus on John's (2003: 488) 'institutions, networks, socioeconomic process, choices, and ideas'. We identify not only the role of individual policymakers (making choices), but also the wider importance of institutions such as bureaucracies and political parties, and the role of interest groups and other pressure participants within networks or sub-systems. We highlight the importance of socio-economic influences or structural factors on these actors, and discuss the role of ideas to demonstrate that policymaking relates to much more than the exercise of power. Our aim is to generate questions relating to these causal processes, gather the evidence and use multiple theories to interpret the evidence.

This approach is exemplified by Cairney, Studlar and Mamudu's study of global tobacco policy (2012; Cairney, 2007a). First, they identify fourteen policy instruments, including the use of legislation to ban tobacco advertising and smoking in public places, economic penalties such as tobacco taxation, public education and smoking cessation services. Second, they analyse these instruments to produce narratives of policy change with three main elements: was change sudden or incremental; was it voluntary or enforced; and which countries are leaders and which are laggards? Narratives provide competing accounts of policy change based on the explanatory weight we attach to different policy instruments, the timeframe we adopt, the institutional focus of analysis, the level of change we expect to occur and the actors that we identify as most powerful. Third, they use the focus on institutions, choices, networks, socio-economic processes and ideas to produce a range of research questions relevant to each region-based chapter: who has responsibility for tobacco policy? How important is tobacco control as a policy issue and how high is it on the policy agenda? Has there been a shift in power between pressure participants? What is the role of 'external' factors and have they contributed to shifts in power and agenda-status? What is the role of ideas and to what extent is policy driven by transfer?

The answer to some questions is similar in many regions. For example, in most we find a shift in policy responsibility from finance and trade departments to health departments. In others, the answers differ. For example, the departmental shift generally accelerated the replacement of the dominant pro-tobacco coalition by the anti-smoking coalition within 'developed' countries, but tobacco companies were able to maintain strong governmental links in many 'developing' countries. In turn, the process of policy transfer differs. Within the leading tobacco control countries there is a strong professional network for the exchange of ideas; the main link between developed and developing countries is the Framework Convention for Tobacco Control – a tool developed by leading countries to combat the influence of tobacco companies in developing regions. There are also similarities and differences within developed countries. For example, while there is a general trend towards reduced smoking prevalence, a reduction in the economic power of tobacco companies (paying fewer taxes and relied upon less by governments) and increased public support for tobacco control, the levels vary from country to country and produce different levels of pressure. Similarly, while tobacco control is based on the same basic idea (the scientific evidence linking smoking to ill health), there is marked variation in receptivity to that idea and therefore the speed with which political systems have adopted control measures.

Our final aim is to use multiple theories to interpret the results of such studies. The advantage of comparative analysis is that it shows the comparative advantage of different theories in different cases. For example, punctuated equilibrium theory may explain changing agendas within developed countries, as the promotion of the scientific evidence helps reframe the issue of tobacco (from a product that generates government revenue to a health epidemic that must be addressed) and prompts new audiences to become interested in tobacco control. However, such analysis may not be as applicable in developing countries which often display a lack of media interest, low levels of public attention to the effects of smoking and, in countries such as China, a direct government interest in tobacco production that minimizes receptivity to the idea of tobacco control. Instead, a focus on policy transfer may better explain the recent trajectory of policy in developing countries, with the agenda set not by domestic public health interests, but international policy networks prompting developed country leaders to influence their developing country counterparts. This approach suggests that, in practice, the complementary/contradictory issue is not an intractable problem. Few, if any studies, reject one theory out of hand following extensive case study research. Rather, they explain why one is relatively valuable in particular circumstances.

Conclusion

From our review of the literature, we can build a clear picture of the modern policy process, the key issues in public policy and the main ways to study them. We live in a 'post-Machiavellian' era in which politics is not centralized to the extent that it excludes most actors. There is no single, authoritative decision maker. The policy process is marked by a diffusion of power from the centre towards other levels of government and, in many cases, quasi and non-governmental actors. The lines are blurry between power exercised by executives, based on their formal roles and responsibilities, and influence pursued by other actors, based on their resources and experience of the process. Access to policymakers is not controlled by a small elite. The group–government world is not small, 'clubby' and insulated. Rather, there are multiple channels of access to policymaking, and policy participants have access to a range of policymaking venues. At the same time, the policy world is clearly specialized. The logic of government is to divide the policy process into a large number of smaller units and to devolve policymaking responsibility from the 'top' towards sub-systems (and, in many cases, local or policy-specific arrangements at the 'bottom'). Consequently, the logical step for pressure participants is to specialize in a small number of policy areas and to participate within a small number of sub-systems or policy networks. Policymakers devolve responsibility to officials who, in turn, seek information and advice from pressure participants. The currency of government may be power, in which people marshal their resources to represent groups and influence policy delivery, but it is also information and expertise which can be used to build reputations and trust.

The modern policy process therefore contains sources of stability and instability; of policy continuity and change. Stable arrangements are a common feature of sub-systems. The same small group of participants may be involved for long periods, at the expense of other actors, because they have the ability to exclude those actors. They have resources, based on their socio-economic position: for example, businesses are central to the functioning of efficient, productive economies and the ability of governments to raise tax revenue, while doctors take centre stage in the treatment of illness. They also have resources based on their knowledge and expertise, which allows them to develop reputations valued within government and society. Such resources allow them to pursue privileged access to policymakers and positions within sub-systems. They may also have the power to protect their positions by helping create policy monopolies: defining issues in particular ways to ensure that only certain groups are interested or deemed to have the necessary expertise, and presenting an image in which the policy problem has been solved in principle, with only the implementation to be discussed. Or, coalitions exercise power to further their beliefs and ensure that they have the dominant position within sub-systems necessary to translate beliefs into policy action. These arrangements are often institutionalized: the frequent contact between officials and certain groups becomes routine, while the dominant ways to consider and address policy problems become taken for granted and rarely questioned. Further, policymakers are often unable or unwilling to challenge these arrangements. Paying attention to one issue means ignoring most others, while policy innovation (and termination) often requires more political will than succession.

Yet, there are also many sources of instability. Policy participants, dissatisfied with existing policy and institutional arrangements, can seek influence by identifying more sympathetic audiences in other venues; by lobbying policymakers who may be more willing to consider policy problems in a different way and take action. Policy action taken in other jurisdictions can change overall policy (in systems where policymaking responsibilities overlap and multiple venues are involved) or act as a source of pressure for change. External shocks – such as major economic or environmental events, significant policy failures or changes of government – can prompt dominant advocacy coalitions to reconsider their beliefs or minority coalitions to exploit their position and increase their influence. Institutional barriers may be strong, but they can also be overcome, as new ideas are used to reframe policy problems and events prompt policymakers to reconsider their assumptions, process information in a different way and seek alternative sources of information and advice. Finally, and perhaps most importantly, individuals make a difference. Some policymakers simply do not accept the existing arrangements and seek to challenge institutions and change policy.

In short, policy processes are complex and often unpredictable. We can use theories and concepts to guide study and explanation, but must also recognize their limitations. The identification of the conditions required for comprehensively rational decision making serves primarily to show what actually happens when those conditions are not met. The division of policymaking into stages helps us analyse the process, not show us that it works in this way. The identification of individuals making choices, institutional constraints and socio-economic pressures shows us that models focusing on only one of these aspects will not tell us the whole story. Theories based on the exercise of power are incomplete without theories that explain how ideas are promoted and accepted within government. We can combine the insights of these theories and account for most outcomes with reference to our five pillars of explanation: institutions, networks, ideas, socio-economic factors and choices. However, we must also allow for an element of serendipity, as unpredictable events change how policy participants see the world and behave within it, and windows of opportunity open to allow policy change when, under other circumstances, it would not. These constraints to our knowledge and understanding of the world are shared by all of the sciences and should not be taken to suggest that public policy analysis is uniquely problematic. Rather, the public policy literature contains a rich and fascinating source of information on what happens and a variety of theories that help us explain how and why it happened.

References

Abbott, P., Wallace, C. and Tyler, M. (2005) *Introduction to Sociology: Feminist Perspectives* (London: Routledge).

Adcock, R., Bevir, M. and Stimson, S. (2006) 'Historicizing the New Institutionalisms' in R. Adcock, M. Bevir and S. Stimson (eds) *Modern Political Science: Anglo-American Exchanges since 1880* (Princeton, NJ: Princeton University Press).

Adler, E. and Haas, P. (1992) 'Conclusion: Epistemic Communities, World Order, and the Creation of a Reflective Research Program', *International Organization*, 46, 1: 367–90.

Allison, G. (1969) 'Conceptual Models and the Cuban Missile Crisis', *American Political Science Review*, 63, 3: 689–718.

Allison, G. (1971) *Essence of Decision: Explaining the Cuban Missile Crisis* (Boston, MA: Little Brown).

Alter, K. and Meunier, S. (2009) 'The Politics of International Regime Complexity', *Perspectives on Politics*, 7, 1: 13–24.

Althaus, C., Bridgman, P. and Davis, G. (2007) *The Australian Policy Handbook* 4th edn (Sydney: Allen & Unwin).

Anderson, J.A. (1975) *Public Policy Making* (London: Thomas Nelson & Sons).

Andrews, R. and Martin, S. (2007) 'Has Devolution Improved Public Services?' *Public Money and Management*, 27, 2: 149–56.

Arendt, H. (1986) 'Communicative Power' in Lukes, S. (ed.) *Power* (New York, NY: New York University Press).

Armstrong, A. (1998) 'A Comparative Analysis: New Public Management – The Way Ahead?', *Australian Journal of Public Administration*, 57, 2: 12–24.

Arrow, K. (1963) *Social Choice and Individual Values* 2nd edn (New York, NY: John Wiley & Sons) http://cowles.econ.yale.edu/P/cm/m12-2/index.htm.

Asare, B., Cairney, P. and Studlar, D. (2009) 'Federalism and Multilevel Governance in Tobacco Control Policy: The European Union, United Kingdom, and Devolved Institutions', *Journal of Public Policy*, 29, 1: 79–102 .

Atkinson, M. and Coleman, W. (1989) 'Strong States and Weak States: Sectoral Policy Networks in Advanced Capitalist Economies', *British Journal of Political Science*, 19, 1: 47–67.

Avery, G. (2004) 'Bioterrorism, Fear, and Public Health Reform: Matching a Policy Solution to the Wrong Window', *Public Administration Review*, 64, 3: 275–88.

Axelrod, R. (1984) *The Evolution of Cooperation* (New York, NY: Basic Books).

Axelrod, R. (1986) 'An Evolutionary Approach to Norms', *American Political Science Review*, 80, 4: 1095–111.

Bache, I. (1999) 'The Extended Gatekeeper: Central Government and the Implementation of EC Regional Policy in the UK', *Journal of European Public Policy*, 6, 1: 28–45.

Bache, I. and Flinders, M. (2004a) 'Multi-Level Governance and the Study of the British State', *Public Policy and Administration*, 19, 1: 31–51.

Bache, I. and Flinders, M. (2004b) 'Themes and Issues in Multi-level Governance' in I. Bache and M. Flinders (eds) *Multi-Level Governance* (Oxford: Oxford University Press).

Bachrach, P. and Baratz, M. (1962) 'Two Faces of Power', *American Political Science Review*, 56, 4: 947–52.

Bachrach, P. and Baratz, M. (1963) 'Decisions and Nondecisions: An Analytical Framework', *The American Political Science Review*, 57, 3: 632–42.

Bachrach, P. and Baratz, M. (1970) *Power and Poverty* (New York, NY: Oxford University Press).

Bale, T. (2008) *European Politics*, 2nd edn (Basingstoke: Palgrave Macmillan).

Bardach, E. (2006) 'Policy Dynamics' in M. Moran, M. Rein and R. Goodin (eds) *The Oxford Handbook of Public Policy* (Oxford: Oxford University Press).

Bardach, E. (2009) *A Practical Guide for Policy Analysis: The Eightfold Path to More Effective Problem Solving* (Washington, DC: CQ Press).

Barrett, S. (2004) 'Implementation Studies: Time for a Revival?' *Public Administration*, 82, 2: 249–62.

Barrett, S. and Fudge, C. (eds) (1981) *Policy and Action* (London: Methuen).

Barry, B. (1980a) 'Is it Better to be Powerful or Lucky: Part 1', *Political Studies*, XXVIII, 2: 183–94.

Barry, B. (1980b) 'Is it Better to be Powerful or Lucky: Part 2', *Political Studies*, XXVIII, 3: 338–52.

Barry, B. (2002) 'Capitalists Rule Ok? Some Puzzles About Power', *Politics Philosophy Economics*, 1: 155–84.

Barzelay, M. and Gallego, R. (2010) 'The Comparative Historical Analysis of Public Management Policy Cycles in France, Italy, and Spain: Symposium Conclusion', *Governance*, 23, 2: 297–307.

Baumgartner, F. and Jones, B. (1993) *Agendas and Instability in American Politics* (Chicago, IL: Chicago University Press).

Baumgartner, F. and Jones, B. (eds) (2002) *Policy Dynamics* (Chicago, IL: University of Chicago Press) .

Baumgartner, F. and Jones, B. (2009) *Agendas and Instability in American Politics* 2nd edn (Chicago, IL: Chicago University Press).

Baumgartner, F. and Mahoney, C. (2005) 'Social Movements, the Rise of New Issues, and the Public Agenda' in D. Meyer, V. Jenness and H. Ingram (eds) *Routing the Opposition: Social Movements, Public Policy, and Democracy* (University of Minnesota Press).

Baumgartner, F., Green-Pedersen, C. and Jones, B. (eds) (2006) 'Comparative Studies of Policy Agendas', special issue of the *Journal of European Public Policy*, 13: 7.

Baumgartner, F., Breunig, C., Green-Pedersen, C., Jones, B., Mortensen, P., Nuytemans, M. and Walgrave, S. (2009) 'Punctuated Equilibrium in Comparative Perspective', *American Journal of Political Science*, 53, 3: 603–20.

Baumol, W. (1987) 'Microeconomics: A Comment on the Realism of Assumptions', *Journal of Economic Education*, 18, 2: 155.

BBC News (2008) 'G7 Passes Plan to Ease Credit Woe', 11 April, http://news.bbc.co.uk/1/hi/business/7342419.stm.

Beaumont, P. (2007) 'Amputations Bring Health Crisis to Iraq' 29 July, *Observer,* http://www.guardian.co.uk/world/2007/jul/29/iraq.peterbeaumont.

Becker, G. (1976) *The Economic Approach to Human Behavior* (Chicago, IL: Chicago University Press).

Béland, D. (2010) 'The Idea of Power and the Role of Ideas', *Political Studies Review*, 8, 2:145–54.

Béland, D. and Cox, R. (2010) 'Introduction: Ideas and Politics' in D. Béland and R. Cox (eds) *Ideas and Politics in Social Science Research* (Oxford: Oxford University Press).

Bell, S., Hindmoor, A. and Mols, F. (2010) 'Persuasion as Governance: A State-centric Relational Perspective', *Public Administration*, 88, 3: 851–70.

Bendor, J. and Hammond, T. (1992) 'Rethinking Allison's Models', *American Political Science Review*, 86, 2: 301–22.

Bennett, C. (1991a) 'What is Policy Convergence and What Causes It?', *British Journal of Political Science*, 21, 2: 215–33.

Bennett, C. (1991b) 'How States Utilize Foreign Evidence", *Journal of Public Policy*, 11, 1: 31–54.

Bennett, C. and Howlett, M (1992) 'The Lessons of Learning: Reconciling theories of policy learning and policy change', *Policy Sciences*, 25: 275–94.

Berry, F. and Berry, W. (2007) 'Innovation and Diffusion Models in Policy Research' in P. Sabatier (ed.) *Theories of the Policy Process* (Cambridge, MA: Westview).

Bevir, M. (2009) 'Anti-Foundationalism' in M. Flinders, A. Gamble, C. Hay and M. Kenny (eds) *The Oxford Handbook of British Politics* (Oxford: Oxford University Press).

Bevir, M. and Rhodes, R. (1999) 'Studying British Government', *British Journal of Politics and International Relations*, 1, 2: 215–39 .

Bevir, M. and Rhodes, R.A.W. (2003) *Interpreting British Governance* (London: Routledge).

Biersteker, T. (1990) 'Reducing the Role of the State in the Economy: A Conceptual Exploration of IMF and World Bank Prescriptions', *International Studies Quarterly*, 34: 477–92.

Birkland, T. (1997) *After Disaster: Agenda Setting, Public Policy and Focusing Events* (Washington, DC: Georgetown University Press).

Birkland, T. (2005) *An Introduction to the Policy Process: Theories, Concepts and Models of Public Policy Making*, 2nd edn (London: M.E. Sharpe).

Blackman, T. (2001) 'Complexity theory and the new public management', *Social Issues* (2).

Blomquist, W. (2007) 'The Policy Process and Large-N Comparative Studies' in P. Sabatier (ed.) *Theories of the Policy Process 2* (Cambridge, MA: Westview).

Blyth, M. (1997) 'Any More Bright Ideas: The Ideational Turn in Comparative Political Economy', *Comparative Politics*, 29, 2: 229–50.

Blyth, M. (2002) *Great Transformations: Economic Ideas and Institutional Change in the Twentieth Century* (Cambridge: Cambridge University Press).

Bock, G. and James, S. (1992) *Beyond Equality and Difference: Citizenship, Feminist Politics, and Female Subjectivity* (London: Routledge).

Boin, A., 'T Hart, P., McConnell, A. and Preston, T. (2010) 'Leadership Style, Crisis Response and Blame Management: The Case of Hurricane Katrina', *Public Administration*, 88, 3: 706–20.

Bovaird, T. (2008) 'Emergent Strategic Management and Planning Mechanisms in Complex Adaptive Systems', *Public Management Review*, 10, 3: 319–40.

Bovens, M., 'T Hart, P., Peters, B.G., Albaek, E., Busch, A., Dudley, G., Moran, M. and Richardson, J. (2001) 'Patterns of Governance: Sectoral and National Comparisons' in M. Bovens, P. 'T Hart and B.G. Peters (eds) *Success and Failure in Public Governance* (Cheltenham: Edward Elgar).

Bovens, M., 'T Hart, P. and Kuipers, S. (2006) 'The Politics of Policy Evaluation' in M. Moran, M. Rein and R. Goodin (eds) *The Oxford Handbook of Public Policy* (Oxford: Oxford University Press).

Braithwaite, J. (2006) 'The Regulatory State' in R. Rhodes, S. Binder and B. Rockman, (eds) *The Oxford Handbook of Political Institutions* (Oxford: Oxford University Press).

Braybrooke, D. and Lindblom, C. (1963) *A Strategy of Decision* (New York, NY: Free Press).

Brennan, G. (1996) 'Selection and the Currency of Reward' in R. Goodin (ed.) *The Theory of Institutional Design* (Cambridge; Cambridge University Press).

Brewer, G. and deLeon, P. (1983) *The Foundations of Policy Analysis* (Chicago, IL: Dorsey Press).

Bridgman, P. and Davis, G. (2003) 'What Use is a Policy Cycle? Plenty, if the Aim is Clear', *Australian Journal of Public Administration*, 62, 3: 98–102.

Brinkmann, S. (2009) 'Facts, Values, and the Naturalistic Fallacy in Psychology', *New Ideas in Psychology*, 27, 1: 1–17.

Buchanan, J. (1988) 'Market Failure and Political Failure', *Cato Journal*, 8, 1: 1–13, http://www.cato.org/pubs/journal/cj8n1/cj8n1-1.pdf.

Buchanan, J. (2005) 'Public Choice: The Origins and Development of a Research Program', paper to Public Choice Society, http://sb.cofc.edu/pv_obj_cache/pv_obj_id_4ECD266F12BDD0CFDC97260213CA09AA2CE10700/filename/Public%20Choice%20Origins%20Buchanan.pdf.

Budge, I. (2006) in R. Rhodes, S. Binder. B. Rockman (eds) *The Oxford Handbook of Political Institutions* (Oxford: Oxford University Press).

Burgess, M. (2006) *Comparative Federalism: Theory and Practice* (London: Routledge).

Burns, J. (1963) *The Deadlock of Democracy* (Englewood Cliffs, NJ: Prentice-Hall).

Busch, P. and Jörgens, H. (2005) 'The International Sources of Policy Convergence: Explaining the Spread of Environmental Policy Innovations', *Journal of European Public Policy*, 12, 5: 860–84.

Cafruny, A. and Rosenthal, G. (eds) *The State of the European Community: The Maastrict Debate and Beyond* (Boulder, CO: Lynne Rienner).

Cairney, P. (1997) 'Advocacy Coalitions and Political Change', in G. Stoker and J. Stanyer (eds) *Contemporary Political Studies 1997* (Belfast: Political Studies Association) http://www.informaworld.com/index/792976384.pdf.

Cairney, P. (2002) 'New Public Management and the Thatcher Health Care Legacy', *British Journal of Politics and International Relations*, 4, 3: 375–98.

Cairney, P. (2006) 'Venue Shift Following Devolution: When Reserved Meets Devolved in Scotland', *Regional and Federal Studies*, 16, 4: 429–45.

Cairney, P. (2007a) 'A 'Multiple Lenses' Approach to Policy Change: the Case of Tobacco Policy in the UK', *British Politics*, 2, 1: 45–68.

Cairney, P. (2007b) 'Using devolution to set the agenda? Venue shift and the smoking ban in Scotland', *British Journal of Politics and International Relations*, 9: 73–89.

Cairney, P. (2008) 'Has Devolution Changed the British Policy Style?, *British Politics*, 3, 3: 350–72.

Cairney, P. (2009a) 'Implementation and the Governance Problem: A Pressure Participant Perspective', *Public Policy and Administration*, 24, 4: 355–77.

Cairney, P. (2009b) "The 'British Policy Style' and Mental Health: Beyond the Headlines", *Journal of Social Policy*, 38, 4: 1–18.

Cairney, P. (2009c) 'The Role of Ideas in Policy Transfer: The Case of UK Smoking Bans since Devolution', *Journal of European Public Policy*, 16, 3: 471–88.

Cairney, P. (2010a) 'Complexity Theory in Public Policy', Paper to the Political Studies Associations Conference, University of Edinburgh, April.

Cairney, P. (2010b) 'Complexity Theory and Mixed Methods in Political Science', paper to seminar of 'Methodological Pluralism', European University Institute, December.

Cairney, P. (2012) 'Intergovernmental Relations in Scotland before and after the SNP', *British Journal of Politics and International Relations*, forthcoming.

Cairney, P., Keating, M. and Hepburn, E. (2009) 'Policy Convergence, Learning and Transfer in the UK under Devolution', Political Studies Association Annual Conference, Manchester, April.

Cairney, P., Studlar, D. and Mamudu, H. (2012) *Global Tobacco Control: Power, Policy, Governance and Transfer* (Basingstoke: Palgrave Macmillan).

Caldwell, D. (1977) 'Bureaucratic Foreign Policy-Making', *American Behavioral Scientist*, 21: 87–110.

Cammack, P. (2004) 'What the World Bank Means by Poverty Reduction, and Why it Matters', *New Political Economy*, 9, 2: 189–211.

Campbell, J. (2002) 'Ideas, Politics and Public Policy', *Annual Review of Sociology*, 28: 21–38.

Capoccia, G. and Kelemen, D. (2007) 'The Study of Critical Junctures: Theory, Narrative, and Counterfactuals in Historical Institutionalism', *World Politics*, 59, 3: 341–69.

Chalmers, A. (1999) *What is this Thing Called Science?* 3rd edn (Buckingham: Open University Press).

Church, C. and Dardanelli, P. (2005) 'The Dynamics of Confederalism and Federalism: Comparing Switzerland and the EU', *Regional and Federal Studies*, 15, 2: 163–85.

Chwaszcza, C. (2008) 'Game Theory' in D. Della Porta and M. Keating (eds) *Approaches and Methodologies in the Social Sciences: A Pluralist Approach* (Cambridge: Cambridge University Press).

Clancy, P. (1996) 'The New Zealand Experiment: A Canadian Perspective', *Electronic Journal of Radical Organization Theory*, 2, 1: http://www.mngt. waikato.ac.nz/ejrot/Vol2_1/clancy.pdf.

Cobb, R. and Elder, C. (1972) *Participation in American Politics: The Dynamics of Agenda-Building* (Boston, MA: Allyn & Bacon).

Cohen, M., March, J. and Olsen, J. (1972) 'A Garbage Can Model of Organizational Choice', *Administrative Science Quarterly*, 17, 1: 1–25.

Colebatch, H. (1998) *Policy* (Buckingham: Open University Press).

Colebatch, H. (2006) 'Mapping the Work of Policy' in H. Colebatch (ed.) *Beyond the Policy Cycle: the Policy Process in Australia* (Crow's Nest, New South Wales: Allen & Unwin).

Common, R.K. (1998) 'Convergence and Transfer: A Review of the Globalisation of New Public Management', *International Journal of Public Sector Management*, 11, 6: 440–50.

Cook, F.L. and Skogan, W.G. (1991) 'Convergent and Divergent Voice Models of the Rise and Fall of Policy Issues' in D.L. Protess, and M. McCombs (eds) *Agenda Setting* (London: LEA).

Craib, I. (1992) *Anthony Giddens* (London: Routledge).

Crenson, M. (1971) *The Un-politics of Air Pollution: A Study of Non-decision-making in the Cities* (London: Johns Hopkins Press).

Dahl, R. (1957) 'The Concept of Power', *Behavioral Science*, 2, 3: 201–15.

Dahl, R. (1958) 'A Critique of the Ruling Elite Model', *The American Political Science Review*, 52, 2: 463–9.

Dahl, R. (1961) *Who Governs? Democracy and Power in an American City* (New Haven, CT: Yale University Press).

Davidson, D. (1980) *Essays on Actions and Events* (Oxford: Clarendon Press).

Dawkins, R. (1976) *The Selfish Gene* (New York, NY: Oxford University Press).

Dawson, R. and Robinson, J. (1963) Inter-Party Competition, Economic Variables and Welfare Policies in the American States', *Journal of Politics*, 25: 265–89.

Day, P. and Klein, R. (2000) 'The Politics of Managing the Health Service' in (ed.) R. Rhodes (ed.) *Transforming British Government Vol. 1* (London: Macmillan).

DBERR (Department for Business, Enterprise and Regulatory Reform) (2008) *Understanding the Public Services Industry: How Big, How Good, Where Next?* (The Julius Report) http://www.berr.gov.uk/files/file46965.pdf.

Dearing, J.W. and Rogers, E.M. (1996) *Agenda Setting* (London: Sage).

deLeon, P. (1978) 'A Theory of Policy Termination' in J. May and A. Wildavsky (eds) *The Policy Cycle* (London: Sage).

deLeon, P. (1999) 'The Missing Link Revisited', *Review of Policy Research*, 16, 3–4: 311–38.

deLeon, P. and deLeon, L. (2002) 'Whatever Happened to Policy Implementation? An Alternative Approach', *Journal of Public Administration Research and Theory*, 12, 4: 467–92.

Della Porta, D. and Keating, M. (2008a) 'Introduction' in D. Della Porta and M. Keating (eds) *Approaches and Methodologies in the Social Sciences* (Cambridge: Cambridge University Press).

Della Porta, D. and Keating, M. (2008b) 'How Many Approaches in the Social Sciences? An Epistemological Introduction', in D. Della Porta and M. Keating (eds) *Approaches and Methodologies in the Social Sciences* (Cambridge: Cambridge University Press).

Deutsch, K. (1970) *Politics and Government* (Boston, MA: Houghton Mifflin).

Dewan, T., Dowding, K., and Shepsle, K. (2009) 'Editors' introduction: Rational Choice Classics in Political Science' in K. Dowding, T. Dewan and K. Shepsle (eds) *Rational Choice Politics Volume 1* (London: Sage).

DiMaggio, P. and Powell, W. (1983) 'The Iron Cage Revisited: Institutional Isomorphism and Collective Rationality in Organizational Fields', *American Sociological Review*, 48, 2: 147–60.

Dinan, D. (2004) *Europe Recast: A History of European Union* (Boulder, CO: Lynne Rienner).

Dolowitz, D. (2000) 'Introduction', *Governance*, 13, 1: 1–4.

Dolowitz, D. (2003) 'A Policy-Maker's Guide to Policy Transfer', *Political Quarterly*, 74, 1: 101–8.

Dolowitz, D. (2010) 'Learning, Information and Policy Transfer Process: What do Governments Learn when Shopping for Ideas?', Conference paper, *Policy Learning and Policy Transfer in Multilevel Systems*, Edinburgh, January .

Dolowitz, D. and Marsh, D. (1996) 'Who Learns What From Whom: A Review of the Policy Transfer Literature', *Political Studies*, XLIV: 343–57.

Dolowitz, D. and Marsh, D (2000) 'Learning from Abroad: The Role of Policy Transfer in Contemporary Policy-Making', *Governance*, 13, 1: 5–24.

Dolowitz, D., Greenwold, S. and Marsh, D (1999) 'Policy Transfer: Something Old, Something New, Something Borrowed, but why Red, White And Blue?', *Parliamentary Affairs*, 52, 4: 719–30.

Dowding, K. (1991) *Rational Choice and Political Power* (Aldershot: Edward Elgar).

Dowding, K. (1994) 'The Compatibility of Behaviouralism, Rational Choice and 'New Institutionalism', *Journal of Theoretical Politics*, 6, 1: 105–17.

Dowding, K. (1995a) 'Interpreting Formal Coalition Theory' in K. Dowding and A. King (eds) *Preferences, Institutions and Rational Choice* (Oxford: Oxford University Press).

Dowding, K. (1995b) 'Model or Metaphor? A Critical Review of the Policy Network Approach', *Political Studies*, 43, 2: 136–58.

Dowding, K. (1995c) *The Civil Service* (London: Routledge).

Dowding, K. (1996) *Power* (Buckingham: Open University Press).

Dowding, K. (2000) 'How not to use Evolutionary Theory in Politics: A Critique of Peter John', *British Journal of Politics and International Relations*, 2, 1: 72–80.

Dowding, K. (2001) 'There Must be End to Confusion: Policy Networks, Intellectual Fatigue, and the need for Political Science Methods Courses in British Universities', *Political Studies*, 49, 1: 89–105.

Dowding, K. (2003) 'Resources, Power and Systematic Luck: A Response to Barry', *Politics Philosophy Economics*, 2: 305–12.

Dowding, K. (2009) 'Luck, Equality and Responsibility', *Critical Review of International Social and Political Philosophy*, 12, 4: 561–82.

Dowding, K. (2010) 'Rational Choice Theory' in M. Bevir (ed.) *Sage Handbook of Governance* (Beverly Hills, CA: Sage).

Dowding, K. and James, O. (2004) 'Analysing Bureau-Shaping Models: Comments on Marsh, Smith and Richards, *British Journal of Political Science*, 34, 1: 183–9.

Dowding, K. and King, A. (1995) 'Introduction' in K. Dowding and A. King (eds) *Preferences, Institutions and Rational Choice* (Oxford: Oxford University Press).

Downs, A. (1967) *Inside Bureaucracy* (Boston, MA: Little, Brown).

Downs, A. (1972) 'Up and Down With Ecology: The "Issue-Attention Cycle"', *The Public Interest*, 28 (Summer): 38–50, http://www.anthonydowns.com/upand-down.htm.

Dror, Y. (1964) 'Muddling Through – "Science" or Inertia?', *Public Administration Review*, 24: 153–7.

Duina, F. (1997) 'Explaining Legal Implementation in the European Union', *International Journal of the Sociology of Law*, 25: 155–79 .

Dunleavy, P. (1985) 'Bureaucrats, Budgets and the Growth of the State: Reconstructing an Instrumental Model', *British Journal of Political Science*, 15, 3: 299–328.

Dunleavy, P. (1986) 'Explaining the Privatization Boom: Public Choice versus Radical Approaches', *Public Administration*, 64, 1: 13–34.

Dunleavy, P. (1990) 'The Westland Affair: Theories of the State and Core Executive Decision Making', *Public Administration*, 68, 1: 29–60.

Dunleavy, P. (1991) *Democracy, Bureaucracy and Public Choice* (Hemel Hempstead: Harvester Wheatsheaf).

Dunsire, A. (1973) *Administration* (Buckingham: Open University Press) .

Durant, R. and Diehl, P. (1989) 'Agendas, Alternatives, and Public Policy: Lessons from the U.S. Foreign Policy Arena', *Journal of Public Policy*, 9, 2: 179–205.

Dye, T. (1966) *Politics, Economics and the Public* (Chicago, IL: Rand McNally).

Easton, D. (1953) *The Political System* (New York, NY: Albert Knopf).

Easton, D. (1965) *A Systems Analysis of Political Life* (New York, NY: Wiley) .

Elazar, D. (1971) 'From the Editor: The Themes of a Journal of Federalism', *Publius*, 1, 1: 3–9.

Eller, W. and Krutz, G. (2009) 'Editor's Notes: Policy Process, Scholarship and the Road Ahead: An Introduction to the 2008 Policy Shootout!', *Policy Studies Journal*, 37, 1: 1–4.

Elster, J. (1985) *Making Sense of Marx* (Cambridge: Cambridge University Press).

Elster, J. (1986) 'Introduction' in J. Elster (ed.) *Rational Choice* (Oxford: Blackwell).

Epstein, D. and O'Halloran, S. (1999) *Delegating Powers: A Transactions Cost Politics Approach to Policy Making under Separate Powers* (Cambridge: Cambridge University Press).

Eriksson, L. (2012) *Rational Choice Theory: Potential and Limits* (Basingstoke: Palgrave Macmillan).

Etzioni, A. (1967) 'Mixed Scanning: A "Third" Approach to Decision Making', *Public Administration Review*, 27: 385–92.

European Commission (2011) 'Policy cycle, EU policy cycle', http://ec.europa. eu/governance/better_regulation/glossary_en.htm#_P.

Evans, M. and Davies, J. (1999) 'Understanding Policy Transfer: A Multi-Level, Multi-Disciplinary Perspective", *Public Administration*, 77, 2: 361–85.

Everett, S. (2003) 'The Policy Cycle: Democratic Process or Rational Paradigm Revisited?', *Australian Journal of Public Administration* 62, 2: 65–70.

Exadaktylos, T. and Radaelli, C. (2009) 'Research Design in European Studies: The Case of Europeanization', *Journal of Common Market Studies*, 47, 3: 507–30.

Eyestone, R. (1977) 'Confusion, Diffusion, and Innovation', *American Political Science Review*, 71, 2: 441–7.

Fabbrini, S. and Gilbert, M.F. (2000) 'When Cartels Fail: The Role of the Political Class in the Italian Democratic Transition', *Government and Opposition* 35, 1: 27–48.

Falkner, G., Hartlapp, M., Leiber, S. and Treib, O. (2004) 'Non-Compliance with EU Directives in the Member States: Opposition through the Backdoor?', *West European Politics*, 27, 3: 452–73.

Feldman, E. and Bayer, R (2004) 'Introduction' in E. Feldman, and R. Bayer, (eds) *Unfiltered: Conflicts Over Tobacco Policy and Public Health* (London: Harvard University Press).

Fenger, M. and Klok, P. (2001) 'Interdependency, Beliefs, and Coalition Behavior: A Contribution to the Advocacy Coalition Framework', *Policy Sciences* 34, 2: 157–70.

Finer, S. (1972) *Adversary Politics and Electoral Reform* (London: Wigram).

Finkelstein, L. (1995) 'What is Global Governance?', *Global Governance* 1, 1: 367–92.

Fischer, F. (2003) *Reframing Public Policy* (Oxford: Oxford University Press).

Fischer, F. and Forester, J. (eds) (1993) *The Argumentative Turn in Policy Analysis* (London: UCL Press).

Flinders, M. (2008) *Delegated Governance and the British State* (Oxford: Oxford University Press).

Foucault, M. (1977) *Discipline and Punish* (Harmondsworth: Penguin).

Freeman, G. (1985) 'National Styles and Policy Sectors: Explaining Structured Variation', *Journal of Public Policy*, 5, 4: 467–96.

Freeman, G. (2006) 'Politics and Mass Immigration' in M. Moran, M. Rein and R. Goodin (eds) *The Oxford Handbook of Public Policy* (Oxford: Oxford University Press).

Friedman, M. (1953) 'The Methodology of Positive Economics' in *Essays in Positive Economics* (Chicago, IL: University of Chicago Press).

Friedman, T. (2000) *The Lexus and the Olive Tree: Understanding Globalization* (New York, NY: Anchor Press).

Galligan, B. (2006) 'Comparative Federalism' in R. Rhodes, S. Binder. B. Rockman (eds) *The Oxford Handbook of Political Institutions* (Oxford: Oxford University Press).

Gamble, A. (1990) 'Theories of British Politics', *Political Studies*, 38, 3: 404–20.

Gamble, A. (2000) 'Policy Agendas in a Multi-Level Polity' in Dunleavy *et al.* (eds) *Developments in British Politics 6* (Basingstoke: Palgrave Macmillan).

Genieys, W. and Smyrl, M. (2008a) 'The Problem of Policy Change' in W. Genieys and M. Smyrl (eds) *Elites, Ideas and the Evolution of Public Policy* (Basingstoke: Palgrave Macmillan).

Genieys, W. and Smyrl, M. (2008b) 'Competing Elites, Legitimate Authority, Structured Ideas' in W. Genieys and M. Smyrl (eds) *Elites, Ideas and the Evolution of Public Policy* (Basingstoke: Palgrave Macmillan).

Genieys, W. and Smyrl, M. (2008c) 'Accounting for Change: The Role of Programmatic Elites' in W. Genieys and M. Smyrl (eds) *Elites, Ideas and the Evolution of Public Policy* (Basingstoke: Palgrave Macmillan).

Geva-May, I. (2004) 'Riding the Wave of Opportunity: Termination in Public Policy', *Journal of Public Administration Research and Theory*, 14, 3: 309–33,.

Geyer, R. and Rihani, S. (2010) *Complexity and Public Policy* (London: Routledge).

Giddens, A. (1984) *The Constitution of Society* (Cambridge: Polity).

Goggin, M., Bowman, A., Lester, J. and O'Toole, L. (1990) *Implementation Theory and Practice: Towards a Third Generation* (Boston, MA: Little, Brown).

Goldfinch, S. and Wallis, J. (2010) 'Two Myths of Convergence in Public Management Reform', *Public Administration*, 88, 4: 1099–115.

Goldsmith, M. and Page, E. (1997) 'Farewell to the British State?' in J. Lane (ed.) *Public Sector Reform* (London: Sage).

Goodin, R. and Tilly, C. (2006) *The Oxford Handbook of Contextual Political Analysis* (Oxford: Oxford University Press).

Gramsci, A. (1971) *Selections from Prison Notebooks* (London: Lawrence & Wishart).

Gray, C. (2000) 'A "Hollow State"?' in R. Pyper and L. Robins (eds) *United Kingdom Governance* (Basingstoke: Palgrave Macmillan).

Green, D. and Shapiro, I. (1994) *Pathologies of Rational Choice Theory* (New Haven, CT: Yale University Press).

Green, D. and Shapiro, I. (2005) 'Revisiting the Pathologies of Rational Choice' in I. Shapiro (ed.) *The Flight from Reality in the Human Sciences* (Princeton, NJ: Princeton University Press).

Greenaway, John, S. Smith and J. Street (1992) *Deciding Factors in British Politics* (London: Routledge).

Greener, I. (2002) 'Understanding NHS Reform: The Policy-Transfer, Social Learning and Path-Dependency Perspectives', *Governance*, 15, 2: 161–83.

Greener, I. (2005) 'The Potential of Path Dependence in Political Studies', *Politics*, 25, 1: 62–72.

Greenwood, J., Pyper, R. and Wilson, D. (2001) *New Public Administration in Britain* (London: Routledge).

Greer, P. (1994) *Transforming Central Government: The Next Steps Initiative* (Buckingham: Open University Press).

Greer, S. (2004), *Territorial Politics and Health Policy* (Manchester: Manchester University Press).

Gregory, R. (1993) 'Political Rationality or Incrementalism' in M. Hill (ed.) *The Policy Process: A Reader* (Hemel Hempstead: Harvester Wheatsheaf) .

Grey, J. (1973) 'Innovation in the States: A Diffusion Study', *American Political Science Review*, 67, 4: 1174–85.

Griggs, S. (2007) 'Rational Choice Theory in Public Policy: The Theory in Critical Perspective' in F. Fischer, G. Miller and M. Sidney (eds) *Handbook of Public Policy Analysis* (London: CRC Press).

Haas, E. (1958) *The Uniting of Europe: Political, Economic, and Social Forces 1950–1957* (Stanford, CA: Stanford University Press).

Haas, E.B. (1975) *The Obsolescence of Regional Integration Theory* (Institute of International Studies, University of California, Research Series No. 25) .

Haas, P.M. (1992) 'Introduction: Epistemic Communities and International Policy Coordination', *International Organization*, 46, 1: 1–35.

Hale, D. (1988) 'What is a Policy, Anyway? And Who's Supposed to Make it? A Survey of the Public Administration and Policy Texts', *Administration & Society*, 4: 423–52.

Hall, P. (1986) *Governing the Economy* (Oxford: Oxford University Press).

Hall, P. (1993) 'Policy Paradigms, Social Learning, and the State: The Case of Economic Policymaking in Britain', *Comparative Politics*, 25, 3: 275–96.

Hall, P. and Taylor, R. (1996) 'Political Science and the Three New Institutionalisms', *Political Studies*, 44, 4: 936–57.

Hampsher-Monk, I. and Hindmoor, A. (2010) 'Rational Choice and Interpretive Evidence: Caught Between a Rock and a Hard Place?', *Political Studies*, 58, 1: 47–65.

Hann, A. (1995) 'Sharpening up Sabatier: Belief Systems and Public Policy', *Politics*, 15, 1: 19–26.

Hardin, G. (1968) 'The Tragedy of the Commons', *Science*, 162, December: 1243–8.

Harsanyi, J. (1986) 'Advances in Understanding Rational Behavior' in J. Elster (ed.) *Rational Choice* (Oxford: Blackwell).

Hay, C. (2002) *Political Analysis: A Critical Introduction* (Basingstoke: Palgrave Macmillan).

Hay, C. (2004a) 'Theory, Stylized Heuristic or Self-fulfilling Prophecy? The Status of Rational Choice Theory in Public Administration', *Public Administration*, 82, 1: 39–62.

Hay, C. (2004b) '"Taking Ideas Seriously" in Explanatory Political Analysis', *British Journal of Politics and International Relations*, 6: 142–9.

Hay, C. (2006a) 'Constructivist Institutionalism', in R. Rhodes, S. Binder and B. Rockman, (eds) *The Oxford Handbook of Political Institutions* (Oxford: Oxford University Press).

Hay, C. (2006b) 'Globalization and Public Policy' in M. Moran, M. Rein and R. Goodin (eds) *The Oxford Handbook of Public Policy* (Oxford: Oxford University Press).

Hay, C. and Wincott, D. (1998) 'Structure, Agency and Historical Institutionalism', *Political Studies*, 46: 951–7.

Hayes, M.T. (2001) *The Limits of Policy Change: Incrementalism, Worldview, and the Rule of Law* (Washington, DC: Georgetown University Press).

Haynes, P. (2008) 'Complexity Theory and Evaluation in Public Management', *Public Management Review*, 10, 3:401–19.

Head, B. (2008) 'Three Lenses of Evidence-Based Policy', *Australian Journal of Public Administration*, 67, 1: 1–11.

Heclo, H. (1978) 'Issue Networks and the Executive Establishment', in A. King (ed.) *The New American Political System* (Washington, DC: American Enterprise Institute).

Heichel, S., Pape, J. and Sommerer, T. (2005) 'Is there Convergence in Convergence Research? An Overview of Empirical Studies on Policy Convergence', *Journal of European Public Policy*, 12, 5: 817–40.

Heyward, C. (2007) 'Revisiting the Radical View: Power, Real Interests and the Difficulty of Separating Analysis from Critique', *Politics*, 27,1: 48–54.

Hill, K. (1997) 'In Search of Policy Theory', *Policy Currents*, 7, 1: 1–9, http://apsapolicysection.org/vol7_1/71.pdf.

Hill, M. (2005) *The Public Policy Process* 4th edn (Harlow: Pearson).

Hill, M. (2009) *The Public Policy Process* 5th edn (Harlow: Pearson).

Hill, M. and Hupe, P. (2002) *Implementing Public Policy* (London: Sage).

Hill, M. and Hupe, P. (2009) *Implementing Public Policy*, 2nd edn (London: Sage).

Hindess, B. (1988) *Choice, Rationality and Social Theory* (London: Unwin Hyman).

Hindess, B. (1996) *Discourses of Power: From Hobbes to Foucault* (Oxford: Blackwell).

Hindmoor, A. (2003) 'Public Policy: The 2002 Spending Review and Beyond', *Parliamentary Affairs*, 56, 2: 205–18.

Hindmoor, A. (2006a) *Rational Choice* (Basingstoke: Palgrave Macmillan).

Hindmoor, A. (2006b) 'Public Choice' in C. Hay, M. Lister and D. Marsh (eds) *The State: Theories and Issues* (Basingstoke: Palgrave Macmillan).

Hindmoor, A. (2010) '"Major Combat Operations Have Ended?" Arguing about Rational Choice, 1994–2009', *British Journal of Political Science*, 41, 1: 191–210.

Hjern, B. (1982) 'Implementation Research – the Link Gone Missing', *Journal of Public Policy*, 2, 3: 301–8.

Hjern, B. and Porter, D. (1981) 'Implementation Structures: A New Unit of Administrative Analysis', *Organizational Studies*, 2: 211–27.

Hoberg, G. (1991) 'Sleeping with an Elephant: The American Influence on Canadian Environmental Regulation' *Journal of Public Policy*, 11, 1: 107–31.

Hoberg, G. (1996) 'Putting Ideas in Their Place: A Response to "Learning and Change in the British Columbia Forest Policy Sector"', *Canadian Journal of Political Science*, 29, 1: 135–44.

Hoberg, G. (2001) 'Globalization and Policy Convergence: Symposium Overview', *Journal of Comparative Policy Analysis: Research and Practice*, 3: 127–32.

Hofferbert, R. (1974) *The Study of Public Policy* (Indianapolis, IN: Bobbs-Merrill).

Hogwood, B. (1987) *From Crisis to Complacency* (Oxford: Oxford University Press).

Hogwood, B. (1992a) *Trends in British Public Policy* (Buckingham: Open University Press).

Hogwood, B. (1992b) 'Ups and Downs: Is There an Issue-Attention Cycle in Britain?', *Strathclyde Papers on Government and Politics*, 89 (Glasgow University of Strathclyde).

Hogwood, B. (1997) 'The Machinery of Government 1979–97', *Political Studies*, XLV: 704–15.

Hogwood, B. and Gunn, L. (1984) *Policy Analysis for the Real World* (Oxford: Oxford University Press).

Hogwood, B. and Peters, B.G. (1982) 'The Dynamics of Policy Change: Policy Succession', *Policy Sciences*, 14: 225–45.

Hogwood, B. and Peters, B.G. (1983) *Policy Dynamics* (New York, NY: St Martin's Press).

Hogwood, B., Judge, D. and McVicar, M. (2001) 'Agencies, Ministers and Civil Servants in Britain' in B.G. Peters and J. Pierre (eds) *Politicians, Bureaucrats and Administrative Reform* (London: Routledge).

Holland, K., Morton, F. and Galligan, B. (1996) *Federalism and the Environment* (Westport, CT: Greenwood Press).

Holliday, I. (2000) 'Is the British State Hollowing Out?', *Political Quarterly*, 71, 2: 167–76 .

Holzinger, K. and Knill, C. (2005) 'Causes and Conditions of Cross-National Policy Convergence', *Journal of European Public Policy*, 12, 5: 775–96.

Hood, C. (1976) *The Limits of Administration* (London: Wiley).

Hood, C. (1995) 'The "New Public Management" in the 1980s: Variations on a Theme', *Accounting, Organizations and Society*, 20, 2/3: 93–109.

Hood, C. (2007) 'Public Service Management by Numbers', *Public Money and Management*, 27, 2: 95–102.

Hood, C., Scott, C., James, O., Jones, G. and Travers, T. (1999) *Regulation Inside Government* (Oxford: Oxford University Press).

Hooghe, L. and Marks, G. (2001) *Multi-Level Governance and European Integration* (London: Rowman & Littlefield).

Hooghe, L. and Marks, G. (2003) 'Unraveling the Central State, but How? Types of Multi-Level Governance', *American Political Science Review*, 97, 2: 233–43.

Hooghe, L. and Marks, G. (2004) 'Contrasting Visions of Multi-Level Governance' in I. Bache and M. Flinders (eds) *Multi-Level Governance* (Oxford: Oxford University Press).

Hopkins, R., Powell, A., Roy, A. and Gilbert, C. (1997) 'The World Bank and Conditionality', *Journal of International Development*, 9, 4: 507–16.

Hoque, K., Davis, S. and Humphreys, M. (2004) 'Freedom to Do What You Are Told', *Public Administration*, 82, 2: 355–75.

Horgan, G. (2004) 'Inter-institutional Relations in the Devolved Great Britain: Quiet Diplomacy', *Regional and Federal Studies*, 14, 1: 113–35.

Horn, M. (1995) *Political Economy of Public Administration* (Cambridge: Cambridge University Press).

Howard, C. (2005) 'Policy Cycle: A Model of Post-Machiavellian Policy Making?' *Australian Journal of Public Administration*, 3: 3–13.

Howlett, M. and Ramesh, M. (2003) *Studying Public Policy: Policy Cycles and Policy Subsystems* (Oxford: Oxford University Press).

Howlett, M., Ramesh, M. and Perl, A. (2009) *Studying Public Policy: Policy Cycles and Policy Subsystems* (Oxford: Oxford University Press).

Huber, J. (2000) 'Delegation to Civil Servants in Parliamentary Democracies', *European Journal of Political Research* 37: 397–413.

Huber, J. and Shipan, C. (2002) *Deliberate Discretion? The Institutional Foundations of Bureaucratic Autonomy* (Cambridge: Cambridge University Press).

Hudson, B. (1993) 'Michael Lipsky and Street-level Bureaucracy: A Neglected Perspective' in M. Hill (ed.) *The Policy Process: A Reader* (Hemel Hempstead: Harvester Wheatsheaf).

Hueglin, T. and Fenna, A. (2006) *Comparative Federalism: A Systematic Inquiry* (Peterborough, ON: Broadview Press).

Hunter, F. (1953) *Community Power Structure* (Chapel Hill, NC: University of North Carolina Press).

Hunter, F. (1980) *Community Power Succession* (Chapel Hill, NC: University of North Carolina Press).

Hupe, P. and Hill, M. (2007) 'Street-Level Bureaucracy and Public Accountability', *Public Administration*, 85, 2: 279–99.

Immergut, E. (1998) 'The Theoretical Core of the New Institutionalism', *Politics Society*, 26, 1: 5–34.

Ingram, H., Schneider, A. and deLeon, P. (2007) 'Social Construction and Policy Design' in P. Sabatier (ed.) *Theories of the Policy Process 2* (Cambridge, MA: Westview).

Jachtenfuchs, M. (2001) 'The Governance Approach to European Integration', *Journal of Common Market Studies*, 39, 2: 245–64.

Jacobsen, J.K. (1995) 'Much Ado About Ideas: The Cognitive Factor in Economic Policy', *World Politics*, 47, 2: 283–310.

James, O. (1995) 'Explaining the Next Steps in the Department of Social Security: The Bureau-Shaping Model of Central State Reorganisation', *Political Studies*, 43, 4: 614–29.

James, O. (2001) 'Business Models and the Transfer of Businesslike Central Government Agencies', *Governance*, 14, 2: 233–52.

James, O. and Lodge, M. (2003) 'The Limitations of "Policy Transfer" and "Lesson Drawing" for Public Policy Research', *Political Studies Review*, 1: 179–93.

Jann, W. and Wegrich, K. (2007) 'Theories of the Policy Cycle', in F. Fischer, G. Miller and M. Sidney (eds) *Handbook of Public Policy Analysis* (London: CRC Press).

Jenkins, W. (1978) *Policy Analysis* (London: Martin Robertson).

Jenkins-Smith, H. and Sabatier, P. (1993a) 'The Study of Public Policy Processes' in P. Sabatier and H. Jenkins-Smith, (eds) *Policy Change and Learning: An Advocacy Coalition Approach* (Boulder, CO: Westview Press).

Jenkins-Smith, H. and Sabatier, P. (1993b) 'The Dynamics of Policy-Oriented Learning' in P. Sabatier and H. Jenkins-Smith, (eds) *Policy Change and Learning: An Advocacy Coalition Approach* (Boulder, CO: Westview Press).

Jenkins-Smith, H. and Sabatier, P. (1993c) 'Methodological Appendix' in P. Sabatier and H. Jenkins-Smith, (eds) *Policy Change and Learning: An Advocacy Coalition Approach* (Boulder, CO: Westview Press).

Jenkins-Smith, H. and Sabatier, P. (1994) 'Evaluating the Advocacy Coalition Framework', *Journal of Public Policy*, 14, 2: 175–203.

Jervis, R. (1998) *System Effects: Complexity in Political and Social Life* (Princeton, NJ: Princeton University Press).

Jessop, B. (2004) 'Multi-Level Governance and Multi-Level Metagovernance' in I. Bache and M. Flinders (eds) *Multi-Level Governance* (Oxford: Oxford University Press).

Jobert, B. and Muller, P. (1987) *L'Etat en Action: Politiques Publiques et Corporatismes* (Paris: Presses Universitaires de France).

John, P. (1998) *Analysing Public Policy* (London: Continuum).

John, P. (1999) 'Ideas and Interests; Agendas and Implementation: An Evolutionary Explanation of Policy Change in British Local Government Finance', *British Journal of Politics and International Relations*, 1, 1: 39–62.

John, P. (2000) 'The Uses and Abuse of Evolutionary Theory in Political Science: A reply to Alan McConnell and Keith Dowding', *British Journal of Politics and International Relations*, 11: 89–94.

John, P. (2003) 'Is There Life After Policy Streams, Advocacy Coalitions, and Punctuations: Using Evolutionary Theory to Explain Policy Change?' *Policy Studies Journal*, 31, 4: 481–98.

John, P. (2006) 'The Policy Agendas Project: A Review', *Journal of European Public Policy*, 13, 7: 975–86.

John, P. (2012) *Analysing Public Policy*, 2nd edn (London: Routledge).

John, P. and Margetts, H. (2003) 'Policy Punctuations in the UK: Fluctuations and Equilibria in Central Government Expenditure Since 1951', *Public Administration*, 81, 3: 411–32.

Jones, B. (1994) *Reconceiving Decision-Making in Democratic Politics: Attention, Choice and Public Policy* (Chicago, IL: Chicago University Press).

Jones, B. (1999) 'Bounded Rationality', *Annual Review of Political Science*, 2: 297–321.

Jones, B. (2003) 'Bounded Rationality and Political Science: Lessons from Public Administration and Public Policy' *Journal of Public Administration Research and Theory*, 13, 4: 395–412 .

Jones, B. and Baumgartner, F. (2005) *The Politics of Attention* (Chicago, IL: University of Chicago Press).

Jones, B., Baumgartner, F., Breunig, C., Wleizen, C., Soroka, S., Foucault, M., Francois, A., Green-Pedersen, C., Koski, C., John, P., Mortensen, P., Varone, F., Walgrave, S. (2009) 'A General Empirical Law of Public Budgets: A Comparative Analysis', *American Journal of Political Science*, 53, 4: 855–73.

Jones, C. (1970; 1984) *An Introduction to the Study of Political Life*, 3rd edn (Berkeley, CA: Duxberry Press).

Jones, M. and Jenkins-Smith, H. (2009) 'Trans-Subsystem Dynamics: Policy Topography, Mass Opinion, and Policy Change', *Policy Studies Journal*, 37, 1: 37–59.

Jordan, A.G. and J.J. Richardson (1987) *British Politics and the Policy Process* (London: Allen & Unwin).

Jordan, A.G. and Maloney, W.A. (1997) 'Accounting for Subgovernments: Explaining the Persistence of Policy Communities', *Administration and Society*, 29, 5: 557–83.

Jordan, A.G. and Richardson, J.J. (1982) 'The British Policy Style or the Logic of Negotiation?' in J.J. Richardson (ed.) *Policy Styles in Western Europe* (London: Allen & Unwin).

Jordan, A.G. and Richardson, J.J. (1987) *British Politics and the Policy Process* (London: Allen & Unwin).

Jordan, A.G. and Stevenson, L. (2000) 'Redemocratizing Scotland. Towards the Politics of Disappointment?', in A. Wright (ed.) *Scotland: The Challenge of Devolution* (Aldershot: Ashgate).

Jordan, G. (1981) 'Iron Triangles, Woolly Corporatism and Elastic Nets: Images of the Policy Process', *Journal of Public Policy* 1, 1: 95–123.

Jordan, G. (1990a) 'Policy Community Realism versus "New" Institutionalist Ambiguity', *Political Studies*, 38: 470–84.

Jordan, G. (1990b) 'The Pluralism of Pluralism: An Anti-Theory?', *Political Studies*, 38, 2: 286–301.

Jordan, G. (2005) 'Bringing Policy Communities Back In? A Comment on Grant', *British Journal of Politics and International Relations*, 7: 317–21.

Jordan, G. and Maloney, W. (2004) 'Defining Interests: Disambiguation and the Need for New Distinctions?' *British Journal of Politics and International Relations*, 6, 2: 195–212.

Jordan, G. and Maloney, W. (1995) 'Policy Networks Expanded: A Comment on Cavanagh, Marsh and Smith', *Public Administration*, 73: 630–4.

Jordan, G. and Maloney, W. (1996) 'How Bumble Bees Fly: Accounting for Public Interest Participation', *Political Studies*, 44, 4: 668–85.

Jordan, G. and Schubert, K. (1992) 'A Preliminary Ordering of Policy Network Labels', *European Journal of Political Research*, 21, 1: 7–27.

Judge, D. (1993) *The Parliamentary State* (London: Sage).

Judge, D. (2005) *Political Institutions in the United Kingdom* (Oxford: Oxford University Press).

Just, R., Hueth, D. and Schmitz, A. (2004) *The Welfare Economics of Public Policy* (Cheltenham: Edward Elgar).

Karp, J. and Banducci, S. (2008) 'Political Efficacy and Participation in Twenty-Seven Democracies: How Electoral Systems Shape Political Behaviour', *British Journal of Political Science*, 38, 2: 311–34.

Kaufman, H. and Jones, V. (1954) 'Review: The Mystery of Power', *Public Administration Review*, 14, 3:205–12.

Kay, A. (2006) *The Dynamics of Public Policy* (Cheltenham: Edward Elgar).

Keating, M. (2005) *The Government of Scotland* (Edinburgh: Edinburgh University Press).

Keating, M., Cairney, P. and Hepburn, E. (2009) 'Territorial Policy Communities and Devolution in the United Kingdom', *Cambridge Journal of Regions, Economy and Society*, 2, 1: 51–66.

Keating, M., Stevenson, L. Cairney, P. and MacLean, K. (2003) 'Does Devolution Make a Difference? Legislative Output and Policy Divergence in Scotland', *Journal of Legislative Studies*, 9, 3: 110–39.

Keleman, R. D. (2004) *The Rules of Federalism: Institutions and Regulatory Politics in the EU and Beyond* (Cambridge: Harvard University Press).

Keohane, R. and Ostrom, E. (1995) *Local Commons and Global Independence* (London: Sage).

Kernick, D. (2006) 'Wanted – New Methodologies for Health Service Research. Is Complexity Theory the Answer?' *Family Practice* 23: 385–90.

Kettell, S. and Cairney, P. (2010) 'Taking the Power of Ideas Seriously: The Case of the 2008 Human Fertilisation and Embryology Bill', *Policy Studies*, 31, 3: 301–17.

Kettl, D. (2006) 'Public Bureaucracies' in R. Rhodes, S. Binder. B. Rockman (eds) *The Oxford Handbook of Political Institutions* (Oxford: Oxford University Press).

Kikeri, S., Nellis, J. and Shirley, M. (1992) *Privatization: The Lessons of Experience* (Washington, DC: The World Bank) http://www-wds.worldbank.org/servlet/main?menuPK=64187510&pagePK=64193027&piPK=64187937&theSitePK=523679&entityID=000178830_9810191113028.

Kim, Y. and Roh, C. (2008) 'Beyond the Advocacy Coalition Framework in Policy Process', *International Journal of Public Administration*, 31, 6: 668–89.

Kingdon, J. (1984) *Agendas, Alternatives and Public Policies* (New York, NY: Harper Collins).

Kingdon, J. (1995) *Agendas, Alternatives and Public Policies*, 2nd edn (New York, NY: HarperCollins).

Kitschelt, H. and Streeck, W. (2003) 'From Stability of Stagnation: Germany at the Beginning of the Twenty-First Century', *West European Politics*, 26, 4: 1–34.

Kjaer, A. (2004) *Governance* (Cambridge: Polity).

Klijn, E. (2008) 'Complexity Theory and Public Administration: What's New?' *Public Management Review*, 10, 3: 299–317.

Kooiman, J. (1993) 'Socio-political Governance: Introduction' in (ed.) J. Kooiman, *Modern Governance* (London: Sage).

Kooiman, J. (2003) *Governing as Governance* (London: Sage).

Kratochwil, F. (2008) 'Constructivism' in D. Della Porta and M. Keating (eds) *Approaches and Methodologies in the Social Sciences* (Cambridge: Cambridge University Press).

Krauss, E. and Pekkanen, R. (2004) 'Explaining Party Adaptation to Electoral Reform: The Discreet Charm of the LDP?', *Journal of Japanese Studies*, 30, 1: 1–34.

Kriesi, H., Adam, S. and Jochum, M. (2006) 'Comparative Analysis of Policy Networks in Western Europe', *Journal of European Public Policy* 13, 3: 341–61.

Kuhn, T. (1970) *The Structure of Scientific Revolutions* (Chicago, IL: University of Chicago Press). (For a handy summary: http://www.des.emory.edu/mfp/Kuhn.html.)

Larsen, T., Taylor-Gooby, P. and Kananen, J. (2006) 'New Labour's Policy Style: A Mix of Policy Approaches', *Journal of Social Policy*, 35, 4: 629–49.

Larsen, J., Vrangbaek, K. and Traulsen, J. (2006) 'Advocacy Coalitions and Pharmacy Policy in Denmark', *Social Science and Medicine*, 63, 1: 212–24.

Lasswell, H. (1936) *Politics: Who Gets What, When, How* (Cleveland, OH: Meridian Books).

Lasswell, H. (1956) *The Decision Process: Seven Categories of Functional Analysis*, (College Park, MD: University of Maryland Press).

Laver, M. (1997) *Private Desires, Political Action* (London: Sage).

Lavis, J., Ross, S., Hurley, J. *et al.* (2002) 'Examining the Role of Health Services Research in Public Policymaking', *Milbank Quarterly*, 80, 1: 125–54.

Le Grand, J. (2003) *Motivation, Agency and Public Policy: Of Knights and Knaves, Pawns and Queens* (Oxford: Oxford University Press).

Leach, W. and Sabatier, P. (2005) 'To Trust an Adversary: Integrating Rational and Psychological Models of Collaborative Policymaking', *American Political Science Review*, 99, 4: 491–503.

Lerner, D. and Lasswell, H. (1951) *The Policy Sciences* (Stanford, CA: Stanford University Press).

Lichbach, M. (2003) *Is Rational Choice Theory All of Social Science?* (Ann Arbor, MI: University of Michigan Press).

Lieberman, R.C. (2002) 'Ideas, Institutions and Political Order: Explaining Political Change', *American Political Science Review*, 90, 4: 691–712.

Lijphart, A. (1999) *Patterns of Democracy* (New Haven, CT: Yale University Press).

Lindblom, C. (1959) 'The Science of Muddling Through', *Public Administration Review*, 19: 79–88.

Lindblom, C. (1964) 'Contexts for Change and Strategy: A Reply', *Public Administration Review*, 24, 3: 157–8.

Lindblom, C. (1965) *The Intelligence of Democracy* (New York, NY: Free Press).

Lindblom, C. (1968) *The Policy-Making Process* (Englewood Cliffs, NJ: Prentice-Hall).

Lindblom, C. (1977) *Politics and Markets* (New York: Basic Books).

Lindblom, C. (1979) 'Still Muddling, Not Yet Through', *Public Administration Review*, 39: 517–25.

Linder, S. and Peters, B.G. (2006) 'Coming to Terms with Intramural Differences over Policy Frameworks', *Policy Sciences* 39, 1: 19–40.

Lindquist, E. (2004) 'Organizing for Policy Implementation: The Emergence and Role of Implementation Units in Policy Design and Oversight', *Journal of Comparative Policy Analysis: Research and Practice*, 8, 4: 311–24.

Lipsky, M (1980) *Street-Level Bureaucracy* (New York, NY: Russell Sage Foundation).

Litfin, K. (2000) 'Advocacy Coalitions Along the Domestic-Foreign Frontier: Globalization and Canadian Climate Change Policy', *Policy Studies Journal*, 28, 1: 236–52.

Lodge, M. and Gill, D. (2011) 'Toward a New Era of Administrative Reform? The Myth of Post-NPM in New Zealand', *Governance*, 24, 1: 141–66.

Lowi, T. (1964) 'An American Business, Public Policy, Case-Studies, and Political Theory', *World Politics*, 16, 4: 677–715.

Lowi, T. (1972) 'Four Systems of Policy, Politics and Choice', *Public Administration Review*, 32, 4: 298–310.

Lowi, T. (1988) 'Comment', *Policy Studies Journal*, 16: 725–8.

Lowndes, V. (2010) 'The Institutional Approach' in D. Marsh and G. Stoker (eds) *Theory and Methods in Political Science* (Basingstoke: Palgrave Macmillan).

Lukes, S. (1974) *Power: A Radical View* (London: Macmillan).

Lukes, S. (ed.) (1986) *Power* (New York, NY: New York University Press).

Lukes, S. (2005) *Power: A Radical View*, 2nd edn (Basingstoke: Palgrave Macmillan).

Lukes, S. and Haglund, L. (2005) 'Power and Luck', *European Journal of Sociology*, 46, 1: 45–66.

Lundin, M. (2007) 'When Does Cooperation Improve Public Policy Implementation?', *Policy Studies Journal*, 35, 4: 629–52.

Lynas, M. (2008) 'Six Degrees, but no PhD' *Guardian*, 18 June, http://blogs.guardian.co.uk/books/2008/06/six_degrees_but_no_phd.html.

MacDonald, P. (2003) 'Useful Fiction or Miracle Maker: The Competing Epistemological Foundations of Rational Choice Theory', *American Political Science Review*, 97, 4: 551–65.

Machin, A. (2004) 'Comparisons between Unemployment and the Claimant Count', *Labour Market Trends February 2004*, 59–62.

Macleavy, J. and Gay, O. (2005) *The Quango Debate*, House of Commons Research Paper 05/30 (April).

Majone, G. (1980) 'Policies as theories', *Omega* 8, 2: 151–62.

Majone, G. (1989) *Evidence, Argument and Persuasion in the Policy Process* (New Haven, CT: Yale University Press).

Majone, G. (1993) 'The European Community Between Social Policy and Social Regulation', *Journal of Common Market Studies*, 31, 2: 153–70.

Majone, G. (1994) 'The Rise of the Regulatory State in Europe', *West European Politics*, 17, 3: 77–101.

Majone, G. (1996) *Regulating Europe* (London: Routledge).

Majone, G. (2006) 'Agenda Setting' in M. Moran, M. Rein and R. Goodin (eds) *The Oxford Handbook of Public Policy* (Oxford: Oxford University Press).

Maloney, W.A. and Richardson, J.J. (1995a) *Managing Policy Change in Britain: The Politics of Water* (Edinburgh: Edinburgh University Press).

Maloney, W.A. and Richardson, J.J. (1995b) 'Water Policy-Making in England and Wales: Policy Communities Under Pressure?' in H. Bressers, L.J. O'Toole Jr and

J.J. Richardson (eds) *Networks For Water Policy: A Comparative Perspective* (London: Frank Cass).

Maloney, W., Jordan, G. and McLaughlin, A. (1994) 'Interest Groups and Public Policy: The Insider/Outsider Model Revisited', *Journal of Public Policy*, 14, 1: 17–38.

March, J. and Olsen, J. (1984) 'The New Institutionalism: Organizational Factors in Political Life', *The American Political Science Review*, 78, 3: 734–49.

March, J. and Olsen, J. (1996) 'Institutional Perspectives on Political Institutions', *Governance*, 9, 3: 247–64.

March, J. and Olsen, J. (2006a) 'Elaborating the "New Institutionalism"' in R. Rhodes, S. Binder and B. Rockman (eds) *The Oxford Handbook of Political Institutions* (Oxford: Oxford University Press).

March, J. and Olsen, J. (2006b) 'The Logic of Appropriateness' in M. Moran, M. Rein and R. Goodin (eds) *The Oxford Handbook of Public Policy* (Oxford: Oxford University Press).

Marchildon, G. (2001) 'Royal Commissions and the Policy Cycle in Canada', Public Lecture at the Saskatchewan Institute of Public Policy, http://www.uregina.ca/sipp/documents/pdf/ssgm.pdf.

Marcussen, M. (2005) 'Central Banks on the Move', *Journal of European Public Policy*, 12, 5: 903–23.

Marinetto, M. (2003) 'Governing beyond the Centre: A Critique of the Anglo-Governance School', *Political Studies*, 51: 592–608.

Marks, G. (1993) 'Structural Policy and Multi-Level Governance in the EC', in A. Cafruny and G. Rosenthal (eds) *The State of the European Community: The Maastrict Debate and Beyond* (Boulder, CO: Lynne Rienner).

Marks, G. and Hooghe, L. (2000) 'Optimality and Authority: A Critique of Neoclassical Theory', *Journal of Common Market Studies*, 38, 5: 795–816.

Marsh, D. (1991) 'Privatisation under Mrs Thatcher', *Public Administration*, 69, 4: 459–80.

Marsh, D. (2008) 'Understanding British Government: Analysing Competing Models', *British Journal of Politics and International Relations*, 10, 2: 251–69.

Marsh, D. and McConnell, A. (2010) 'Towards a Framework for Establishing Policy Success', *Public Administration*, 88, 2: 564–83.

Marsh, D. and Rhodes, R.A.W. (eds) (1992a) *Implementing Thatcherite Policies* (Buckingham: Open University Press).

Marsh, D. and Rhodes, R.A.W. (1992b) 'Policy Communities and Issue Networks: Beyond Typology' in D. Marsh and R.A.W. Rhodes (eds) *Policy Networks in British Government*(Oxford: Oxford University Press).

Marsh, D. and Smith, M. (2000) 'Understanding Policy Networks: Towards a Dialectical Approach', *Political Studies*, 48, 1: 4–21.

Marsh, D. and Smith, M. (2001) 'There is More Than One Way to do Political Science: On Different Ways to Study Policy Networks' *Political Studies*, 49, 3: 528–41.

Marsh, D., Richards, D. and Smith, M.J. (2001) *Changing Patterns of Governance in the United Kingdom* (Basingstoke: Palgrave Macmillan).

Marsh, D., Richards, D. and Smith, M.J. (2003) 'Unequal Plurality: Towards an

Asymmetric Power Model of British Politics', *Government and Opposition*, 38, 306–32.

Marsh, D., Richards, D. and Smith, M.J. (2004) 'Understanding and Explaining Civil Service Reform: A Reply to Dowding and James', *British Journal of Political Science*, 34, 1: 189–92.

Marsh, D., Smith, M. and Richards, D. (2000) 'Bureaucrats, politicians and reform in Whitehall: Analysing the Bureau-Shaping Model', *British Journal of Political Science*, 30, 3: 461–82.

Martin, C.J. and Swank, D. (2004) 'Does the Organization of Capital Matter?', *American Political Science Review*, 98, 4: 593–611.

Martin, C.J. and Thelen, K. (2007) 'The State and Coordinated Capitalism', *World Politics*, 60, 1: 1–36.

Massey, A. (2001) 'Policy, Management and Implementation' in S. Savage and R. Atkinson (eds) *Public Policy Under Blair* (London: Palgrave Macmillan).

Massey, A. (2010) 'Lessons from Africa: New Public Management and the Privatization of Kenya Airways', *Public Policy and Administration*, 25, 2: 194–215.

Mastenbroek, E. (2005) 'EU Compliance: Still a Black Hole', *Journal of European Public Policy*, 12, 6: 1103–20.

Matland, R. (1995) 'The Implementation Literature: The Ambiguity-Conflict Model of Policy Implementation', *Journal of Public Administration Research and Theory: J-PART*, 5, 2: 145–74.

Maxwell, S. (1999) 'The Meaning and Measurement of Poverty', Overseas Development Institute Poverty Briefing, http://www.odi.org.uk/publications/briefing/pov3.html.

May, P. (1992) 'Policy Learning and Failure', *Journal of Public Policy*, 12, 4: 331–54.

Mazey, S. and Richardson, J. (2006) 'Interest groups and EU Policy-Making: Organisational Logic and Venue Shopping' in J. Richardson (ed.) *European Union: Power and Policy-Making*, 3rd edn (London: Routledge).

McConnell, A. (2000) 'Local taxation, Policy Formation and Policy Change: A Reply to Peter John', *British Journal of Politics and International Relations*, 2, 1: 81–8.

McConnell, A. (2010) *Understanding Policy Success: Rethinking Public Policy* (Basingstoke: Palgrave Macmillan).

McCool, D. (1995) *Public Policy Theories, Models and Concepts: An Anthology* (Englewood Cliffs, NJ: Prentice-Hall).

McCool, D. (1998) 'The Subsystem Family of Concepts: A Critique and a Proposal', *Political Research Quarterly* 51, 2: 551–70.

McGarvey, N. and Cairney, P. (2008) *Scottish Politics* (Basingstoke: Palgrave Macmillan).

McKay, D. (2000) 'Policy Legitimacy and Institutional Design: Comparative Lessons for the European Union', *Journal of Common Market Studies*, 38, 1: 25–44.

McLean, I. (1987) *Public Choice* (Oxford: Basil Blackwell).

McLean, I. (2002) 'Review Article: William H. Riker and the Invention of Heresthetic(s)', *British Journal of Political Science*, 32, 3: 535–58.

McPherson, A.M. and Raab, C.D. (1988) *Governing Education: a Sociology of Policy Since 1945* (Edinburgh: Edinburgh University Press).

Meier, K. (2009) 'Policy Theory, Policy Theory Everywhere: Ravings of a Deranged Policy Scholar', *Policy Studies Journal*, 37,1: 5–11.

Meseguer, C. (2003) 'Learning and Economic Policy Choices: A Bayesian Approach', EUI Working Paper RSC No. 2003/5 (San Domenico: European University Institute), http://cadmus.iue.it/dspace/bitstream/1814/1847/1/03_05.pdf.

Mills, C. W. (1956) *The Power Elite* (New York: Oxford University Press).

Mintrom, M. and Norman, P. (2009) 'Policy Entrepreneurship and Policy Change', *Policy Studies Journal*, 37, 4: 649–67.

Mintrom, M. and Vergari, S. (1996) 'Advocacy Coalitions, Policy Entrepreneurs and Policy Change', *Policy Studies Journal*, 24, 3: 420–34.

Mitchell, M. (2009) *Complexity* (Oxford: Oxford University Press).

Mitleton-Kelly, E. (2003) 'Ten Principles of Complexity and Enabling Infrastructures' in E. Mitleton-Kelly (ed.) *Complex Systems and Evolutionary Perspectives of Organisations* (Amsterdam: Elsevier).

Monbiot, G. (2008) 'Credit Crunch? The Real Crisis is Global Hunger. And If You Care, Eat Less Meat', 15 April, *Guardian,* http://www.guardian.co.uk/comment-isfree/2008/apr/15/food.biofuels.

Moran, M. (2005) *Politics and Governance in the UK* (Basingstoke: Palgrave Macmillan).

Moran, M. (2006) 'Economic Institutions' ' in R. Rhodes, S. Binder and B. Rockman (eds) *The Oxford Handbook of Political Institutions* (Oxford: Oxford University Press).

Moravscik, A. (1993) 'Preferences and Power in the European Community: A Liberal Intergovernmentalist Approach', *Journal of Common Market Studies*, 31, 4: 473–524.

Moser, P. (1990) 'Rationality in Action: General Introduction' in P. Moser (ed.) *Rationality in Action: Contemporary Approaches* (Cambridge: Cambridge University Press).

Mueller, D. (2003) *Public Choice III* (Cambridge: Cambridge University Press).

Newig, J. and Fritsch, O. (2009) 'Environmental Governance: Participatory, Multi-Level – and Effective?' *Environmental Policy and Governance*, 19: 197–214.

Newton, K. and van Deth, J. (2010) *Foundations of Comparative Politics* (Cambridge: Cambridge University Press).

Niskanen, W. (1971) *Bureaucracy and Representative Government* (Chicago, IL: Aldine Atherton).

Niskanen, W. (1975) 'Bureaucrats and Politicians', *Journal of Law and Economics,* 18, 3: 617–43.

Norris, P. (1997) 'Choosing Electoral Systems: Proportional, Majoritarian and Mixed Systems' *International Political Science Review*, 18, 3: 297–312.

O'Neill, F. (2000) 'Health: The "Internal Market" and Reform of the National Service' in D. Dolowitz (ed.) *Policy Transfer and British Social Policy* (Buckingham: Open University Press).

O'Toole, B. and Jordan, G. (1995) *Next Steps* (Aldershot: Dartmouth).

Oaksford, M. and Chatter, N. (2007) *Bayesian Rationality* (Oxford: Oxford University Press).

OECD, Organisation for Economic Co-operation and Development (1995) *Governance in Transition: Public Management Reforms in OECD Countries* (Paris: OECD).

Oleman, J. (1999) 'Unified Government, Divided Government and Party Responsiveness', *American Political Science Review*, 93, 4: 821–35.

Olsen, J. (2009) 'Change and Continuity: An Institutional Approach to Institutions and Democratic Government', *European Political Science Review*, 1, 1: 3–32.

Olson, M. (1971) *The Logic of Collective Action*, 2nd printing (Cambridge, MA: Harvard University Press).

Olson, M. (1982) *The Rise and Decline of Nations* (New Haven, CT: Yale University Press).

OPSR (Office of Public Services Reform) (2002) *Better Government Services*, http://archive.cabinetoffice.gov.uk/opsr/documents/pdf/opsr-agencies.pdf.

Ormond, D. and Löffler, E. (1998) 'New Public Management: What To Take And What To Leave', III Congreso Internacional del CLAD sobre la Reforma del Estado y de la Administración Pública, Madrid, 14–17 October, http://bvc.cgu.gov.br/bitstream/123456789/1758/1/Derry+Ormond.pdf.

Ostrom, E. (1990) *Governing the Commons: The Evolution of Institutions for Collective Action* (Cambridge: Cambridge University Press).

Ostrom, E. (2007) 'Institutional Rational Choice' in P. Sabatier (ed.) *Theories of the Policy Process 2* (Cambridge, MA: Westview Press).

Page, E. (2000) 'Future Governance and the Literature on Policy Transfer and Lesson Drawing', ESRC Future Governance Workshop, 28 January.

Page, E. (2006) 'The Origins of Policy' in M. Moran, M. Rein and R. Goodin (eds) *The Oxford Handbook of Public Policy* (Oxford: Oxford University Press).

Parker, C., Stern, E., Paglia, E. and Brown, C. (2009) 'Preventable Catastrophe? The Hurricane Katrina Disaster Revisited', *Journal of Contingencies and Crisis Management*, 17, 4: 206–20.

Parsons, S. (2005) *Rational Choice and Politics: A Critical Introduction* (London: Continuum).

Parsons, T. (1938) 'The Role of Ideas in Social Action', *American Sociological Review*, 3, 5: 652–64.

Parsons, W. (1995) *Public Policy* (Aldershot: Edward Elgar). .

Peters, B.G. (2005) *Institutional Theory in Political Science: The 'New Institutionalism'*, 2nd edn (London: Continuum).

Peters, B.G. and Hogwood, B.W. (1985) 'In Search of the Issue-Attention Cycle', *Journal of Politics*, 47, 1: 238–53.

Peters, B.G. and Pierre, J. (2004) 'Multi-level Governance and Democracy' in I. Bache and M. Flinders (eds) *Multi-Level Governance* (Oxford: Oxford University Press).

Peters, B.G., Pierre, J. and King, D. (2005) 'The Politics of Path Dependency: Political Conflict in Historical Institutionalism', *Journal of Politics*, 67, 4: 1275–300.

Pidd, H. and Goldenberg, S. (2011) 'Germany Suspends Power Station Extension Plans as Nuclear Jitters Spread', *Guardian* 14 March, http://www.guardian.co.uk/environment/2011/mar/14/germany-japan-nuclear-industry.

Pierre, J. and Peters, B.G. (2000) *Governance, Politics and the State* (Basingstoke: Palgrave Macmillan).

Pierre, J. and Stoker, G. (2000) 'Towards Multi-Level Governance' in P. Dunleavy *et al.* (eds) *Developments in British Politics 6* (Basingstoke: Palgrave Macmillan).

Pierson, P. (2000a) 'Increasing Returns, Path Dependence, and the Study of Politics', *The American Political Science Review*, 94, 2: 251–67.

Pierson, P. (2000b) 'Introduction: Investigating the Welfare State at Century's End' in P. Pierson (ed.) *The New Politics of the Welfare State* (Oxford: Oxford University Press).

Pierson, P. (2000c) 'Post-Industrial Pressures on the Mature Welfare States' in P. Pierson (ed.) *The New Politics of the Welfare State* (Oxford: Oxford University Press).

Pollack, M. (2001) 'International Relations Theory and European Integration', *Journal of Common Market Studies*, 39, 2: 221–44.

Polsby, N. (1960) 'How to Study Community Power: The Pluralist Alternative', *Journal of Politics*, 22, 3: 474–84.

Polsby, N. (1968) 'On Intersections between Law and Political Science', *Stanford Law Review*, 21, 1: 142–51.

Polsby, N. (1980) *Community Power and Political Theory*, 2nd edn (New Haven, CT: Yale University Press).

Poulantzas, N. (1986) 'Class Power' in S. Lukes (ed.) *Power* (New York, NY: New York University Press).

Pressman, J. and Wildavsky, A. (1973) *Implementation* (Berkeley, CA: University of California Press).

Pressman, J. and Wildavsky, A. (1979) *Implementation*, 2nd edn (Berkeley, CA: University of California Press).

Princen, S. (2007) 'Advocacy Coalitions and the Internationalization of Public Health Policies', *Journal of Public Policy*, 27, 1: 13–33.

Pülzl, H. and Treib, O. (2007) 'Implementing Public Policy' in F. Fischer, G. Miller and M. Sidney (eds) *Handbook of Public Policy Analysis* (London: CRC Press).

Putnam, R. (2001) *Bowling Alone: The Collapse and Revival of American Community* (London: Simon & Schuster).

Quiggin, J. (2006) 'Economic Constraints on Public Policy' in M. Moran, M. Rein and R. Goodin (eds) *The Oxford Handbook of Public Policy* (Oxford: Oxford University Press).

Radaelli, C. (1995) 'The Role of Knowledge in the Policy Process', *Journal of European Public Policy*, 2, 2: 159–83.

Radaelli, C. (1999) 'Harmful Tax Competition in the EU: Policy Narratives and Advocacy Coalitions', *Journal of Common Market Studies*, 37, 4: 661–82.

Radin, B. (2000) *Beyond Machiavelli: Policy Analysis Comes of* Age (Washington, DC: Georgetown University Press).

Ramia, G. and Carney, T. (2010) 'The Rudd Government's Employment Services Agenda: Is it Post-NPM and Why is that Important?' *Australian Journal of Public Administration*, 69, 3: 263–73.

Rayner, J., M Howlett, J Wilson, B Cashore, G Hoberg (2001) 'Privileging the sub-sector', *Forest Policy and Economics* 2: 319–32.

Read, M. (1996) *The Politics of Tobacco: Policy Networks and the Cigarette Industry* (Aldershot: Avebury).

Reich, R. (1988) 'Introduction' in R. Reich (ed.) *The Power of Public Ideas* (Cambridge, MA: Ballinger).

Rhodes, R.A.W. (1994) 'The Hollowing Out of the State', *Political Quarterly*, 65: 138–51.

Rhodes, R.A.W. (1997) *Understanding Governance* (Open University Press).

Rhodes, R.A.W. (2006a) 'Old Institutionalisms' in R. Rhodes, S. Binder. B. Rockman (eds) *The Oxford Handbook of Political Institutions* (Oxford: Oxford University Press).

Rhodes, R.A.W. (2006b) 'Policy Network Analysis' in M. Moran, M. Rein and R. Goodin (eds) *The Oxford Handbook of Public Policy* (Oxford: Oxford University Press).

Rhodes, R.A.W. (ed.) (2009) *The Australian Study of Politics* (Basingstoke: Palgrave Macmillan).

Rhodes, R., Binder, S. and Rockman, B. (2006) 'Preface' in R. Rhodes, S. Binder. B. Rockman (eds) *The Oxford Handbook of Political Institutions* (Oxford: Oxford University Press).

Richards, D. and Smith, M. (2002) *Governance and Public Policy in the UK* (Oxford: Oxford University Press).

Richards, D. and Smith, M. (2004) 'The "Hybrid State"' in S. Ludlam and M. Smith (eds) *Governing as New Labour* (Basingstoke: Palgrave Macmillan).

Richardson, J. J. (1982a) 'Convergent Policy Styles in Europe?' in J.J. Richardson, (ed.) *Policy Styles in Western Europe* (London: Allen & Unwin).

Richardson, J. J. (ed.) (1982b) *Policy Styles in Western Europe* (London: Allen & Unwin).

Richardson, J. J. (2000) 'Government, Interest Groups and Policy Change', *Political Studies*, 48: 1006–25.

Richardson, J. J. (2008) 'Policy-making in the EU: Interests, Ideas and Garbage Cans of Primeval Soup' in J.J. Richardson (ed.) *European Union: Power and Policymaking*, 3rd edn (London: Routledge).

Richardson, J. and Jordan, G. (1979) *Governing under Pressure: The Policy Process in a Post-Parliamentary Democracy* (Oxford: Robertson).

Richardson, J. and Jordan, G. (1983) 'Overcrowded Policymaking: Some British and European Reflections', *Policy Sciences*, 15, 3: 247–68.

Richardson, J. J., Gustafsson, G. and Jordan, G. (1982) 'The Concept of Policy Style' in J. J. Richardson (ed.) *Policy Styles in Western Europe* (London: Allen & Unwin).

Richardson, J. J., Maloney, W.A., and Rüdig, W. (1992) 'The Dynamics of Policy Change: Lobbying and Water Privatization', *Public Administration*, 70: 157–75.

Riker, W. (1980) 'Implications from the Disequilibrium of Majority Rule for the Study of Institutions', *American Political Science Review*, 74, 2: 432–46.

Riker, W. (1982) *Liberalism Against Populism* (San Francisco, CA: Freeman).

Ringquist, E. (2005) 'Assessing Evidence of Environmental Inequities: A Meta-Analysis', *Journal of Policy Analysis and Management*, 24, 2: 223–47.

Rochefort, D.A. and Cobb, R.W. (1994) 'Problem Definition: An Emerging Perspective' in D.A. Rochefort and R.W. Cobb (eds) *The Politics of Problem Definition* (Kansas City, KS: University Press of Kansas).

Roemer, J. (1988) *Free to Lose: An Introduction to Marxist Economic Philosophy* (London: Radius).

Rosamond, B. (2000) *Theories of European Integration* (Basingstoke: Palgrave Macmillan).

Rose, R. (1984) *Do Parties Make a Difference?* (London: Macmillan).

Rose, R. (1986) 'Steering the Ship of State: One Rudder but Two Pairs of Hands', Appendix 15 of HC 92-II, Civil Servants and Ministers: Duties and Responsibilities, Seventh Report from the Treasury and Civil Service Committee, Session 1985–86.

Rose, R. (1987) *Ministers and Ministries: A Functional Analysis* (Oxford: Clarendon Press).

Rose, R. (1990) 'Inheritance Before Choice in Public Policy', *Journal of Theoretical Politics*, 2, 3: 263–91.

Rose, R. (1991) 'What Is Lesson-Drawing?' *Journal of Public Policy*, 11, 1: 3–30.

Rose, R. (1993) *Lesson-Drawing in Public Policy* (New York, NY: Chatham House).

Rose, R. (2005) *Learning From Comparative Public Policy: A Practical Guide* (London: Routledge) .

Rose, R. and Davies, P. (1994) *Inheritance in Public Policy: Change Without Choice in Britain* (New Haven, CT: Yale University Press).

Ross, D. (2005) *Economic Theory and Cognitive Science: Microexplanation* (Cambridge, MA: MIT Press).

Sabatier, P. (1986) 'Top-Down and Bottom-Up Approaches to Implementation Research: A Critical Analysis and Suggested Synthesis', *Journal of Public Policy*, 6, 1: 21–48.

Sabatier, P. (1988) 'An Advocacy Coalition Framework of Policy Change and the Role of Policy-Oriented Learning Therein', *Policy Sciences*, 21, 2–3: 129–68.

Sabatier, P. (1991) 'Towards Better Theories of the Policy Process', *PS: Political Science and Politics*, 24, 2: 147–56.

Sabatier, P. (1993) 'Policy Change over a Decade or More' in P. Sabatier and H. Jenkins-Smith (eds) *Policy Change and Learning: An Advocacy Coalition Approach* (Boulder, CO: Westview Press).

Sabatier, P. (1998) 'The Advocacy Coalition Framework: Revisions and Relevance for Europe', *Journal of European Public Policy*, 5, 1: 98–130.

Sabatier, P. (2007a) 'The Need for Better Theories' in P. Sabatier (ed.) *Theories of the Policy Process 2* (Cambridge, MA: Westview).

Sabatier, P. (2007b) 'Fostering the Development of Policy Theory' in P. Sabatier (ed.) *Theories of the Policy Process 2* (Cambridge, MA: Westview).

Sabatier, P. and Jenkins-Smith, H. (1993) 'The Advocacy Coalition Framework: Assessment, Revisions and Implications for Scholars and Practitioners' in Sabatier, P. and Jenkins-Smith, H. (eds) *Policy Change and Learning: An Advocacy Coalition Approach* (Boulder, CO: Westview Press).

Sabatier, P. and Weible, C. (2007) 'The Advocacy Coalition Framework: Innovations and Clarifications' in Sabatier, P. (ed.) *Theories of the Policy Process* (Boulder, CO: Westview Press).

Sanders, D. (2010) 'Behaviouralism' in D. Marsh and G. Stoker (eds) *Theory and Methods in Political Science* (Basingstoke: Palgrave Macmillan).

Sanders, E. (2006) 'Historical Institutionalism' in R. Rhodes, S. Binder. B. Rockman (eds) *The Oxford Handbook of Political Institutions* (Oxford: Oxford University Press).

Sanderson, I. (2009) 'Intelligent Policy Making for a Complex World: Pragmatism, Evidence and Learning', *Political Studies*, 57: 699–719.

Sandler, T. (1997) *Global Challenges: An Approach to Environmental, Political and Economic Problems* (Cambridge: Cambridge University Press).

Sandler, T. (2004) *Global Collective Action* (Cambridge: Cambridge University Press).

Sandler, T. and Enders, W. (2004) 'An Economic Perspective on Transnational Terrorism', *European Journal of Political Economy*, 20, 2: 301–16.

Schain, M. and Menon, A. (eds) (2007) *Comparative Federalism: The European Union and the United States* (New York: Oxford University Press).

Scharpf, F. (1988) 'The Joint-Decision Trap: Lessons from German Federalism and European Integration', *Public Administration*, 66, 3: 239–78.

Scharpf, F. (1997) 'Introduction: The Problem-Solving Capacity of Multi-level Governance', *Journal of European Public Policy*, 4, 4: 520–38.

Schattschneider, E.E. (1960) *The Semi-Sovereign People* (Fort Worth, TX: Harcourt Brace, 1975 edition).

Schlager, E. (1995) 'Policy Making and Collective Action: Defining Coalitions within the Advocacy Coalition Framework', *Policy Sciences*, 28, 3: 243–70.

Schlager, E. (2007) 'A Comparison of Frameworks, Theories, and Models of Policy Processes' Theory' in P. Sabatier (ed.) *Theories of the Policy Process 2* (Cambridge, MA: Westview).

Schmidt, V. (2006) 'Institutionalism' in C. Hay, M. Lister and D. Marsh (eds) *The State: Theories and Issues* (Basingstoke; Palgrave Macmillan).

Schmidt, V. (2008) 'Discursive Institutionalism: The Explanatory Power of Ideas and Discourse', *Annual Review of Political Science*, 11: 303–26.

Schmidt, V. (2010) 'Taking Ideas and Discourse Seriously: Explaining Change through Discursive Institutionalism as the Fourth "New Institutionalism"', *European Political Science Review*, 2, 1: 1–25.

Schmidt, V. and Radaelli, C. (2004) 'Policy Change and Discourse in Europe: Conceptual and Methodological Issues', *West European Politics*, 27, 2: 183–210.

Schofield, J. (2004) 'A Model of Learned Implementation', *Public Administration*, 82, 2: 283–308.

Schofield, J. and Sausman, C. (2004) 'Symposium on Implementing Public Policy', *Public Administration*, 82, 2: 235–48.

Schultz, K. (1995) 'The Politics of the Business Cycle', *British Journal of Political Science*, 25, 1: 79–99.

Schumpeter, J. (1942) *Capitalism, Socialism and Democracy* (London: Allen & Unwin).

Seager, A. (2008) 'Ministers Risk Missing Key Labour Target' *Guardian*, 11 June, http://www.guardian.co.uk/society/2008/jun/11/socialexclusion.children1.

Self, P. (1993) *Government by the Market: The Politics of Public Choice* (London: Macmillan).

Selznick, P. (1996) 'Institutionalism "Old" and "New"', *Administrative Science Quarterly*, 41, 2: 270–7.

Sementelli (2007) 'Distortions of Progress: Evolutionary Theories and Public Administration', *Administration & Society*, 39, 6: 740–60.

Sharkansky, I. (1972) *Public Administration*, 2nd edn (Chicago, IL: Markham).

Sharman, J. (2008) 'Power and Discourse in Policy Diffusion: Anti-Money Laundering in Developing States', *International Studies Quarterly*, 52, 3: 635–56.

Sharman, J. (2010) 'Dysfunctional Policy Transfer in National Tax Blacklists', *Governance*, 23, 4: 623–9.

Shepsle, K. (2006) 'Rational Choice Institutionalism' in R. Rhodes, S. Binder and B. Rockman (eds) *The Oxford Handbook of Political Institutions* (Oxford: Oxford University Press).

Shepsle, K. and Bonchek, M. (1997) *Analyzing Politics: Rationality, Behaviour and Institutions* (London: Norton).

Shugart, M. (2006) 'Comparative Executive-Legislative Relations' in R. Rhodes, S. Binder and B. Rockman (eds) *The Oxford Handbook of Political Institutions* (Oxford: Oxford University Press).

Simon, H, (1957) *Models of Man: Social and Rational* (New York, NY: John Wiley).

Simon, H. (1960) *The New Science of Management Decisions* (Englewood Cliffs, NJ: Prentice-Hall) .

Simon, H. (1976) *Administrative Behavior*, 3rd edn (London: Macmillan).

Simon, H. (1983) *Reason in Human Affairs* (Oxford: Blackwell).

Sinclair, J. (2004) 'Globalization, Supranational Institutions and Media', in J.D.H. Downing, D. McQuail, P. Schlesinger and E. Wartella (eds) *The Sage Handbook of Media Studies* (Thousand Oaks, CA: Sage).

Slaughter, A. (2004) *A New World Order* (Princeton, NJ: Princeton University Press).

Smith, A. (2000) 'Policy Networks and Advocacy Coalitions: Explaining Policy Change and Stability in UK Industrial Pollution Policy?' *Environment and Planning C: Government and Policy 2000*, 18, 1: 95–114.

Smith, G. and May, D. (1993) 'The Artificial Debate Between Rationalist and Incrementalist Models of Decision Making' in M. Hill (ed.) *The Policy Process: A Reader* (Hemel Hempstead: Harvester Wheatsheaf).

Smith, K. (2002) 'Typologies, Taxonomies and the Benefits of Policy Classification', *Policy Studies Journal*, 30, 3: 379–95.

Smith, K. and Larimer, C. (2009) *The Public Policy Theory Primer* (Boulder, CO: Westview Press).

Smith, M. (2009) *Power and the State* (Basingstoke: Palgrave Macmillan).

Stein, M. and Turkiewitsch, L. (2008) 'The Concept of Multi-level Governance in Studies of Federalism', Paper Presented at the 2008 International Political Science Association International Conference, Montréal, May, http://montreal 2008.ipsa.org/site/images/PAPERS/section3/RC%2028-%20Stein%20Turkewit sch%203.4.pdf.

Steinberger, P. (1980) 'Typologies of Public Policy: Meaning Construction and the Policy Process', *Social Science Quarterly*, 61, 2: 185–97.

Steinmo, S. (2008) 'Historical Institutionalism' in D. Della Porta and M. Keating (eds) *Approaches and Methodologies in the Social Sciences* (Cambridge: Cambridge University Press).

Stolfi, F. (2010) 'Testing Structuralist and Interpretative Explanations of Policy Change: The Case of Italy's Budget Reform', *Governance*, 23, 1: 109–32.

Stoker, G. (2004) *Transforming Local Governance: From Thatcherism to New Labour* (Basingstoke: Palgrave Macmillan).

Stoker, G. and Marsh, D. (2002) 'Introduction' in D. Marsh and G. Stoker (eds) *Theory and Methods in Political Science* (Basingstoke: Palgrave Macmillan).

Stone, D. (1989) 'Causal Stories and the Formation of Policy Agendas', *Political Science Quarterly*, 104: 281–300.

Stone, D. (1999) 'Learning Lessons and Transferring Policy across Time, Space and Disciplines', *Politics*, 19, 1: 51–9.

Stone, D. (2000) 'Non-Governmental Policy Transfer: The Strategies of Independent Policy Institutes', *Governance*, 13, 1: 45–62.

Stone, D. (2002) *Policy Paradox: The Art of Political Decision Making*, rev. edn (London: Norton).

Stone, D. (2004) 'Transfer Agents and Global Networks in the 'Transnationalization' of Policy, *Journal of European Public Policy*, 11, 3: 545–66.

Streek, W. and Thelen, K. (2005) 'Introduction: Institutional Change in Advanced Political Economies' in W. Streek and K. Thelen (eds) *Beyond Continuity: Institutional Change in Advanced Political Economies* (Oxford: Oxford University Press).

Strøm, K. (1990) *Minority Government and Majority Rule* (Cambridge: Cambridge University Press).

Studlar, D. (2002) *Tobacco Control: Comparative Politics in the United States and Canada* (Peterborough, Ontario: Broadview Press).

Studlar, D. (2004) Tobacco Control Policy in a Shrinking World: How Much Policy Learning?' in E. Vigoda-Gadot and D. Levi-Faur (eds) *International Public Policy and Management: Policy Learning and Policy Beyond Regional, Cultural and Political Boundaries* (New York, NY: Marcel Dekker).

Studlar, D. (2007a) 'What Explains Policy Change in Tobacco Control Policy in Advanced Industrial Democracies?', paper to PSA Conference, Bath, April, http://www.psa.ac.uk/2007/pps/Studlar.pdf.

Studlar, D. (2007b) 'Ideas, Institutions and Diffusion: What Explains Tobacco Control Policy in Australia, Canada and New Zealand?', *Commonwealth and Comparative Politics*, 45, 2: 164–84.

Taylor, D. and Balloch, S. (2005) 'The Politics of Evaluation: An Overview', in D. Taylor and S. Balloch (eds) *The Politics of Evaluation: Participation and Policy Implementation* (Bristol: The Policy Press) 1–17.

Teisman, G. and Klijn, E. (2008) 'Complexity Theory and Public Management', *Public Management Review*, 10, 3: 287–97.

Thelen, K. and Steinmo, S. (1992) 'Historical Institutionalism in Comparative Politics' in S. Steinmo, K. Thelen and F. Longstreth (eds) *Structuring Politics: Historical Institutionalism in Comparative Analysis* (Cambridge: Cambridge University Press).

True, J.L., Jones, B.D. and Baumgartner, F.R. (2007) Punctuated Equilibrium Theory' in P. Sabatier (ed.) *Theories of the Policy Process*, 2nd edn (Cambridge, MA: Westview Press).

Tsebelis, G. (1990) *Nested Games: Rational Choice in Comparative Politics* (Berkeley, CA: California University Press).

Tsebelis, G. (2002) *Veto Players: How Political Institutions Work* (Princeton, NJ: Princeton University Press).

Tullock, G. (1967) 'The Welfare Costs of Tariffs, Monopolies and Theft', *Western Economic Journal*, 5, 3: 224–32.

Udehn, L. (1996) *The Limits of Public Choice* (London: Routledge).

Wade, R. (2002) 'US hegemony and the World Bank: The Fight over People and Ideas', *Review of International Political Economy*, 9, 2: 215–43.

Wade, R. (2006) 'The Invisible Hand of the American Empire', *Ethics and International Affairs*, 17, 2: 77–88.

Walker, J.L. (1969) 'The Diffusion of Innovations among the American States', *American Political Science Review*, 63, 3: 880–99.

Walsh, J. (2000) 'When Do Ideas Matter? Explaining the Successes and Failures of Thatcherite Ideas' *Comparative Political Studies*, 33, 4: 483–516.

Ward, H. (1987) 'Structural Power – A Contradiction in Terms?' *Political Studies*, 35, 4: 593–610.

Ward, H. (2002) 'Rational Choice' in D. Marsh and G. Stoker (eds) *Theory and Methods in Political Science* (Basingstoke: Palgrave Macmillan).

Ward, H. and Weale, A. (2010) 'Is Rule by Majorities Special?', *Political Studies*, 58, 1: 26–46.

Watts, R. (2007), 'The United Kingdom as a Federalized or Regionalized Union', in A. Trench (ed.) *Devolution and Power in the United Kingdom* (Manchester: Manchester University Press).

Weaver, R. and Rockman, B. (1993) 'Assessing the Effects of Institutions' in R. Weaver and B. Rockman (eds) *Do Institutions Matter?* (Washington, DC: The Brookings Institution).

Weber, M. (with G. Roth and C. Wittich) (1978) *Economy and Society: An Outline of Interpretive Sociology, Volume 1* (London: University of California Press).

Webster, D. (2002) 'Unemployment: How Official Statistics Distort Analysis and Policy, and Why', *Radical Statistics Journal*, No. 79, http://www.radstats.org.uk/no079/webster.htm.

Weible, C. and Sabatier, P. (2005) 'Comparing Policy Networks: Marine Protected Areas in California', *Policy Studies Journal*, 33, 2: 181–204.

Weible, C., Sabatier, P. and McQueen, K. (2009) 'Themes and Variations: Taking Stock of the Advocacy Coalition Framework', *Policy Studies Journal*, 37, 1: 121–41.

Weiss, T. (2009) 'What Happened to the Idea of World Government', *International Studies Quarterly*, 53, 2: 253–71.

Welch, S. and Kennedy-Pipe, C. (2004) 'Multi-Level Governance and International Relations' in I. Bache and M. Flinders (eds) *Multi-Level Governance* (Oxford: Oxford University Press).

Wheeler, N. (2000) *Saving Strangers* (Oxford: Oxford University Press).

WHO, World Health Organization (2008) 'WHO Framework Convention on Tobacco Control', http://www.who.int/fctc/en/.

Wildavsky, A. (1980) *The Art and Craft of Policy Analysis* (London: Macmillan).

Wilks, S. and Wright, M. (1987) 'Conclusion: Comparing Government-Industry Relations: States, Sectors, and Networks', in S. Wilks and M. Wright (eds) *Comparative Government-Industry Relations* (Oxford: Clarendon Press).

Wilson, D. (2003) 'Unravelling Control Freakery: Redefining Central-Local Government Relations', *British Journal of Politics and International Relations*, 5, 3: 317–46.

Wilson, J. (1980) *American Government: Institutions and Policies* (Lexington, MA: D.C. Heath).

Wistow, G. (1992) 'The Health Service Policy Community: Professionals Preeminent or Under Challenge?' in D. Marsh and R.A.W. Rhodes (eds) *Policy Networks in British Government* (Oxford: Oxford University Press).

Wolfinger, R. (1960) 'Reputation and Reality in the Study of "Community Power"', *American Sociological Review*, 25, 5: 636–44.

World Bank (2008) 'Understanding Poverty', http://web.worldbank.org/WBSITE/EXTERNAL/TOPICS/EXTPOVERTY/0,,contentMDK:20153855~menuPK:373757~pagePK:148956~piPK:216618~theSitePK:336992,00.html.

Wright, B., Caspi, A., Moffitt, T. and Paternoster, R. (2004) 'Does the Perceived Risk of Punishment Deter Criminally Prone Individuals? Rational Choice, Self-Control and Crime', *Journal of Research in Crime and Delinquency*, 41, 2: 180–213 .

Yanow, D. (1996) *How Does a Policy Mean* (Washington, DC: Georgetown University Press).

Zafonte, M. and Sabatier, P. (2004) 'Short-Term versus Long-Term Coalitions in the Policy Process: Automotive Pollution Control, 1963–1989', *Policy Studies Journal*, 1: 75–107.

Zahariadis, N. (1999) 'Ambiguity, Time and Multiple Streams', in P. Sabatier (ed.) *Theories of the Policy Process* (Boulder, CO: Westview Press).

Zahariadis, N. (2003) *Ambiguity and Choice in Public Policy* (Washington, DC: Georgetown University Press).

Zahariadis, N. (2007) 'The Multiple Streams Framework' in P. Sabatier (ed.) *Theories of the Policy Process* (Cambridge, MA: Westview).

Index